China-EU Law Series

Volume 2

More information about this series at http://www.springer.com/series/11933

Niels Philipsen • Stefan E. Weishaar •
Guangdong Xu
Editors

Market Integration: The EU Experience and Implications for Regulatory Reform in China

Springer

Editors
Niels Philipsen
Faculty of Law
Maastricht University
Maastricht, The Netherlands

Stefan E. Weishaar
Faculty of Law
University of Groningen
Groningen, The Netherlands

Guangdong Xu
Centre for Law and Economics
China University of Political Science and Law
Beijing, China

ISSN 2198-2708 ISSN 2198-2716 (electronic)
China-EU Law Series
ISBN 978-3-662-48272-8 ISBN 978-3-662-48273-5 (eBook)
DOI 10.1007/978-3-662-48273-5

Library of Congress Control Number: 2015953626

Springer Heidelberg New York Dordrecht London

Printed on acid-free paper

Springer-Verlag GmbH Berlin Heidelberg is part of Springer Science+Business Media (www.springer.com)

List of Abbreviations

ABS	Alternative business structure
AIC	Administration of Industry and Commerce
ALL	Administrative License Law
AML	Anti-Monopoly Law
API	American Petroleum Institute
APL	Administrative Procedure Law
ASME	American Society of Mechanical Engineers
BOC	Bank of China
BSI	British Standards Institution
CCBE	Council of Bars and Law Societies of Europe
CCR	Command and Control Regulation
CER	Corporate environmental responsibility
CFI	Court of First Instance
CFP	Corporate financial performance
CGO	Central government owned
CNY	Renminbi
COE	Collectively owned enterprise
CPC	Communist Party of China
CSOE	Central State Owned Enterprises
CSP	Corporate social performance
CSR	Corporate social responsibility
CSRC	China Securities Regulatory Commission
DECC	Department of Energy and Climate Change
DNV	Det Norske Veritas
DRC	Development and Reform Commission
DSJI	The Dow Jones Sustainability Indices
ECJ	European Court of Justice
ECSC	European Coal and Steel Community
EEC	European Economic Community
EIA	Environmental Impact Assessment

EU	European Union
EUR	Euro
FIE	Foreign invested enterprise
GATI	Germany Trade & Invest
GDP	Gross domestic product
GMO	Genetically modified organism
GPL	Government Procurement Law
IGC	Intergovernmental Conference
IMF	International Monetary Fund
ISO	International organization for Standardization
ISPC	Institution-Structure-Conduct-Performance
LGO	Local government owned
MDP	Multi-disciplinary partnership
MEW	Margolis, Elfenbein and Walsh (authors)
MNC	Multinational corporation
MOFCOM	Ministry of Commerce
MoU	Memorandum of Understanding
NCS	National Competition Strategy
NDRC	National Development and Reform Commission
NGO	Non-governmental organization
NPC	National's People Congress
NPL	Non-performing loans
NSB	National Standards Body
NSGP	Nord Stream Gas Pipeline
OECD	Organization for Economic Co-operation and Development
PB	Private Background
PBOC	People's Bank of China
PPP	People, Profit, Planet
PR	Public relations
PRC	People's Republic of China
RMB	Renminbi
ROE	Return on equity
RP	Revenue Producing
SAIC	State Administration of Industry and Commerce
SASAC	State-owned Assets Supervision and Administration Commission
SETC	State Economic and Trade Commission
SGEI	Services of General Economic Interest
SIC	Schwarz information criterion
SME	Small and medium enterprise
SOE	State-owned enterprise
TEC	Treaty of Amsterdam
TEU	Treaty on European Union
TFEU	Treaty on the Functioning of the European Union
TVE	Township and village enterprises

U.K.	United Kingdom
UN	United Nations
U.S.	United States
USD	United States Dollar
USDA	United States Department of Agriculture
VAT	Value added tax
WTO	World Trade Organization
WWF	World Wildlife Fund

Contents

Contributors

Michael Faure Maastricht University Faculty of Law, Maastricht, The Netherlands

Erasmus School of Law, Rotterdam, The Netherlands

Binwei Gui Center for Law and Economics at the China University of Political Science and Law, Beijing, China

Jiye Hu Center for Law and Economics at the China University of Political Science and Law, Beijing, China

Wenjing Li Center for Law and Economics at the China University of Political Science and Law, Beijing, China

Mengxing Lu Maastricht University Faculty of Law, Maastricht, The Netherlands

Jingyuan Ma Central University of Finance and Economics, Beijing, China

Mel Marquis European University Institute, Florence, Italy

Niels Philipsen Faculty of Law, Maastricht University, Maastricht, The Netherlands

Mehdi Piri Damagh Maastricht University Faculty of Law, Maastricht, The Netherlands

Guang Shen Faculty of Law, Maastricht University, Maastricht, The Netherlands

Shouji Sun University of International Business and Economics, Beijing, China

Stefan E. Weishaar Faculty of Law, University of Groningen, Groningen, The Netherlands

Guangdong Xu Center for Law and Economics at the China University of Political Science and Law, Beijing, China

Qi Zhou University of Leeds School of Law, Leeds, UK

Tianshu Zhou Center for Law and Economics at the China University of Political Science and Law, Beijing, China

Introduction

Stefan E. Weishaar, Niels Philipsen, and Guangdong Xu

1 Market Integration and Economic Growth

China has long been admired for its ability to achieve double-digit economic growth figures. The economic growth literature describes such phenomena in terms of a 'catch up effect'.[1] The underlying argument is that the rise in the economic welfare and productivity of less developed economies will be larger than those of more advanced economies. Price convergence in this catch-up process is *inter alia* driven by advances in the economic production capacity of a country, and also by inflation and wage increases. The recent slowing of Chinese economic growth rates bears testimony to this catch-up effect. Moreover, various authors, such as Xu (2014), have pointed out that the current economic growth in China is not sustainable because it is the result not only of catching up but also of distorted factor prices (of, e.g., land and labour) and financial repression (such as regulated interest rates and managed credit allocation).[2]

---

[1] Barro and Sala-i-Martin (1995).

[2] Xu (2014), pp. 141–168.

S.E. Weishaar (✉)
Faculty of Law, University of Groningen, Groningen, The Netherlands
e-mail: S.E.Weishaar@rug.nl

N. Philipsen
Faculty of Law, Maastricht University, Maastricht, The Netherlands
e-mail: niels.philipsen@maastrichtuniversity.nl

G. Xu
Center for Law and Economics at the China University of Political Science and Law, Beijing, China
e-mail: guangdongx@cupl.edu.cn

N. Philipsen et al. (eds.), *Market Integration: The EU Experience and Implications for Regulatory Reform in China*, China-EU Law Series 2,
DOI 10.1007/978-3-662-48273-5_1

With an expanding economic potency of China, it is apparent that China cannot rely upon exports as the main driver of economic growth, nor should it rely on legal interventions that cause further distortions of factor prices. Demand for goods and services will also have to derive from China itself. This is particularly important at times of a less favourable global economic climate such as the global financial crisis of 2008, which has challenged China's mode of economic growth.[3] The Chinese legislator has identified sustainable domestic growth as an important long-term policy goal.[4]

A way for China to unleash its economic forces and to foster non-export-led economic growth is 'market integration' and regulatory reform. Economic theory suggests that integrating similar national or regional markets generally leads to (more) economic growth and societal prosperity.[5] Similarly, ensuring that regulation is setting the right incentives for regulated entities to follow rules can help to foster economic growth and allow for increases in social welfare.

Building upon the EU's experience with market integration, this book aims to unravel the role regulation can play in permitting market integration and in unleashing more economic prosperity in China. By taking an interdisciplinary 'Law and Economics' and comparative law (China and EU) approach, we aim to analyse several impediments to market integration and domestic economic growth.

Regulatory interventions can occur at all levels of government (central authorities, provincial authorities, local authorities) and may also take the form of self-regulation. Regulation can either positively or negatively impact market integration and competition, and will thereby influence trade flows. Examples of national rules that can (positively or negatively) impact the free flow of goods and services within China include competition law, public procurement rules and financial regulation. At the provincial level, restrictions to the freedom of establishment can obstruct the move of efficient firms and prevent them from taking advantage of low-cost production factors. At the local level, regulatory restrictions can impede competition on the merits (for example, in the local taxi market) leading to unnecessary high prices and hence to a lower level of social welfare. Such restrictions to market integration and economic prosperity can be routed in inefficiency-inducing regulation itself—either on national, provincial or local level—or are routed in undesirable administrative practices. The latter are sometimes referred to as administrative monopolies, alluding that the culprit that obstructs the creation of a competitive and integrated domestic market is associated with public administration. Various contributions to this book examine whether regulation can be improved to allow for better integrated markets in China and for more economic prosperity.

Some contributions focus more particularly on self-regulation by examining whether (and if so, how) the virtues of self-regulation can be combined with a

[3] Wen (2010).

[4] 12th Five Year Plan (2011–2015), adopted by the National People's Congress on 14 March 2011.

[5] See, e.g., Wagener and Eger (2009).

competitive environment, also in the specific case of China, in order to overcome obstacles to market integration and to provide stimuli for economic growth. Interesting examples in this respect include the case of professional regulation (such as lawyers and accountants) and environmental law.

2 Importance of the Book

Despite impressive economic growth rates, it has been suggested that China's economic system is fragmented and that this fragmentation of the largest market in the world inhibits growth. Economic fragmentation in China is closely linked to the 1994 tax reforms that created the need for the provinces to raise funds to stimulate economic progress (Lu 2008; Jiang 2007). The costs of this strong rise in GDP of the local economies came in the form of regional protectionism and facilitated the creation of administrative monopolies.

Economic theory suggests that the integration of similar[6] regional markets can lead to a reinvigoration of economic growth and societal prosperity—something that may in particular be of interest during times of a world economic slowdown. The EU has a rich experience in market integration and encountered a multitude of obstacles in the creation of the European internal market, in particular related to the four freedoms (free movements of goods, services, labour and capital) and competition law as its 'natural complement' (following the *Consten Grundig* case before the European Court of Justice).

This book approaches obstacles to market integration and regulation that impedes economic growth from the perspectives of Law and Economics and comparative law. It will do so by addressing impediments in a wide area of fields, ranging from competition law, public procurement rules and financial regulation to freedom of establishment, local transportation and self-regulation, e.g. in the areas of liberal professions and the environment. Each is discussed in turn below, although of course these fields are to some extent overlapping.

[6] If regions are not similar, the economic theory of federalism suggests that further integration in the form of harmonization of laws is only efficient when (1) there are transboundary externalities, (2) this leads to economies of scale, (3) harmonization reduces transaction costs and (4) there is a genuine risk of a 'race to the bottom' (i.e., when governments actively try to attract industry at the expense of, e.g., environmental or consumer protection). After all, the starting point is a bottom-up approach, because regional (or national regulation) is better able to serve people's preferences than national (or transnational) regulation and leaves room for regulatory competition and learning effects. See Faure (2003) and various contributions to this book, including the chapter by Zhou and Philipsen.

2.1 Competition Law

The Chinese Anti-Monopoly Law entered into force on August 1st, 2008. Its creation constituted an important step in China's movement towards a more market-oriented socialist economy. It is expected that the strengthening of competition will not only lead to increased levels of welfare for the public at large but at the same time work towards a stronger legal and economic integration. This does not apply only to competition between private firms; the expectation also applies to situations where (semi-)public undertakings are competing with private undertakings. Furthermore, government intervention with competition on the merits may obstruct economic integration and give rise to inefficiencies.

In its development, the Chinese Anti-Monopoly Law was much inspired by the European (EU) competition law. One area that the Chinese legislator did not take up is government support schemes. In the EU there are so-called 'State aid' rules which prevent a 'subsidy race' between EU Member States. These State aid rules aim to prevent direct support measures (e.g., subsidies for research, land purchases, rescue and restructuring aid, etc.) that undermine competition on the merits.

One particularly important aspect regarding the establishment of a more market-oriented socialist economy in China is the role that administrative monopolies play, and to what extent they inhibit market integration. Closely related to this question is the legal relationship between the Anti-Monopoly Law and administrative law that constitutes the basis of administrative monopolies. Some scholars suggest that the Anti-Monopoly Law is not an efficient or effective tool to address such monopolies but that more efficient tools—in the fight against corruption—should be employed.[7] Law and Economics theory can be used to examine the role administrative monopolies play in cementing economic fragmentism and the pros and cons of different approaches to reduce the negative welfare effects of administrative monopolies.

2.2 Public Procurement Rules

As pointed out above, competition law is directed not only at (private and public) undertakings but also at governments granting aid to undertakings. Governments can also impact the economy in another way, namely by how they conduct their purchases of goods or services in procurement tenders. It is more particularly in this context that the European experience may offer interesting insights for China, taking into account that China is a large unitary State with many provinces. Despite all well-meant attempts, the European public procurement market remains an area that continues to resist market integration. The link between public procurement

[7] See Weishaar (2011) for a review.

and competition is a growing field of research. A detailed analysis of the European situation will not only provide much-needed novel insights into the relationship between the two fields in Europe, but it may also generate insights for the Chinese legislative reform process, and it may allow European scholars to learn from the analysis of how the issue could be addressed in the Chinese context. The last point is of particular importance since China enjoys unitary contract and public procurement laws and may therefore also provide new arguments to the discussion on market integration in Europe.

2.3 *Financial Regulation*

Government interference with the economy can also extend to the way it supports particular companies, e.g. by means of financial regulation in the broader sense. Financial support can extend to monetary policy, granting preferential access to loans and contracts, or shaping enforcement efforts of regulatory authorities to favour certain companies.

Capital is the lifeblood of any market-oriented economy. Regulation addressing how banks, in particular central banks, are to conduct their business is decisively influencing money supply in the economy. Furthermore, the (mis)allocation of financial resources in an economy is influenced by the practices of commercial banks and other credit-issuing institutions, which is in turn influenced by central banks' monetary supply, the economy's credit policy and culture, and other regulatory arrangements. For example, in China, as a result of financial repression, which distorts interest rates and favours State-owned banks, scarce financial resources have been systematically and continually allocated to less profitable but more politically preferable entities, especially State-owned enterprises (SOEs), whereas private firms, which have become the driving force of China's economic growth, are forced to rely on informal and even underground credit channels to finance their survival.

Another way in which government entities can impact how companies are doing economically is through the actual application of rules, i.e. enforcement of law. Preferential or dissimilar treatment of companies leads to a distortion of the level playing field and is likely to lead to a reduction of social welfare.

2.4 *Freedom of Establishment*

As described above, the European internal market is based on the free movement of goods, services, labour and capital, as well as on competition law as its 'natural complement'. Closely associated with the freedom to provide services is the freedom of establishment (see Articles 49–55 TFEU). This freedom allows companies to move from one EU Member State to another without obstruction.[8]

The internal market in the EU thus does not only allow goods and services to freely move across borders, but also factors of production such as workers, service providers or capital. This is important because, from an economic perspective, the benefits from trade in goods and services can also be achieved by trade in factors of production. Both lead to similar benefits of trade and hence to more market integration and economic prosperity.

In the EU, the freedom of establishment encompasses the right to take up and pursue activities as a self-employed person and to set up and manage undertakings without being discriminated on the basis of, e.g., nationality. Nationality does of course not play a role in a unitary country such as China, but discrimination against companies from other provinces or even from other cities—in whichever form or with whatever motivation—would impede market integration and thus be likely to undermine economic prosperity.

2.5 *Self-Regulation*

The literature on self-regulation has indicated that self-regulation may, from an economic perspective, have several advantages over public regulation. These advantages are more particularly related to lower costs (especially the costs of complying with new regulation), more flexibility and—most importantly—superior information of self-regulatory bodies (e.g., professional associations) when compared to the government. Thus, self-regulation, provided it is accompanied with an appropriate institutional infrastructure, can fit into a competitive environment. However, economists equally warn that there is always a risk that self-regulation may be abused by, e.g., professional bodies to engage in behaviour that in fact restricts competition (e.g., limiting the entry into the profession, restrictions on the execution of the profession, etc.). The crucial question therefore has been how the benefits of self-regulation can be kept whereby the potential disadvantages can be avoided. Some solutions, like organizing a competition between self-regulatory bodies, have in that respect been suggested. The role of self-regulation of the professions in a competitive environment is even more challenging in the context of China's adoption of the Anti-Monopoly Law and its simultaneous developments in professional regulation. So far, within the Chinese context professional regulation has been strongly state driven and has thus not yet created a competitive environment for professional services. However, steps towards self-regulation of the professions are also taken in China now, such as the Licensing Act of 2003 and

---

[8] Although we should point out that sometimes the goals of market integration and economic efficiency, both of which are goals of EU competition law, conflict. See on this Bishop and Walker (2010), pp. 4–8.

the recent amendments to the Lawyer's Act.[9] Hence, the question arises how these steps towards self-regulation can fit into the equally interesting tendency towards an effective competition law and policy.

Self-regulation encompasses regulatory power that derives from the authority given to self-regulatory bodies. There is, however, also the possibility that companies choose to self-impose rules of conduct upon themselves. In recent years, there has been an increase in not legally binding rules in the EU, particularly related to production standards and the environment. While in the EU and the US a lot has been written about voluntary self-restraints of companies, it is yet unclear to what extent such practices are present in China and if they are similarly effective.

3 History and Origins of This Book

This is the third book that originates from a long-standing cooperation between various Chinese and European institutions. The editors have worked together for a long time through collaboration between the Research Centre for Law and Economics (RCLE) of the China University of Political Science and Law (CUPL), to which Guangdong Xu is connected; the Maastricht European Institute for Transnational Legal Research (METRO), where Niels Philipsen is Vice Director; and the Department of Law and Economics at the University of Groningen, to which Stefan Weishaar is affiliated. Both Niels Philipsen and Stefan Weishaar are teaching courses also at the China–EU School of Law (CESL) at CUPL.

It is within the framework of this collaboration that a first joint seminar entitled 'Using Economics to Improve Regulation' was organized in May 2012 in Beijing. The papers that were presented at this seminar were later compiled into a book under the title 'Economics and Regulation in China', which was published by Routledge (Faure and Xu 2014). A follow-up seminar entitled 'Law and Finance: The Role of Law and Regulations in Sustaining Financial Markets' was organized in May 2013. This gave rise to another publication, 'The Role of Law and Regulation in Sustaining Financial Markets', with Routledge (Philipsen and Xu 2015). Both of these books also included contributions by invited experts from the United States, Europe and China.

The conference that lies at the basis of the underlying book was held in May 2014 and was co-financed by the China–EU School of Law. The audience not only consisted of invited international experts and senior staff from various Chinese universities but also included CUPL students.[10] The contributions to this seminar are included in this volume, which examines how regulation can be improved to

[9] See also Philipsen (2010).

[10] In addition to the people who contributed to this book, also Prof. Hildegard Schneider (Maastricht University, Dean of the Law Faculty), Prof. Zhang Qing (CUPL) and Prof. Cao Fuguo (CUFE) presented at the seminar in Beijing.

allow for better market integration and/or economic growth in China, and if experiences in Europe may be providing useful insights (of what to do or what not to do).

4 Methodology

4.1 Multidisciplinary and Interdisciplinary Approach

In addition to Law and Economics, which will be relied upon in the current book as the main tool for studying law and regulation, other disciplines such as legal analysis, financial economics, political science and sociology will also be applied. Given that law and (economic) regulation are embedded in highly sophisticated institutional environments in which political, economic and social factors influence, complement and strengthen one another, a mono-disciplinary approach may fail to provide relevant answers. Therefore, a multidisciplinary and interdisciplinary approach is desirable.

4.2 Comparative Law

This book not only discusses general theory of market integration but also—and perhaps more importantly—compares the regulatory philosophies and practices of the EU and China. This comparative approach will provide opportunities for mutual learning and understanding. The formation, operation and evolution of economic regulation in the EU may be used as a useful reference source for policymakers in China as they design and implement their own regulatory framework. Conversely, the lessons that the Chinese have learned from market integration and regulatory reform may enrich the understanding of their counterparts in the EU regarding the connection among law, regulation and economic growth.

4.3 Positive Analysis

Many of the studies in this volume can be classified as positive analyses, in the sense that these studies attempt to explain legal rules and outcomes as they are rather than to evaluate them on the basis of subjective criteria or to provide some institutional proposals to improve them. With no intention of underestimating the importance of normative analysis, this book prefers factual issues that are related to positive analysis to the value judgments that are associated with normative analysis, which inevitably generates controversy owing to its subjectivity. Furthermore, convincing positive analyses may contribute in clarifying existing normative issues and hence makes it more likely that a consensus will be reached. Nevertheless, some contributions will go beyond a mere positive analysis, by providing (carefully defined) policy recommendations, e.g. indicating how particular legal rules may be better able to stimulate market integration or enhance domestic demand and welfare.

5 Structure of the Book

This book is divided into four parts. Part I addresses competition law and public procurement. The chapter by Ma Jingyuan describes the role of market integration as a policy goal of competition in both the EU and China. The chapter by Mel Marquis also addresses competition law and examines state action in EU competition law and draws comparisons to Chinese competition law. Subsequently, Stefan Weishaar examines the role of public procurement in the market integration process in Europe and draws inferences for China.

Financial regulation is the subject of Part II. Hu Jiye and Sun Shouji address the implications of the European debt crisis for China. The chapter by Gui Binwei and Xu Guangdong addresses the impact of financial regulation on the profitability of SOEs. Finally, Li Wenjing and Zhou Tianshu examine the public and private enforcement of securities law in China.

Part III deals with freedom of establishment, professional regulation and self-regulation. Freedom of establishment is addressed *inter alia* by Shen Guang and Niels Philipsen. The authors take a private interest approach to assess the rules governing the freedom of establishment between provinces in China. Professional regulation is addressed by Niels Philipsen and Zhou Qi. In their chapter, Philipsen and Zhou examine alternative business structures of legal services, also from the perspective of the freedom of establishment (market integration).

Self-regulation can also take the form of self-imposed codes of conduct that are not legally binding. Lu Mengxing and Michael Faure consider these in the context of corporate environmental responsibility. In the last chapter of Part III, Mehdi Piri Damagh and Michael Faure consider the trade-off between self-regulation and public regulation by considering the specific case of regulation of cross-border pipelines.

Part IV (consisting of only one chapter) contains a set of comparative and concluding remarks by the editors.

6 Contributors

The contributors to this book are from various universities in China and in Europe. Many of the Chinese scholars, including Gui Binwei, Hu Jiye, Li Wenjing, Xu Guangdong and Zhou Tianshu, are connected to the RCLE of CUPL. Ma Jingyuan is associated with the Central University of Finance and Economics (CUFE) in Beijing. Sun Shouji is associated with the University of International Business and Economics (UIBE) in Beijing.

Several Chinese scholars are currently residing abroad. Zhou Qi is associated with the University of Leeds (UK), and Lu Mengxing and Shen Guang (both former students at CUPL) are now pursuing a PhD degree at Maastricht University (Netherlands).

The European scholars include Mel Marquis, associated with the European University Institute (Florence, Italy); Niels Philipsen from Maastricht University (Netherlands); and Stefan Weishaar from the University of Groningen (Netherlands). Michael Faure is associated with the Erasmus University Rotterdam and Maastricht University and is also a 'foreign distinguished professor' at CUPL. Mehdi Piri Damagh is a PhD researcher from Iran, currently associated with Maastricht University.

Acknowledgements As editors, we are grateful to the many people who made this book and the preceding seminar possible. We are especially grateful to all the contributors for their willingness to participate in this highly interesting and challenging project and for meeting the strict deadlines that we imposed upon them.

We are also grateful to the people who helped us in organizing the seminar on 'Market Integration: The EU experience and implications for regulatory reform in China'. Our thanks in this respect go to Professor Xi Tao, director of RCLE, for his continuous support and to Ms. Liang Min and Ms. Wang Yao for their efficient practical support in organizing the seminar.

Furthermore, we would like to thank the Student Fellows at METRO, as well as one of our former students, who helped us in proofreading and pre-editing many chapters. We would like to especially mention Amelie Draper, Joanna Switalska and Mariam Pathan here.

We are grateful to the China–EU School of Law at CUPL and Hamburg University for the financial support that made this research project possible. Finally, we are grateful to our publisher, Springer, for their kind, professional and efficient support in the publication of this book.

Finally, we would like to point out that in this introduction we adhered to the Chinese custom of mentioning family names of Chinese authors first. In the remainder of the book we will, however, follow the European (and our publisher's) custom.

April 2015

References

Barro R, Sala-i-Martin X (1995) Economic growth. MIT Press, New York

Bishop S, Walker M (2010) The economics of EC competition law: concepts, application and measurement, 3rd edn. Sweet & Maxwell, London

Faure M (2003) How law and economics may contribute to the harmonisation of tort law in Europe. In: Zimmerman R (ed) Grundstrukturen des Europäischen Deliktsrechts. Nomos, Baden-Baden, pp 31–82

Faure M, Xu G (eds) (2014) Economics and regulation in China. The Economics of Legal Relationships Series, Routledge

Jiang L (2007) Interpreting the AML on abuse of dominance – an interview with a member of the expert group on AML Drafting, Prof. Huang Yong. Administration of Industrial and Commerce 18, 37

Lu M (2008) The most serious weakness of the AML. Shanghai Security Daily, 14 April 2008

Philipsen NJ (2010) Regulation and competition in the legal profession: developments in the EU and China. J Competition Law Econ 6(2):203–231

Philipsen NJ, Xu G (eds) (2015) The role of law and regulation in sustaining financial markets. The Economics of Legal Relationships Series, Routledge

Wagener HJ, Eger T (2009) Europäische Integration, Wirtschaft und Recht: Geschichte und Politik. Vahlen, München, pp 240–250

Weishaar S (2011) Administrative monopolies, state aid, barriers to entry and market integration: challenges for the Chinese Anti-Monopoly Law. In: Faure M, Zhang X (eds) Competition policy and regulation: recent developments in China, the US and Europe. Edward Elgar, Cheltenham/Northampton, pp 98–129

Wen J (2010) Increasing domestic demand a long-term strategy: China's premier. Xinhua, Beijing, 22 March. http://www.china-embassy.org/eng/xw/t674551.htm

Xu G (2014) Does law matter for economic growth: a re-examination of the legal origin hypothesis. European Studies in Law and Economics No. 14. Intersentia, Antwerpen-Groningen

Part I
Competition Law and Public Procurement

Market Integration as the Goal of Competition Law: The EU Experience and Its Implications for China

Jingyuan Ma

1 Introduction

Both in China and in Europe, competition law plays a crucial role in establishing an integrated market. Chinese economists and lawyers have long acknowledged that administrative monopolies generate considerable efficiency losses and consumer welfare losses;[1] provisions on prohibiting administrative monopolies entered into force even decades before the promulgation of the Chinese Anti-Monopoly Law (hereinafter the AML). However, the enforcement of these provisions was rather ineffective.[2]

During the 13-year legislative history of the AML, it remained a debated issue whether prohibiting administrative monopolies should be included as one of its main objectives. Some commentators argued that administrative monopolies were *the* monopoly problem in China that the competition law should tackle,[3] whereas others proposed that given the specific economic and political characteristics of China during its transition from a centrally planned system to a market economy, the AML could only play a limited role in preventing governmental agencies from imposing anti-competitive restrictions.[4] Being influenced by this debate, provisions on prohibiting administrative monopolies were first included in several drafts of the AML that were released for comments after 2002; however, in the draft of December 2005, the entire chapter on "prohibiting administrative monopolies"

[1] Chan (2009), p. 267; Guo and Hu (2004), p. 277; Yu and Yu (2011).

[2] Owen et al. (2008), p. 235; Liu and Qiao (2012), p. 79.

[3] Wang (2004), p. 286.

[4] Owen et al. (2008), pp. 256–257.

J. Ma (✉)
Central University of Finance and Economics, Beijing, China
e-mail: jingyuan.ma@edle-phd.eu

N. Philipsen et al. (eds.), *Market Integration: The EU Experience and Implications for Regulatory Reform in China*, China-EU Law Series 2,
DOI 10.1007/978-3-662-48273-5_2

was completely deleted by the State Council. This chapter was reinserted in 2006 when the draft was submitted to the Standing Committee of the National People's Congress (NPC) for its first reading, and was kept until this law was promulgated in August 2007.[5]

Although the chapter on administrative monopolies was included in the final version of the AML, the current competition law system in China still faces some obstacles to combat administrative monopolies, therefore to foster integration within the domestic market. Foremost, among the five objectives that are listed in Article 1 of the AML,[6] the goal of breaking down trade barriers between regions was not explicitly mentioned. Although it seems to be obvious that to achieve any of these five goals, such as the objective of "safeguarding the interests of consumers and social public interest" or "promoting the healthy development of the socialist market economy", monopolistic conduct by administrative agencies should be prohibited, it remains both a theoretical and practical question how these broad competition goals are connected and, among all of these goals, whether the market integration goal should be prioritized.

This chapter draws attention to EU competition law. For over 60 years, competition law and policy in Europe has played a crucial role in the process of European integration. EU competition law has been considered as the essential legal instrument to break down trade barriers that are raised by both public and private powers. According to Barry Hawk, market integration is the "first principle" of the competition law in the European Community, and it is to be applied to eliminate restrictive practices that may impede the process of market integration.[7] Competition Commissioner Karel van Miert made clear that "*competition policy is not an end in itself, to be pursued dogmatically. Rather it is an instrument, a crucial one, to make the best of one's economic potential and to serve the common good. In doing so, in the EC, competition policy has been and remains also a major tool for integration*".[8] Starting from the Treaty of Paris in 1951, the goal of establishing an integrated common market has been clearly stated in EU treaties, and to achieve this goal, a complete competition law system has been developed to prohibit anti-competitive restrictions imposed both by public power at the Member States' level and by private enterprises.

This chapter explains how market integration has become the primary goal of EU competition law and how this goal can be achieved by developing a competition law framework. On the one hand, competition law should be implemented together with other EU laws in order to eliminate restrictions on the free movement of economic resources. On the other hand, provisions on dealing with governmental

---

[5] Owen et al. (2008), pp. 254–255.

[6] See Article 1 of the AML: "This Law is enacted for the purpose of preventing and restraining monopolistic conducts, protecting fair competition in the market, enhancing economic efficiency, safeguarding the interests of consumers and social public interest, promoting the healthy development of the socialist market economy". This translation is adopted from http://en.people.cn/90001/90776/90785/6466798.html. Accessed 6 March 2015.

[7] Hawk (1972), p. 231.

[8] Van Miert (1993), p. 135.

conduct on restricting competition should be developed and enforcement mechanisms of such provisions must be strengthened. This chapter shows that we can learn from the EU experience: if market integration is indeed a main goal of competition law in China, a more complete legal framework should be developed to deal with different types of administrative monopolies, and to secure an effective enforcement of the competition law, both public and private enforcement instruments should be enhanced.

The structure of this chapter is as follows. After this introduction, Sect. 2 will introduce administrative monopolies in China and their anti-competitive effects. Also, it will discuss the weak enforcement of competition law provisions on administrative monopolies. Section 3 will summarize how the market integration goal has been incorporated in the EU treaties and how the competition law system has developed in order to achieve this goal. Section 4 analyses the implications of EU experiences for China. The last section concludes.

2 Market Fragmentation and Administrative Monopolies in China

2.1 Administrative Monopolies

As a general definition, administrative monopolies usually refer to monopolistic behaviour that is supported by government or regulatory agencies at both central and regional levels. The governmental agencies and departments tend to protect certain sectors or industries through exercising their administrative power and thus impede competition in these sectors.

Administrative monopolies have developed due to historical reasons. Prior to the Market Reform in 1978, the Chinese economy was organized through a system of national planning.[9] State-owned enterprises (SOEs), which played a dominant role in almost all industries, were under the direct control of the central authority.[10] Learning from the former Soviet Union, before the reform, in every major industry in China, there was a "corresponding ministry" to ensure government control and management.[11] The State directly regulated production, price, supply of raw materials, entry and exit into the market, even the salary of enterprises' managers and employees.[12] SOEs had to produce according to central plans, and to deliver all outputs and revenues to the State.[13] The tight control over industries was gradually relaxed after the 1978 Market Reform. SOEs were allowed to retain part of their

[9] Shang (2009), p. 4.
[10] Lin et al. (1998), p. 423.
[11] Owen et al. (2008), p. 240; Berry (2005), p. 133; Yang (2002), p. 170.
[12] Lin et al. (1998), p. 423.
[13] Lin et al. (1998), p. 423.

profits. Nevertheless, because the Market Reform followed a top-down, planned approach,[14] one of the most challenging tasks during the transition was the "separation of the administration from the enterprise".[15] By implementing certain economic regulatory policies, governments in all regions are often involved in activities that have anti-competitive effects.[16]

Yang defines three types of administrative monopolies in China: sectorial monopolies, regional monopolies and public utilities.[17] Sectorial monopolies refer to large enterprise groups affiliated with government ministries that may receive favourable treatment, because government departments often play a regulatory role in industries such as non-ferrous metal, electronics, shipbuilding, tobacco and freight transport. Regional monopolies refer to local governments and administrative agencies, which may establish trade barriers in order to prevent the flow of goods and services from a particular local region to other regions. Such behaviour is also called local protectionism. Public utility monopolies refer to sectors that are considered as natural monopolies, such as water, power, heat, gas, postal services, telecommunications, civil aviation and railways. Their monopolistic position is often protected.[18]

Although, in general, administrative monopolies include monopolistic conduct by both central and local governments, it is more likely that the central government tends to conduct sectorial monopolies, and local governments are involved in regional monopolies. According to Chan,[19] in the analysis of administrative monopolies, restrictive behaviour by the central government is often excluded, because many scholars perceive such behaviour as implementing a type of national industrial policy. In most cases, administrative monopolies refer to the abusive conduct by local governments, which impose territorial restrictions on the free flow of economic resources or tend to protect local enterprises. Administrative monopolies can also refer to the abusive conduct by ministries and departments subordinated to the central government, which protect certain industries or sectors by restricting market entry.[20]

The underlying motivation for local protectionism is that, starting from the 1970s, the control over SOEs has been to a large extent decentralized to local governments; at the same time, as a result of the 1994 tax reform, the fiscal power was also decentralized.[21] The profits of SOEs could contribute to the tax revenues of local regions, and the performance of these companies could also partially

[14] Yang (2002), p. 175.
[15] Guo and Hu (2004), p. 272.
[16] Guo and Hu (2004), p. 272.
[17] Yang (2002), p. 172.
[18] Yang (2002), p. 172.
[19] Chan (2009), p. 264.
[20] Guo and Hu (2004), p. 273.
[21] Qian and Weingast (1996), p. 162.

determine how likely it is that local political leaders would be promoted.[22] As a consequence, local governments were incentivised to promote economic growth in their own region,[23] and some of them were willing to set up trade barriers to block the inflow of products and services from other regions in order to support the development of SOEs in their own region.

2.2 *Anti-competitive Effects of Administrative Monopolies*

Both lawyers and economists in China have acknowledged that administrative monopolies create anti-competitive effects, and a few empirical studies have been conducted to measure the efficiency losses that are caused by administrative monopolies. Many have agreed that the most significant effect of administrative monopolies is market fragmentation.[24] The empirical study by Poncet shows that the trade flow between provinces in China decreased significantly from 1987 to 1997. In 1987, consumers purchased products that were produced in the local region 12 times more than those that were produced in other provinces. This number increased to 16 in 1992 and 27 in 1997.[25] By applying the institution-structure-conduct-performance (ISCP) framework, Yu and Yu claimed that market segmentation could be significantly reduced by implementing a successful regional development policy and a cross-region competition policy.[26] For example, between 1985 and 2006, the degree of regional administrative monopoly in eastern provinces decreased more significantly than in western provinces.[27] One reason to explain such observations, according to their study, was that the regional development policy implemented during the Market Reform reduced the level of administrative monopolies in eastern provinces.[28]

In addition to the market fragmentation problem, it was argued that administrative monopolies may impose harm on consumer welfare, because administrative monopolies may incentivise inefficient firms to provide expensive products and services for local consumers, since the efficient ones in other regions are often prohibited from entering the local market.[29] Imposing restrictions on the free movement of economic resources may also lead to allocative inefficiency.[30]

---

[22] Jung and Hao (2003), p. 115; Chen and Zhu (2014), p. 230. See also the contribution by Shen and Philipsen to this volume.

[23] Saich (2011); Ip and Law (2011), p. 358.

[24] Chan (2009), p. 267; Guo and Hu (2004), p. 277.

[25] Poncet (2003).

[26] Yu and Yu (2011).

[27] Yu and Yu (2011), p. 94.

[28] Yu and Yu (2011), p. 94.

[29] Chan (2009), p. 267; Yang (2002), p. 172.

[30] Yu and Yu (2011), p. 79; Chen and Zhu (2012), p. 203.

The empirical study conducted by Yu and Zhang shows that in the industries of electricity, telecommunications, oil and railway, administrative monopolies cause substantial efficiency losses at both the micro and macro levels.[31] Lastly, some commentators have raised the issue that administrative monopolies not only cause economic losses but also generate other social costs, since they may incentivise business operators to engage in rent-seeking activities.[32]

2.3 Competition Rules Prohibiting Administrative Monopolies

The earliest competition provisions in China are the Provisional Rules on the Development and Protection of Socialist Competition—an administrative regulation that was adopted by the State Council on 17 October 1980.[33] In 1987, a more detailed administrative regulation on price control was adopted by the State Council.[34] Since the early 1990s, several administrative provisions have been promulgated in order to break down trade barriers established by local governments. The earliest rule was the Notice Concerning the Breaking of Local Market Blockades and Further Encouraging Commodity Circulation, issued by the State Council in November 1990.[35] In April 2001, the State Council enacted the Provisions of the State Council on Prohibiting Regional Blockade in Market Economic Activities.[36] In the same month, the State Council enacted Decisions of the State Council on Rectifying and Standardizing the Order in the Market Economy.[37] Administrative

---

[31] Yu and Zhang (2013), p. 216.

[32] Chan (2009), p. 267; Ding (2011), p. 119; Wang (2014), p. 6.

[33] GuanyuKaizhan He BaohuShehuizhuyiJingzheng De ZanxingGuiding (关于开展和保护社会主义竞争的暂行规定) [Provisional Rules on the Development and Protection of Socialist Competition] (promulgated by the State Council on 17 October 1980, effective on 17 October 1980, and repealed on 6 October 2001). Available at http://finance.sina.com.cn/g/20050418/12411526820.shtml (in Chinese). Accessed 6 March 2015.

[34] ZhonghuaRenminGongheguoJiageGuanliTiaoli (中华人民共和国价格管理条例) [Regulations of the People's Republic of China on Price Control] (promulgated by the State Council on 11 September 1987, effective on 11 September 1987), available at http://en.pkulaw.cn/display.aspx?cgid=3479&lib=law. (in English and Chinese). Accessed 6 March 2015.

[35] Mehra and Meng (2009), pp. 388 and 401.

[36] GuowuyuanGuanyuJinzhiZaiShichangJingjiHuodongZhongShixingDiquFengsuo De Guiding (国务院关于禁止在市场经济活动中实行地区封锁的规定) [Provisions of the State Council on Prohibiting Regional Blockade in Market Economic Activities] (promulgated by the State Council on 21 April 2001, effective on 21 April 2001), available at http://en.pkulaw.cn/display.aspx?cgid=35595&lib=law (in English and Chinese). Accessed 6 March 2015.

[37] GuowuyuanGuanyuZhengdun He GuifanShichangZhixu De Jueding (国务院关于整顿和规范市场秩序的决定) [Decisions of the State Council on Rectifying and Standardizing the Order in the Market Economy] (promulgated by the State Council on 27 April 2001, effective on 27 April 2001) available at http://en.pkulaw.cn/display.aspx?cgid=35594&lib=law. Accessed 6 March 2015.

monopoly and local protectionism were both prohibited by Article 11 of this decision.

Administrative regulations prohibiting monopolistic conduct have also been promulgated by the State Administration for Industry and Commerce (SAIC). It should be highlighted that the enforcement agency for the Law of Countering Unfair Competition is the SAIC and its local branches, AICs.[38] Therefore, the SAIC was empowered to enact and implement regulations in accordance with the Law of Countering Unfair Competition.[39] In 1994, both the SAIC and the AIC set up their offices to deal with fair trade issues.[40] In December 1993, the SAIC promulgated the Certain Regulations on Prohibiting Anti-competitive Practices of Public Enterprises.[41] This administrative provision specifically dealt with anti-competitive conduct by public utilities and administrative agencies. To strengthen the enforcement power of the SAIC, the State Council upgraded the SAIC to a ministerial level department in April 2001.[42] After the promulgation of the AML, SAIC became one of the enforcement agencies of the AML under the supervision of the State Council.[43]

2.4 *Laws Prohibiting Administrative Monopolies*

2.4.1 The Law for Countering Unfair Competition

The Law of the People's Republic of China for Countering Unfair Competition[44] was promulgated in 1993. It prohibits predatory pricing, which will restrict competition (Article 11), and forced tying and bundling (Article 12). This law also

[38] Jung and Hao (2003), p. 128.

[39] Jung and Hao (2003), p. 128.

[40] Mehra and Meng (2009), p. 403.

[41] GuanyuJinzhiGongyongQiyeXianzhiJingzhengXingwei De Ruogan Guiding (关于禁止公用企业限制竞争行为的若干规定) [Certain Regulations on Prohibiting Anti-competitive Practices of Public Enterprises] (promulgated by the State Administration for Industry and Commerce, 24 December 1993, effective on 24 December 1993), available at http://en.pkulaw.cn/display.aspx?cgid=8847&lib=law (in English and Chinese). Accessed 6 March 2015.

[42] Jung and Hao (2003), p. 130.

[43] GuowuyuanBangongtingGuanyuYinfaGuojiaGongshangXingzhengGuanliZongjuZhuyaoZhizeNeisheJigou He RenyuanBianzhi Guiding De Tongzhi (国务院办公厅关于印发国家工商行政管理总局主要职责,内设机构和人员编制规定的通知) [Notice of the General Office of the State Council on Major Duties, Internal Organization and Administration of the SAIC] 11 July 2008.

[44] ZhonghuaRenminGongheguoFanbuzhengdangjingzhengFa (中华人民共和国反不正当竞争法) [Anti-Unfair Competition Law of the People's Republic of China] (promulgated by the Standing Committee of the National People's Congress on 2 September 1993, effective 2 September 1993), available at http://tfs.mofcom.gov.cn/aarticle/date/i/s/200503/20050300027909.html (in Chinese). Accessed 15 March 2015; English translation is available at http://en.pkulaw.cn/display.aspx?cgid=6359&lib=law. Accessed 15 March 2015.

prohibits public utilities or other enterprises from holding monopolistic positions that may restrict competition by forcing others to purchase specific commodities (Article 6). Article 7 deals with the issue of administrative monopoly. It states that governmental agencies should not abuse administrative power to restrict competition by forcing others to purchase products.[45] This law is by no means a comprehensive competition law, because the major issues that this law addresses such as bribery, false advertisement, prohibition of fraudulent practices and coercive sales are more related to consumer protection, and it does not include competition rules on mergers.[46]

2.4.2 The Price Law

Articles 23 and 45 of the Price Law of 1997[47] are the provisions on prohibiting administrative monopolies.[48] Article 23 stipulates that when setting prices for public utilities that are important for public welfare, the governmental price regulatory agencies should organize public hearings, in order to collect opinions from consumers, business operators and other relevant departments.[49] Article 45 holds that local governments and governmental agencies at all levels should not set or adjust prices beyond their duties and shall not refuse to implement price intervention measures or emergency measures. This law also specifies administrative sanctions in case of infringement.[50] The enforcement of the Price Law relies on the National Development and Reform Commission (NDRC) and its local branches, DRCs, which later became one of the enforcement agencies of the AML.[51]

---

[45] Article 7 of the Countering Unfair Competition Law of the People's Republic of China: "The government and its organ shall not abuse its authority to force the others to purchase the commodities from the pointed seller or prohibit the fair competition from the others. The government and its organ shall not abuse its authority to prohibit outside commodities from going into home market, or prohibit domestic commodities from going to outside market". English translation is based on http://en.pkulaw.cn/display.aspx?cgid=6359&lib=law. Accessed 6 March 2015.

[46] Owen et al. (2005), p. 139; Owen et al. (2008), p. 233.

[47] ZhonghuaRenminGongheguoJiageFa (中华人民共和国价格法) [Price Law of the People's Republic of China] (promulgated by the Standing Committee of the National People's Congress, 29 December 1997, and effective on 1 May 1998) available at http://www.pkulaw.cn/fulltext_form.aspx?Db=chl&Gid=19158&keyword=%E4%BB%B7%E6%A0%BC%E6%B3%95&EncodingName=&Search_Mode=accurate (in English and Chinese). Accessed 6 March 2015. This law was enforced by the National Development and Reform Commission (NDRC) and local price administration agencies. Article 14 in Chapter 1 of this law prohibits price fixing, dumping sales at below cost prices and price discrimination.

[48] Chan (2009), p. 268.

[49] Article 23 of the Price Law.

[50] Article 45 of the Price Law.

[51] Liu and Qiao (2012), p. 79.

2.4.3 The Bidding Law

Articles 6 and 63 of the Bidding Law of 1999[52] prohibit the abuse of administrative power in bidding activities.[53] Article 6 prohibits administrative restrictions on the participation of bidding activities. Neither entity nor individual is allowed to impose illegal restrictions in order to exclude legal persons or organizations in other regions or sectors from participating in bidding activities. Article 6 also prohibits illegal interference with bidding activities.[54] Article 63 states that staff members at governmental organs who are responsible for the supervision over bidding activities should not abuse their administrative duties. This law provides both administrative and criminal sanctions in order to deter infringement.[55]

2.5 *The Weak Enforcement of Provisions on Prohibiting Administrative Monopolies*

Many commentators have claimed that the enforcement of these provisions on prohibiting administrative monopolies has been ineffective.[56] Provisions on prohibiting administrative monopolies are often overlapping and even contradict each other,[57] and different enforcement agencies may apply different standards in investigating administrative monopolies. For example, although the SAIC and its local branches (AICs) are the enforcement agencies of the Law for Countering Unfair Competition, Article 3 of this law states that the enforcement competence may be shared with other government departments, if the exercise of supervising monopolistic conduct in certain sectors is allowed by other administrative rules.[58] Meanwhile, the NDRC and its local branches (DRCs) are responsible for enforcing the Price Law, which may apply a different criterion in detecting administrative

[52] ZhonghuaRenminGongheguoZhaobiaoToubiaoFa (中华人民共和国招标投标法) [The Bidding Law of the People's Republic of China] (promulgated by the Standing Committee of the National People's Congress on 30 August 1999, effective on 1 January 2000), available at http://en.pkulaw.cn/display.aspx?cgid=23176&lib=law (in English and Chinese). Accessed 06.12.2014. See Article 32 in Chapter 3, "Tenderers shall not collude with each other in setting bidding prices, nor shall they exclude other tenderers from fair competition and harm the lawful rights and interests of the tenderee and other tenderers. Tenderers shall not collude with the tenderee in injuring the interests of the state, general public and other people. Tenderers shall be forbidden to win any bid by offering any bribe to the tenderee or any member of the bid-evaluation committee".

[53] Chan (2009), p. 268.

[54] Article 6 of the Bidding Law.

[55] Article 63 of the Bidding Law.

[56] Owen et al. (2008), p. 235; Liu and Qiao (2012), p. 79; Lin (2003), p. 10.

[57] Chan (2009), p. 268.

[58] Jung and Hao (2003), p. 129.

monopolies. Moreover, these enforcement agencies may apply different standards with regard to the assessment of damages and sanctions.[59]

Another reason for the weak enforcement of these provisions is that the enforcement agencies are mainly governmental agencies; therefore, the independence and authority of these agencies are rather weak.[60] The enforcement agencies, either the SAIC, the NDRC or other competition authorities, all function within the administrative system, and it is highly likely that the investigation will be interfered with and challenged by other governmental authorities.[61]

2.6 *The Anti-Monopoly Law*

During the legislative process of the AML, the question of whether prohibiting administrative monopolies should be taken as one of the objectives of the AML has been intensively debated.[62] Proponents have argued that given the substantial social harm that administrative monopolies create, a chapter on prohibiting administrative monopolies is an "indispensable part" of the AML.[63] Moreover, by including provisions on prohibiting abuse of administrative power, the AML could contribute to the political regulatory reform by drawing attention from government officials on anti-monopoly issues.[64] Opponents claimed that administrative monopolies would be better dealt with by administrative law or constitutional law rather than by competition law.[65] For example, Huang Yong, an advisory expert on the AML, argued that the ultimate solution for administrative monopolies is economic and political reform. Given the difficulty and the long process of such reform, adopting provisions restraining administrative power in the AML may be only a "second-best option".[66] Jung and Hao argued that the goal of tackling monopolistic behaviour by administrative power is "far-reaching" and "ambitious".[67] Some foreign scholars expressed similar views. For example, Fox argued that the abusive administrative restraints on economy should be dealt with by other legal instruments rather than an antitrust law.[68] Haley expressed his worries of applying an antitrust model that originated in the US and Europe to developing countries, because none of these

[59] Liu and Qiao (2012), p. 84.

[60] Chan (2009), p. 268, Jung and Hao (2003), p. 130; Sun (2010), p. 8.

[61] Chan (2009), p. 270; Jung and Hao (2003), p. 130.

[62] Chan (2009), p. 271.

[63] Wang (2008), p. 149

[64] Wang (2004), p. 294.

[65] Chan (2009), p. 275; Li and Wu (2006), pp. 73–75.

[66] Huang (2008), p. 122.

[67] Jung and Hao (2003), p. 134.

[68] Fox (2008), p. 173.

models were designed to deal with the state power or the need for state actions to create "conditions for effective market competition".[69]

In 2002, the drafting team of the AML, consisting of staff members from the State Economic and Trade Commission (SETC),[70] submitted a draft version to the Legislative Affairs Office of the State Council.[71] The 2002 Draft Anti-Monopoly Law included provisions prohibiting administrative monopolies in the fifth chapter, and the enforcement competence of these provisions is shared by "administrative authority at the higher level" and the Anti-Monopoly Management Body of the State Council.[72] The 2002 draft clearly reveals the concern of establishing a legislative framework to tackle the administrative obstacles for a competitive market.[73] However, the argument opposing the inclusion of administrative monopolies in the draft gained wide support during the legislative process[74] and the chapter on prohibiting administrative monopolies was completely deleted in the draft of the AML that was published in 2005.[75] Harris argued that there were two major reasons for excluding provisions against administrative monopolies: one was that, as it was argued by many commentators at that time, administrative monopolies might be better dealt with by a separate legal instrument or through regulatory reforms in the future rather than by an Anti-Monopoly Law. Another major issue was that administrative monopolies were often conducted to support the development of SOEs, and including provisions combating administrative monopolies would receive significant political pressure.[76] However, after receiving criticisms, in the draft published in 2006 this chapter was reinserted[77] and kept until the final version of the AML.

In the first chapter (General Provisions) of the AML, Article 8 states that it was prohibited for any administrative organ to abuse its administrative power to eliminate or restrict competition.[78] Chapter V (Articles 32–37) of the AML prohibits abuse of administrative power to eliminate or restrict competition.[79] Administrative

[69] Haley (2004), p. 277.

[70] After the SETC was abolished during the government agency reform in 2003, the Ministry of Commerce (MOFCOM) was responsible for many of the duties of the former Ministry of Foreign Trade and Economic Cooperation (MOFTEC) and the SETC. Since then, the MOFCOM participated in the drafting of the AML. *See* Owen et al. (2008), p. 260.

[71] Harris (2006), p. 178; Wang (2004), p. 285.

[72] Harris (2006), p. 178; Wang (2004), p. 290.

[73] Jung and Hao (2003), p. 108.

[74] Huang (2008), p. 131.

[75] New Changes on the Draft of the AML—Provisions on Prohibiting Administrative Monopolies were deleted (反垄断法面临新变数,禁止行政性垄断条款被删除), *Xinhua News*, 04 April 2006, available at http://news.xinhuanet.com/newscenter/2006-04/04/content_4383884.htm. Accessed 6 March 2015.

[76] Harris (2006), p. 214.

[77] Owen et al. (2008), p. 255.

[78] Article 8 of the AML.

[79] Chapter V of the AML.

organs or organizations are not allowed to abuse administrative power to restrict entities and individuals to operate, purchase or use certain commodities provided by business operators selected by these organs (Article 32). Administrative agencies or organizations are not allowed to create trade barriers between regions through imposing discriminative terms and technical requirements, exerting administrative licensing or setting barriers on the free distribution of commodities between regions (Article 33). Administrative organs or organizations are not allowed to abuse administrative power by imposing restrictions on business operators from outside regions to participate in the tendering and bidding activities in the local region (Article 34). Governmental agencies should not impose restrictions on business operators from other regions on the investment in or set up of branches in the local region through granting unequal treatment on outside business operators compared with local operators (Article 35). Administrative agencies are not allowed to abuse administrative power to urge business operators to conduct monopolistic activities (Article 36) or to issue provisions to eliminate or restrict competition between regions (Article 37).

The issue of how Chapter V of the AML is enforced is dealt with by Article 51 of the AML. Article 51 states that when the abuse of administrative power occurs, "the superior authority shall order it to make correction, and impose punishments on the directly liable person(s)-in-charge and other directly liable persons". According to Article 51, the enforcement competence of the anti-monopoly authority with respect to administrative monopoly is that it may provide suggestions for the relevant superior authority regarding how to handle the case.[80] From Article 51 of the AML, it seems that the enforcement competence of administrative monopoly remains the same as the previous legal rules and administrative regulations, that is, the "superior authority".[81] It is highly uncertain which governmental agency should be considered as a "superior authority", what the "punishment" will be and how the "liable persons" can be detected. From this article, it also remains unclear how individuals or firms can file administrative lawsuits in case of suffering a loss due to the anti-competitive conduct of administrative organs.[82] Given the weak enforcement of the competition rules before the AML prohibiting administrative monopolies, commentators have expressed the worry that administrative monopolies may not be effectively restrained even if it is included in an Anti-Monopoly Law.[83] For example, Fox argued that the enforcement powers against administrative abuses are "so weak as to nearly undermine the effort".[84] Huang

[80] Article 51 of the AML, English translation available at http://english.peopledaily.com.cn/90001/90776/90785/6466813.html. Accessed 6 March 2015.

[81] Chan (2009), p. 270; Wang (2014), p. 7.

[82] Sun (2010); Ip and Law (2011), p. 365.

[83] Howell et al. (2009), p. 84; Huang (2008), p. 131; Wang (2007).

[84] Fox (2008), p. 173.

stated that the provisions on administrative monopolies are "so mild that no meaningful enforcement can be foreseen".[85]

3 Market Integration as the Goal of EU Competition Law

3.1 Market Integration as the Goal of EU Competition Law: A Historical Overview

The process of European integration was first initiated by the Treaty of Paris in 1951, which established the European Coal and Steel Community (ECSC). The six founding countries are France, Germany, Italy, Belgium, the Netherlands and Luxembourg. From the late 1940s to the early 1950s, there was an intense debate at the policy level in Europe regarding the unification of Europe and the ECSC was considered one of the plans. As other proposals, such as establishing a European Political Community or a European Defence Community, all failed, uniting Europe through economic functions was seen as the last option to strengthen the economic cooperation between countries and to stimulate economic growth in Europe.[86] The economic cooperation had a strong responsibility to build a "new Europe".[87] In 1955, the plan of creating a Common Market in Europe gained political support during the conference in Messina.[88] In 1956, the Foreign Ministers of the six founding states of the ECSC had a meeting in Brussels. In the same year, the "Spaak Report" was drafted by the Heads of Delegations to the Foreign Ministers,[89] which laid the foundations for the Treaty of Rome.

According to the Spaak report, there are two plans to be accomplished during the process of European integration.[90] As a political goal, the economic integration between European countries would to a certain extent resolve the potential conflicts and wars. As an economic goal, the increased cooperation between Member States would contribute to economic prosperity in Europe. Both business entities and consumers would benefit from the increased trade between countries within the common market.[91] The foundation for the common market is the free movement of goods, services, capital and labour, that is, the "four-freedoms". In addition to breaking down the tariff barriers, restrictions on competition that are imposed by

[85] Huang (2008), p. 131.

[86] Gerber (1994), pp. 101–102.

[87] Gerber (1998), pp. 345–347.

[88] Gerber (1998), p. 343.

[89] Intergovernmental Committee of the Messina Conference, Report by the Heads of Delegations to the Foreign Ministers ("Spaak Report"), April 21, 1956. Akman (2009), p. 278.

[90] Gerber (1998), p. 343.

[91] Gerber (1998), p. 343.

private enterprises must be prohibited, and competition provisions are taken as the instrument to prohibit abusive conduct by private powers.[92]

This consensus of establishing a common market has been reflected in Article 2 of the Treaty of Paris as well as Article 2 of the Treaty of Rome. As shown in Table 1, this mission remained unchanged throughout the development of EU treaties. Nevertheless, the goals that this common market strives to achieve have been extended in later years. In particular, the Treaty on European Union (TEU) signed in Maastricht in 1992 extended the economic integration goal to broader concerns of political and monetary integration. Article 3(3) of the TEU states that an internal market must be established within the European Union and the objectives that the internal market strives to achieve include broad social and environmental considerations. Article 2(3) of the Treaty on the Functioning of the European Union (TFEU) clarified that the internal market should promote "balanced economic growth", "price stability" and "a highly competitive social market economy", and such economic development would lead to full employment and social progress, as well as the improvement of environment quality and technological progress.

3.2 Developing a Competition Law System to Achieve the Market Integration Goal

As discussed in the previous section, starting from the Treaty of Paris in 1951, all EU treaties sought to further integrate the common market. To achieve this goal, trade barriers and territorial restrictions have to be eliminated; then economic resources could be allocated optimally within the European Community, and consumers could be served by the product with the best quality irrespective of its origin.[93] Territorial restrictions on the flow of economic resources imposed by Member States are prohibited by the fundamental "four freedoms" under the EU law. Provisions on the "four freedoms" prohibit Member States from imposing restrictions on cross-border trade, such as the discrimination of services, goods or labour provided by other countries (Article 18 TFEU); restrictions on the freedom to provide services (Article 56 TFEU); restrictions on the free movement of goods (Articles 34–36 TFEU), capital (Article 63 TFEU) and workers (Articles 45–48 TFEU). Territorial restrictions that are imposed by undertakings are addressed by competition law.[94]

[92] Gerber (1998), p. 343.

[93] Craig and de Búrca (2008), p. 605.

[94] Craig and de Búrca (2008), p. 605; Weishaar (2011), p. 111; European Commission Enterprise and Industry (2010), "Free Movement of Goods: Guide to the Application of Treaty Provisions Governing the Free Movement of Goods", Luxembourg: Publications Office of the European Union, available at http://ec.europa.eu/enterprise/policies/single-market-goods/files/goods/docs/art34-36/new_guide_en.pdf. Accessed 7 March 2015.

Table 1 Market integration goal in EU treaties

EU treaty	Market integration goal
Treaty of Paris 1951, established the European Coal and Steel Community (ECSC)	Article 2: "The mission of the European Coal and Steel Community is to contribute to economic expansion, the development of employment and the improvement of the standard of living in the participating countries through the institution, in harmony with the general economy of the member States, of a common market".
Treaty of Rome 1957, established the European Economic Community (EEC)	Article 2: "The Community shall have as its task, by establishing a common market and progressively approximating the economic policies of Member States, to promote throughout the Community a harmonious development of economic activities, a continuous and balanced expansion, an increase in stability, an accelerated raising of the standard of living and closer relations between the States belonging to it".
Treaty on European Union (TEU)	Article 3(3): "The Union shall establish an internal market. It shall work for the sustainable development of Europe based on balanced economic growth and price stability, a highly competitive social market economy, aiming at full employment and social progress, and a high level of protection and improvement of the quality of the environment. It shall promote scientific and technological advance. It shall combat social exclusion and discrimination, and shall promote social justice and protection, equality between women and men, solidarity between generations and protection of the rights of the child. It shall promote economic, social and territorial cohesion, and solidarity among Member States. It shall respect its rich cultural and linguistic diversity, and shall ensure that Europe's cultural heritage is safeguarded and enhanced".
Treaty of Amsterdam (TEC)	Article 2: "The Community shall have as its task, by establishing a common market and an economic and monetary union and by implementing common policies or activities referred to in Articles 3 and 3a, to promote throughout the Community a harmonious, balanced and sustainable development of economic activities, a high level of employment and of social protection, equality between men and women, sustainable and non-inflationary growth, a high degree of competitiveness and convergence of economic performance, a high level of protection and improvement of the quality of the environment, the raising of the standard of living and quality of life, and economic and social cohesion and solidarity among Member States".

(continued)

Table 1 (continued)

EU treaty	Market integration goal
Treaty on the Functioning of the European Union (TFEU)	Article 2(3): "The Union shall establish an internal market. It shall work for the sustainable development of Europe based on balanced economic growth and price stability, a highly competitive social market economy, aiming at full employment and social progress, and a high level of protection and improvement of the quality of the environment. It shall promote scientific and technological advance".

Cross-regional trade barriers imposed by undertakings can be constructed either through public authorities or by private restrictions. If competition law and policy only prohibit distortive conduct by private powers, undertakings may seek protection from public authorities in order to obtain monopoly benefits. Restrictions on competition imposed by public authorities tend to be more stable than private measures. Ineffective enforcement of rules prohibiting public abusive conduct may also incentivise enterprises to engage in lobbying in order to obtain monopoly rights, which further leads to regulatory capture or administrative or government failure.[95] Therefore, the competition law system must be *complete*, that is, competition provisions must be developed to combat both public and private sources of anti-competitive practices.[96]

When the Treaty of Paris was signed, competition provisions on prohibiting anti-competitive practice by private undertakings were included: Article 65 prohibits anti-competitive agreements, and Article 66 deals with abuses of economic power. Including competition provisions in the treaty was an important milestone during the process of European integration. Articles 65 and 66 were also considered as a precedent for Articles 85 and 86 of the Treaty of Rome, which was signed in 1957 and created the European Economic Community (EEC).[97] In the Treaty of Rome, Articles 85 and 86 follow the same structure as Articles 65 and 66 of the Treaty of Paris and prohibit anti-competitive restrictions imposed by private entities, including monopolistic agreements and abuse of dominance. Article 90 of the Treaty of Rome (now 106 TFEU) was added in order to prohibit government interferences in economic activities through undertakings[98] and covers both public undertakings and undertakings that have been granted exclusive rights by the Member States.

If, by relying on the monopolistic rights and privileges that it has received from the State, the undertaking could be released from competition, the State bears the obligation that such protective measure should not be enacted or maintained and

[95] Marquis (2013), pp. 77 and 81.

[96] Marquis (2013), p. 80.

[97] Gerber (1998), p. 341.

[98] Gerber (1998), p. 344. On Article 106 TFEU, see also the contribution to this volume by Mel Marquis.

existing measures should be removed.[99] Already the Treaty of Paris contained provisions relating to state aids (Article 67). Similar provisions were contained in subsequent treaties and are now enshrined in Article 107 TFEU. This provision prevents the granting of state aid, including aid that is given to public undertakings or private ones, such as direct subsidies, favourable interest rates, loan guarantees, special terms for public ordering and tax exemptions. It makes clear that state aid is "incompatible" with the principle of the common market, since granting aid to certain undertakings will give them a financial advantage over their competitors, and such conduct would distort competition and affect trade between Member States. Only under specific circumstances, aid granted by the Member States may be considered as "compatible" with the internal market. For example, Article 107 (2) TFEU provides that aid to "make good the damage caused by natural disasters or exceptional occurrences" shall be "compatible" with the internal market. Article 107 (3) (c) states that aid to "facilitate the development of certain economic activities or of certain economic areas", "where such aid does not adversely affect trading conditions to an extent contrary to the common interest", may be considered to be "compatible" with the common market.

4 Implications for China

The discussion of the market integration goal under EU competition law is highly relevant for China, given the fact that competition laws in China and Europe face a similar challenge of dealing with geographic and institutional barriers that impede trade between regions.[100] Moreover, since the drafting process of the AML has been significantly influenced by EU competition law,[101] it becomes important to pay attention to the EU experience in respect of how the market integration goal has been incorporated and how it is enforced. The EU experience has implications for China in three aspects: firstly, the EU competition law prioritized market integration and presents the challenges on how this goal could be connected with other goals of the competition policy as well as the mission of the European Union. Secondly, the EU experience indicates that to achieve the market integration goal, a complete competition law framework should be developed to prohibit distortive conduct by both public authorities and private enterprises. Thirdly, the EU experience could show that the enforcement instruments of the AML need to be strengthened to implement the competition provisions.

---

[99] Craig and de Búrca (2008), p. 1075.

[100] Marquis (2013), p. 91.

[101] Jung and Hao (2003), p. 124; Samuels (2007), p. 184.

4.1 Market Integration as the Goal of Competition Law

As discussed above, during the legislation process of the AML, the question of whether prohibiting administrative monopolies should be considered as one of the objectives of the AML has been debated. The drafting process of the AML corresponded to the development of the openness of the market, and there is, in fact, no consensus among Chinese scholars and policymakers regarding which goal the AML should prioritize.[102] To find a solution, the AML has included a multitude of policy goals, including both economic and non-economic considerations. The goals of contributing to the development of a socialist market economy and protecting public interest, however, may on certain occasions contradict the goal of market integration. Foremost, given the close connection between SOEs and administrative agencies, it is highly possible that administrative monopolies may be conducted to support the development of SOEs.[103] Moreover, administrative organs may implement industrial policies that give rise to anti-competitive effects. For example, according to Yu and Zhang's study, in the sectors of electricity and telecommunications and in the railway industry and the mining industry, the intensity of administrative monopolies is the highest.[104] In these sectors, the dominant enterprises are often SOEs and most of them are under the supervision of industry regulators.[105] In some cases, it is not entirely clear whether an entity is a commercial enterprise or an administrative agency.[106] Therefore, if market integration is considered as the goal of competition law in China, questions remain with respect to how this goal could be connected with the goal of developing a socialist market economy and the goal of protecting public interest and, more importantly, how the AML can be implemented if the administrative monopolies are related to SOEs.

In Europe, the legislative history of EU competition law showed a strong tendency toward prioritizing market integration. Explicitly focusing on market integration contributed to the development of a well-structured EU competition law system and gave competition authorities a clear criterion that could be applied in competition cases. However, market integration never became the *sole* aim of EU competition law. Although goals of EU competition law have not been described precisely in any political documents or decisions,[107] European scholars generally agree that EU competition law pursues both market integration and competition goals. This includes promoting consumer welfare and total welfare and protecting the "freedom to compete" by following the German Ordo-liberal

[102] Ma (2014), pp. 45–57.

[103] Marquis (2013), p. 88; Furse (2009), pp. 92–93.

[104] Yu and Zhang (2013), p. 215.

[105] Yang (2002), pp. 170–171.

[106] Marquis (2013), p. 88; Furse (2009), pp. 92–93.

[107] Ahlborn and Padilla (2008), p. 40.

approach.[108] The goal of market integration remained the central concern of EU competition law until the 1990s.[109] It was accepted in the literature that competition law could be utilized to serve the integration goal and competition goals simultaneously.[110] Since the 1980s, economic goals have gained popularity in the US and the view of prioritizing economic goals has also been exported from the US to Europe.[111] Some European scholars argued that EU competition policy has shifted from the integration goal towards the competition goal, and this trend was first observed in the 1990s when the European Commission advocated a "more economic approach".[112] According to Roeller, the recent increasing use of economics is regarded as one of the "most significant trends" in EU competition policy.[113] The goal of promoting consumer welfare under EU competition law has been emphasized during the promotion of a "more economic approach" and an "effect-based" analysis of competition issues, which focuses on the competitive effects on the market and consumers.[114]

Given the long pluralist tradition of EU competition law, the recent trend of shifting from the integration goal towards economic goals may encounter a few challenges.[115] Firstly, law and economics literature shows that the goals of market integration and competition are not always consistent. For example, to achieve the market integration goal, imposing a *per se* ban on territorial protection may give rise to substantial loss of efficiency savings resulting from intra-brand restrictions; another example is that prohibiting price discrimination may be beneficial to achieve the market integration goal, while at the same time it may reduce welfare gain for consumers. Based on the theoretical analysis, there is a tension between protecting consumer welfare, efficiency and the market integration goal, and a successful move towards a "more economic approach" would require more attention to be given to economic goals.[116] Secondly, the relationship between the market integration goal and competition goals is ultimately subject to political interpretations. As the Treaty of Lisbon moved Article 3 (1) (g) on "a system ensuring competition in the internal market is not distorted" into a Protocol, it raised doubts about whether competition goal could be *separated* from the market integration goal.[117] In this aspect, both Chinese Anti-Monopoly Law and EU competition policy face the challenge of aligning the political consensus with theoretical analysis on what role competition law could play in the development

[108] Kirchner (1998), pp. 513–523.

[109] Aydin and Thomas (2012), p. 537.

[110] Kirchner (1998), p. 516; Kirchner (2007), p. 15.

[111] Fox (2006), p. 725.

[112] Monti (2001); Kirchner (2007), p. 7.

[113] Roeller (2011), p. 289.

[114] Roeller (2011), p. 289.

[115] Van den Bergh (2007), p. 31.

[116] Van den Bergh (2007), p. 33.

[117] Jones and Sufrin (2010), p. 43.

of a market economy and how market integration could be connected with other goals of competition law.

4.2 Developing a Competition Law System to Achieve the Market Integration Goal

The EU experience indicates that if market integration is the goal, competition policy can be taken as an essential instrument to achieve this goal. In particular, the EU experience shows that to establish an integrated market, trade barriers must be eliminated and it is important to protect competition between regions. Increased competition between regions will not only promote allocative and productive efficiency at the national level but will also generate benefits to business operators and consumers in all regions. As a country with a rather weak development of competition culture, China could draw lessons from the EU in how protecting competition could benefit the national economy. The EU experience shows that by reducing trade barriers, consumers in all regions could benefit from lower prices, increased product choices and improved quality, as well as the development of new technology. Promoting competition rules would increase consumer welfare and would contribute to the goal of enhancing economic integration.

Under the current competition law system in China, the linkage between the market integration goal and provisions on prohibiting administrative monopolies is weak. In particular, the definition of the term "administrative monopoly" should be clarified. To take a closer examination on the conduct of "administrative monopolies" itself, it leads to two different problems. One type of administrative monopolies refers to territorial control; for example, local governments tend to abuse their administrative power in order to restrict the inflow or outflow of economic resources (including capital, technology, labour and product) from the local region to other regions. The other main type of administrative monopolies refers to granting privileges to government-affiliated companies; for example, government agencies tend to protect companies in their local region or in their sector by granting exclusive rights, or by providing subsidies, or forcing local consumers to purchase products or services provided by certain companies. These two different types of monopolistic behaviour should be dealt with by two different sets of legal rules. In the EU, state actions restricting the free movement of economic resources are prohibited under the general provisions on the four freedoms, and the trade barriers established by undertakings are prohibited under competition provisions. In particular, Article 106 TFEU on public undertakings deals with the situation when a government grants exclusive rights to undertakings and Article 107 TFEU on state aid, which deals with the abusive conduct of granting subsidies or giving favourable treatment to government-affiliated undertakings.[118]

[118] Weishaar (2011), p. 111.

Under the current Chinese competition law system, different types of administrative monopolies have not yet been distinguished and clearly defined. It would be difficult to enforce these provisions if "administrative monopolies" are treated as one thing since they refer to different types of behaviour and lead to different effects. The monopolistic conduct of administrative agencies themselves, such as abusing administrative power in order to erect local trade barriers and impede market integration, is certainly beyond the capacity of a single competition law. Like formulating the fundamental rights of four freedoms under the EU law, a whole set of administrative rules and regulations have to be implemented, and a more comprehensive legal framework has to be developed to prevent local governments from imposing distortive restrictions. With respect to the distortive conduct of government intervention through granting exclusive rights to government-affiliated undertakings, competition provisions should be further clarified in order to distinguish between different types of monopolistic behaviour, such as developing rules prohibiting the granting of exclusive rights on undertakings and prohibiting giving favourable treatment to undertakings. In this way, the linkage between the market integration goal and competition provisions provided by the AML could be strengthened, and the enforcement mechanisms for these provisions could be developed.

4.3 Enhancing Enforcement Mechanisms

The EU experience would also have implications for China in respect of improving the enforcement of the AML. The EU experience also shows that to achieve the goal of market integration, the enforcement of Chapter V of the AML should be strengthened. Under the current enforcement system of the AML, the SAIC and the NDRC—two administrative organs—are only granted the power to provide suggestions to the superior authority when administrative monopoly occurs. In the EU, provisions on prohibiting Member States from granting distortive privileges on public undertakings have been effectively enforced. On the one hand, both the Commission[119] and the European Court of Justice have actively worked together to prioritize market integration in competition cases;[120] on the other hand, the EU competition law system granted natural and legal persons the right to undertake

[119] For example, in 1972, in the first annual report on competition policy, the Commission clearly stated that the primary goal was to protect market integration: "Concerning the competition applicable to enterprises, Community policy in the first place must prevent the substitution of state restrictions and obstacles to trade which have been abolished, by private measures with similar consequences". Premier rapport sur la politique de concurrence (1972), at 13. The Report was originally written in French. The quoted text was translated by Hawk. Hawk (1972), p. 231.

[120] Gerber (1994), p. 108.

private actions for compensating damages at national courts.[121] In the case of China, Chapter VII of the AML on legal liabilities does not provide provisions on how private victims of administrative monopolies could seek damage compensation. Compared with the EU competition law system, both public enforcement and private enforcement of the AML on prohibiting administrative monopolies are rather weak.[122]

5 Conclusion

Administrative monopolies are one of the major obstacles for China to establish an integrated and competitive domestic market. Local governments tend to establish entry barriers in order to support enterprises in their local region, resulting in substantial efficiency losses and consumer welfare losses. Since the beginning of the 1980s, several administrative provisions and laws have been implemented to prohibit administrative monopolies, and this concern has also been incorporated in the Anti-Monopoly Law when it was promulgated in 2007. However, many commentators have expressed their concerns that the enforcement of provisions on prohibiting administrative monopolies in China is rather ineffective. This chapter introduced how market integration became the primary goal of the EU competition policy and how competition policy could play a crucial role during the process of European integration. The EU experiences have implications for China, this being that if market integration is considered as the goal of competition law, the linkage between this goal and corresponding legal provisions must be strengthened. In particular, different conduct of administrative monopolies should be distinguished and more clearly defined by the AML. The EU experience shows that by aligning the anti-competitive conduct with competition provisions, and by providing both public and private enforcement instruments for these provisions, a complete competition law framework could be established. In this way, competition law and policy in China could be better implemented in order to foster economic integration between regions and contribute to the development of a market economy.

Acknowledgement I am indebted to Stefan Weishaar and Niels Philipsen for their helpful and insightful comments and suggestions. My sincere gratitude also goes to Michael Faure, Roger van den Bergh and Mel Marquis for their help and encouragement. Profound thanks to all the participants at the conference on "Market Integration: The EU Experience and Implications for Regulatory Reform in China" held at China University of Political Science and Law (CUPL) on 12 May 2014.

---

121 Marquis (2013), p. 113.

122 Marquis (2013), p. 116.

References

Ahlborn C, Padilla J (2008) From fairness to welfare: implications for the assessment of unilateral conduct under EC competition law. In: Ehlermann CD, Marquis M (eds) European competition law annual 2007: a reformed approach to Article 82 EC. Hart, Oxford, pp 37–54

Akman P (2009) Searching for the long-lost soul of Article 82 EC. Oxf J Legal Stud 29 (2):267–303

Aydin U, Thomas KP (2012) The challenges and trajectories of EU competition policy in the twenty-first century. J Eur Integration 34(6):531–547

Berry JA (2005) Anti-Monopoly Law in China: a socialist market economy wrestles with its antitrust regime. Int Law Manag Rev 2:129–152

Chan GYM (2009) Administrative monopoly and the Anti-Monopoly Law: an examination of the debate in China. J Contemp China 18(59):263–283

Chen L, Zhu W (2012) The economic performance of regional administrative monopoly: an empirical research based on the instrumental variable method (中国地区性行政垄断与区域经济绩效——基于工具变量法的实证研究). Comp Econ Soc Syst (经济社会体制比较) 2012(4):195–204

Chen L, Zhu W (2014) Causes and governance of regional administrative monopoly (中国地区性行政垄断的成因与治理). J Syst Manag (系统管理学报) 23(2):229–237

Craig P, De Búrca G (2008) EU Law: text, cases and materials, 4th edn. Oxford University Press, Oxford

Ding Q (2011) Research on the formation and reformation of administrative monopoly (行政垄断的形成机制及改革思路研究). Ind Econ Rev (产经评论) 2011(3):119–132

European Commission, Enterprise and Industry (2010) Free movement of goods: Guide to the application of Treaty provisions governing the free movement of goods, Luxembourg: Publications Office of the European Union

Fox EM (2006) Monopolization, abuse of dominance, and the indeterminacy of economics: The U.S./E.U. divide. Utah Law Rev 3:725–740

Fox EM (2008) An Anti-Monopoly Law for China – scaling the walls of government restraints. Antitrust Law J 75(1):173–194

Furse M (2009) Antitrust law in China, Korea and Vietnam. Oxford University Press, Oxford

Gerber DJ (1994) The transformation of European Community competition law? Harv Int Law J 35(1):97–148

Gerber DJ (1998) Law and competition in twentieth century Europe: protecting prometheus. Clarendon, Oxford

Guo Y, Hu A (2004) The administrative monopoly in China's economic transition. Communist Post-Communist Stud 37(2):265–280

Haley JO (2004) Competition policy for East Asia. Wash Univ Global Stud Law Rev 3:277–284

Harris HS Jr (2006) The making of an antitrust law: the pending Anti-Monopoly Law of the People's Republic of China. Chic J Int Law 7(1):169–230

Hawk BE (1972) Antitrust in the EEC – the first decade. Fordham Law Rev 41(2):229–292

Howell TR, Wolff AW, Howe R, Oh D (2009) China's new Anti-Monopoly Law: a perspective from the United States. Pacific Rim Law Policy J 18(1):53–95

Huang Y (2008) Pursuing the second best: the history, momentum and remaining issues of China's Anti-Monopoly Law. Antitrust Law J 75(1):117–132

Ip EC, Law MKH (2011) Decentralization, agency costs, and the new economic constitution of China. Constit Polit Econ 22:355–372

Jones A, Sufrin B (2010) EU competition law: texts, cases and materials, 4th edn. Oxford University Press, Oxford

Jung YJ, Hao Q (2003) The new economic constitution in China: a third way for competition regime? Northwestern J Int Law Bus 24:107–172

Kirchner C (1998) Future competition law. In: Ehlermann CD, Laudati L (eds) European competition law annual 1997 – objectives of competition policy. Hart, Oxford, pp 513–523

Kirchner C (2007) Goals of antitrust and competition law revisited. In: Schmidtchen D, Albert M, Voigt S (eds) The more economic approach to European competition law. Mohr Siebeck, Tübingen, pp 7–26

Li B, Wu Y (2006) Administrative monopolies – a perspective from the Anti-Monopoly Law (行政垄断的反垄断法反思). Guangxi Soc Sci (广西社会科学) 2:73–75

Lin P (2003) Competition policy in East Asia: the cases of Japan, People's Republic of China, and Hong Kong. Lingnan University Working paper series 133

Lin YF, Cai F, Li Z (1998) Policy burdens, and state-owned enterprise reform. Am Econ Rev 88 (2):422–427

Liu Z, Qiao Y (2012) Abuse of market dominance under China's 2007 Anti-Monopoly Law: a preliminary assessment. Rev Ind Organ 41:77–107

Ma J (2014) Comparative analysis of merger control policy – lessons for China. Intersentia, Antwerpen-Groningen

Marquis M (2013) Abuse of administrative power to restrict competition in China: four reflections, two ideas and a thought. In: Faure M, Zhang X (eds) The Chinese Anti-Monopoly Law: new developments and empirical evidence. Edward Elgar, Cheltenham, pp 73–141

Mehra SK, Meng Y (2009) Against antitrust functionalism: reconsidering China's Anti-Monopoly Law. V J Int Law 49(2):379–430

Monti M (2001) Foreword, XXXth report on competition policy 2000, European Commission, Brussels, Luxembourg

Owen BM, Sun S, Zheng W (2005) Antitrust in China: the problem of incentive compatibility antitrust in China. J Competition Law Econ 1(1):123–148

Owen BM, Sun S, Zheng W (2008) China's competition policy reforms: the Anti-monopoly Law and beyond. Antitrust Law J 75(1):231–266

Poncet S (2003) Measuring Chinese domestic and international integration. China Econ Rev 14:1–21

Qian Y, Weingast BR (1996) China's transition to markets: market-preserving federalism, Chinese style. J Policy Reform 1(2):149–185

Roeller L (2011) Challenges in EU competition policy. Empirica 38(3):287–314

Saich T (2011) Governance and politics of China, 3rd edn. Palgrave Macmillan, New York

Samuels JR (2007) "Tain't what you do" effect of China's proposed Anti-Monopoly Law on State owned enterprises. Pa State Int Law Rev 26:169–202

Shang M (2009) Antitrust in China – a constantly evolving subject. Competition Law Int 5:4–11

Sun J (2010) On the defects of administrative monopoly in China's "Anti-Monopoly Law" and its improvement. Can Soc Sci 6(2):1–19

Van den Bergh R (2007) The "more economic approach" and the pluralist tradition of European competition law (comment). In: Schmidtchen D, Albert M, Voigt S (eds) The more economic approach to European competition law. Mohr Siebeck, Tübingen, pp 27–36

Van Miert K (1993) Global forces affecting competition policy in a post-recessionary environment. World Competition 17(2):135–149

Wang X (2004) Issues surrounding the drafting of China's Anti-Monopoly Law. Wash Univ Global Stud Law Rev 3:285–296

Wang X (2007) Four main obstacles of Anti-Monopoly Law enforcement (反垄断法实施面临四大瓶颈), Cai Jing Magazine, 27 December 2007. http://www.caijing.com.cn/2007-12-05/100040265.html

Wang X (2008) Highlights of China's new anti-monopoly law. Antitrust Law J 75:133–150

Wang X (2014) Difficulties and implications of regulating administrative monopoly (行政垄断规制的困境与展望). China Price (中国物价) (3):6–8

Weishaar SE (2011) Administrative monopolies, state aid, barriers to entry and market integration: challenges for the Chinese Anti-Monopoly Law. In: Faure M, Zhang X (eds) Competition policy and regulation: recent developments in China, the US and Europe. Edward Elgar, Cheltenham, pp 98–129

Yang J (2002) Market power in China: manifestations, effects and legislation. Rev Ind Organ 21 (2):167–183

Yu L, Yu D (2011) The measure of regional administrative monopoly in China. In: Faure M, Zhang X (eds) Competition policy and regulation: recent developments in China, the US and Europe. Edward Elgar, Cheltenham, pp 79–97

Yu L, Zhang W (2013) Research on the intensity and effect of industrial administrative monopoly in China. In: Faure M, Zhang X (eds) The Chinese Anti-Monopoly Law: new developments and empirical evidence. Edward Elgar, Cheltenham, pp 194–217

The State of State Action in EU Competition Law (Post-*Greek Lignite*) and a National Competition Strategy for China

Mel Marquis

1 Introduction

Europe has never adopted the term Anti-Monopoly Law. In the EU, stress is laid on the "competitive process". This term often refers not to hard-nosed competition with entry and exit in the name of maximising output and productivity gains; but to a dynamic process of rivalry in markets thought to be generally incapable of self-correction and thus in need of vigilant tutelage. The aim of keeping markets open and rivalry alive is reflected in the credo that competition must be protected "as an institution". To those who view competition law in (purely or largely) utilitarian terms as serving ulterior objectives such as the public interest, efficiency, consumer welfare, economic growth, and/or the (imperfect) alleviation of poverty, the idea that the ultimate aim of competition law is preserving openness and rivalry may seem unsatisfactory. Yet this distinctive, semi-deontological interpretation of competition law persists, and it is understandable in light of the intellectual history of European competition law. To abbreviate that story, the idea is that freedom should be denied one act of liberty: the act of transforming freedom into power that is hostile to freedom and liable to trample on it. To prevent economic liberty from cancelling itself out so that only a monopolistic tyrant remains, market regulation in the form of (*inter alia*) competition law must be an integral part of the economic order. There are competing conceptions of competition law in Europe, but the one just described has been very influential. The superimposition upon this rivalry- and freedom-based canvass of a utilitarian understanding of competition law has left EU competition law with a split personality in which efficiency concerns might drive the law in some areas while efficiency is trumped in other areas by quasi-egalitarian

M. Marquis (✉)
European University Institute, Florence, Italy
e-mail: Mel.Marquis@EUI.eu

N. Philipsen et al. (eds.), *Market Integration: The EU Experience and Implications for Regulatory Reform in China*, China-EU Law Series 2,
DOI 10.1007/978-3-662-48273-5_3

notions of openness, or the notion that a dominant firm has a special responsibility not to impair effective competition.[1]

Is a special responsibility not to impair competition also ascribed to the *State*? In particular, is (should) the State (be) bound by specific competition law constraints where its administrative or legislative interventions create a "legal" monopoly? Transposed roughly to terms familiar to Chinese experience, this is akin to asking: how does EU competition law regulate the European version of administrative monopoly?[2] As I have discussed the Chinese variant of the problem in an earlier essay,[3] this chapter mainly focuses on the EU while at the same time offering input as to how a *national competition strategy* in China might impose enhanced legal-institutional-cultural discipline on administrative monopolies (bearing in mind that the problem in China has distinct political overtones,[4] which suggests that strictly legal-doctrinal approaches can only be part of an effective strategy, and cannot in the end *constitute* the strategy).

With regard to Europe, if EU law really cares about the competitive process, then a central concern must logically be the harm caused to that process by legal monopolies (exclusive rights) and similar privileges (special rights). Indeed, legal monopolies are the *antithesis* of the competitive process. Here one finds common ground between the deontological and utilitarian visions of competition law: each should be concerned about exclusive and special rights because such rights reduce competition and undermine its positive aggregate consequences for welfare, productivity and innovation. Furthermore, in a system of fragmented national markets, exclusive and special rights discourage trade and may encourage further grants of such rights in the Westphalian tradition of reciprocity and tit-for-tat. The same observations may be made with regard to subsidies and state aid. These

[1] A crucial goal of the EU's competition regime is the integration of national markets and the idealized "unity" of the single, EU-wide market. The integration objective is partly economic and partly political, and may be consistent with both the (semi-)deontological understanding of EU competition law and the efficiency/consumer welfare understanding. But these different conceptions are ultimately incompatible. This chapter does not grapple with the eternal "goals" debate but only raises the issue incidentally. For further (comparative) discussion of the EU model, see Marquis (2015).

[2] The term *xingzheng longduan* can have different meanings in different contexts. See Wang (2014), for example at p. 113 or p. 266, and generally Chapter 13. In another essay I expressed dissatisfaction with its English translation, preferring the bulkier but clearer "abuse of administrative power to restrict competition". See Marquis (2013).

[3] Marquis (2013).

[4] See Cheng (2014), referring to the views of Shi Jichun. The somewhat pessimistic conclusions of commentators such as Cheng, Shi and others (e.g., Wenton Zheng) are understandable, and I share the view that China's Antimonopoly Law alone cannot resolve the problem of administrative monopoly. However, the limits of the current legal apparatus and the related challenges (e.g., as regards the special characteristics of China's judicial system) do not justify the conclusion that legal instruments and law-based enforcement are futile in this field. Rather, it is necessary to develop better legal, institutional and political mechanisms, as well as educational and cultural transmission approaches, to enhance compliance incentives. For a fuller examination of these issues, see Marquis (2013).

considerations were understood by the authors of the Treaty of Rome when the Treaty was being negotiated in 1956–1957. They also realised that the effectiveness of mere legal rules depends on robust enforcement. Although the jargon was not current in the 1950s, the Treaty authors sought to establish credible commitment mechanisms. The radical idea of a supranational "prosecutor" dragging sovereign states into a supranational court wherein the court might condemn the state for failure to respect its Treaty obligations could only be accepted because the original six Member States of the European Economic Community (EEC) recognised that the benefits of credible commitments justified the courageous step of submitting to supranational authority. The Member States did not fully anticipate that Community law (now EU law) would develop in such a way that private traders could seek relief and even damages against them in their own national courts for erecting impermissible obstacles to trade, but this parallel mechanism has undoubtedly made the Member States' commitments more credible still.

However, the EU Member States have always been able to invoke public interest justifications to justify reasonably tailored trade barriers, state aid, and exclusive and special rights. It is therefore inaccurate to portray the EU as having run amok and deprived Member States of all their regulatory prerogatives. Nevertheless, state measures often do create tensions with the objectives of market integration, efficiency/welfare and competition "as such". The EU competition rules discussed in this chapter leave some space for Member States to exercise their prerogatives as regulators of economic life, but they impose outer limits and establish a superordinate rationality upon state measures when they step over those boundaries.

This chapter surveys the most important tool available under EU law in this context—namely Article 106 of the Treaty on the Functioning of the European Union (TFEU). Article 106 allows legitimate and proportionate state action while filtering out unjustified parochial measures that restrict competition. Although other instruments of EU law may be relevant where the state intervenes in the economy, Article 106 and its complex substantive components will be the main point of focus here, in part because it is a major topic unto itself, and in part because there is new jurisprudence in this area: part 2 of this chapter thus offers a detailed analysis and critique of *Commission v. DEI* (also known as *Greek lignite*), decided in July 2014, and the views of the Commission, the General Court and the Court of Justice are all examined. As will be respectfully suggested, this case has been decided by the Court of Justice in error.

It will be apparent that the term state action is not used here (e.g., in the chapter title) to denote an exemption from competition law rules on the ground that states acting as sovereigns fall outside the scope of EU law, or that business operators acting pursuant to clear state policies and effectively supervised by state officials are likewise immune. The term is thus not used as it is in U.S. antitrust parlance; in the U.S., the same term is often used as a reference to exemptions developed in *Parker v. Brown* and *Midcal*.[5]

[5] U.S. Supreme Court, *Parker v. Brown*, 317 U.S. 341, 4 January 1943; U.S. Supreme Court, *Calif. Retail Liquor Dealers Ass'n v. Midcal Aluminum*, 445 U.S. 97, 3 March 1980.

No attempt is made here to embark on detailed comparisons between U.S. law and EU law in relation to the lawfulness of state measures. But the differences between the two regimes should not be underestimated. Whereas the conditions for the *Parker/Midcal*-based exemptions in the U.S. serve as a check of procedural character to ensure transparency, adequate representation and political accountability, EU law goes farther and to some extent even allows judges to substitute their own assessments of appropriateness for those of the legislatures and executive actors at national, regional and local level.[6] In this regard, a degree of caution is desirable, and two fundamental points should be kept in mind. First, the authors of the Treaty of Rome "constitutionalised" the legal restraints on anticompetitive regulation with greater intensity than U.S. authorities have done. There is both symbolic and practical significance in the fact that, whereas, in the U.S., the Sherman Act is an instrument of "secondary" law, in the EU the competition rules are hierarchically superior legal rules of primary law. It is equally significant, as the U.S. Supreme Court noted in *Parker*, that the Sherman Act was never intended to function as a framework for the sovereign activities of the American states.[7] By 1890, commercial integration in the U.S. was advancing rapidly, and the increasingly integrated economy probably cannot be compared to the state of affairs in Europe in 1957. Among the EEC countries, outright tariff barriers and discriminatory taxes persisted until the end of the 1960s; non-tariff barriers, including those cutting against the competition rules (but many of which may be justified), are built and rebuilt routinely by today's legislatures. The second point is that while *Parker* reflected the anti-*Lochnerian* spirit of the times (which has generally endured) and the rejection of substantive due process,[8] the very *raison d'être* of the Treaty of Rome (today, the TFEU) is to trigger a radical and irreversible unification of previously fragmented national markets. Substantive due process at least arguably never had a firm foundation in the U.S. federal Constitution but the Treaty of Rome was replete with prohibitions addressed to Member States to promote market unification and to avoid re-fragmentation. In its most expansive interpretation, the dormant Commerce Clause doctrine in U.S. constitutional law is roughly analogous to the free movement rules in Europe, but the impact of that doctrine has been tempered since the 1990s for reasons of federalism (i.e., in the typical U.S. sense of states' rights) by the U.S. Supreme Court.

The irony of this brief comparison between U.S. and EU constitutional law is that, in some ways, state sovereignty is more potent in the U.S. than it is in the EU. This is quite startling from an international law perspective, under which EU

---

[6] See, e.g., Crane (2013) (contrasting the "representation reinforcement" model with the "substantive review" model).

[7] Because of the "spillover" effects of the California legislation at issue in *Parker*, a reasonable application of the dormant Commerce Clause doctrine probably should have resulted in the Supreme Court striking down the legislation. See further Fox (2004) and Inman and Rubinfeld (1997).

[8] Cooper and Kovacic (2010), pp. 1570–1571 and 1589, with references; Verkuil (1975), pp. 330–341.

Member States are fully sovereign actors while American states are not. However, one should guard against facile comparisons, because, e.g., many state measures may fall within the scope of the EU Treaties but may be perfectly compatible with them—possibly based on Treaty rules providing for derogation.

The present contribution focuses on the EU's approach to these problems, with emphasis on legal principles applied to cases (negative integration), as opposed to other topics that could also be of interest, such as legislative initiatives (positive integration) designed to liberalise markets (e.g., postal services, telecoms, transportation, energy, etc.). One should note, however, that if a case is brought by the European Commission (as opposed to preliminary reference cases), this may reflect a specific litigation strategy to supplement the EU's legislative efforts to open up a previously monopolised sector to competition.

Section 2 of this chapter presents, in some detail, Article 106 TFEU. This provision is relevant in situations involving state measures granting exclusive and special rights. The discussion covers developments through the fall of 2014. Section 3 shifts from Europe to China. No attempt is made to engage in analysis of law and cases concerning administrative monopoly in China, as I have conducted such analysis elsewhere. Rather, the aim is to suggest how China should build on the steps it has taken already with regard to the administrative monopoly problem and to construct a comprehensive and credible *national competition strategy* that will produce important benefits for the Chinese economy and for society.

2 Article 106 TFEU: State Measures Granting Exclusive and Special Rights

A first contextual point is that Article 4(3) of the Treaty on European Union (TEU) provides that Member States may not jeopardise the attainment of the objectives of the Treaties. This principle—the duty of sincere cooperation—has been quite versatile. It has been interpreted as meaning, *inter alia*, that Member States may not undermine the "effectiveness" of EU law. The relevance of Article 4(3) TEU goes well beyond competition law, but in this field it can also be read with Article 101 TFEU. Together, the two provisions restrict state-compelled and state-facilitated collusion. A retreat from this doctrine by the Court has diminished its impact, and it will not be discussed in depth in this chapter; but the doctrine is not entirely dormant.[9]

The Treaty's authors, wishing to preclude Member States from adopting or maintaining measures that compromise the Treaty's competition rules, might have limited themselves to Article 4(3) as a general clause establishing a duty of

[9] See European Court of Justice, *API – Anonima Petroli Italiana SpA and Others v. Ministero delle Infrastrutture e dei Trasporti and Ministero dello Sviluppo economico*, 4 September 2014, Case C-184/13.

sincere cooperation, which could be read together with the antitrust rules. As Article 101 TFEU prohibits cartels and other anticompetitive agreements and concerted practices, and because Article 102 TFEU prohibits the abuse of dominance, it might have been thought that state measures contrary to the aims of those provisions addressed to undertakings would breach an implicit duty attaching to the Member States themselves. This was in fact the basic position of the Court of Justice when it first constructed the state action doctrine in the 1970s.[10] But the working group responsible for the Treaty provisions establishing a common market (i.e., the free movement rules and the competition rules) decided to introduce another provision of greater specificity and complexity—Article 106 (originally, Article 90 EEC).

Article 106(1) prohibits Member States from enacting or maintaining measures contrary to the rules of the Treaty, including the competition rules where they apply. Article 106(2) makes derogation available for proportionate state measures that ensure the adequate provision of services of general economic interest (SGEIs); the same derogation applies in favour of the undertakings responsible for the relevant SGEI tasks. Article 106(3) empowers the Commission to enforce Article 106 through administrative and legislative instruments. The particular features of this complex of rules should not obscure the broader point that the authors of the Treaty—the same authors that drafted the Treaty's free movement rules—thought it prudent to introduce a specific injunction and potentially far-reaching enforcement apparatus against state measures that are incompatible with the Treaty and in particular with the competition rules addressed to undertakings. Furthermore, as a consequence of the judicial development of Community/EU law, it was not just the Commission that was authorised to enforce Article 106; national courts were likewise empowered to do so (within the limits of their judicial powers) to ensure that the rights accruing to individuals under the Treaty could be invoked and enjoyed[11]—requesting, when in doubt, legal interpretations from the Court of Justice. Consequently, the deliberate or negligent anticompetitive acts of national authorities may trigger: (i) Commission action; and/or civil remedies including damages; or, in certain limited cases, as explained later, (ii) administrative action by a national competition authority under national law.

2.1 Article 106(1) TFEU

Article 106(1) TFEU provides that "[i]n the case of public undertakings and undertakings to which Member States grant special or exclusive rights, Member

[10] European Court of Justice, *SA G.B.-INNO-B.M. v. Association des détaillants en tabac (ATAB)*, 16 November 1977, Case 13/77.

[11] This point was already implicit in European Court of Justice, *Giuseppe Sacchi*, 30 April 1974, Case 155/73, para. 18.

States shall neither enact nor maintain in force any measure contrary to the rules contained in this Treaty, in particular [the rules on competition]". This provision contains several elements. The first clause specifies its scope, while the second clause describes the substance of the obligation itself, which is a prohibition against state measures incompatible with the provisions of the Treaty. Because Article 106 refers to the other rules of the Treaty, it is applied in conjunction with other Treaty provisions that govern competition or free movement. For this reason, the provision has been described as a *règle de renvoi* (i.e., a "reference rule") with variable legal content in different spheres of application.[12] In the case of the free movement rules, the content of Article 106(1) does not differ from the content of those rules, which are addressed to Member States. Article 106 would therefore be superfluous in the free movement context if it were not for the fact that Article 106 (3) confers on the Commission certain advantages such as greater discretion and relatively efficient procedures. By contrast, where competition law is concerned, the application of Article 106(1) against a state measure must presuppose a duty to which Member States are bound which is distinct from the duties imposed on undertakings by the competition rules contained in Articles 101 and 102 TFEU. In this context, Article 106(1) assumes a dual nature, at once dependent on another Treaty provision (almost always Article 102[13]) and containing independent substance regulating not the conduct of an undertaking but the conduct (or omission) of public authorities. As will be discussed, the question of whether the nature of Article 106(1) is evolving (or has already evolved) away from this dualism toward a fully liberated autonomy is at the heart of the current debate relating to this provision.

2.1.1 Scope and Application of Article 106(1)[14]

In the following sections, the elements of Article 106(1) will be elaborated in further detail. First, it is necessary to consider the scope of the provision. Questions of whether a given scenario fall within the scope of Article 106 sometimes turn on the basic issue of whether the public entity, or the entity enjoying exclusive or

---

[12] See Buendía Sierra (2014).

[13] Because Article 106 applies "in the case of" public undertakings and undertakings enjoying exclusive and special rights, the undertaking in question may be dominant within the meaning of Article 102. For this reason, in the vast majority of competition cases where Article 106 has been applied, the host provision has been Article 102. To date, the only notable judgment concerning the combined application of Article 106(1) and Article 101 is European Court of Justice, *Ahmed Saeed Flugreisen and Silver Line Reisebüro GmbH v. Zentrale zur Bekämpfung unlauteren Wettbewerbs eV*, Case 66/86, 11 April 1989.

[14] The literature discussing Article 106 is abundant. See, e.g., Monti (2014); Buendía Sierra (2014); Schweitzer (2011); Holmes (2007); Maíllo (2007), pp. 596–603; Wainwright and Bouquet (2004), pp. 563–568; Buendia Sierra (1999), Chapters 4, 5 and 6; Kovar (1996); Edward and Hoskins (1995); Ehlermann (1993).

special rights, is properly characterised as an "undertaking", as the competition rules only apply *ratione personae* if the contested acts are carried out by an undertaking (or undertakings).

2.1.2 The Concept of an Undertaking

The term "undertaking" refers to a natural or legal person engaged in *economic activity*, regardless of its legal status or the way it is financed.[15] This involves offering goods or services on a market,[16] and it is likely to involve financial risk.[17] Conversely, the economic provisions of the Treaty do not apply to *non-economic* activities.[18] An entity which enjoys exclusive rights is *not* bound to respect Article 102 if it pursues activities of an *exclusively social function* (such as compulsory social security or the provision of health services,[19] on condition that principles of solidarity predominate over market-logic principles such as capitalisation), or if it carries out tasks of sovereign authority such as police or justice functions, national defence, diplomacy, or air traffic control.[20] Where a Member State delegates regulatory powers to a professional association, the association's rules may be regarded as state measures if the State defines the public interest criteria and essential principles to which those rules conform and if the State retains the power to adopt decisions in the last resort.[21] The line between economic and

[15] See European Court of Justice, *Klaus Höfner and Fritz Elser v. Macrotron GmbH*, Joined Cases C-6/90 and C-9/90, 23 April 1991.

[16] See European Court of Justice, *Commission v. Italy (Transparency Directive)* Case 118/85, 16 June 1987, para. 7; European Court of Justice, *Commission v. Italy*, Case C-35/96, 16 June 1998, para. 36. See also European Court of Justice, *Pavel Pavlov and Others v Stichting Pensioenfonds Medische Specialisten*, Joined Cases 180/98 to 184/98, 12 September 2000, para. 75.

[17] See European Court of Justice, *Commission v. Italy*, Case C-35/96, 18 June 1998, para. 37. See also European Court of Justice, *Wouters and others v Algemene Raad van de Nederlandse Orde van Advocaten*, Case C-309/99, 19 February 2002, para. 48.

[18] See Baquero Cruz (2005), p. 179.

[19] See, e.g., European Court of Justice, *AOK Bundesverband and others v. Ichtyol-Gesellschaft Cordes, Hermani & Co.*, Joined Cases C-264/01, C-306/01, C-354/01 and C-355/01, 16 March 2004, paras 47–57.

[20] The leading cases, with respect to tasks typical of a public authority, are European Court of Justice, *SAT-Fluggellschaft mbH v. Eurocontrol*, Case C-364/92, 19 January 1994 (air traffic control); and European Court of Justice, *Diego Calì v. Servizi ecologici porto di Genova SpA*, Case C-343/95, 18 March 1997 (anti-pollution surveillance). The fact that an entity acts as regulatory body does not necessarily mean that its activities will be typical of those of a public authority. See European Court of Justice, *Ordem dos Técnicos Oficiais de Contas v. Autoridade da Concorrência*, Case C-1/12, 28 February 2013, para. 46.

[21] See *Wouters*, cited above note 17, para. 68; *Ordem dos Técnicos Oficiais de Contas*, previous footnote, paras 54–56.

non-economic activities may be slender,[22] and sometimes an entity may be an undertaking for some purposes but not for others.[23]

2.1.3 Undertakings with Special or Exclusive Rights ("Privileged" Undertakings)

In general, the concept of exclusive rights is straightforward. They are granted by public authorities acting as such, and it is assumed that the granting authority acts with some margin of discretion. By contrast, if exclusive rights are granted automatically upon satisfaction of objective criteria, as in the case of intellectual property rights or non-discretionary procurement procedures, Article 106(1) is thought not to apply.[24]

If a public entity is engaged in the sale of goods or services on a market, then it is acting as a public undertaking. If the authority is engaged only in *purchasing,* it may be subject to procurement rules but as for the competition rules, it would have to be ascertained whether the entity qualifies as an undertaking, in particular to determine whether such purchasing is ancillary to activities of an exclusively social function.[25]

To cite only a few examples from a long (open) list of exclusive rights, the Court of Justice has considered the following kinds of privileges to be relevant under Article 106: a monopoly covering broadcasting activities[26]; a monopoly granted to a port undertaking to carry out port operations[27]; exclusive concessions (covering

---

[22] For example, while procurement of goods or services on a *purchasing market* might seem as "economic" as *sales* of goods or services, purchasing activities need to be considered in light of the end use of the products procured. An entity buying goods or services in a manner ancillary to an otherwise exclusively social function is unlikely to be regarded as engaged in an economic activity. See General Court, *Federación Nacional de Empresas de Instrumentación Científica, Médica, Técnica y Dental (FENIN) v. Commission*, Case T-319/99, 4 March 2003, *upheld on appeal:* 11 June 2006.

[23] See, e.g., *AOK Bundesverband,* cited above note 19, para. 58; European Court of Justice, *Aé roports de Paris v Commission*, Case C-82/01 P, 24 October 2002, paras 78–82; General Court, *SELEX Sistemi Integrati SpA*, Case T-155/04, 12 December 2006, para. 54.

[24] The grant of IPRs is automatic and non-discretionary where objective criteria are fulfilled. Furthermore, once granted, IPRs generally cannot be revoked before their expiry, which would tend to diminish the influence of the State over the right holder. Thus, while some observers have argued that IPRs should be considered exclusive rights for purposes of Article 106(1), on a better view they should not be thus understood. Similarly, see Buendía Sierra (2014) p. 819.

[25] See above note 22.

[26] *Sacchi,* cited above note 11. See also European Court of Justice, *Elliniki Radiophonia Tilèorassi AE (ERT) v. Dimotiki Etairia Pliroforissis and Sotirios Kouvelas and Nicolaos Avdellas*, Case C-260/89, 18 June 1991.

[27] European Court of Justice, *Merci convenzionali porto di Genova SpA v. Siderurgica Gabriella SpA* Case C-179/90, 10 December 1991.

discrete regional territories) granted to funeral enterprises[28]; a monopoly granted in respect of the collection, transport and distribution of mail[29]; *et cetera.*

Special rights typically involve Member States taking steps to restrict the number of players in a market, e.g., by way of a licensing regime. In a (now defunct) Directive concerning the satellite communications sector in 1994,[30] the Commission indicated that special rights could be defined as—rights that are granted by a Member State to a limited number of undertakings, through any legislative, regulatory or administrative instrument which, within a given geographical area: limits to two or more, otherwise than according to objective, proportional and non-discriminatory criteria, the number of undertakings which are authorised to provide any such service; designates, otherwise than according to such criteria, several competing undertakings as those which are authorised to provide any such service; or confers on any undertaking or undertakings, otherwise than according to such criteria, legal or regulatory advantages which substantially affect the ability of any other undertaking to provide the same telecommunications service in the same geographical area under substantially equivalent conditions. This definition is carried forward by Directive 2002/77 on competition in the markets for electronic communications networks and services.[31]

2.1.4 Public Undertakings

The element that distinguishes a public undertaking from private undertakings is that the former is directly or indirectly subject to the *dominant influence* of a public administration (whether national, regional or local). Such influence may result from owning shares in the undertaking, or from the rules that govern it. For example, an undertaking governed by private law will nevertheless qualify as a public undertaking if it is wholly owned by the State.[32] Majority shareholdings or majority voting rights enjoyed by a public administration effectively give rise to a presumption of dominant influence.[33]

[28] European Court of Justice, *Bodson v. Pompes Funèbres des Régions Libérées*, Case C-30/87, 4 May 1988.

[29] European Court of Justice, *Prosecutor v. Paul Corbeau,* Case C-320/91, 19 May 1993.

[30] Commission Directive 94/46 amending Directive 88/301 and Directive 90/388 in particular with regard to satellite communications, OJ 1994 L268/15, Article 1 and recital 11.

[31] Commission Directive 2000/52/EC of 26 July 2000, OJ 2000 L193/75 (Article 1(6)). See also the definition of special rights in Article 2(f) of Commission Directive 2006/111 (the "Transparency Directive"), OJ 2006 L318/17.

[32] *Express Delivery Services in the Netherlands*, OJ 1990 LI0/47, p. 49. See also *International Express Courier Services in Spain*, OJ 1990 L233/19.

[33] See, e.g., European Commission, *BdKEP – restrictions on mail preparation,* Case COMP/ 38.745, 20 October 2004, *on appeal:* General Court, *Germany v. Commission* Case T-490/04 (removed from the register 7 May 2008).

2.1.5 State Measures

A state measure—yet another undefined term in the Treaty—can be any measure taken by any public authority (national, regional or local) acting as such. An entity acting as a private undertaking is by definition incapable of adopting a *state* measure because it is engaged in an economic activity.[34] By contrast and as noted above, to the extent that an otherwise private entity exercises regulatory powers typical of those of a public authority, and assuming there is no improper delegation, the entity will not normally be considered an undertaking.[35] If the private entity is *obliged* by law to carry out such tasks, the entity will lack the capacity for autonomous behaviour, which is a precondition for the application of Articles 101 and 102. In these scenarios, which may coincide, application of the competition rules to the private entity will be precluded.

In examining whether a given act adopted by a public body is a state measure, the form of the relevant instrument (e.g., a law or decree versus a contract governed by private law) is relevant but not decisive.[36] If the act regulates the market to advance the public interest it will qualify as a state measure, regardless of its form. If the act is of a purely commercial nature, then even if it is formally an instrument of public law, Article 101 or 102 may potentially apply but Article 106(1) will not.

2.1.6 State Measures Contrary to Article 106(1): Background and Four Strands of Case Law

Article 106(1) combined with Article 102 functions as an instrument of *negative* integration: it is capable of breaking down barriers to competition, but it is not typically a basis on which to lay down common rules for a given sector.[37] The Commission may use it, for example, as a bargaining chip to elicit the cooperation of its sister political institutions. From the perspective of private litigants, Article 106(1) expands the possibilities of challenging state measures by asserting Treaty-

---

[34] *Cf.* the dichotomy elaborated by the Court of Justice in *Wouters,* cited above note 17, paras 68–69.

[35] See European Court of Justice, *Diego Calì & Figli Srl v. Servizi ecologici porta di Genova SpA*, Case C-343/95, 18 March 1997, para. 23.

[36] See Buendía Sierra (2014), pp. 813–814. As Buendía Sierra explains, different Member States may employ different instruments to achieve the same results, which militates against a strictly formal approach.

[37] In the spheres of (i) transparency in the financing of public undertakings, and (ii) telecoms/electronic communications, the Commission has used Article 106(3) as a legal base for liberalising directives. This approach is controversial, as it excludes the Council and the Parliament. The Commission thus avoids this route, even if, for tactical purposes, it occasionally professes its willingness to resort to Article 106(3) if the Member States are uncooperative.

based rights as part of their "legal heritage" (*patrimoine juridique*) and potentially recovering damages from public authorities caused by the breach of EU law.[38]

By reason of the variety of factual settings that have arisen, and because of ambivalence on the part of the Court of Justice reflecting an insoluble tension between the sovereign prerogatives of the Member States and the integration-driven Community interest, the jurisprudence under Article 106 has at times been uneven; different legal tests have been devised by the Court in different cases. Commentators thus routinely organise this jurisprudence according to various categories of cases. One approach that has resonated with some observers[39] was elaborated by Advocate General Jacobs in his Opinion in *Albany*.[40] Jacobs referred to three scenarios that arise under Article 106(1): (i) cases where the undertaking concerned, merely by exercising the exclusive rights granted to it, cannot avoid abusing its dominant position (*manifest incapacity to satisfy demand* cases); (ii) cases where the Court has made the peremptory assumption that the contested state measure was *prima facie* in breach of Article 106(1) without any analysis, proceeding directly to consider the possibility of a justification under Article 106 (2) (*burden-shifting* cases); and (iii) cases where a public or privileged undertaking faces a conflict of interest liable to prejudice the ability of third parties to compete, often because of the accumulation of exclusive rights in favour of the undertaking concerned, or because of a delegation of regulatory powers which places the undertaking in a gatekeeper role (*conflict of interest* cases). In subsequent case practice, and in a notable recent case (*Greek lignite*—discussed later in detail), a fourth scenario has emerged which shares some features with conflict of interest cases: (iv) cases in liberalising sectors where a state does not accumulate exclusive rights or delegate regulatory powers but nevertheless through the grant of exclusive or special rights puts an undertaking in a position of *obvious competitive advantage vis-à-vis* would-be challengers (*inequality of opportunity* cases). Category (iv) is broader than (iii), and in my view effectively has subsumed it. In other words, a conflict of interest case (category (iii)) is necessarily an inequality of opportunity case (category (iv)) but the reverse is not necessarily true. However, the niceties of these categories should not distract from the fundamental issue of whether the State has taken steps to limit or defeat the effectiveness of the competition rules and, if so, whether there is a relevant justification or exclusion on which the State may rely.

The case law on which these categories are based is discussed below. But first we need to flesh out an important principle that has its roots in the centripetal-centrifugal tension between the normative constraints imposed by Europe's integration process and the natural desire, on the part of Member States, to control

[38] EU law is rather far-reaching as regards the possibility of holding Member States liable for damages. See European Court of Justice, *Ministero dell'Industria, del Commercio e dell'Artigianato v. Lucchini SpA*, Case C-119/05, 18 June 2007.

[39] See, e.g., Monti (2014); Szyszczak (2007), pp. 125–127.

[40] European Court of Justice, Opinion of the Advocate General, *Albany International BV v. Stichting Bedrijfspensioenfonds Textielindustrie*, Case C-67/96 28 January 1999, paras 395 *et seq*.

commerce that affects their territories and to manage competition where it is expedient to do so.

Grant of Special or Exclusive Rights Acceptable *in Principle*

The wording of Article 106(1)—"in the case of undertakings to which Member States grant special or exclusive rights"—seems to presuppose that Member States can confer such rights. Thus, in *Sacchi*,[41] where Italy had reserved to a public undertaking the right to broadcast cable television transmissions, the Court of Justice stated that Article 106(1) "permits Member States *inter alia* to grant special or exclusive rights to undertakings. Nothing in the Treaty prevents Member States, for considerations of public interest, of a non-economic nature, from removing radio and television transmissions, including cable transmissions, from the field of competition by conferring on one or more establishments an exclusive right to conduct them".[42] This proposition was arguably called into question 20 years later by the *Corbeau* judgment.[43] In *Corbeau*, the Court did not linger on the question of whether exclusive rights covering all collection and delivery of mail in Belgium infringed any of the rules referred to in Article 106(1), but merely stated that the latter provision was to be read with Article 106(2) and proceeded to assess whether the exclusive rights could be justified. A common interpretation of *Corbeau* is that it reversed the burden of proof established in *Sacchi*, thereby bringing the approach under Articles 106(1) and 102 closer to the *Dassonville*/*Cassis de Dijon* approach in the free movement of goods context.[44] This position seems odd considering that, following the confusion caused by the *Sunday Trading* cases,[45] the Court was keen to "re-examine" and "clarify" that approach. One may therefore doubt that *Corbeau* was an attempt by the Court to unify these two fields of law. In any event, *Corbeau* does not offer a satisfying analysis under Article 106(1), and it muddied up the jurisprudence insofar as that provision was concerned. In *La Crespelle*,[46] decided the following year, the Court sought to restore some rigour, and it was more careful to avoid conflating Article 106(1) and Article 106(2). The Court insisted that the "mere creation of [. . .] a dominant position by the granting of an exclusive right within the meaning of Article [106(1)] *is not as such incompatible* with Article [102] of the Treaty. A Member State contravenes the prohibition contained in those

---

[41] *Sacchi*, cited above note 11.

[42] *Sacchi*, cited above note 11, para. 14. See also *ERT v. Dimotiki*, cited above note 26, para. 10; European Court of Justice *Société Civile Agricole du Centre d'Insémination de la Crespelle v. Coopérative d'Elevage et d'Insémination Artificielle du Département de la Mayenne*, Case C-323/93, 21 September 1999, para. 18.

[43] *Corbeau*, cited above note 29.

[44] See, e.g., Buendía Sierra (2014), p. 832; Whish (2008), p. 227.

[45] To cite just one of the cases, see European Court of Justice, *Torfaen Borough Council v. B & Q plc*, Case C-145/88, 23 November 1989.

[46] *La Crespelle*, cited above note 42.

two provisions *only if, in merely exercising the exclusive right granted to it, the undertaking in question cannot avoid abusing its dominant position*".[47]

Not only did the Court forcefully reaffirm the burden of proof as understood before *Corbeau*, it also seemed deliberately to omit reference to the possibility (seen in earlier case law) that a Member State may also infringe Articles 106(1) and 102 where it creates a situation in which the dominant undertaking to which it grants exclusive rights is *led* to abuse its dominant position,[48] a test more likely to result in close scrutiny of state measures than the more lenient "cannot avoid" standard. Although the passage *La Crespelle* was only a partial statement of the law (as it neglected important cases like *ERT*—see below), the Court's clear intention was to re-establish the need for a (causal) *link* between the contested state measure and an abuse by an undertaking of its dominant position.[49] The judgments since *La Crespelle* have wavered somewhat between the rigorous approach in that judgment[50] and the burden-shifting approach adopted in *Corbeau*.[51]

Notwithstanding cases such as *Sacchi* and *La Crespelle*, this chapter will later suggest that the Court of Justice no longer regards such a link as necessary for the application of Article 106(1).

Grant of Special or Exclusive Rights *Impermissible* in Some Circumstances

Given the far-reaching impact that exclusive and special rights can have on competition, with all the negative consequences that artificially restricted competition implies for consumer welfare, productivity and innovation, and considering furthermore the principle of the effectiveness (*effet utile*) of the Treaty rules underlying Article 106(1), the discretion of the Member States to grant such rights is not unlimited.[52] As the Court of Justice explained in the *Terminal equipment*

[47] *La Crespelle,* cited above note 42, para. 18 (emphasis added; citing *Höfner,* cited above note 15, para. 29; *Merci convenzionali,* cited above note 27, para. 17). On the facts of *La Crespelle,* the public authorities did not infringe Articles 106(1) and 102 because the challenged state measure left the monopolist in question free to determine its own prices. Thus, any pricing abuse that might occur could not be said to be a "direct consequence" of the grant of exclusive rights.

[48] *ERT v. Dimotiki* cited above note 26, para. 37. In later cases the Court returned to the formula used in *ERT* many times. See, e.g., *Pavlov,* cited above note 16, para. 127; European Court of Justice, *Deutsche Post AG v Gesellschaft für Zahlungssysteme mbH GZS and Citicorp Kartenservice GmbH*, Joined Cases C-147/97 and C-148/98, 28 May 2005, para. 48.

[49] See the Opinion of Advocate General Jacobs in *Albany,* cited above note 40, para. 388 (Article 106(1) can only be infringed "where there is a causal link between a Member State's legislative or administrative intervention on the one hand and anti-competitive behaviour of undertakings on the other hand").

[50] See European Court of Justice, *Giorgio Domingo Banchero*, Case C-387/93, 14 December 1995.

[51] See European Court of Justice, *Chemische Afvalstoffen Dusseldorp BV and others v. Minister van Volkshuisvesting, Ruimtelijke Ordening en Milieubeheer*, Case C-203/96, 25 June 1998. See further Buendía Sierra (2014), pp. 832–833.

[52] *Cf.* the Opinion of Advocate General Jacobs in *Albany,* cited above note 40, paras 389–393.

case, "even though [Article 106(1)] presupposes the existence of undertakings which have certain special or exclusive rights, it does not follow that *all* the special or exclusive rights are necessarily compatible with the Treaty. That depends on different rules, to which [Article 106(1)] refers".[53] This passage highlights the balance the Court has sought to strike. As it does in other areas of the law, the Court recognises a zone of national sovereignty as a matter of principle, but it insists on ultimate supervisory control and marks the outer boundaries (although in a loose way that leaves room for a degree of case-by-case analysis) of a Member State's sovereign power to restrict competition.[54]

The following (abbreviated) exposition of case law sheds further light on the way in which Article 106(1) is applied in practice. The cases are organised first of all according to the typology proposed by Advocate General Jacobs in *Albany* (see above): manifest incapacity cases, burden-shifting cases and conflict of interest cases. Subsequently, the emerging fourth category—inequality of opportunity cases—is discussed. As will be seen, the latter category has been contested, with the European Commission and the General Court adopting opposed positions. This debate was resolved in 2014 by the European Court of Justice.

Manifest Incapacity to Satisfy Demand Cases

Exemplary Case: Höfner v. Macrotron (Headhunting Services in Germany)

Höfner[55] concerned recruitment services assigned exclusively to a public agency, the *Bundesanstalt für Arbeit*. The Court of Justice stated that a Member State only breaches Article 106(1) where "the undertaking in question, merely by exercising the exclusive rights granted to it, cannot avoid abusing its dominant position". Here, the *Bundesanstalt* was manifestly incapable of supplying the full range of market demand for headhunting services.[56] Its inability to supply the market, together with the inability of private headhunting firms to enforce their recruitment contracts to satisfy the surplus demand (because they were in breach of the legal monopoly),

[53] European Court of Justice, *France v. Commission (Terminal equipment)*, Case C-202/88, 19 March 1991, para. 22 (emphasis added).

[54] Again, it can be seen that EU law is not aimed at ensuring that the political process functions according to appropriate democratic standards of representation and accountability; it imposes, rather, a framework of substantive review in which both objectives and means are assessed by judges.

[55] *Höfner,* cited above note 15. See also European Court of Justice, *Job centre coop. arl (Job Centre II)*, Case C-55/96, 11 December 1997 (an Italian version of *Höfner*); European Court of Justice, *Giovanna Carra and others*, Case C-258/98, 8 June 2000.

[56] Indeed, the market had previously sustained the operations of more than 700 private placement agencies, and unlawful executive recruitment services were openly tolerated.

limited output to the prejudice of customers, a practice proscribed by Article 102.[57] In this sense, the state measure necessarily resulted in "conduct" contrary to that provision.[58]

Burden-Shifting Cases

Exemplary Case: Corbeau (Belgian Postal Monopoly)

Although *Corbeau*[59] was important for its approach to Article 106(2) (see Sect. 2.3), another remarkable feature of the case is the Court's (non-)handling of the question whether Article 106(1) applied to Belgian legislation reserving exclusive rights to the provision of postal services in favour of the Régie des Postes (state postal service). On this issue, the Court merely stated that Article 106(1) had to be read in conjunction with Article 106(2), and with haste it proceeded directly to a discussion of the latter provision.

Corbeau was a controversial judgment. According to Buendía Sierra, "[I]f the grant of exclusive rights was only permitted under Article 106 to the extent that it came within the exception contained in Article 106(2), that meant that in principle all grants of exclusive rights were contrary to Article 106(1) unless they were objectively justified".[60] This approach reverses the oft-repeated principle, best elaborated in *Terminal equipment,* that Article 106(1) presupposes that a Member State may in principle remove an activity from the field of competition.[61] Yet it may be doubted whether the Court really intended to adopt a *Dassonville*-type, "automatic abuse" standard to govern all grants of exclusive rights. Such a proposition cuts against the wording of Article 106(1) itself, and as suggested earlier it would imply the improbable conclusion that *Dassonville* and *Cassis* were driving forward the Court's Article 106 jurisprudence precisely when the Court was seeking to "re-examine and clarify" those judgments in the field of the free movement of goods (although the Court later retreated, to an extent, from its "clarification" in *Keck*).

The Court's rush to discuss services of general economic interest in the *Corbeau* judgment is more comprehensible if it is seen as simply reflecting the Court's view

---

[57] *Cf. Terminal equipment,* cited above note 53, where the European Court of Justice found an infringement in respect of the grant by the French State of exclusive rights for the importation, marketing, connection and/or maintenance of terminal equipment.

[58] *Cf.* the Opinion of Advocate General van Gerven in European Court of Justice, *Netherlands and Koninklijke PTT Nederland NV and PTT Post BV v. Commission*, Joined Cases C-48/90 and C-66/90, 12 February 1992.

[59] *Corbeau*, cited above note 29.

[60] Buendía Sierra (2014), p. 831. Similarly, see Hancher (1994); Jones and Sufrin (2007), pp. 640–641.

[61] According to Buendía Sierra (2014), p. 832, *Corbeau* brought "the approach in relation to Articles 106(1) and 102 into line with that concerning free movement. That is, restrictions [...] were in principle prohibited unless they existed because of mandatory requirements of general interest and they respected the principle of proportionality".

that the contested legislative framework undeniably created a situation in which the Régie des Postes was abusing its dominant position by failing to respond to emerging demand among corporate customers for value-added services such as express delivery, on-site collection and so on.[62] This impression is arguably reinforced by the Court's later judgment in *Job Centre II*, which underlined the inability of a monopolist to keep pace with the needs of a sector as dynamic and diverse as placement services.[63] In any event, subsequent cases seem to show that the burden-shifting methodology seen in *Corbeau* occasionally resurfaces, but it has not been adopted as a blanket standard.[64]

Conflict of Interest Cases, Including Delegation of Regulatory Powers Cases

This category has proved to be rather more typical than the other categories described above. The discussion here will therefore dwell a bit longer on the relevant case law.

(i) ERT v. DEP (Greek Television Broadcaster)

In *ERT*,[65] Greece had granted exclusive rights to transmit/retransmit television broadcasts to an undertaking that subsequently brought an action in the Greek courts against an upstart competitor. The Court of Justice found that Greece had infringed Article 106(1) and Article 102 because of the *accumulation* of exclusive rights granted to the same undertaking. The fatal aspect of those rights was that they created a situation in which the monopolist could discriminate against foreign programs in favour of its own. The Court explained that the grant of exclusive rights would be regarded as contrary to Article 106(1) "where those rights are liable to create a situation in which [the] undertaking is led to infringe [Article 102] of the Treaty by virtue of a discriminatory broadcasting policy which favours its own programmes".[66] One way to understand this judgment is that the Court implicitly considers whether the contested state measure puts the incumbent in a position

[62] It is true, however, that the Court in *Corbeau* did not specify which aspects of the Belgian postal legislation it found offensive to Article 106(1). See Opinion of the Advocate General in *Albany,* cited above note 40, para. 417.

[63] *Job centre II,* cited above note 55.

[64] Reaching a similar conclusion, see Sauter and Schepel (2009), p. 161: "Admittedly, [in] the 1993 *Corbeau* Case concerning the legality of the Belgian postal monopoly [...] [t]he Court seemed to suggest – albeit ambiguously – that statutory monopolies which lack (or extend beyond) a public interest justification under Article [106(2) TFEU] are contrary to Community law. However, there is no evidence that the Court intended this dictum to extend beyond services of general economic interest to cover exclusive rights at large". (footnotes omitted).

[65] *ERT v. Dimotiki,* cited above note 26.

[66] *ERT v. Dimotiki,* cited above note 26, para. 37.

where it has both the ability and incentive to distort competition by means of discrimination.

(ii) Raso (Temporary Dock Labour)

In *Raso,*[67] the contested legislation was an Italian law granting a port authority the exclusive right to supply temporary labour for dock work in the port of La Spezia. The port authority was also licensed to operate on the market for dock work services, and it thus competed on that market against the same firms that depended on it for their temporary labour. Significantly, the Court underlined that the fact that the national court had not identified an actual abuse by the port authority did not preclude the application of Article 106(1). Both *ERT* and *Raso* involved an accumulation of rights which *prima facie* create a situation liable to lead the incumbent to abuse its dominant position (either by entrenching its position on the home market or by extending its power into a neighbouring market).[68] In this sense, each case involved a conflict of interest.

(iii) RTT v GB-Inno-BM (Belgian Telecoms Incumbent: Telephone Equipment)

In *RTT,*[69] Belgium had empowered the incumbent telecoms operator, the RTT, to dictate specifications for telephone equipment, and to grant approvals to suppliers of equipment and authorise connections despite the fact that the RTT itself was also active as a supplier on the same market. The Court recalled that a dominant firm abuses its position where it reserves to itself, without any objective justification, an ancillary activity which could be carried out by a third party on a neighbouring market, with the aim of eliminating competition on that market.[70] If such an "extension" of the dominant firm's power into the neighbouring market results from a state measure, the State breaches Article 106(1) in combination with Article 102. The Court stressed that the RTT's power to authorise the connection of telephones to the public network, which placed the RTT at an "obvious advantage" relative to its competitors, was sufficient to establish a breach without any need to verify that the monopoly had in fact been exercised in a discriminatory manner.[71] One may wonder if the issue of whether a state measure puts a dominant firm in a

[67] European Court of Justice, *Silvano Raso and others*, Case C-163/96, 12 February 1998.

[68] See also European Court of Justice, *Firma Ambulanz Glöckner v. Landkreis Südwestpfalz*, Case C-475/99, 25 October 2001.

[69] European Court of Justice, *RTT v. GB-Inno-BM,* Case C-18/88, 13 December 1991. See also European Court of Justice, *Francine Gillon, née Decoster,* Case C-69/91, 27 October 1993; *Spain, Belgium and Italy v. Commission*, Joined Cases C-271/90, C-281/90 and C-289/90, 17 November 1992.

[70] See European Court of Justice, *Centre belge d'études de marché – Télémarketing (CBEM) v. SA Compagnie luxembourgeoise de télédiffusion (CLT) and Information publicité Benelux (IPB)*, Case C-311/84, 3 October 1985.

[71] *RTT,* cited above note 69, para. 24. *Cf.* also *Terminal equipment,* cited above note 53, para. 51.

situation where it has both the ability and incentive to abuse its dominance is, in the eyes of the Court, a necessary condition for state liability. A standard of "obvious advantage" would constitute a significant change of emphasis, and seems to be a farther-reaching criterion. However, *RTT* was not decisive in this regard because, on the facts, the RTT had both the incentive and the ability to abuse its dominant position by degrading its rivals' capacity to compete.

The difference between the *RTT* and *ERT* cases is that in *RTT* the incumbent network operator was in a position to use its regulatory powers (offensively) to strengthen its position on a neighbouring market, whereas in *ERT* the incumbent's exclusive rights over retransmission of television programs shielded its *own* monopoly (defensively) against would-be direct competitors. In both cases the essence of the breach is that the contested legislation was *liable to create a situation* in which the privileged undertaking in question would be led to abuse its dominant position because of a strong temptation (incentive and ability) to discriminate against rivals. Thus, where there is a serious conflict of interest, the potential for abuse will *ordinarily* suffice as a basis for state liability; it is not necessary to wait for an abuse to materialise in fact. However, with respect to the application of Articles 106(1) and 102 to the delegation of regulatory powers, the *RTT* judgment must be read in light of the cases mentioned below (see (v) and (vi)).

(iv) MOTOE v. Elliniko Dimosio (Motorcycle Races)

In *MOTOE*,[72] the Court held that Article 106(1) precluded a Greek law that conferred on ELPA, an entity which organised motorcycling competitions and engaged in such activities on a commercial (albeit non-profit) basis by concluding sponsorship, advertising and insurance contracts, the power to authorise applications made by competing organisations to organise their own motorcycling competitions. In light of ELPA's incentive to favour its own activities, the Court was quite explicit that "it is not necessary that any abuse should actually occur", and that a "risk of an abuse" sufficed.[73] Allowing ELPA to act as both market participant and regulator amounted "*de facto* to conferring upon it the power to designate the persons authorised to organise those events and to set the conditions in which those events are organised, thereby placing that entity at an obvious advantage over its competitors".[74] If the Court had stopped there, the implication might have been merely that creating or maintaining a competitive advantage was a distortion of competition contrary to Article 106(1). This would have made exclusive rights illegal in the absence of justification. Additional language leans in that direction:

[72] European Court of Justice, *Motosykletistiki Omospondia Ellados NPID (MOTOE) v. Elliniko Dimosio* Case C-49/07, 1 July 2008.

[73] European Court of Justice, *Motosykletistiki Omospondia Ellados NPID (MOTOE) v. Elliniko Dimosio* Case C-49/07, 1 July 2008, paras 49 and 50 respectively.

[74] European Court of Justice, *Motosykletistiki Omospondia Ellados NPID (MOTOE) v. Elliniko Dimosio* Case C-49/07, 1 July 2008, para. 51.

"That situation of unequal conditions of competition is [. . .] highlighted by the fact [. . .] that, when ELPA organises or participates in the organisation of motorcycling events, it is not required to obtain any consent".[75] This distortion theory appears to be offered, however, as an add-on to the more fundamental point that the power to authorise motorcycling events may "lead the undertaking which possesses it to deny other operators access to the relevant market",[76] which would normally constitute an abuse under Article 102. Similarly, the Court adds, in an *ERT*-type vein, that ELPA's two hats could lead it "to distort competition by favouring events which it organises or those in whose organisation it participates".[77] In a sense, Greece made the case an easy one because it had failed to impose any limits on ELPA's consent powers whatsoever, such as conditions, provisions for administrative or judicial appeal, or a corresponding responsibility to provide services of general economic interest.[78]

(v) Lagauche (Belgian Telecoms Incumbent: Communications Equipment)

Lagauche, another preliminary reference from Belgium, involved facts similar to those in *RTT,* but on this occasion the technical specifications for type-approval of communications equipment, and the detailed parameters of approval, were determined by the competent minister. The "only" task remaining for the RTT was to verify that the equipment of its competitors complied with those requirements.[79] The judgment thus suggests that, where a potential conflict of interest is created by the delegation of regulatory powers, such a potential will not in itself trigger Article 106(1) if the State has ensured that minimum safeguards are in place to obviate the risk of anticompetitive discrimination. Here the Court presumes this is so because of the minimal discretion of the RTT under the national rules. At the present stage of internal market legislation in specific sectors, regulators must be independent of operators active on the markets concerned. In practice, therefore, and depending on the sector concerned, situations such as that in *Lagauche* may be increasingly exceptional.

[75] European Court of Justice, *Motosykletistiki Omospondia Ellados NPID (MOTOE) v. Elliniko Dimosio* Case C-49/07, 1 July 2008, para. 51.

[76] European Court of Justice, *Motosykletistiki Omospondia Ellados NPID (MOTOE) v. Elliniko Dimosio* Case C-49/07, 1 July 2008, para. 51.

[77] European Court of Justice, *Motosykletistiki Omospondia Ellados NPID (MOTOE) v. Elliniko Dimosio* Case C-49/07, 1 July 2008, para. 52.

[78] In applying Article 101 to regulations adopted by an association of undertakings, the Court adopted a similar approach in *Ordem dos Técnicos Oficiais de Contas,* cited above note 20, para. 91.

[79] European Court of Justice, *Procureur du Roi v. Jean-Marie Lagauche and others,* Joined Cases C-46/90 and C-93/91, 27 October 1993, para. 49. The aspect of the case described here concerns events up until 1 July 1989, at which time Commission Directive 88/301 entered into force and precluded the RTT from engaging simultaneously in both commercial and regulatory activities.

(vi) Albany (Sectoral Pension Fund)

Albany[80] reflects some sensitivity to the choices of Member States in the sphere of social policy. Here the Court decided not to call into question certain sectoral pension fund rules in the Netherlands despite a clear a conflict of interest. Under Dutch law, textile firms had to subscribe to a particular sectoral pension fund. The law also authorised the fund itself to decide whether to grant exemptions, thus allowing an exempted firm to seek better terms through other pension schemes. Plainly, the fund had financial incentives to deny such exemptions, thereby reinforcing its own position to the detriment of alternative providers. However, a complex assessment had to be undertaken to ascertain whether the criteria for an exemption were satisfied. In addition, the grant of exemptions had important implications for the financial equilibrium of the fund, which was obliged by law to accept any firm operating in the sector as a subscriber. Furthermore, and significantly, an undertaking operating in the sector had recourse to appeals before a judge if the fund denied its application for such an exemption. In those circumstances, despite the fund's gatekeeper role, and notwithstanding its greater degree of discretion compared to that of the RTT in *Lagauche,* the Court held that the Netherlands was not obliged to assign authority to grant exemptions to a separate, independent entity.

(vii) Summary of Principles in Cases of "Conflict of Interest" and "Delegation of Regulatory Powers"

In principle, Article 106(1) and Article 102 preclude the delegation of regulatory powers to an undertaking with special or exclusive rights where doing so would create a conflict of interest and a significant risk of anticompetitive discrimination which raises rivals' costs or excludes them from competing with it. A level playing field can thus generally be ensured only where a regulator has sufficient *independence.*[81] However, a Member State can potentially tailor the delegation of authority to mitigate the risk of distortion. Independence might be ensured where the instrument of delegation is transparent and leaves only minimal discretion to the delegee. Or, particularly in the social sphere where the requirements of solidarity are taken rather seriously, the nature of the regulation may be sufficiently complex and may be so closely linked to the financial equilibrium of the delegee's operations that a wider margin of discretion is permissible so long as the applicable rules provide for judicial scrutiny.[82] Despite the Court's optimism, in the latter case, the costs of

[80] *Albany,* cited above note 40.

[81] In the case of a public undertaking, such independence is *not* ensured where the entity with regulatory authority is legally separate but nevertheless belongs to the same administration. See *Decoster,* cited above note 69, para. 21.

[82] The possibility of appeal seems to make the Court more tolerant of potentially discriminatory decision-making structures. In the context of Article 4(3) TEU and Article 101 TFEU, see European Court of Justice, *Autotrasporti Librandi Snc di Librandi F. & C. v. Cuttica spedizioni e servizi internationali Srl*, Case C-38/97, 1 October 1998.

appeal may be too significant for certain operators. If that is so, then the playing field will in fact *not* be level. Quite apart from fairness issues, this could be harmful for investment in the relevant industry.

Inequality of Opportunity Cases

According to the Court of Justice, a "system of undistorted competition" can be guaranteed "only if *equality of opportunity* is secured as between the various economic operators".[83] One problem that emerges here is that, if that phrase were taken literally, Member States would face quite strict constraints: any state measure directly or indirectly conferring a competitive advantage, in the presence of exclusive and special rights, would be *prima facie* incompatible with the Treaty, and would have to be justified as a proportionate means to protect a legitimate public interest. An issue that requires clarity is whether the language of "equality of opportunity" is appreciably broader than the formulae that have been discussed above. In that connection, it is necessary to consider two cases, *Connect Austria* and *Greek lignite*, in which the ideas of competitive advantage for incumbents and, conversely, disadvantageous conditions for challengers, have been particularly prominent.

(i) Connect Austria (Mobile Telecoms Licences)

In *Connect Austria*,[84] the relevant public undertaking Mobilkom (i.e., the successor to the historical monopolist, Post & Telekom) had in 1996 been granted a licence to exploit the GSM 900 standard for a mobile telecommunications network in Austria, and in 1998 it was allocated, at no charge, DCS 1800 frequencies.[85] This made it the only provider capable of offering the full range of mobile telecommunications services. By 1999, Mobilkom's share of the Austrian GSM market was 70 %. The complainant in the main proceedings, Connect Austria, claimed that it had been treated in a discriminatory manner because in 1997 it was obliged, unlike Mobilkom, to pay a fee of 2.3 billion ATS to the regulator for a licence to provide telecoms services on the DCS 1800 frequency band. The Court instructed the Austrian court to resolve a factual dispute by determining whether the fees paid

---

[83] See, e.g., *MOTOE v. Elliniko Dimosio,* cited above note 72, para. 51 (emphasis added). In a different context, see also *Ordem dos Técnicos Oficiais de Contas,* cited above note 20, para. 88.

[84] European Court of Justice, *Connect Austria Gesellschaft für Telekommunikation GmbH v. Telekom-Control-Kommission, and Mobilkom Austria AG*, Case C-462/99, 22 May 2003.

[85] DCS 1800 was a digital mobile telecoms system based on the GSM standard. This system used a frequency band around 1800 MHz rather than 900 MHz. Because there were more frequencies in the DCS 1800 band compared to the GSM 900 band, the DCS 1800 system was able to accommodate more subscribers and more traffic.

by the two companies for the two different kinds of licences were economically equivalent. However, if the national court were to find that there had in fact been asymmetric treatment in favour of Mobilkom, then, according to the Court, Austria would have failed to ensure equal opportunity among operators.[86] In rather apodictic terms, the Court stated that, "[i]f inequality of opportunity between economic operators, and therefore distorted competition, results from a State measure, such a measure constitutes an infringement of Article [106(1) TFEU] in conjunction with Article [102 TFEU]".[87] But if Mobilkom had been treated favourably under Austrian law, it could either "extend its dominant position in the digital mobile telecommunications services market according to the DCS 1800 standard or to reinforce its dominant position in the digital mobile telecommunications services market or in the [analogue and digital] mobile telecommunications services market, depending on how the market at issue is defined, by distorting competition, and therefore to infringe Article [102 TFEU]".[88] More specifically, an incumbent already enjoys advantages such as market presence and a large customer base, and with the benefit of favourable treatment it "could find itself in a situation which would lead it, *inter alia*, to offer reduced rates, in particular to potential subscribers to the DCS 1800 system, and to carry out intensive publicity campaigns in conditions with which Connect Austria would find it difficult to compete".[89]

The *Connect Austria* judgment may be criticised for ascribing too much significance to the notion of equality of opportunity. Arguably, the judgment set the bar for bringing claims at quite a low level. The question is whether the Court was adding "inequality of opportunity" as a separate theory of liability. When the judgment is read as a whole, one could take the view that the Court was concerned that discrimination in favour of the incumbent could lead the dominant firm to take steps to protect its dominant position by competing aggressively against a rival forced to bear higher costs to reduce or eliminate the threat posed by a competitive threat based on a different technology. If this reasoning were correct, then despite the "equality of opportunity" rhetoric the application of Article 106(1) would remain anchored in (actual or likely) conduct that falls within the scope of rules addressed to undertakings. But the latest case law suggests that the Court is attenuating the importance of the issue of abuse, and may even be uncoupling it entirely from the issue of state liability. It is thus necessary to turn to these more recent developments.

[86] *Connect Austria*, cited above note 84, paras 83, 87 and 95.

[87] *Connect Austria*, cited above note 84, para. 84.

[88] *Connect Austria*, cited above note 84, para. 85.

[89] *Connect Austria*, cited above note 84, para. 86.

(ii) DEI v. Commission (Greek Lignite): *Judgments of the General Court and the Court of Justice*

The *Greek lignite* case[90] gave the Court the opportunity to decide on the potency and breadth of Article 106(1).[91] Here the Commission alleged that Greece had granted to DEI, a public undertaking, quasi-exclusive and long-term rights to extract and exploit lignite (brown coal), and that these rights gave DEI a competitive advantage on Greece's *de jure* liberalised wholesale electricity market because lignite was the cheapest input for electricity. The Commission emphasized repeatedly that DEI's privileged access to lignite created an inequality of opportunity which allowed DEI to maintain or reinforce its dominant position in wholesale electricity. From the pleadings before the General Court, one could interpret the Commission's position as reflecting two somewhat different legal theories. The first theory was that Greece had created a situation in which DEI was led to or was liable to abuse its dominant position upstream on the market for lignite extraction by extending its dominance from that market and reserving to itself the downstream wholesale electricity market.[92] However, on this theory the extension (leveraging) would not have been aimed at capturing a dominant position downstream because DEI was already the dominant supplier, with a market share exceeding 85 %. DEI's aim would have been, rather, to maintain or reinforce its dominance.[93] If the case had centred on this extension theory, it would seem less significant, as past precedents had already indicated that, if the possibility to extend dominance from one market to another is attributable to a state measure, Article 106(1) may be triggered. But the Commission probably saw this case as an opportunity to test the boundaries of the "(in)equality of opportunity" concept. The temptation is easy to understand, because, as already suggested, inequality of opportunity is potentially a very broad concept, and because on a broad reading it sits uneasily beside the maxim that dominance, without more, is compatible with Article 102.

It is worth considering the judgment of the General Court which, although quashed on appeal, is at least as interesting as the judgment that overruled it. DEI had contended, *inter alia*, that there had been no "undermining" of competition because it had not, for example, raised rivals' costs or otherwise engaged in abusive conduct. According to DEI, the Commission had failed to "state precisely the conduct to which the applicant was allegedly led by the alleged [*sic*] inequality of

---

[90] General Court, *Dimosia Epicheirisi Ilektrismou AE (DEI) v. Commission*, Case T-169/08, 20 September 2012, *set aside on appeal and remanded:* European Commission, *Commission v. Dimosia Epicheirisi Ilektrismou AE (DEI)*, Case C-553/12 P, 17 July 2014.

[91] The dispute did not involve any real or alleged SGEIs, and thus no issues arose under Article 106 (2).

[92] For example, see paras 17 and 20 of the General Court's judgment.

[93] This distinction might explain why, as the General Court noted, "the Commission does not accuse the applicant of having, without objective justification, extended its dominant position on the market for the supply of lignite to the wholesale electricity market". General Court, *Dimosia Epicheirisi Ilektrismou AE (DEI) v. Commission*, cited above note 90, para. 92. Extension in this sense appears to have meant leveraging dominance in one market to capture an adjacent market.

opportunities".[94] The Commission maintained that the relevant case law (in particular, *Telecommunications equipment, Raso* and *Connect Austria*) "recognised the existence of an infringement of Article [106(1) TFEU], read in combination with Article [102 TFEU], when State measures distort competition by creating an inequality of opportunities between operators, *without at the same time requiring the definition of an actual abusive practice – real or potential.* Consequently, the Commission disputes the claim that it should also have established, beyond the inequality of opportunities, an actual abusive practice [by DEI]".[95] It was this far-reaching proposition of the Commission—i.e., not only that the dominant firm need not have carried out the abuse but that no actual or potential abuse need even be identified—that the General Court decided to refute.[96]

Unlike the Commission, the General Court interpreted the relevant case law under Article 106(1) as requiring the identification of the abuse to which the public or privileged undertaking in question has been led, or could have been led, by the contested state measure.[97] The court then embarked on a short but remarkable *tour d'horizon* of relevant cases (*Raso, MOTOE, Höfner, Job centre II, Merci convenzionali, RTT, Connect Austria* and *Telecommunications equipment*). On the General Court's reading of these cases, the Court of Justice had been careful in each instance to make reference to an actual or potential abuse within the meaning of Article 102. With regard to *RTT*, for example, the Court of Justice pointed out that an undertaking with a monopoly in the market for the operation of the public telecommunications network infringes Article 102 if it reserves to itself a neighbouring market (such as the importation, marketing, connection and maintenance of equipment for connection to that network), thereby eliminating all competition on that neighbouring market. Belgian law made the RTT a gatekeeper, able "to determine at will which terminal equipment might be connected to the public network".[98] With regard to *Connect Austria*, the Court considered that "the public undertaking could find itself in a situation which would lead it, *inter alia*, to offer reduced rates, in particular to potential subscribers to the DCS 1800 system, and to carry out intensive publicity campaigns in conditions with which [the new entrant] would find it difficult to compete (paragraph 86). Thus, the Court also took into consideration the conduct of the public undertaking on the market".[99] And referring

[94] General Court, *Dimosia Epicheirisi Ilektrismou AE (DEI) v. Commission*, cited above note 90, para. 63. Greece's similar position is reported in para. 67.

[95] General Court, *Dimosia Epicheirisi Ilektrismou AE (DEI) v. Commission*, cited above note 90, para. 75 (emphasis added). Similarly, see para. 108.

[96] General Court, *Dimosia Epicheirisi Ilektrismou AE (DEI) v. Commission*, cited above note 90, paras 85–86.

[97] General Court, *Dimosia Epicheirisi Ilektrismou AE (DEI) v. Commission*, cited above note 90, para. 93.

[98] General Court, *Dimosia Epicheirisi Ilektrismou AE (DEI) v. Commission*, cited above note 90, para. 109.

[99] General Court, *Dimosia Epicheirisi Ilektrismou AE (DEI) v. Commission*, cited above note 90, para. 111.

to the *Dusseldorp* judgment, the General Court stated: "It is true that, as the Commission argues, the restriction of outlets found in that case derived from the granting by the Netherlands statute of an exclusive right to process dangerous waste in favour of AVR Chemie, which prevented any other outlet to ensure the processing of the product in question, and not from the manner in which that undertaking exercised that exclusive right. The fact remains, however, that the Court identified the abuse to which the Netherlands statute led the undertaking holding a dominant position, namely the limitation of outlets to the detriment of consumers within the meaning of Article [102(b) TFEU]".[100]

Accordingly, the General Court annulled the Commission's decision, stating that the case law on which the Commission had relied did not allow it to "base its argument solely on the question whether the inequality of opportunities between economic operators, thereby distorting competition, is the result of a State measure. Thus, the Commission cannot maintain that it was not required to identify and establish the abuse of a dominant position to which the State measure in question led, or could lead, the applicant [DEI]".[101] Perhaps a more frank assessment of the jurisprudence of the Court of Justice would have admitted that it has not always been crystal clear. The *Dusseldorp* case is a good example where the restriction of outlets mentioned by the Court may have been more plausibly attributable to the effective exclusivity enjoyed by AVR Chemie (i.e., to the contested state measure), and not to the company itself. One must concede that there is a fine line here, but the General Court was undoubtedly loath to muddy up an otherwise clear normative position according to which, essentially, a challenge brought against a state measure under Article 106(1) must articulate a theory of abuse and show either that such an abuse has occurred, or that its potential meets some threshold of probability.

The debate that the Court of Justice had to resolve was whether Article 106 (1) should be transformed so that it is no longer a reference rule but an autonomous prohibition. It began by recalling some of the basic principles associated with the Article 106 case law, and then stated that "although the mere fact that a Member State has created a dominant position by the grant of exclusive rights is not as such incompatible with Article [102 TFEU, the Treaty] none the less requires the Member States not to adopt or maintain in force any measure which might deprive that provision of its effectiveness".[102] It added, consistent with judgments such as *RTT* and *Raso*, that an infringement of Articles 106(1) and 102 is possible irrespective of whether an actual abuse has been committed by the dominant firm in question.[103] The Court then held that:

[100] General Court, *Dimosia Epicheirisi Ilektrismou AE (DEI) v. Commission*, cited above note 90, para. 117.

[101] General Court, *Dimosia Epicheirisi Ilektrismou AE (DEI) v. Commission*, cited above note 90, para. 118.

[102] *Commission v. DEI* (judgment of the ECJ), cited above note 90, para. 45.

[103] See *Commission v. DEI* (judgment of the ECJ), cited above note 90, para. 46.

> All that is necessary is for the Commission to identify a potential or actual anticompetitive consequence liable to result from the State measure at issue. Such an infringement may thus be established where the State measures at issue affect the structure of the market by creating unequal conditions of competition [...], by allowing the public undertaking or the undertaking which was granted special or exclusive rights to maintain (for example by hindering new entrants to the market), strengthen or extend its dominant position over another market, thereby restricting competition, without it being necessary to prove the existence of actual abuse.[104]

Consequently, the General Court had erred in deciding that the Commission had failed to identify or establish the abusive conduct to which the contested quasi-exclusive rights had led or could have led the dominant company, DEI. A prominent commentator in this area of the law, Buendía Sierra, has already welcomed the final outcome.[105] As he says, the Court "has not merely confirmed the traditional case law; it has also complemented it by leading the effects doctrine to its logical consequence. Indeed, the judgment states that *any State measure* producing anti-competitive consequences would infringe Articles 106 and 102 TFEU. Contrary to previous judgments, this statement is not confined to the extension of a dominant position from one market to another caused by an exclusive or special right. It also applies to the *original* grant of a stand-alone exclusive or special right to a company".[106] But it is worth reflecting critically on this judgment. Earlier it was suggested that the Court's older case law was implicitly consistent with the idea that state liability should be limited to the creation or maintenance by the State of situations in which a dominant firm has both the ability and the incentive to abuse its dominant position. Following *Greek lignite*, it seems that this link to actual or potential abuse is no longer essential. Endorsing a strong version of the "effects" doctrine, the Court seems to consider that the core issue is not abusive conduct but the (potentially) distortive effects of the contested state measure. The wisdom of this move can be questioned: to unhinge Article 106(1) from the need to demonstrate an actual or potential abuse within the meaning of Article 102 amounts to a judicial rewrite of the Treaty. At least in theory such a "rewrite" could have an additional unexpected consequence, in the following sense. In a related but separate context, the combined application of Article 4(3) TFEU (the duty of sincere cooperation) and Article 101 TFEU (the standard rule against unjustified anticompetitive agreements) is subject to a condition according to which the two rules can only be applied to challenge state measures with anticompetitive effects if an agreement or concerted practice contrary to Article 101 has been concluded. Article 4(3) TEU is in this sense completely dependent on Article 101 TFEU.[107] But a fully

---

[104] *Commission v. DEI* (judgment of the ECJ), cited above note 90, para. 46.

[105] Buendía Sierra (2016). For a short and critical case note, see Davilla (2014).

[106] Buendía Sierra (2016). He would further welcome enhanced enforcement activity under Article 106, where the Commission has generally been reluctant to take action.

[107] See European Court of Justice, *Prosecutor v. Wolf W. Meng*, Case C-2/91, 17 November 1993; European Court of Justice, *Prosecutor v. Ohra Schadeverzekeringen*, Case C-245/91, 17 November 1993.

autonomous Article 106(1) could potentially be applied—absent a public interest justification—to state measures with effects equivalent to collusion (horizontal or vertical price fixing, output or innovation limitations, etc.) irrespective of whether the specific criteria of Article 101 are satisfied.

Returning to the combined application of Articles 106(1) and 102, there is another difficulty. If Article 106(1) may be applied even when no actual or likely abusive conduct is shown, why should its application still be tethered to a demonstration that the privileged undertaking occupies a dominant position?

These latter two issues point to the fundamental paradox: Article 106(1) was designed as a norm supporting the effectiveness of the competition (and other Treaty) rules. But as the Court has interpreted it, the provision can arguably now be applied without necessarily having to demonstrate that the effectiveness of those rules is jeopardised.

Reinterpreting the Treaty in a manner not obvious from its wording is certainly not unprecedented. The Court of Justice has been doing this in many fields of Community/Union law for half a century, in accordance with its self-understanding as, in substance although not in form, a constitutional court. Still, the legal and political consequences of a "steroidal" reading of Article 106(1) could be profound. A beefed up Article 106(1) that could apply generally in cases of state measures that artificially distort market structures via the grant of special and exclusive rights would not necessarily render unlawful the whole spectrum of such rights because they could still be found to be exempt in particular under Article 106(2) (see below Sect. 2.3). Nevertheless, one may now argue that most if not all exclusive and special rights are presumptively contrary to the Treaty (because by nature they tend to confer competitive advantage), absent a specific justification.

2.2 *Exemptions from and Exceptions to the Application of Article 106(1) TFEU*

Given the potency of Article 106(1), it is particularly important that Member States may invoke Article 106(2), which provides an exemption from the Treaty rules if the application of those rules would obstruct the adequate provision of services of general economic interest entrusted to an undertaking by the public authorities. The scope, application and limitations of this exemption are discussed below. Second, although this is not an exemption, if a state measure advances a legitimate public interest and if a restriction of competition is an inherent consequence of the measure and could not be moderated via less restrictive means, then the measure may fall within a *Wouters*-type of immunity.[108] The existence of Article 106(2) renders this type of argumentation unnecessary in many cases. In other cases the rationale for state measures may relate not to services of *economic* interest but to the pursuit of

[108] *Wouters*, cited above note 17.

non-economic interests—the protection of public health or public morals, for example. This type of justification has not yet been confirmed in the jurisprudence of the Court of Justice in a case involving Article 106(1), but it seems clear from a judgment decided in a different context that *Wouters* is indeed a possible basis for justifying state measures as well.[109] Third, where Article 106(1) is applied with Article 102, a Member State should have the opportunity to plead efficiency justifications.[110] This would be consistent with the legal position in routine abuse of dominance cases, where the Court has confirmed that a dominant firm may seek to justify apparently abusive conduct on efficiency grounds, provided strict conditions are satisfied.[111] Likewise, if Article 106(1) is applied in conjunction with Article 101,[112] and if the exemption under Article 106(2) is unavailable, a Member State should have the opportunity to demonstrate that the conditions of Article 101 (3) are satisfied.[113]

Of the exemptions and exceptions just described, Article 106(2) stands out as the most frequently invoked. It is therefore useful to examine the meaning and application of Article 106(2) in further detail.

2.3 *Article 106(2) TFEU*

2.3.1 Introduction

Article 106(1) and Article 106(2) often concern a common subject matter, namely the relationship between state measures and a dominant undertaking, public or private. But there is another important aspect of the relationship between Articles 106(1) and 106(2). Whereas Article 106(1) addresses Member States, the text of Article 106(2) does not. It is addressed exclusively to undertakings entrusted with the provision of SGEIs and to revenue-producing monopolies. Member States are alluded to only in the sense that entrusted undertakings must have been entrusted by public authorities. Yet in the case of SGEIs it would seem unacceptable to withhold the possibility of an exemption from a Member State where it has been shown

---

[109] See *API – Anonima Petroli Italiana SpA*, cited above note 9.

[110] As explained above, it can be seen from the judgment of the European Court of Justice in *Greek lignite* that Article 106(1) can apply even where no actual or potential abuse is identified with precision. In this light, allowing a defendant Member State to defend its actions based on pro-competitive arguments would become all the more important to avoid type I errors.

[111] European Court of Justice, *Post Danmark A/S v. Konkurrencerådet*, Case C-209/10, 27 March 2012.

[112] For the only notable case thus far, see *Ahmed Saeed,* cited above note 13.

[113] This is not to suggest that the exemptions provided for in Articles 106(2) and 101(3) are mutually exclusive. If their respective criteria are satisfied then an undertaking should be able to invoke both of them. See European Court of Justice, *Metropole télévision SA and Reti Televisive Italiane SpA and Gestevisión Telecinco SA and Antena 3 de Televisión (Eurovision I) v. Commission*, Joined Cases T-528, 16 January 2014, paras 114–126.

prima facie to breach Article 106(1). Nor would it be coherent to embrace a legal standard that recognises an SGEI defence for the undertaking concerned but refuses to exempt the national authorities on the same facts. These considerations seem to explain why the Court has interpreted Article 106(2) in a typically creative way that allows not only undertakings but also Member States to invoke it, for example in the context of infringement proceedings per Article 258 TFEU.[114]

Article 106(2) is a provision of constitutional importance, and its interpretation and application have unsurprisingly attracted controversy. The wording of the provisions is as follows:

> Undertakings entrusted with the operation of services of general economic interest or having the character of a revenue-producing monopoly shall be subject to the rules in this Treaty [...] in so far as the application of such rules does not obstruct the performance, in law or in fact, of the particular tasks assigned to them. The development of trade must not be affected to such extent as would be contrary to the interests of the Union.

The first clause affirms that undertakings entrusted to provide SGEIs "*shall be subject*" to the Treaty rules. It is only "insofar as the application of such rules" would *obstruct* the performance of the particular tasks assigned to those undertakings that the "shall be subject" commandment is negated, and then only apparently on condition that non-application of the rules would not unduly prejudice the development of trade from the perspective of the interests of the EU. *Mutatis mutandis,* as applied to *Member States* in cases involving SGEIs, rather than to the undertakings themselves, the Treaty rules would again be overridden only where their application would obstruct the performance by the undertakings of their assigned SGEI tasks, and, again, only where the Union's interest in the development of trade is not unduly prejudiced.

One observer, reading Articles 106(1) and 106(2) together, has suggested that Article 106(2) "appears not to be a justification nor an exception [to Article 106(1)], but rather a binary- or switch-rule that establishes the conditions for the application or non-application of the Treaty with regard to situations involving undertakings entrusted with the operation of services of general economic interest".[115] This conclusion is largely based on a comparison with Articles 34 and 36 TFEU (free movement of goods) and other free movement rules, the structure and wording of which are strikingly different.[116] The methodology just outlined is questionable. The Treaty contains other clear "rule and exception" constructions, such as Article 101(1) and Article 101(3), which bear little likeness to Articles 34 and 36.[117] The contrary view, retained here, is that the Treaties impose a plenary framework for a

[114] See, e.g., European Court of Justice, *Commission v. France*, Case C-159/94, 23 October 1997, paras 44–50; *Dusseldorp,* cited above note 51, para. 67.

[115] Baquero Cruz (2005), p. 176.

[116] See Baquero Cruz (2005), p. 175.

[117] See Baquero Cruz (2005), where Baquero Cruz takes note of Articles 101(1) and 101(3) but reaches the very different conclusion that the latter construction reinforces the argument based on Articles 34 and 36.

market economy in Europe that is based on free competition and free trade, the economic provisions of which apply in the sphere of all "economic activities" and deviation from which—e.g., on the grounds contained in Article 34, or under mandatory requirements—must be limited to situations where specific and controlled criteria are satisfied. The latter view seems compatible with the views of certain other commentators,[118] and with at least the rhetoric of the Court.[119] However, I have to acknowledge that the actual practice is not so simple.[120]

The prevailing view—i.e., the view that Article 106(2) derogates from the Treaty and thus must be narrowly interpreted[121]—has an important practical consequence. In principle, it is the Member State (or the undertaking concerned) invoking the exemption that must show that the necessary criteria justifying its operation are met.[122] However, in an Article 258 proceeding, the Commission bears the burden of persuasion at all times. If a defendant Member State presents plausible *prima facie* arguments to the effect that the application of the Treaty rules would obstruct the provision of SGEI by an entrusted undertaking, then the Member State has discharged its burden of *production,* and it is then incumbent on the Commission to rebut those arguments based on *specifically tailored* responses,

---

[118] The "austere" interpretation of Article 106(2) is shared by, *inter alia,* Waelbroeck and Frignani (1999), p 283. See also Whish (2008), p. 233; Sauter (2008), p. 186.

[119] See *Terminal equipment*, cited above note 53, para. 12 ("In allowing *derogations* to be made *from the general rules* of the Treaty *on certain conditions,* [Article 106(2)] seeks to reconcile the Member States' interest in using certain undertakings [...] as an instrument of economic policy with the Community's interest in ensuring compliance with the rules on competition and the preservation of the unity of the common market".) (emphasis added).

[120] See Baquero Cruz (2005), p. 176 ("the strict interpretation was traditionally limited to the definition of an undertaking entrusted with (SGEI) [see European Court of Justice, *BRT v. SABAM*, Case C-127/73, 27 March 1974, para. 19] – an element of Article [106(2)] for which a strict interpretation is indeed justified as it obliges public authorities to be transparent in their decisions – but it was extended to the provision as a whole in [European Court of Justice, *Commission v. Netherlands*, Case C-157/94, 23 October 1997, para. 37], even though in that judgment the interpretation [...] was anything but strict") (footnotes omitted). As I will argue below, in the second case to which Baquero Cruz refers, *Commission v Netherlands,* although it is true that the ECJ displays deference to the defendant Member States, the judgment should be read in light of its sensitive political context and in light of the fact that the Commission failed to discharge its burdens of argumentation and proof under Article 258 TFEU (at that time, Article 226 EC). Understood in those terms, the juxtaposition of (i) the Court's rhetoric concerning the fact that Article 106(2) is to be narrowly construed because it derogates from the general obligations imposed by the Treaty, and (ii) the apparent generosity of the Court in favour of the Netherlands and the other defendant Member States, may not be as inconsistent as it seems.

[121] See, e.g., General Court, *Aéroports de Paris*, Case T-128/98, 12 December 2000, para. 227, *upheld on appeal:* European Court of Justice, Case C-82/01, 24 October 2002. See also *Commission v. Netherlands,* cited previous footnote, para. 37; *Reims II,* OJ 1999 L275/17, 26 October 1999, recital 92.

[122] *Cf. Sacchi,* cited above note 11, para. 15. See also European Court of Justice, *Italy v Commission,* Case 41/83, 20 March 1985, para. 33; *Commission v Netherlands,* cited above note 120, para. 51; European Court of Justice, *TNT Traco SpA v Poste Italiane*, Case C-340/99, 17 May 2001, paras 56–57; General Court, *Air Inter SA v. Commission*, Case T-260/94, 19 June 1997, para. 138.

or else it will lose the case.[123] Arid or dogmatic legal arguments of a general nature, or hypothetical vignettes, will not suffice.

Whether one adopts a strict reading of Article 106(2) or not, there is broad recognition that Article 106(2) aims at a balance. According to the Court, Article 106(2) "seeks to reconcile the Member States' interest in using certain undertakings, in particular in the public sector, as an instrument of *economic or social policy* with the Community's interest in ensuring compliance with the rules on competition and the preservation of the unity of the common market".[124] This passage reflects the contrasting orientations of the original six Member States as to the roles of the State and the market when their delegates negotiated the form and content of Article 106 (then-Article 86 EEC) in 1956–1957.[125] Following lively negotiations, the compromise that emerged with respect to Article 106 as a whole, and Article 106(2) in particular, inevitably carries with it an ambivalence that remains a distinctive feature of these provisions.

With the foregoing preliminary remarks as a backdrop, the following sections will address: the scope of Article 106(2); the terms "services of general economic interest" and "revenue-producing monopolies"; and the principles that have been developed by the Court in its jurisprudence in these areas.[126] The general focus here will be the relevance of Article 106(2) to state measures and state liability, as opposed to private action and the liability of undertakings. However, the availability of Article 106(2) as an exemption from the application of, in particular, Article 102, will also be discussed incidentally.

[123] The allocation of the burden of proof as described here appears to follow from *Commission v. Netherlands,* cited above note 120. According to officials close to the case, "the Commission has to demonstrate *in concreto* that [the SGEI-based arguments of the defendant Member State] are not founded. To a certain extent the Court has imposed upon the Commission a burden of rebuttal that the undertaking with exclusive rights would not be able to perform its tasks of general interest in the absence of the exclusive right. By this approach, the Court appears to have departed from earlier case law, where the full burden of proof (and not only a burden to invoke) lies upon the party which invokes the exception of Article [106(2) TFEU]". Wainwright and Bouquet (2004), p. 572, with references. The issue of the Member State's burden of proof when it seeks an exemption is discussed below.

[124] European Court of Justice, *Spain v. Commission*, Case C-463/00, 13 May 2003, para. 82 (emphasis added). As seen above (note 119), the Court's earlier formulation referred to economic policy but not to social policy.

[125] See, e.g., Marenco (1983).

[126] For further analysis of Article 106(2) and related issues, see Buendia Sierra (1999), Chapter 8. See also, *inter alia*, Hancher (2014); Whish (2008), pp. 233–239; Sauter (2008); Maíllo (2007); Ross (2007); Baquero Cruz (2005); Holmes (2004), pp. 168–171; Lenaerts (2002); Edward and Hoskins (1995).

2.3.2 The Scope of Article 106(2)

Article 106(2) concerns two types of undertakings: those entrusted with the provision of SGEIs, and those having the character of a revenue-producing monopoly.[127] The first clause of the provision reaffirms the principle that the Treaty rules do apply to both classes of undertakings. However, Article 106(2) is more widely noted for its second clause, which establishes an exemption where SGEIs are at stake. With regard to the second clause, where a (*prima facie*) breach of the Treaty rules by an SGEI provider has been shown, two main substantive criteria must be met to justify an exemption. First, it must be shown that applying the competition rules would obstruct the performance of SGEI tasks under economically acceptable conditions.[128] Second, exempting the conduct must not interfere with the development of trade to a degree contrary to the interests of the EU. These criteria are discussed below.

The Concept of Entrustment

An exemption can only be sought where the undertaking has been *entrusted* by a public authority, acting as such, with the provision of SGEIs.[129] The rationale is an insistence on (national) democratic control over the way in which the objectives, content and modalities of SGEIs are determined.[130] The same criterion also facilitates the transparency necessary to allow adequate review by the Commission and by the European Courts with a view to ensuring conformity with other conditions under Article 106(2)—specifically, the principles of necessity and proportionality. The act of entrustment must spell out the SGEI mission as well as the scope and general conditions related to its performance. An entrustment can be effectuated by

---

[127] A "revenue-producing monopoly", one of the Treaty's many undefined terms, can only be subject to the competition rules if it is engaged in economic activities because that is a necessary condition for the application of Articles 101 and 102. In most circumstances, any such monopoly will likely be engaged in economic activities. The notion of a revenue-producing monopoly is discussed below in the main text.

[128] It seems clear that "economically acceptable conditions" must mean a recovery of costs plus a reasonable profit. Presumably, the principles applying to this concept would be similar to those elaborated in statements by the Court of Justice in European Court of Justice, *AltmarkTrans GmbH and Regierungspraesidium Magdeburg v. Nahverkehrsgesellschaft Altmark GmbH*, Case C-280/00, 24 July 2003, and by the Commission in Article 5 of Commission Decision 2012/21/EU of 20 December 2011 on the application of Article 106(2) [TFEU] to State aid in the form of public service compensation granted to certain undertakings entrusted with the operation of services of general economic interest, OJ 2005 L312/67. The notion of "economically acceptable conditions" is further discussed below in the main text.

[129] See, e.g., *BRT v. SABAM,* cited above note 120, para. 22; *Ahmed Saeed,* cited above note 13, para. 55; *Dusseldorp,* cited above note 51, para. 103.

[130] See Holmes (2004), p. 169.

means of: legislative or regulatory measures[131]; the grant of a concession[132]; a non-exclusive licence governed by public law[133]; a ministerial order[134]; or other comparable means. Neither the mere authorisation by a public authority to operate on a market nor the express approval of activities by the authorities is treated as an entrustment, as neither act imposes an *obligation* to perform the contemplated services.[135] In order for obligations to be regarded as "particular tasks", they must make a direct contribution to the subject matter of the SGEIs.[136] If, in addition to its particular SGEI tasks, the undertaking performs other dissociable (i.e., non-ancillary) duties, the "entrustment" will only be deemed to cover the SGEI tasks.

Services of General Economic Interest (SGEIs)

(a) Introduction

SGEIs are commonly defined as services of an economic nature which the Member States or the EU subject to specific public service obligations by virtue of a general interest criterion. SGEIs are not often unprofitable in economic terms; but they serve essential needs valued by a society or community. Where market forces are unlikely to guarantee the adequate provision of such services—i.e., where there is actual or likely market failure—the public authorities may well require such services on a compulsory basis. In those circumstances, they may prescribe means of partial or total *compensation* for the service provider, possibly in the form of special or exclusive rights and/or other advantages. Sauter has suggested, not unreasonably, that market failure could and should be a key indicator when the substantive test under Article 106(2) is applied and that, if the market could spontaneously and adequately deliver the SGEIs, an anticompetitive state measure would fail the test of necessity or proportionality (harming consumers in the process).[137]

The history of EU policy with respect to SGEIs is described very briefly in this section. More space will then be devoted to an exploration of the nature and scope of the concept of SGEIs, and in that regard more attention will be given to the law (and in particular, to primary law) than to the broader policy debate.

---

[131] See, e.g., *British Telecommunications,* OJ 1982 L360/36, *upheld on appeal: Italy v. Commission,* cited above note 122.

[132] See *Commission v. France,* cited above note 114, para. 66.

[133] See European Court of Justice, *Municipality of Almelo and others v Energiebedrijf IJsselmij,* Case C-393/92, 27 April 1994.

[134] See *IJsselcentrale,* OJ 1991 L28/32, 16 January 1991.

[135] See, respectively, *GVL,* OJ 1981 L370/49, 29 October 1981; *Uniform Eurocheques,* OJ 1985 L35/43, 10 December 1984.

[136] See *Commission v. France,* cited above note 114.

[137] Sauter (2008), p. 180.

The Commission's efforts in the 1980s and early 1990s to liberalise certain regulated sectors such as telecoms and others, were supported by the Court of Justice, both directly in cases where Member States challenged the Commission's competence to pursue such an agenda, and indirectly by confirming, in preliminary reference cases, the constraints placed on the Member States by the Treaty rules on free movement and competition. The high water mark was in 1991, when the Court handed down key judgments (including *Höfner*, *RTT* and *ERT*, all discussed earlier) causing no small anxiety to national authorities. It is doubtful that those judgments posed any *real* threat to SGEIs—a concept which remained largely untested in those cases.[138] But in an atmosphere of trends toward liberalisation and privatisation, what mattered more than the precise legal scope of the 1991 judgments was the *perception* that state prerogatives had come under attack. As already noted, certain judgments from 1993 to 1995 which were generally contemporaneous with the "November revolution" when *Keck,*[139] *Meng*[140] and *Ohra*[141] were decided, allowed the Court to establish that in cases of SGEIs it would accept an intermediate standard of review when applying the "obstruction" clause of Article 106(2), rather than substituting its own judgment for that of a defendant Member State.

As for the Commission, by 1996 it had issued its first policy Communication on SGEIs,[142] and in 1996–1997 the IGC at Amsterdam, following vain attempts by some Member States to dilute the original Article 90 EEC (today's Article 106 TFEU), inserted what became Article 16 EC. This provision was all but eviscerated on the road to consensus, but it should not be written off too hastily.[143] In 2000, the Commission amended its 1996 text,[144] and by 2002–2003, momentum was building for a Community legal framework. The Commission responded in 2003 with a Green Paper on the organisation and financing of SGEIs,[145] followed

[138] The underlying facts did not seem to suggest the possibility of redemption under Article 106(2), although the submissions did not enter into the full range of arguments under that provision, undoubtedly because of its relatively limited impact in the jurisprudence of the 1970s and 1980s.

[139] European Court of Justice, *Bernard Keck and Daniel Mithouard,* Joined Cases C-267/91 and C-268/91, 24 November 1993.

[140] *Meng,* cited above note 107.

[141] *Meng,* cited above note 107. See also *Ohra Schadeverzekeringen,* cited above note 107.

[142] See Communication on Services of General Interest in Europe, OJ 1996 C281/3, 26 September 1996.

[143] In incorporating Article 16 EC, an additional cautionary measure was taken in the form of Declaration 13 to the Final Act: "The provisions of [Article 16 EC] on public services shall be implemented with full respect for the jurisprudence of the Court of Justice, *inter alia* as regards the principles of equality of treatment, quality and continuity of such services".). Other commentators were generous in their reading of Article 16 EC and Declaration 13, pointing out that it signified the imposition on the Member States and the Community of a positive *obligation,* even if the exact nature of that obligation is obscure. See, e.g., Lenaerts (2002), pp. 427–428.

[144] The amended version was published in OJ 2001 C17/4.

[145] Green Paper on Services of General Interest, COM(2003) 270 final, 21 May 2003.

by a White Paper in 2004 and more consultation.[146] The White Paper reflected the Commission's lack of enthusiasm for a future framework directive. The Commission's attention presently is on practical steps to consolidate the current framework while advancing its information and consultation activities.[147] On the other hand, the *potential* for an EU law framework took a hesitant step forward with the Lisbon round of amendments, which established a new legal base (in addition to Article 106(3)) in Article 14 TFEU.[148]

(b) Analysing the Term "Services of General Economic Interest" (SGEIs)

The concept of SGEIs consists of the three following elements. First, it relates to *services*. Second, these services must be in the *general interest*. Services performed purely for private interests will not qualify. In *BRT v SABAM*,[149] the Court held that a copyright collecting society, to which the State had not assigned any SGEI task and which managed private interests, could not be regarded as providing SGEIs. The fact that private interests might *benefit* from a service does not preclude it from qualifying as an SGEI if the other relevant requirements (entrustment; general interest criterion) are satisfied. Third, SGEIs are by definition *economic* in nature. To the extent that services are *non-economic*, the economic provisions of the Treaty, in particular the free movement and competition rules, would not normally apply.

(c) A Creature of EU Law

SGEIs are regarded loosely as equivalent to "public service". While the latter term can have quite different meanings in different Member States, as a matter of common parlance even the EU Courts seem to use "public service" as a shorthand for SGEIs.[150] However, the SGEI concept should be distinguished from that of *service public*.[151] It is an autonomous concept of EU law, deliberately unhinged from national doctrines.

---

[146] White Paper on Services of General Interest, COM(2004) 374 final, 12 May 2004.

[147] See Communication on services of general interest, including social services of general interest: a new European Commitment, COM(2007) 725 final, 20 November 2007. The concept of *social* services of general interest is elaborated in Commission, Implementing the Community Lisbon programme: social services of general interest in the European Union, COM(2006) 177 final, 26 April 2006.

[148] See below notes 154–155.

[149] *BRT v. SABAM*, cited above note 120.

[150] For example, the General Court seems to accept that the term "public service" in the *Altmark* judgment of the Court of Justice in the field of state aid is equivalent to the concept of SGEI under Article 106(2). See General Court, *British United Provident Association Ltd (BUPA) v Commission*, Case T-289/03, para. 162.

[151] See, e.g., Braconnier (2007) and Nistor (2011).

(d) Article 14 TFEU and the Role of Subsidiarity

Although the notion of SGEIs is an autonomous concept, EU law itself recognises an active role for the Member States in defining and supporting such services. Article 14 TFEU (ex-Article 16 EC) provides that "the Union and the Member States, each within their respective powers and within the scope of application of the Treaties, shall take care that such services operate based on principles and conditions, particularly economic and financial conditions, which enable them to fulfil their missions". From one perspective, this provision is a "monument of vagueness".[152] It is explicitly subject to a "without prejudice" clause that preserves the integrity of specific rules, namely Article 107 TFEU (state aids generally), Article 93 TFEU (reimbursement for public service in transport) and Article 106. Article 14 is in part a legacy of Amsterdam, where, as noted above, certain governments at the 1996–1997 IGC tried and failed to amend and weaken what was at that time Article 90 EEC (Article 106 TFEU).[153]

Article 14 was bolstered, however, by the Treaty of Lisbon[154] with its Protocol 26 on Services of General Interest.[155] With the entry into force of the TFEU in late 2009, the provision has ripened from quasi-aspirational language into a concrete legal base (even if the value added *vis-à-vis* Article 114 TFEU may be mostly symbolic). Article 36 of the European Charter of Human Rights, which focuses on respect for *access* to SGEIs, might be seen in a similar vein. Furthermore, while it is true that, by its own terms, Article 14 TFEU cannot modify or limit Article 106, it can nevertheless help to identify areas, i.e., "principles and conditions", where subsidiarity operates at high intensity. According to the principle of subsidiarity as

---

[152] Sauter and Schepel (2009), p. 164.

[153] See, e.g., Wainwright and Bouquet (2004), p. 569; Baquero Cruz (2005), p. 177; Sauter and Schepel (2009), p. 175, footnote 32.

[154] Article 14 TFEU carries forward the contents of Article III-122 of the Constitutional Treaty, including the new legal base for adopting regulations. Both of these provisions are without prejudice not only to Articles 93, 106 and 107 TFEU but also to Article 4 TEU, which includes the duty of sincere cooperation (4(3)) and which also states (4(2)) that the Union "shall respect the equality of Member States before the Treaties as well as their national identities, inherent in their fundamental structures, political and constitutional, inclusive of regional and local self-government".

[155] Protocol 26 amplifies Article 14 TFEU (see previous footnote) and underlines the subsidiarity principle: "[t]he shared values of the Union in respect of services of general economic interest within the meaning of Article 14 [TFEU] include in particular: *the essential role and the wide discretion* of national, regional and local authorities in providing, commissioning and organising services of general economic interest *as closely as possible to the needs of the users;* the diversity between various services of general economic interest and the *differences in the needs and preferences* of users that may result from *different geographical, social or cultural situations;* a high level of quality, safety and affordability, equal treatment and the promotion of universal access and of user rights". (emphasis added) Subsidiarity in the context of SGEIs is discussed below in the main text. For the Commission's interpretation of Protocol 26, see Communication on services of general interest, including social services of general interest: a new European Commitment, COM(2007) 725 final, 20 November 2007, pp. 9–11.

expressed in Article 5(3) TEU, in fields where the EU does not have exclusive competence, EU action is justified only if the relevant objectives cannot be sufficiently achieved by the Member States. In areas where EU rules have not been adopted, the considerable diversity across the Member States suggests that the essential needs of citizens at the heart of the concept of SGEIs can in general be identified and served at national or local level. In principle, therefore, and subject to possible harmonisation by the EU, Member States are free to decide which public services are made available for their citizens.

However, the competition rules apply, and the freedom of Member States to define SGEIs is subject to the control of the EU institutions. This raises the issue of the nature and intensity of that control.

(e) EU Control of Nationally Defined SGEIs

As suggested above, Member States enjoy some latitude in deciding how to define the nature and scope of SGEI tasks. The Court underlined this discretion in *Commission v. Netherlands,*[156] where it stated that Member States "cannot be precluded, when defining the SGEIs which they entrust to certain undertakings, from taking account of *objectives pertaining to their national policy* or from endeavouring to attain them by means of obligations and constraints which they impose on such undertakings".[157]

In *BUPA,*[158] the General Court (CFI) explained that "Member States have a wide discretion to define what they regard as SGEIs and that the definition of such services by a Member State can be questioned only in the event of *manifest error*".[159] Seeking to operationalise the concept of subsidiarity in this context, the court then added that: "The determination of the nature and scope of an SGEI mission in specific spheres of action which either do not fall within the powers of the Community, within the meaning of the first paragraph of Article 5 EC, or are based on only limited or shared Community competence, within the second paragraph of that article, remains in principle, within the competence of the Member States".[160] As the health sector fell "almost exclusively" within the competence of the Member States,[161] the CFI considered that the determination of SGEI

[156] *Commission v Netherlands,* cited above note 120.

[157] *Commission v Netherlands,* cited above note 120, para. 40 (emphasis added).

[158] See *BUPA v. Commission,* cited above note 150.

[159] See *BUPA v. Commission,* cited above note 150, para. 166 (citing General Court, *Fred Olsen v. Commission*, Case T-17/02, 15 June 2005, para. 216; Communication from the Commission on services of general interest in Europe, OJ 2001 C17/4, 19 January 2001, para. 22) (emphasis added). See also General Court, *FFSA and others v. Commission*, Case T-106/95, 27 February 1997, para. 192, *appeal dismissed:* Case C-174/97 P, 25 March 1998; *Olsen,* Case T-17/02, cited above in this footnote, paras 215–228.

[160] See *BUPA v. Commission,* cited above note 150, para. 167.

[161] The CFI referred specifically to Articles 152(1) and 152(5) EC (see now Article 168 TFEU), according to which, in the field of health services and medical care, the EU is limited to taking

obligations (relating to guaranteed private medical insurance) was likewise primarily within their domain of authority. Still, a State must ensure that the SGEI mission satisfies "certain minimum criteria common to every SGEI mission within the meaning of the EC Treaty [...] and to demonstrate that those criteria are indeed satisfied in the particular case".[162] This includes not only a demonstration of entrustment by an act of a public authority and a showing of the "universal"[163] and compulsory[164] nature of the obligations but also an indication of the reasons why the service, "because of its specific nature", should qualify as an SGEI as distinguished from other (non-SGEI) economic activities.[165]

(f) Examples of SGEIs Defined at National Level and Recognized or Upheld by the EU Courts

Among others, the following have been found by the EU Courts to be SGEIs under Article 106(2):

- the maintenance of the navigability of a Member State's most important waterway[166];
- the operation of television broadcasting[167];
- the operation of a public telephone network,[168] but not the provision of telephone equipment[169];

action that is not legally binding, and it must fully respect the responsibilities of the Member States for the organisation and provision of such services.

[162] See *BUPA v. Commission,* cited above note 150, para. 172.

[163] *BUPA v. Commission,* cited above note 150, paras 186–187 (noting, despite the misplaced word "universal", that obligations of a limited territorial or material application, or the fact that the recipients of the services in question constitute a relatively limited group of users does not preclude them from qualifying as SGEI obligations).

[164] *BUPA v. Commission,* cited above note 150, paras 188–190 (requirement of compulsory nature of the service does not mean it must have a clearly predetermined content, as a certain latitude may be left to the service provider regarding, e.g., content and pricing; "compulsory" criterion established if the provider is obliged to conclude contracts with users on consistent conditions).

[165] *BUPA v. Commission,* cited above note 150, para. 172 (citing *Merci convenzionali,* cited above note 27, para. 27; European Court of Justice, *Enirisorse SpA v. Ministero delle Finanze*, Joined Cases C-34/01 to C-38/01, 27 November 2003, paras 33–34).

[166] See European Court of Justice, *Ministère public luxembourgeois v. Madeleine Muller, Veuve J.P. Hein and others (Port de Mertert)*, Case 10/71, 14 July 1971.

[167] See, e.g., *Sacchi,* cited above note 11; General Court, *Radio Telefis Eireann v. Commission,* Case T-69/89, 10 July 1991. The ECJ upheld the CFI's judgment on appeal without addressing its findings with regard to SGEIs. See European Court of Justice, *Radio Telefis Eireann v. Commission*, Joined Cases C-241/91 P and C-242/91 P, 6 April 1995.

[168] See *Italy v. Commission,* cited above note 122.

[169] *RTT,* cited above note 69, paras 16 and 22. Notably, the ECJ held that the public telephone network was an SGEI given the state of Community development *at that time,* thus giving a sense of the dynamism of the concept of SGEIs.

- the operation of unprofitable air routes necessary for reasons of general interest[170];
- the provision of basic postal services[171];
- the operation of the public electricity supply and associated tasks such as uninterrupted service[172];
- the provision of universal and continuous mooring services[173]; and
- the wholesale distribution of pharmaceutical medicines subject to an obligation to maintain stocks within a given territory.[174]

In contrast to the services listed above, in *Porto di Genova*[175] the Court did not consider undertakings carrying out dock work (loading, unloading, etc.) in a major seaport to be entrusted with SGEIs. As noted earlier, copyright collecting societies have also failed to qualify as SGEI providers, in particular because they serve private interests.[176] In the banking sector, the Court was prepared to accept that international money transfers were among the "special tasks" of banks, but the argument that such services were SGEIs failed because there had been no official act of entrustment.[177]

Revenue-Producing Monopolies

An undertaking that "has the character" of a revenue-producing (RP) monopoly, within the meaning of Article 106(2), is an undertaking to which national authorities have granted exclusive rights and which generates revenue for the State through its activities. The practice of the EU authorities in this area is scant indeed,[178] and the concept has not been fleshed out. Examples of RP monopolies would include, *inter alia,* the tobacco and alcohol monopolies used as fiscal devices in some countries.

---

[170] *Ahmed Saeed,* cited above note 13; *Air Inter,* cited above note 122.

[171] See, e.g., *Corbeau,* cited above note 29; *FFSA and others v. Commission,* cited above note 159.

[172] See *Commission v Netherlands,* cited above note 114.

[173] European Court of Justice, *Corsica Ferries France SA v. Gruppo Antichi Ormeggiatori del Porto di Genova*, Case C-266/96, 18 June 1998.

[174] European Court of Justice, *Ferring v. Agence centrale des organismes de sécurité sociale (ACOSS)*, Case C-53/00, 22 November 2001.

[175] *Merci convenzionali,* cited above note 27, para. 28.

[176] See *BRT v. SABAM,* cited above note 120.

[177] See European Court of Justice, *Gerhard Züchner v. Bayerische Vereinsbank AG*, Case C-172/80, 14 July 1981, para. 7.

[178] For rare EEC specimens, see Recommendation à la République française au sujet de l'aménagement du monopole des allumettes (*French match monopoly*), JO 1962 48/1502; Recommendation à la République italienne au sujet de l'aménagement du monopole des allumettes (*Italian match monopoly*), JO 1962 48/1505.

The reason why this type of monopoly was introduced in Article 106(2) is identical to the rationale for including undertakings entrusted with SGEIs, namely: to make clear that, *in principle,* the Treaty rules do indeed apply to them. Because RP monopolies engaged in economic activity are undertakings, they are bound to respect Articles 101 and 102. If an RP monopoly may be qualified as a "state monopoly of a commercial character", the relevant Member State is bound by Article 37 TFEU to make the necessary adjustments to ensure that the conditions in which goods are procured and marketed do not discriminate against nationals of other Member States. Other free movement rules might apply in other cases.[179]

The exemption, according to which the Treaty rules are set aside if their application would obstruct the performance of SGEI tasks,[180] literally covers RP monopolies just as it does SGEI providers. Where an RP monopoly provides no SGEI tasks, this exemption appears perhaps unduly generous, as it is not based on the general interest. This seems incompatible with the spirit of the Treaty. Further support for that contention derives from the following argument. The second sentence of Article 106(2) provides that "[t]he development of trade must not be affected to such an extent as would be contrary to the interests of the Union". Although the Court has not yet decided exactly how this proviso is to be interpreted, the interests of the EU seem to impose an outer boundary on the exemption. In particular, the proviso might subject the exemption to a proportionality requirement which could in practice preclude its operation in cases of trade barriers the State cannot justify under the free movement rules. The constraints placed on the undertaking and on the State, in other words, should be aligned. Somewhat different reasoning has likewise led other commentators to conclude that the proportionality principle fully applies in the context of revenue-producing monopolies. According to Buendía Sierra, "[t]here is a general consensus [...] that exclusive rights the *only* objective of which is the generation of revenue would in principle never be justified under Article 106(2). This is because revenue-producing monopolies would normally fail to satisfy the proportionality test, as there are less restrictive means available for obtaining such revenue, such as fiscal measures".[181]

---

[179] For example, in European Court of Justice, *Harry Franzén*, Case C-189/95, 23 October 1997, Article 34 TFEU (then-Article 28 EC) was infringed by the rules in Sweden governing the Swedish alcohol monopoly. According to the ECJ, the protection of public health against alcohol consumption did not justify the restrictive measures placed upon the importation and sale of alcohol. The Court explained that the structures and fees of state monopolies must be both proportionate to the public interest being pursued and must employ the method that is the least restrictive to trade between Member States.

[180] The exemption is discussed below in the next section.

[181] Buendía Sierra (2014), p. 852 (emphasis added; footnotes omitted).

2.3.3 Justification for the Non-application of the Competition Rules

As noted above, under Article 106(2) the application of the Treaty's competition rules can be avoided in situations where: those rules would prevent an undertaking entrusted with the provision of SGEIs from carrying out its assigned tasks; and the non-application of those rules would not affect trade in a way that would be contrary to the interests of the Union. These criteria, of which the first has been the more important by far, are discussed in the following two sections.

Obstruction of the Performance by an Entrusted Undertaking of Its Particular SGEI Tasks: Necessity and Proportionality of the State Measure

(a) Introduction

Article 106(2) states that SGEI providers and RP monopolies "shall be subject to the rules in this Treaty, in particular to the rules on competition, in so far as the application of such rules does not obstruct the performance, in law or in fact, of the particular tasks assigned to them". As explained above, the design of this rule suggests that any non-application of Treaty provisions *derogates* from the general rule, i.e., from the rule that entrusted undertakings "shall be subject" to those provisions. As a derogation, the exemption is to be narrowly construed. If a defendant undertaking or Member State invokes the exemption, it must be demonstrated that if the provisions of the Treaty were enforced this would compromise the proper performance of the SGEI tasks entrusted to the undertaking under economically acceptable conditions.

(b) Proper Performance of SGEIs Presupposes Economically Acceptable Conditions

SGEI providers must be able to carry out their entrusted tasks under "economically acceptable conditions".[182] This means that the undertaking should not be expected to bear net losses generated by their performance.[183] In the absence of public intervention to restrict or eliminate competition, such losses might result in

[182] See *Corbeau,* cited above note 29, paras 14–16.

[183] This raises questions concerning the efficiency of the entrusted undertaking because a rule allowing *any* restrictions of competition necessary to offset losses might remove incentives to control costs. In *Corbeau,* cited previous footnote, Advocate General Tesauro had stated at paragraph 16 of his Opinion that Articles 106 and 102 "cannot constitute a means of evaluating the economic efficiency of this or that national monopoly". Strictly speaking, the European Court of Justice does not appear to have deviated significantly from that generous point of view. However, whereas the Court does not appear to control the undertaking's efficiency forensically in terms of costs, the exemption from application of the Treaty rules will not be available in the case of a hopelessly *ineffective* undertaking that is manifestly unable to respond to market demand. (See the discussion above; see also specifically *Ambulanz Glöckner,* cited above note 79, para. 62.)

particular (but not only) from the imposition by the authorities of *universal service* obligations on a given undertaking, a common form of SGEIs.[184] In that scenario, rivals unburdened by the same *de jure* obligation to maintain services irrespective of profitability and by the *de facto* need to spread the costs of those services might concentrate their competitive efforts on the most lucrative parts of the market (unless precluded from doing so, e.g., by long-term contracts), leaving the dregs to the hapless universal service provider.[185] In this context, the Court of Justice has rejected the proposition that the exemption should only be available if the economic survival of the entrusted undertaking is threatened.[186] The benchmark, rather, is the economic *equilibrium* of the services, considering the net costs the undertaking has to bear to provide them and any relevant regulatory burdens.[187] On the other side of the ledger, economic *benefits* accruing from the responsibility for carrying out the SGEI tasks should also be considered, including advantages qualifying as state aid within the meaning of Article 107 TFEU.

Furthermore, if the services in question are to be performed in economic equilibrium, then, at least in the absence of sector-specific EU legislation,[188] the

[184] Typical universal service obligations may be seen in *Corbeau* (discussed above). There the Court stated that "it cannot be disputed that the Régie des Postes is entrusted with a service of economic interest consisting in the obligation to collect, carry and distribute mail on behalf of all users *throughout the territory* of the Member State concerned, *at uniform tariffs and on similar quality conditions, irrespective of the specific situations or the degree of economic profitability of each individual operation*". *Corbeau,* cited above note 29, para. 15 (emphasis added).

[185] See *Corbeau,* cited above note 29, paras 17–18. See also *Ambulanz Glöckner,* cited above note 68.

[186] See, e.g., *Commission v. France,* cited above note 114, paras 53–59. At paragraph 95 the Court explained that, "contrary to the Commission's contention [...] [i]t is sufficient that, in the absence of the rights at issue, it would not be possible for the undertaking to perform the particular tasks entrusted to it, defined by reference to its public-service obligations". The Commission's "economic survival" theory might have been consistent with the exemption if the latter had been formulated more stringently, so that the application of the Treaty rules could only be avoided if it would render the performance of the SGEI *impossible*. However, in English the verb "to obstruct" has two possible meanings: not only "to block or prevent" but also the less demanding "to hinder". (But see *Air Inter,* cited above note 122, para. 138 ("it was not sufficient for [the performance of the SGEI at issue] to be simply hindered or made more difficult")). In any case, the "economic survival" theory is draconian and unnecessary to support the aim of the exemption, which is to set aside Treaty rules insofar as necessary to ensure the provision of SGEIs under acceptable economic conditions.

[187] *Almelo,* cited above note 133, para. 49.

[188] The presence or absence of EU legislation, and the consequent "pre-emption" of conflicting action by national authorities, is presented by Sauter as a major factor which should determine whether a "least restrictive means" test or a more lenient "manifestly disproportionate" standard applies. See Sauter (2008), pp. 186–188. However, the *Energy* cases of 1997 were litigated outside the confines of the First Electricity Directive, Directive 96/92, adopted in 1996 (because the case involved past infringements—not to mention the fact that the deadline for transposition had not passed), and even in the "absence" of Community rules, the Court signalled that it would at least have been willing to *entertain* an argument based on less restrictive means. The *Energy* cases are discussed below.

State may in some cases be able to justify reserving for the entrusted undertaking a zone of protection from competition that is *broader* than the entrusted SGEI tasks themselves.[189] A classic case is where the additional protection yields extra profits necessary to offset losses resulting from universal service obligations. Yet there must be limits to the State's ability to extend the reserved sector, not only because the exemption should be interpreted strictly but, more fundamentally, because otherwise entire spheres of economic activity could be insulated from competition. Identifying precisely where those limits fall is a difficult area of the law; it defies an abstract description and depends on concrete facts. But before reviewing the relevant jurisprudence, it is necessary to consider two preliminary issues: how closely EU and national judges must scrutinise state measures in cases where the exemption in Article 106(2) is invoked; and how the burden of proof is allocated.

(c) Necessity and Proportionality of State Measures: Intensity of Judicial Review and Burden of Proof

The words "in so far as" in the second clause of Article 106(2) are significant. If they were taken to mean only "if", a defendant would merely have to show that the restriction of competition makes it possible for the undertaking to perform an entrusted SGEI task. For example, if exclusive rights effectively make it impossible for rivals to offer discrete services the entrusted undertaking does not *itself* offer, then reserving those services to the entrusted undertaking would likely fail to meet even this relatively lenient test.[190] The plain language of Article 106(2), however, suggests a different construction: if the exemption applies *in so far as* the adequate provision of SGEIs is threatened, then a restriction of competition that *goes beyond what is necessary* cannot be justified. This would imply a stricter proportionality test. However, proportionality can be an ambiguous term, as it is sometimes applied with different degrees of rigour.[191] A *strong* version of the proportionality test would require the defendant to demonstrate that adequate provision of SGEIs could not have been ensured by any other *less restrictive means* than by restricting or excluding competition in the manner of the case at hand. Some observers believe that this would encroach impermissibly on national discretion to commission and organise SGEIs. Irrespective of the question of disturbing national prerogatives, the Court may be reluctant to liberalise sectors on an uneven, case-by-case basis that could potentially lead to legislative or regulatory disruptions,[192] or legal vacuums.

[189] See *Corbeau,* cited above note 29; *Almelo,* cited above note 133; *Ambulanz Glöckner,* cited above note 68.

[190] *Cf. Corbeau,* cited above note 29, para. 19. This assumes that the dissociable services offered by other firms are not so substitutable that clients would switch until the economic equilibrium of the SGEIs is ultimately compromised.

[191] See especially Baquero Cruz (2005), pp. 194–196.

[192] *Cf.* then-Judge David Edward (1995), pp. 20–21 (ECJ "cannot be expected to define a coherent Community policy for every sector through judgments in *ad hoc* cases. The task of defining policy falls, in varying degrees, to the member states, the Commission, the Council and the Parliament".).

In short, the delicate nature of SGEIs and conceptions of the proper role of the judiciary can influence the intensity of judicial review. At least in Article 258 infringement proceedings, it appears that the Court only expects the defendant Member State to come forward with a plausible claim that the application of the Treaty rules would obstruct the performance of the particular SGEI tasks under economically acceptable conditions. As it stated in the *Energy import and export* cases of 1997, "[w]hilst it is true that it is incumbent upon a Member State which invokes [Article 106(2)] to demonstrate that the conditions laid down in that provision are met, that burden of proof cannot be so extensive as to require the Member States [...] to go even further and prove, positively, that no other conceivable measure, which by definition would be hypothetical, could enable those tasks to be performed under the same [economically acceptable] conditions".[193]

That is not to say that the Member State would never have to engage with the issue of less restrictive alternatives. In Article 258 proceedings in the *Energy* cases, although it was the Member States concerned which invoked Article 106(2) as a justification for alleged breaches of Article 37 TFEU, the ultimate burden of proof was borne by the Commission. In the pre-litigation procedure, once a Member State, in reply to the Commission's letter of formal notice, invokes the exemption and supports it with plausible arguments that the corresponding conditions are satisfied, it is for the Commission to counter those arguments in its reasoned opinion. Abstract and purely legal arguments that do not grapple specifically with the factual arguments of the Member State are insufficient. The *Energy* cases appeared to turn on the Commission's failure to discharge the nuanced burden of proof just described. The Court was "*not in a position, in these proceedings,* to consider whether, by maintaining exclusive import and export rights for [the entrusted undertakings, the defendant Member State] *has in fact gone further than was necessary* to enable those establishments to perform, under economically acceptable conditions, the tasks of general economic interest assigned to them".[194] This passage indicates that, in the future, if the Commission presents more responsive and tailored legal and *factual* arguments demonstrating why less restrictive measures than those adopted by a Member State could have secured the adequate provision of SGEIs, then the State will bear the burden of rebuttal and the Court *will* be in a position to decide on the lawfulness of the State measures.[195] It is also clear from the Court's language that the nature of the inquiry concerns whether those measures *go beyond* what is necessary. That would seem to entail the more rigorous

[193] *Commission v. France,* cited above note 11, para. 101.

[194] *Commission v. France,* cited above note 11, para. 107 (emphasis added).

[195] Before the *Energy* cases were decided, the CFI did not hesitate to apply a less restrictive means test in *Air Inter,* cited above note 122, para. 140. There, binding sectoral rules adopted by the Community (Regulation 2408/92 on access for Community air carriers to intra-Community air routes, entering into force on 1 January 1993) were already in force at the material time, in contrast to the situation surrounding the *Energy* cases of 1997 (formal proceedings opened by the Commission in 1994, more than 2 years before the adoption of the First Electricity Directive on 19 December 1996).

test mentioned above. If the case is argued properly, the Court will not shy away from examining less restrictive alternatives.

This discussion begs the question of what changes, if anything, when issues arise not in an infringement procedure under Article 258 but in proceedings before national courts. Questions of procedure, including rules on burden of proof, are normally a matter of national law.[196] Nevertheless, having regard for the principle of the effectiveness of EU law, the considerations described above should apply *mutatis mutandis*. The party invoking Article 106(2) would need to show that the conditions of the exemption are satisfied, without having to show that all other conceivable alternatives would have been insufficient to ensure the adequate performance of SGEIs. It would then be for the other party to respond and, if need be, to demonstrate concretely how the contested measures exceed what is necessary under the circumstances.

(d) Obstruction of Performance of SGEIs Within the Meaning of Article 106(2): Illustrative Cases

Two cases illustrate how the Court has approached the exemption established in Article 106(2).[197] Reference is made to a "necessity (proportionality)" criterion as a reminder that the intensity of judicial review in this area is ambiguous and appears to vary according to certain factors such as the degree of previous legislative action by the Council and Parliament (Article 114 TFEU) or the Commission (Article 106(3)).

(i) Corbeau

In *Corbeau,*[198] a private courier had been competing illegally with Belgium's incumbent postal service, the Régie des Postes. The State had granted the Régie

[196] See, e.g., European Court of Justice, *Rewe-Zentralfinanz eG and Rewe-Zentral AG v. Landwirtschaftskammer für das Saarland*, Case C-33/76, 16 December 1976; European Court of Justice, *Comet BV v. Produktschap voor Siergewassen*, Case C-45/76, 16 December 1976; European Court of Justice, *Deutsche Milchkontor GmbH and others v. Germany*, Case C-205/82, 21 September 1983.

[197] A host of cases, leaving alone many others in the field of state aid, could also be discussed in this context. See, *inter alia*, *Almelo,* cited above note 133; *Air Inter,* cited above note 122; *Corsica Ferries France,* cited above note 173; *Albany,* cited above note 40; *Deutsche Post,* cited above note 48; European Court of Justice, *Entreprenøforeningens Affalds/Miljøsektion (FFAD) v. Københavns Kommune (Sydhavnens)*, Case C-209/98, 23 May 2000; *Ambulanz Glöckner,* cited above note 68; European Court of Justice, *Krister Hanner*, Case C-438/02, 31 May 2005; *BUPA v. Commission,* cited above note 150; European Court of Justice, *AG2R Prévoyance v. Beaudout Père et Fils SARL*, Case C-437/09, 3 March 2011; General Court, *Coordination bruxelloise d'institutions sociales et de santé (CBI) v. Commission,* Case T-137/10, 7 November 2012,; *Ordem dos Técnicos Oficiais de Contas,* cited above note 20.

[198] *Corbeau,* cited above note 29. Commentary abounds. See, e.g., Wachsmann and Berrod (1994); Hancher (1994); Buendia Sierra (1999), pp. 316–320; Baquero Cruz (2005), pp. 179–182. Before the *Corbeau* judgment, see more generally *Ahmed Saeed,* cited above note 13, para. 55.

the exclusive right to collect and distribute all the mail in Belgium, while also requiring it to provide universal service. The legal grant of monopoly made no distinction between basic and value-added services. The courier, Courbeau, was prosecuted for poaching the Régie's business customers, in particular by collecting parcels at the address of the sender, and guaranteeing next-day (pre-noon) delivery to destinations within the city of Liège. Mr Corbeau, regarded alternatively as a hero (by his customers) or as a "cherry picker" or "cream skimmer" or worse (by the Régie), allegedly jeopardised the Régie's universal service by diverting away lucrative operations in the relatively densely populated area of Liège, without having to sustain loss-making operations. According to the Court of Justice, the central issue was whether a restriction or exclusion of competition was "necessary in order to allow the holder of the exclusive right to perform its task of general interest and in particular to have the benefit of economically acceptable conditions".[199] The Court decided that a broad reserved sector may be justified where necessary to allow cross-subsidies supporting loss-making SGEIs. As it explained: the obligation of the SGEI provider to perform its services in economic equilibrium "presupposes that it will be possible to offset less profitable sectors against the profitable sectors and hence justifies a restriction of competition from individual undertakings where the economically profitable sectors are concerned. Indeed, to authorise individual undertakings to compete with the holder of the exclusive rights in the sectors of their choice corresponding to those rights would make it possible for them to concentrate on the economically profitable operations and to offer more advantageous tariffs [because] they are not bound for economic reasons to offset losses in the unprofitable sectors against profits in the more profitable sectors".[200] If the Court had stopped there, the situation would not have appeared promising for Mr Corbeau. But having established the general proposition that extended reserved sectors may be justified on the foregoing grounds, the Court then added:

> However, the exclusion of competition is not justified as regards specific services dissociable from the service of general interest which meet special needs of economic operators and which call for certain additional services not offered by the traditional postal service, such as collection from the senders' address, greater speed or reliability of distribution or the possibility of changing destination in the course of transit. Such specific services, by their nature and the conditions in which they are offered, including the geographical area in which they are provided, do not compromise the economic equilibrium of the service of general economic interest performed by the holder of the exclusive right.[201]

As some commentators have emphasised,[202] *Corbeau* does *not* stand for the proposition that state measures should be subjected to a strict proportionality test, according to which the state measure would be doomed if less restrictive alternatives are available—consisting in this case, for example, of direct funding to the

---

[199] *Corbeau,* cited above note 29, para. 16.

[200] *Corbeau,* cited above note 29, paras 17–18.

[201] *Corbeau,* cited above note 29, para. 19.

[202] See especially *Corbeau,* cited above note 29, pp. 191–192.

Régie to support its universal service obligation, or an average rate increase for basic services. For this reason, *Corbeau* is regarded as embodying a "flexible" approach to the principles of necessity and proportionality.[203] To that extent it is plainly a landmark judgment with important implications for monopolists in need of cross-subsidies to cover losses they sustain in carrying out their SGEI tasks.[204] At the same time, however, the Court has emphasised that the imposition of cross-subsidies from the competitive sector must not result in *overcompensation*,[205] which by definition would surpass what is necessary to satisfy the criterion of economically acceptable conditions.

(ii) Energy Import and Export Cases

These cases were brought by the Commission under Article 37 TFEU against (in particular) France, Italy and the Netherlands[206] in relation to their exclusive import (and in the case of France, export) regimes in the energy sector. The details are omitted here to conserve space but the judgments are notable for many reasons. First, the Court stressed that Member States may consider national policy objectives when defining SGEIs.[207] Second, the Court specified how the Commission must rebut plausible arguments under Article 106(2) with specific legal, economic and factual arguments. Third, the Court clarified that it need not be shown that an undertaking's very survival is at stake as a prerequisite for the exemption. In keeping with these indicia of restraint, it has been argued that the Court in these cases adopted a "simple necessity test instead of a proportionality test proper".[208] My reading of the case, however, is closer to that of Holmes.[209] Granted, the Court was treading carefully because of the delicate issue of state sovereignty; and due, perhaps above all, to the serious concrete disruptions that an adverse ruling might have had for electricity supply operations in particular. Yet the Court ultimately chose *not* to hand the Member States a clear victory based on Article 106(2). Instead, it held that the arguments of the Commission (concerning, in particular, less restrictive alternatives) had been too general and abstract for it to engage in a meaningful assessment.[210] That appears to leave the door open in future cases for a

---

[203] See, e.g., Maíllo (2007), pp. 596 ff.

[204] See, e.g., *TNT Traco,* cited above note 122, paras 54–55 (upholding postal dues imposed in the competitive express mail sector to finance the incumbent's SGEI mission).

[205] *TNT Traco,* cited above note 122, para. 57.

[206] Respectively, *Commission v. France,* cited above note 114; European Court of Justice, *Italy v. Commission,* Case C-158/94, 23 October 1997; *Commission v. Netherlands,* cited above note 120. Once again, there is plenty of commentary. To cite only one example, see Cameron (2007), pp. 478–488.

[207] More recently, see also European Court of Justice, *Federutility and Others v. AEEG,* Case C-265/08, 20 April 2010.

[208] See Baquero Cruz (2005), pp. 193–194.

[209] See Holmes (2007), pp. 1038ff; Holmes (2004).

[210] *Cf.* Holmes (2007), p. 1061, footnote 146; Holmes (2004), p. 171.

more searching examination of whether the restriction of competition adopted to support an entrusted undertaking's SGEI tasks fits its purpose.

Application of Exemption Under Article 106(2) Must Not Affect the Development of Trade to an Extent Contrary to the Interests of the Union

As already seen, Article 106(2) contains a proviso that "the development of trade must not be affected to such an extent as would be contrary to the interests of the Union".[211] It is increasingly well established that the proviso is not mere surplusage; it appears to be a justiciable condition that imposes real, if often indeterminate, limits on the availability of the exemption.[212] It must be acknowledged, however, that there does not seem to be a consensus among commentators with respect to its function and legal consequences.

In the *Energy* cases,[213] the Commission argued that the exemption contained in Article 106(2) did not apply because the exclusive import and export rights at issue *did* unduly affect the development of trade. But it failed to spell out the interests of the Union in reference to which the development of trade was to be evaluated.[214] What little evidence there was regarding the development of trade suggested that trade was actually increasing.[215] It was thus all the more incumbent upon the

[211] The question of whether this proviso has direct effect remains unsettled. See Buendía Sierra (2014), pp. 864–865. Whish states that "[i]t is arguable that only the Commission should be entitled to carry out the task of assessing the interests of the Community". Whish (2008), p. 239. Whish's contention is consistent with the original understanding in 1957, when direct effect was not foreseen for the *first* sentence of Article 106(2) either. (*Cf. Port de Mertert*, decided in 1971, cited above note 166.) However, now that nearly 60 years have passed, this position is debatable. The "interests of the Union" may not always be obvious (see discussion below in the main text), but where there is doubt a national court may refer the question to the European Court of Justice, in accordance with Article 267 TFEU, or it may request input from the Commission (see Article 15 (1) of Regulation 1/2003). The more traditional view *excluding* direct effect would imply, unsatisfactorily, that parties to national proceedings may invoke the first sentence in national court but not the second, somewhat reminiscent of the fractured application of Article 101 before the adoption of Regulation 1/2003. It is submitted that Article 106(2) is more naturally applied, despite its complex structure, as an indivisible norm, albeit with various elements and conditions. (State aid disputes are quite different, as in the latter context the Commission has exclusive competence to decide compatibility. See European Court of Justice, *Servizi Ausiliari Dottori Commercialisti Srl v. Giuseppe Calafiori*, Case C-451/03, 30 March 2006, para. 71.)

[212] See, e.g., *TNT Traco*, cited above note 122, paras 56–57; *Air Inter*, cited above note 122, para. 52. *Cf.* also *BUPA v. Commission*, cited above note 150, paras 306–309.

[213] *Commission v. France*, cited above note 114; *Commission v Italy*, cited above note 206; *Commission v. Netherlands*, cited above note 120.

[214] See *Commission v. Netherlands*, cited above note 120, para. 113.

[215] See *Commission v. Netherlands*, cited above note 120. This evidence consisted of the sixth recital in the preamble to the Electricity Transit Directive, which stated that trade between the high-voltage systems in Europe was increasing from year to year. See Directive 90/547 on the transit of electricity through transmission grids, OJ 1990 L313/30, 13 November 1990 (now repealed), recital 6.

Commission to clarify exactly which interests had been compromised. In particular, the Commission had not shown how, "in the absence of a common policy in the area concerned, development of direct trade between producers and consumers, in parallel with the development of trade between major networks, would have been possible having regard, in particular to the existing capacity and arrangements for transmission and distribution".[216] The Court was thus sceptical that exclusive import rights could have such a detrimental effect on trade when producers and consumers did not have a right of access to the networks to support cross-border transactions.

It is true that there was no established Community policy in relation to trade in electricity in 1994 when the Commission lodged its legal actions, and that there were no Community-imposed third party access rights at that time. But the Court's judgments were rendered in October 1997—11 months after the adoption of the original Electricity and Gas Directives.[217] The Court made no reference to this new legislative environment. One may take the view that only the facts as they stood in 1994 were relevant. Nonetheless, had the Court been so inclined it could have fashioned a remedy prospectively with no harm done to legal certainty. In appropriate future cases the Court may be willing to consider relevant EU legislation for the purposes of determining the nature of the "interests of the Union", particularly where the latter expression is given some shape in sector-specific regulation. The Court has already taken the important step, in the *Energy* cases, of signalling that the proviso is indeed justiciable and can potentially have some autonomous normative force. On the other hand, in the presence of harmonising (and partially pre-emptive) EU legislation, the scope for Member States to claim an exemption may well be specifically narrowed by the terms of the relevant instrument. If so, then disputes arising in such a setting could potentially be decided at an earlier stage of analysis—i.e., under the first sentence of Article 106(2)—on grounds of proportionality.

3 Building a National Competition Strategy (NCS) in China

In an earlier essay I made several suggestions to strengthen the legal framework governing administrative acts with anticompetitive effects in China.[218] The following remarks partially overlap with, but mostly supplement, the proposals already

[216] *Commission v. Netherlands,* cited above note 120, para. 71.

[217] Directive 96/92 concerning common rules for the internal market in electricity, OJ 1997 L27/20, 30 January 1997; Directive 98/30 of the European Parliament and of the Council concerning common rules for the internal market in natural gas, OJ 1998 L204/1, 22 June 1998. Indeed, the Council had agreed upon the particulars of these directives in June 1996.

[218] See Marquis (2013).

put forward. It should be pointed out that Chinese authorities have not allowed the problem to fade into obscurity. Following the Third Plenum of November 2013, which famously affirmed that the market was to play a decisive role in allocating resources, 12 central ministries (MOFCOM, NDRC, SAIC, etc.) adopted in December 2013 a "Work Program to Eliminate Regional Blockades and Break Industry Monopolies", whose relevant tasks include reforming laws and regulations that impose regional blockades and establish exclusive rights. The Work Program is mainly concerned with inter-regional trade issues—an important component of the administrative monopoly problem, but not the only one. Also, past efforts of this kind to address the administrative monopoly problem yielded few results. Nevertheless, the adoption of such policies at a high level and in a visible manner is to be encouraged.

The first forward-looking observation to be made here is that making changes to China's hard law to ameliorate the pervasive problem of anticompetitive administrative acts will be a long-term process. Unlike the EU, China does not currently have the advantage of relevant legal rules with effective remedies embedded in law of superior rank (i.e., "primary law", in EU jargon). Moreover, while the notion of a hierarchy of laws exists in China,[219] it poses difficulties because constitutional rules are not always respected. In the long-term, China should not only assign constitutional rank to legal rules addressing the administrative monopoly problem, it should also frame those rules in mandatory terms while allowing for appropriate and proportionate justifications. The basic framework seen above in the EU law context may serve as a source of inspiration. That is to say, it should be acknowledged that competition is not a *supreme* value prevailing over all others; but the balance between competition and other values should be determined within a framework of superior law, i.e., a framework that ranks higher than the Anti-Monopoly Law. Anticompetitive rules and regulations of lesser rank should be pre-empted (contrary to the current configuration under the AML).

But again, the suggestion of elevating Chapter V-type rules to a "constitutional" stature could only realistically be pursued as a long-term project. In the meantime, and in recognition of the weaknesses of the current rules that apply to anticompetitive administrative abuse of power, a comprehensive and multidimensional national competition strategy (NCS) should be developed. The NCS should involve a broad and coherent plan that would be implemented at the national, provincial and municipal levels of government. Implementation could be done in stages where appropriate in order for reforms to retain their focus. To make a significant impact, the NCS should include, for example, the following elements:

---

[219] See the Law of Legislation of China (2000), which establishes a hierarchical order beginning with laws (adopted by the NPC or its Standing Committee and signed by the President) and descending to administrative regulations (adopted by the State Cabinet or State Council and signed by the Prime Minister), local regulations (local People's Congress), ministerial ordinances (ministries under the State Council such as MOFCOM) local ordinances (municipalities).

- Steps to reinforce the slow trend toward better-functioning, independent courts free to decide cases according to legal and de-politicised criteria (an issue which is obviously of common importance to multiple fields of law, and not just competition law)[220];
- Dialogue, education and advocacy at all levels, whereby, *inter alia*, competition agency officials and non-agency experts deliver opinions and recommendations concerning new and existing (law-based or policy-based) instruments and initiatives;
- Sweeping and systematic review, employing tools such as Competition Impact Assessments,[221] of significant new and existing laws and administrative rules and acts with a view to assessing their proportionality in light of market and competition logics (taking inspiration from other jurisdictions that have conducted such exercises, including especially Australia,[222,223]);

---

[220] Many have drawn attention to the problem of the divided loyalties of China's judges, and to the scope for manipulation of litigation outcomes. See, e.g., Williams (2013), pp. 96–97. The Third Plenum of November 2013 took some modest steps to acknowledge and improve the situation. More recently, on 28 October 2014, the Communist Party's Central Committee adopted a significant Resolution according to which local courts will be held to higher standards of impartiality and meddling local officials will face punishment. It is to be expected that the new vision will not preclude the Party itself from intervening in a politicised case if it deems such action to be necessary to protect its interests. For recent discussion of the specific issue of adjudication committees, see Chng and Dowdle (2014).

[221] The notion of a Competition Impact Assessment builds on, and is sometimes implemented as part of, the more traditional concept of a Regulatory Impact Assessment. In essence, a Competition Impact Assessment involves scrutiny of new or existing rules and regulations to determine whether the measure in question advances a legitimate aim of general interest in a way which is proportionate and which employs means that are least restrictive of competition. Reasonably available alternative ways of achieving the same ends with less distortive impact on competition should be favoured. Competition Impact Assessments have been used to significant effect in jurisdictions such as Australia, the European Union (the European Commission being the main body responsible in that context), Greece, Hungary, Korea, Mexico, Romania (with a recently launched initiative), the United Kingdom and the United States. The systematic use of this instrument promotes both rationality and transparency with regard to the social costs and benefits of public acts. For detailed discussion, see OECD (2011). More recently, see also the ICN (2014) (Recommended Practices, including a proportionality/less restrictive means analysis; see Recommendation VII).

[222] While other jurisdictions have carried out large-scale regulatory reviews to identify unnecessary anticompetitive distortions, the most well-known and probably the most ambitious screening exercise was that conducted by Australia in the early 1990s. The Australian initiative was spearheaded by the Hilmer Report of 1992, and following its recommendations the Government implemented a National Competition Policy in 1995. The scale of this project can be seen in the decision to exhaustively review *all* national and state laws over a period of 6 years. Some of the main features of the Policy included: removal of barriers to inter-state competition; removal of all national and state laws found to restrict competition without adequate justification; review of publicly owned industries to determine the distortive impact of public ownership; price regulation in those instances where market competition was infeasible; and the establishment of competitive neutrality, with public and privileged operators subject to the same competition rules as private operators.

[223] In Taiwan a large-scale screening exercise was launched in 1994. Meng recommends that mainland China should learn from this experience. Meng (2013), p. 267.

- Promotion of a culture of compliance, which involves a shift in the values of officials of all levels so that they desire to comply with norms against abuse of administrative power not only because they are deterred from misconduct by the threat of detection and sanctions (such as they are) but because they come to understand spontaneous compliance as being part of their own identity;
- Corrective fiscal reforms to reduce local incentives that perversely support mercantilist behaviour and protection of local champions[224];
- Development of additional (hard and soft) legal and institutional tools, e.g., by (i) introducing a real possibility of recovering damages for infringements of Chapter V of China's Anti-Monopoly Law (i.e., by way of inserting specific compensatory provisions in the AML that go beyond the general possibility of seeking damages for direct losses in administrative law disputes[225]) and (ii) adopting guidelines (of the Anti-Monopoly Commission) on how the concept of anticompetitive abuse of administrative power is to be understood and applied[226];
- Filling the administrative remedy gap, e.g., by (i) developing specific powers to challenge other public authorities and organs (ascending a pyramidal remedy ladder), including powers to address recidivism, (ii) moving beyond the increasingly archaic distinction between abstract (i.e., generally applicable) and specific administrative acts,[227] (iii) drawing inspiration from other jurisdictions (such as, in the case of Italy, Article 21-*bis* of Law 287/1990,[228,229]), and (iv) reinforcing

[224] Previous fiscal reforms reinforced local governments' relations with local operators and incentivised the local authorities to promote tax revenue-maximising investments "regardless of the overall market situation". See, e.g., Breslin (2012), p. 42 (citation omitted). While regional competition may also stimulate economic development in some areas, negative externalities have not been adequately internalised.

[225] Direct losses in administrative law disputes may be claimed under Article 67 of China's Administrative Litigation Law. Conciliation procedures may apply.

[226] See Marquis (2013), pp. 129–130.

[227] Xu and Zhang (2013), pp. 281 and 284, are understandably critical of the undue protection accorded to abstract administrative conduct falling short of a regulation. They recommend a right of appeal to a court where a claimant cannot obtain relief through administrative reconsideration. I would go further and expose even abstract regulations to challenge if appropriate conditions are fulfilled in terms of distortive effects and absence of a proportionate public interest justification. See Marquis (2013), p. 129. Such an approach would provide a potential antidote to measures of general application that have been diverted or "hijacked" by private interests.

[228] Italy is a good example of a jurisdiction where growth and productivity have been held back by rigidities in public regulation. In an attempt to improve this situation the Italian Government in December 2011, under then-Prime Minister Mario Monti, introduced an amendment to Italy's competition law which produced Article 21-*bis*. According to this provision, the competition authority (the AGCM) can bring the distortive character of any administrative measure or regulation to the relevant administrative entity. (No distinction between abstract and specific administrative acts is made.) If the latter fails to comply with the AGCM's instructions within 60 days, the AGCM will then have 30 days in which it may file a claim against that entity before the Italian administrative courts. For discussion of the incipient practice under Article 21-*bis*, see Munari (2015).

[229] Other countries besides Italy also have provisions allowing competition authorities to challenge anticompetitive rules and regulations in court. To cite only some European examples, France,

the above measures by deciding, in the long run, to empower a *single* high-level agency, acting on direct delegation from and with the derived authority of the State Council, to take charge of administrative enforcement[230];
- Cultivation of not only a competition culture but an internal market culture.

The foregoing measures and projects can work together, in a mutually reinforcing manner, as a system constituting China's national competition strategy. A piecemeal approach—exemplified by the status quo—is likely to fail because what is required is cultural (and hence behavioural) change. The problem concerns not just a need to shift from a planned or transition economy to a market economy; this can be seen from the fact that the administrative monopoly problem afflicts market economies around the world, including the economies of "rich" jurisdictions. The core issue in China is a different one. It relates to the fact that, if reform efforts are incomplete or piecemeal, then when public authorities knowingly or unknowingly distort competition, there are no adequate corrective mechanisms; national wealth, productivity and dynamism suffer accordingly. The usual mechanisms applying to private conduct—the market itself and antitrust regulation—are of little avail. And this is compounded by the fact that democratic, political and/or bureaucratic mechanisms of correction also tend to be weak, notably because they are often influenced or even dictated by narrow private interests.[231] As a consequence, it may well be the case that there is no effective check on the acts of public officials and public bodies. With no such safeguards, and without the supportive measures indicated above such as advocacy and education, the necessary cultural and behavioural transformations based on revised values, beliefs and self-understanding have no hope of taking hold.

References

Baquero Cruz J (2005) Beyond competition: services of general interest and European Community Law. In: De Búrca G (ed) EU law and the welfare state: in search of solidarity. OUP, Oxford, pp 169–212

Braconnier S (2007) Droit des Services Publics, 2ème édn. Presses Universitaires de France, Paris

Breslin S (2012) Government-industry relations in China: a review of the art of the state. In: Walter A, Zhang X (eds) East Asian capitalism: diversity, continuity, and change. OUP, Oxford, pp 29–47

Buendia Sierra JL (1999) Exclusive rights and state monopolies (trans: Read A). OUP, Oxford

Buendía Sierra JL (2014) Article 106 – exclusive or special rights and other anti-competitive state measures (Chapter 6). In: Faull J, Nikpay A (eds) The EU law of competition, 3rd edn. OUP, Oxford

Hungary, Lithuania and Spain, Sweden all have relevant procedures. For a more complete round-up, see Fox and Healey (2014).

[230] *Cf.* Williams (2013), pp. 110–111.

[231] The argument is presented in detail in Marquis (2013).

Buendía Sierra JL (2016) Enforcement of Article 106(1) TFEU by the European Commission and the EU Courts (Chapter 9). In: Lowe P, Marquis M, and Monti G (eds) Effective and legitimate enforcement of competition law. Hart, Oxford, forthcoming

Cameron P (2007) Competition in energy markets, 2nd edn. OUP, Oxford

Cheng T (2014) Competition and the state in China. In: Cheng T, Lianos I, Sokol DD (eds) Competition and the state. Stanford University Press, Stanford, pp 170–186

Chng M, Dowdle M (2014) The Chinese Debate about the Adjudication Committee: implications for what "Judicial Independence" means in the context of China. Chin J Comp Law 2 (2):233–251

Cooper J, Kovacic W (2010) U.S. convergence with international competition norms: antitrust law and public restraints on competition. Boston Univ Law Rev 90:1555–1610

Crane D (2013) Judicial review of anticompetitive state action: two models in comparative perspective. J Antitrust Enforcement 1(2):418–436

Davilla M (2014) Case note. J Eur Competition Law Pract. Advance Access, doi:10.1093/jeclap/lpu102

Edward D (1995) Article 90 EC-Treaty and the deregulation, liberalisation and privatisation of public enterprises and public monopolies. Speech, Bonn

Edward D, Hoskins M (1995) Article 90: deregulation and EC law; reflections arising from the XVI FIDE conference. Common Mark Law Rev 32:157–186

Ehlermann C-D (1993) Managing monopolies: the role of the state in controlling market dominance in the European Community. Eur Competition Law Rev 14:61–69

Fox E (2004) State action in comparative context: what if *Parker v. Brown* were Italian? (Chapter 19). In: Hawk B (ed) International Antitrust Law & Policy: Fordham Corporate Law 2003. Juris Publishing, Huntington

Fox E, Healey D (2014) When the state harms competition: the role of competition law. Antitrust Law J 79(3):769–820

Hancher L (1994) Case note. Common Mark Law Rev 31:105–122

Hancher L (2014) Public services and EU law (Chapter 18). In: Barnard C, Peers S (eds) European Union law. OUP, Oxford

Holmes J (2004) Fixing the limits of EC competition law: state action and the accommodation of the public services. Curr Legal Probl 57:149–174

Holmes J (2007) The competition rules and the acts of member states (Chapter 11). In: Bellamy and Child, The EC law of competition, 6th edn. Sweet and Maxwell, London

ICN (2014) Recommended Practices on Competition Assessment, http://www.inernationalcompetitionnetwork.org/uploads/library/doc978.pdf

Inman R, Rubinfeld D (1997) Making sense of the antitrust state action doctrine: balancing political participation and economic efficiency in regulatory federalism. Tex Law Rev 75:1203–1300

Jones A, Sufrin B (2007) EC competition law: text, cases, and materials. OUP, Oxford

Kovar R (1996) Droit communautaire et service public: esprit d'orthodoxie ou pensée laïcisée, parts 1 and 2. 32(2) Revue Trimestrielle de Droit Européen 32(2): 215–242 and 32(3): 493–534

Lenaerts K (2002) Les services d'intérêt économique et le droit communautaire. In: Conseil d'Etat, *Rapport public 2002: Collectivités publiques et concurrence,* pp 425 ff.

Maíllo J (2007) Services of general interest and EC competition law. In: Amato G, Ehlermann C-D (eds) EC competition law: a critical assessment. Hart, Oxford, pp 591–615

Marenco G (1983) Public sector and community law. Common Mark Law Rev 20:495–528

Marquis M (2013) Abuse of administrative power to restrict competition in China: four reflections, two ideas and a thought. In: Faure M, Zhang X (eds) Regulation and competition policy in China: new developments and empirical evidence. Edward Elgar, Cheltenham, pp 73–141

Marquis M (2015) Idea merchants and paradigm peddlers in global antitrust. Pacific McGeorge Global Bus Dev Law J 28: 155–208

Monti G (2014) State regulation and EU competition law (Chapter 25). In: Chalmers D et al (eds) European Union Law, 3rd edn. CUP, Cambridge (online supplement)

Munari F (2015) Judicial assessment of anticompetitive behaviour in Italy (Chapter 7). In: Cisotta R, Marquis M (eds) Litigation and arbitration in EU competition law. Edward Elgar, Cheltenham
Nistor L (2011) Public services and the European Union. T.M.C. Asser Press, The Hague
OECD (2011) Competition Assessment Toolkit, Volumes 1 and 2, http://www.oecd.org/competition/assessment-toolkit.htm
Ross M (2007) Promoting solidarity: from public services to the European model of competition? Common Mark Law Rev 44:1057–1080
Sauter W (2008) Services of general economic interest and universal service in EU law. Eur Law Rev 33:167–193
Sauter W, Schepel H (2009) State and market in European Union law. CUP, Cambridge
Schweitzer H (2011) Services of general economic interest: European law's impact on the role of markets and of member states. In: Cremona M (ed) Market integration and public services within the EU. OUP, Oxford, pp 11–62
Szyszczak E (2007) The regulation of the state in competitive markets in the EU. Hart, Oxford
Verkuil P (1975) State action, due process, and antitrust: reflections on *Parker v. Brown*. Columbia Law Rev 75:328–358
Wachsmann A, Berrod F (1994) Les critères de justification des monopoles: un premier bilan après l'affaire Corbeau. Revue Trimestrielle de Droit Européen 30:39–61
Waelbroeck M, Frignani A (1999) European competition law (trans: Gamet-Pol). Transnational Publishers, Ardsley
Wainwright R, Bouquet A (2004) State intervention and action in EC competition law (Chapter 23). In: Hawk B (ed) International Antitrust Law & Policy: Fordham Corporate Law 2003. Juris Publishing, Huntington
Wang X (2014) The evolution of China's Anti-Monopoly Law. Edward Elgar, Cheltenham
Whish R (2008) Competition law, 6th edn. OUP, Oxford
Williams M (2013) China. In: Williams M (ed) The political economy of competition law in Asia. Edward Elgar, Cheltenham, pp 88–118
Xu S, Zhang B (2013) Judicial and administrative remedies against administrative monopoly: cases and analysis. In: Emch A, Stallibrass D (eds) China's Anti-Monopoly Law: the first five years. Wolters Kluwer, Alphen aan den Rijn, pp 271–285
Meng Y (2013) The uneasy relationship between antitrust enforcement and industry-specific regulation in China. In: Emch A, Stallibrass D (eds) China's Anti-Monopoly Law: the first five years. Wolters Kluwer, Alphen aan den Rijn, pp 259–270

Striking an Uneasy Balance Between Competition and Market Integration: The Case of EU Public Procurement

Stefan E. Weishaar

1 Introduction

Shortly after the Second World War the 'European integration project' was fuelled by economic interests[1] that made war 'not merely unthinkable, but materially impossible'.[2] Germany's economic recovery started to threaten France's newly set up steel industry that might have been cut-off from cheap German coal and iron ore supplies as German production slowly expanded again. This episode of market integration that led to the creation of the 'European Coal and Steel Community' in 1952 is a reminder that the rhetoric's of European institutions such as the European Commission often appeal to higher objectives but that the driving force behind policies can very well be of a subtle nature: economic interests.

Market integration, the main driving force behind the ever closer cooperation between Member States of the European Union (EU), is strongly motivated by the desire of economic prosperity. Market integration should allow for more gains from trade and more competition. In the EU market integration has strongly taken root in the form of the four freedoms (goods, services, capital and labour) and thereby greatly shaped the current European Union and lead to significant advancement of economic cooperation and prosperity. Curiously, one policy area has to a large degree resisted market integration: public procurement.

Public procurement rules have been justified on economic grounds—procurement market integration was therefore more a means to an end rather than a goal in itself. It was assumed that introducing competitiveness into the national

[1] Griffiths (2004).

[2] Schumann (1990), p. 13.

S.E. Weishaar (✉)
Faculty of Law, University of Groningen, Groningen, The Netherlands
e-mail: S.E.Weishaar@rug.nl

N. Philipsen et al. (eds.), *Market Integration: The EU Experience and Implications for Regulatory Reform in China*, China-EU Law Series 2,
DOI 10.1007/978-3-662-48273-5_4

procurement markets would give rise to market liberalisation, more integration and the associated benefits.[3] Improvements in competition across national borders in this sector could lead to significant improvements in the budgetary positions of the various Member States because of lower prices paid for procured goods and services.[4] Procurement constitutes a sizable part of each Member State's economy. Although the importance of public procurement differs significantly across EU Member States, according to European Commission estimates it accounts for approximately 16 % of the Union's GDP.[5]

Unlike the EU, China is a unitary state and does not have diverse national public procurement rules albeit implementing regulations on lower governmental levels can differ. Yet China suffers from fragmented[6] and thus not integrated markets. This chapter examines the EU's and China's approach to procurement market integration, particularly with regard to the EU's recent public procurement reform and identifies its similarities and differences.

The space available in this contribution necessarily limits the scope of this research. This chapter is restricted to the most important procurement rules in the EU (Directive 2014/24/EU)[7] and the Chinese Government Procurement Law (GPL)[8] and does not extend to sectorial rules. It also does not assess whether the market integration is beneficial or desirable.

In this contribution, first the evolution of EU market integration in the area of public procurement is concisely presented from a historic perspective (Sect. 2) before studies showing the current degree of integration in the procurement market and the identified obstacles for cross-border procurement are reviewed (Sect. 3). Building upon Sect. 3, the thrust of the latest public procurement reform is contrasted with empirical insights, and the merits of the recent reform for deepening market integration in the area of public procurement are assessed (Sect. 4). Section 5 examines China's approach to public procurement market integration. A comparison and concluding remarks are presented in Sect. 6.

[3] Bovis (2012), p. 482.

[4] See Weishaar (2013).

[5] European Commission (2004), p. 4. Data for all EU 15 Member States ranges from 1995 to 2002 and is robustly above 16 %.

[6] Poncet (2005).

[7] Directive 2014/24/EU of the European Parliament and of the Council (2014) on public procurement and repealing Directive 2004/18/EC. OJ L 94/65, 26 February 2014.

[8] Government Public Procurement law of the People's Republic of China. Adopted at the 28th meeting of the Standing Committee of the Ninth National People's Congress of the People's Republic of China; 29 June 2002.

2 Procurement Market Integration in the EU

Public procurement in the European Union (at that time European Community) dates back to 1971, when the first directive for public works was introduced.[9] A few years later, in 1976 rules on supplies followed.[10] These rules did, however, not give rise to competition on the merits between domestic and foreign undertakings. Foreign undertakings where in practice prevented from entering the domestic markets by favouritism of national undertakings over foreign undertakings as a matter of public policy. There were also a series of malpractices such as subdivision of contracts so as to circumvent procurement publication thresholds under EC rules, standards setting that would be more easily complied with by national undertakings, requiring additional capacity or financial statements of foreign suppliers, unsuitable response times for first-time suppliers, and undue reliance upon special derogations of the directives in cases such as emergencies, etc.

In the 1980s fears in Europe to lose competitiveness *vis-à-vis* the US, Japan and the Newly Industrialized Countries (NICs) highlighted the need for a new economic impulse. This impulse took the form of the Commission's 1985 White Paper, 'Completing the Internal Market'. The thrust of this document was to address both the formal and informal barriers to trade that would open up the national markets in the Member States to invigorated competition and help them prepare for the global competition. This led to the Single European Act in 1986 that encompassed around 300 directives addressing physical, technical and fiscal barriers to trade in the internal market. It also envisaged the creation of a single public procurement market.

The 1988 Cecchini report[11] was an economic report on the single market that also examined the status of the public procurement regime in the Member States. It described the public sector markets as closed and uncompetitive and criticised the regulatory diversity that obstructed cross-border procurement in sectors such as defence, power generation, telecommunications and railways. Moreover, it pointed out that promoting competition between competitors that were uncompetitive at international level was insufficient to prepare Europe for the future. Subsidies for national industries were held to distort competition on the merits and thus to be counterproductive. Other criticism of the Cecchini report relates to the firm sizes and their product markets such as Research and Development being insufficiently concentrated in the economies and that undertakings were insufficiently specialised, entailing that the European firms did not benefit sufficiently from returns to scale.

---

[9] Council Directive 71/305/EEC of 26 July 1971 concerning the co-ordination of procedures for the award of public works contracts, 16 August 1971.

[10] Council Directive 77/62/EEC of 21 December 1976 coordinating procedures for the award of public supply contracts, 15 January 1977.

[11] Commission of the European Communities (1988) Europe 1992, the overall challenge. SEC (88) 524 final, Brussels, 13 April 1988.

Following the Cecchini report until 1993, several directives were introduced to delineate the scope and procedural aspects of public procurement relating to works, supplies and services. The object and purpose of these directives was to foster a more open and fair procurement market that was expected to give rise to enhanced competition, improved international competitiveness and efficiency. Strategic industries would emerge and individual market players would gain in strength as they would progressively gain market share in the European Community to eventually be on par with non-European competitors. In addition, reductions of public procurement costs were desired.

Based on the public procurement Green Paper[12] published in 1996 and its public procurement report in 1998,[13] the European Commission proposed amendments to simplify, clarify and combine existing legislation and modernise the existing public procurement directives.[14] These amendments related to: (1) electronic purchasing, (2) extending the applicability of the negotiation procedure to particularly complex contracts, (3) framework agreements, (4) clarification of technical specifications, (5) strengthening of award and selection criteria, (6) simplification of thresholds and (7) the introduction of a common procurement vocabulary.[15] These amendments were reflected in the 2004 procurement Directives on public works, supply and services (2004/18/EC) and for entities operating in the sectors of water, energy, transport and postal services (2004/17/EC). Both Directives had to be implemented until 31st January 2006[16] and bring national legislation in line, as to help the integration of the European public procurement market.

The revision of public procurement directives in 2004 also examined the impact of the previous procurement rules. According to a Commission study, prices paid by procuring entities fell by 30 %[17] because of the introduction of public procurement directives,[18] which led to both an increase in transparency and effective cross-border competition. Issues identified to contribute to a further reduction of

[12] European Commission (1996a) COM (96) 583 final, 27 November 1996.

[13] European Commission (1998) COM (98) 143 final, 11 March 1998.

[14] European Commission (2000) COM (2000)275 final/2, 30 August 2000, replacing COM(2000) 275 final, 10 May 2000.

[15] European Commission (2000) COM (2000)275 final/2, 30 August 2000, replacing COM(2000) 275 final, 10 May 2000, pp. 4–16.

[16] Article 71 (1) Directive 2004/17/EC of the European Parliament and of the Council (2004) coordinating the procurement procedures of entities operating in the water, energy, transport and postal services sectors. OJ L 134/1, 31 March 2004 and Article 80 (1) Directive 2004/18/EC of the European Parliament and of the Council (2004) on the coordination of procedures for the award of public works contracts, public supply contracts and public service contracts. OJ L 134/114, 31 March 2004.

[17] European Commission (2004), pp. 15–16.

[18] Public procurement legislation in force in 2002 included Council Directive 89/665, Council Directive 92/13/EEC, Council Directive 92/50/EEC, Council Directive 93/36/EEC, Council Directive 93/37/EEC, Council Directive 93/38/EEC.

procurement prices were transaction costs and to a lesser extent social clauses.[19] Environmental clauses were not regarded as problematic.[20]

Not only the legislator at EU level emphasizes the importance of procurement markets but also the European Court of Justice (CJEU) has developed a solid line of case law. The CJEU describes the purpose of EU public procurement legislation as averting both the risk of preference being given to national bidders or applicants whenever a contract is awarded by the contracting authorities and the possibility that a body financed or controlled by the State, regional or local authorities or other bodies governed by public law may choose to be guided by other than economic considerations.[21] Coherent with the Court's understanding that public procurement legislation is directed towards the fostering of competition[22] and the furtherance of the internal market,[23] all relevant Community principles are cited in the directives.

---

[19] European Commission (2004), pp. 21 ff. See also COWI (2003a) and COWI (2003b).

[20] European Commission (2004), p. 21. See also ICLEI (2003).

[21] European Court of Justice, *Korhonen and others*, 22 March 2003, Case C-18/01, para 52, European Court of Justice, *University of Cambridge*, Case C-380/98, 3 October 2000, para 17, European Court of Justice, *Universale-Bau and others*, Case C-470/99, 12 December 2002, para 52, European Court of Justice, *Truley*, Case C-373/00, 27 February 2003, para 42, European Court of Justice, *France v. Commission*, Case C-237/99, 1 February 2001, para 42, European Court of Justice, *Mannesmann Anlagenbau Austria and others*, Case C-44/96, 15 January 1998, para 33, European Court of Justice, *Gemeente Arnhem and Gemeente Rheden*, Case C-360/96, 10 November 1998, para 42–43, European Court of Justice, *Commission v. Spain*, Case C-283/00, 16 October 2003, para 92.

[22] Competition: European Court of Justice, *Commission/Spain*, Case C-214/00, 15 May 2003, para 53, European Court of Justice, *Fabricom SA v. Belgian State*, joined cases C-21/03 and C-34/03, 3 March 2005, para 26, European Court of Justice, *Concordia Bus Finland*, Case C-513/99, 17 September 2002, para 81, European Court of Justice, *Impresa Lombardini SpA – Impresa Generale di Construzioni*, joined cases C-285/99 and C-286/99, 27 November 2001, para 35, European Court of Justice, *Fracasso and Leitschutz*, Case C-27/98, 16 September 1999, para 26, European Court of Justice, *Universale-Bau and others*, Case C-470/99, 12 December 2002, para 89, European Court of Justice, *Sintesi SpA*, Case C-247/02, 7 October 2004, para 35, European Court of Justice, *Commission v. Denmark*, Case C-243/89, 22 June 1993, para 33, European Court of Justice *Ordine degli Architetti delle province di Milano e Lodi and others*, Case C-399/98, 12 July 2001, para 52 and 75, European Court of Justice, *Beentjes*, Case C-31/87, 20 September 1988, para 21.

[23] The ECJ states that Directives 92/50, 93/46 and 93/37 which taken as a whole constitute the core of Community law on public contracts are intended to attain similar objectives in their respective fields and that there is no reason to give a different interpretation to provisions which fall within the same field of community law and have substantially the same wording. See European Court of Justice, *Kauppatalo Hansel Oy*, Case C-244/02, 16 October 2003, para 34–35 and European Court of Justice, *Concordia Bus Finland*, Case C-513/99, 17 September 2002, para 90–91. Consequently former case law falling under any of these directives is cited below. Case law concerning public procurement and the internal market/freedoms: European Court of Justice, *Commission vGermany*, joined cases C-20/01 and C-28/01, 10 April2003, para 60, European Court of Justice, Case C-26/03, *Stadt Halle and RPL Recyclingpark Lochau GmbH*. 11 January 2003, para 46, European Court of Justice, *Commission v. Italy*, Case C-199/85, 10 March 1987, para 12, European Court of Justice, *Holst Italia*, Case C-176/98, 2 December 1999, para 23, European Court of Justice, *Ballast Nedam Groep I*, Case C-389/92, 14 April 1994, para 6, European Court of Justice, *SIAC Construction*, Case C-19/00, 18 October 2001, para 32, European Court of Justice, *Concordia Bus Finland*, Case C-513/99,

These include the principle of free movement of goods, establishment and services and derived from them, the principles of equal treatment,[24] non-discrimination,[25] mutual recognition, proportionality and transparency.[26] Jurisprudence developed

17 September 2002, para 32, European Court of Justice, *Hospital Ingenieure Krankenhaustechnik Planungs GmbH*, Case C-92/00, 18 June 2002, para 43, European Court of Justice, *University of Cambridge*, Case C-380/98, 3 October 2000, para 16, European Court of Justice, *Bent Mousten Vestergaard*, Case C-59/00, 3 December 2001, para 21, European Court of Justice, *Truley*, Case C-373/00, 27 February 2003, para 41, European Court of Justice, *Universale-Bau and others*, Case C-470/99, 12 December 2002, para 51 and 89, European Court of Justice, *France v. Commission*, Case C-237/99, 1 February 2001, para 41, European Court of Justice, *Impresa Lombardini SpA – Impresa Generale di Construzioni*, joined cases C-285/99 and C-286/99, 27 November 2001, para 34, European Court of Justice, *Ordine degli Architetti delle province di Milano e Lodi and others*, Case C-399/98, 12 July 2001, para 52.

[24] Equal treatment: European Court of Justice, *SIAC Construction*, Case C-19/00, 18 October 2001, para 33–34, European Court of Justice, *Commission v. Denmark*, Case C-243/89, 22 June 1993, para 33, European Court of Justice, *Commission v. Belgium*, Case C-87/94, 25 April 1996, para 54, Court of First Instance, *Strabag Benelux v. Council*, Case T-183/00, 25 February 2003, para 39, European Court of Justice, *Fabricom SA v. Belgian State*, joined cases C-21/03 and C-34/03, 3 March 2005, para 26 and 29, European Court of Justice, *Concordia Bus Finland*, Case C-513/99, 17 September 2002, para 81, European Court of Justice, *Parking Brixen GmbH*, Case C-458/03, 13 October 2005, para 48, European Court of Justice, *Universale-Bau and others*, Case C-470/99, 12 December 2002, para 91 and 93, European Court of Justice, *GAT*, Case C-315/01, 19 June 2003, para 73, European Court of Justice, *EVN and Wienstrom*, Case C-448/01, 4 December 2003, para 47, European Court of Justice, *Hospital Ingenieure Krankenhaustechnik Planungs GmbH*, Case C-92/00, 18 June 2002, para 45, European Court of Justice, *ATI EAC and others*, Case C-331/04, 24 November 2005, para 22.

[25] Case law concerning public procurement and non-discrimination: European Court of Justice, *Concordia Bus Finland*, Case C-513/99, 17 September 2002, para 63, European Court of Justice, *Commission v. Germany*, joined cases C-20/01 and C-28/01, 10 April 2003, para 62, European Court of Justice, *Unitron Scandinavia*, Case C-275/98, 18 November 1999, para 29, European Court of Justice, *Commission v. France*, Case C-264/03, 20 October 2005, para 32, European Court of Justice, *Telaustria*, Case C-324/98, 7 December 2000, para 60–61, European Court of Justice, *Hospital Ingenieure Krankenhaustechnik Planungs GmbH*, Case C-92/00, 18 June 2002, para 47, European Court of Justice, *Bent Mousten Vestergaard*, Case C-59/00, 3 December 2001, para 20, European Court of Justice, *Commission v. Denmark*, Case C-243/89, 22 June 1993, para 33, 37–40, 45, European Court of Justice, *Commission v. France*, Case C-225/98 26 September 2000, para 50, European Court of Justice, *Beentjes*, Case C-31/87, 20 September 1988, para 29–30, European Court of Justice, *Parking Brixen GmbH*, Case C-458/03, 13 October 2005, para 48.

[26] See recital 2 and Article 2 and 3 of Directive 2004/18/EC. See European Court of Justice, *Telaustria*, Case C-324/98, 7 December 2000, para 60–62, European Court of Justice, *Commission v. Belgium*, Case C-87/94, 25 April 1996, para 54. For case law addressing preferential treatment of economic operators by contracting authorities see European Court of Justice, *Commission v. Belgium*, Case C-87/94, 25 April 1996, para 56, Court of First Instance, *Adia Interim SA v. Commission*, Case T-19/95, 8 May 1996, para 42 and 47. More specifically for the principle of transparency see European Court of Justice, *Unitron Scandinavia*, Case C-275/98, 18 November 1999, para 31, European Court of Justice, *Commission v. Spain*, Case C-214/00, 15 May 2003, para 53, C European Court of Justice, *SIAC Construction*, Case C-19/00, 18 October 2001, para 41, European Court of Justice, *Hospital Ingenieure Krankenhaustechnik Planungs GmbH*, Case C-92/00, 18 June 2002, para 45, European Court of Justice, *Telaustria*, Case C-324/98, para 61 and 62, European Court of Justice, *Traunfellner*, Case C-421/01, 16 October 2003, para 29, European

by the CJEU plays a central role in limiting the liberty of contracting authorities to address public concerns through the design of award criteria that violate the above principles.[27] While the above holds true for public works contracts, public supply contracts and public service contracts,[28] the legislator has attributed a special position to economic entities operating in the water, energy, transport and postal service sector.[29] Despite of the closed nature of markets in these sectors and the frequent existence of special and exclusive rights, the legislator is also referring to the core legal principles of equal treatment, non-discrimination, mutual recognition, proportionality and transparency.[30]

Despite the use of legal principles and the many attempts of the legislator to improve the public procurement rules, integration in this market remained limited. The main drivers for future growth that are at the centre of the Europe 2020 strategy for smart, sustainable and inclusive growth[31] are research and innovation, including eco-innovation and social innovation. As a market-based instrument, public procurement was deemed instrumental to achieve the Europe 2020 strategy. The 2014 modernisation of the procurement rules envisaged the increase of the efficiency of public spending, to allow small and medium-sized enterprises (SMEs) to take part in public procurement, and to enable procurers to make better use of public procurement in support of common societal goals. The approach towards market integration in the area of procurement markets has therefore shifted under the 2020 strategy. Before examining the impact of the reform on procurement market integration (Sect. 4), Sect. 3 reviews the impediments to market integration in the area of public procurement.

3 Procurement Integration Studies in the EU

After giving a general historic background on market integration in public procurement in the EU, this section of the paper reviews the empirical studies on the state of the procurement market. In recent years there has been a heightening interest in the state of the procurement market integration and in understanding what impedes cross-border procurement. This section therefore reviews procurement market studies and show that current market integration in the public procurement market is quite limited. It also reviews the factors that influence cross-border procurements

Court of Justice, *Parking Brixen GmbH,* Case C-458/03, 13 October 2005, para 49, European Court of Justice, *Universale-Bau and others*, Case C-470/99, 12 December 2002, para 92.

[27] See Directive 2004/18/EC recital 3.

[28] As addressed in Directive 2004/18/EC.

[29] As addressed in Directive 2004/17/EC.

[30] See Directive 2004/17/EC recital 9.

[31] COM(2010) 2020, Brussels, 3 March 2010, Commission Communication, Europe 2020, a strategy for smart, sustainable and inclusive growth'.

(Sect. 3.1). Subsequently Sect. 3.2 examines how procurement laws could be used to address the issues identified in Sect. 3.1.

3.1 Market Integration and Cross-Border Procurements

To determine the degree of cross-border public procurement, several studies have examined how many undertakings established in other Member States have participated in national procurements. Such measures are commonly described as 'direct penetration' of the procurement market. The data shows that market integration as measured by the direct cross-border market penetration is very low. In the examined reports (published during the years 1997–2011) it ranges between 1.1 and 3.5 %. Although a tripling of the magnitude of direct penetration is reflected in Table 1, this should not be taken as conclusive evidence that there have been quantum leaping advances in market penetration in the last decade. The reason for this is of course that the studies are not following the same methodology and do not encompass the same scope. The reports should therefore be viewed as independent observations at particular points in time that do, however, indicate improvements. Despite this, the studies consistently show that undertakings from other EU Member States engage less often in cross-border public procurements and/or are less successful in them. Improving cross border competition was a goal of public procurement reforms and should have led to more market integration.

Overall it can thus be concluded that the degree of procurement market integration in the European Union is very low. Especially if contrasted to the import and export figures of EU Member States.

Some public procurement studies have therefore broadened their methodology to also include more indirect forms of market penetration. Examples of such indirect participation in procurement tenders include participation in domestic public procurements of foreign affiliates but also situations when foreign undertakings are hired as subcontractors or form a consortium together with a domestic firm. In a broader conceptualisation also increased trade via wholesale or distribution

Table 1 Procurement market penetration

Direct penetration	Indirect penetration	Study	Approach
3.0 %	7.0 %	European Commission (Single Market Review) (1996)	Survey
1.8 %	8.5 %	Eurostrategy consultants (1999)	Survey
1.1 %		EIM and KMU Forschung Austria (2004)	Contract data
2.6 %		Bird and Bird (2008)	Survey
1.9 %		GHK and Technopolis (2007)	
3.5 %	25.6 %	Ramboll and HTW Chur (2011)	

Table 2 Determinants of participating in a foreign tender

Direct cross border proc. effects	Percentage effect
Common language	21
Negotiated vs. open procedure	46
Contract value	45
Number of bids	−5
Corruption	−6
Local government	−36
Euro area	97
EU financed	110

activities resulting from domestic public procurements were included in research studies. Although the latter may not strictly speaking indicate the success of foreign undertakings at a particular public procurement, it nevertheless highlights that at least foreign products are not prevented from being used by domestic bidders. This in turn might also reflect the efficacy of the free movement of goods and services. While a more narrow view on indirect forms of market penetration in public procurement may explain the lower indirect penetration figures of 7–8.5 % that were found in the 1990s,[32] a recent study by Ramboll and HTW Chur (2011) estimates an indirect market penetration of 25.6 %. In this study the biggest factors are foreign affiliation accounting for 13.4 % and wholesale/distribution that accounts for 11.9 %. Subcontracting and consortium formation appear with 0.2 and 0.1 % to be negligible.

Applying a regression analysis Ramboll and HTW Chur (2011) identify a number of statistically significant relationships that positively or negatively affect the ability of companies to participate in a foreign public procurements (see Table 2).

Important elements promoting cross-border public procurements are EU financing (110 %), the Euro as a common currency (97 %), and a common language (21 %). While these elements are arguably beyond the scope of public procurement rules, there are other elements that fall within the scope of these laws. For example negotiated procedures and higher contract values attract more competition from other EU Member States than open procedures (46 % and 45 % respectively). The discretion of the procuring entities to opt for one rather than the other may of course be co-determined by the object of the public procurement tender, but it is nevertheless insightful that larger contracts attract more foreign competitors. If there is already a competitive market as indicated by a higher number of bidders foreign bidders tend to shy away (−5 %). Similarly also corruption tends to prevent foreign competitors to cross the border (−6 %). Perhaps somewhat surprisingly, if local governments are organising public procurements there is a strong likelihood that competitors of other EU Member States will not participate (−36 %). This indicates

[32] European Commission (1996b) SEC (96) 2378, p. 47 found 7 % and Eurostrategy consultants (1999) found 8.5 %.

that the administrative level at which procurements are organised in the EU obstructs market integration.

Besides statistical tools, also surveys of economic operators are employed by Ramboll and HTW Chur (2011) to identify what promotes or prevents undertakings to participate in foreign public procurements. Here they identify inter alia a common language as facilitating procurement market integration. Competition in the foreign procurement market deters undertakings to cross the border. Also legal requirements are often perceived as barriers to entry and frequently mentioned to impede foreign participation in public procurements. The survey also indicates that undertakings simply lack experience with doing business abroad and therefore find it difficult to engage in foreign public procurements. The lack of experience is viewed as the most important obstacle to cross-border public procurement (cited by more than 80 % of the companies as a high and medium important obstacle).[33]

Besides the above analysis, there are also a number of interesting descriptive statistics that bear mentioning. It is found that SMEs account for about 47 % of all cross border public procurements although they only account for 18 % of the total value of all direct cross-border awards. Given that most public procurement contracts (domestic and foreign) are awarded to SMEs (around 78 %) while around 99.8 % of all companies in the EU are SMEs, it is apparent that SMEs are underrepresented in direct cross border public procurements.[34] In terms of indirect cross-border procurements SMEs are underrepresented as well (accounting merely for 1 % of all procurements). This can partially be explained by foreign affiliates being generally larger (thus not being qualified as SMEs) and by corporate linkage rules in which foreign affiliates are considered in conjunction with their mother company. Given that there are much more SMEs than large companies and that the success rate in public procurements between large companies and SMEs does not differ statistically,[35] it can be inferred that SMEs are not sufficiently engaging in cross-border public procurement. Perhaps this lack of experience in doing business abroad is deterring SMEs from engaging in cross-border public procurement or perhaps they are simply not interested in engaging in cross-border public procurements.

The above reports suggest that the procurement markets in the EU are not strongly integrated. Determinants that support cross-border participation of undertakings are EU financing, common language, common currency, negotiated procedures and high contract values. Determinants that impede cross-border participation in public procurement tenders are high levels of domestic competition, corruption, local tenders, legal requirements and lack of experience of the associated undertakings. Moreover, SMEs are underrepresented in direct cross border public procurement.

[33] Ramboll and HTW Chur (2011), p. 92.

[34] European Commission (2004) A report on the functioning of public procurement markets in the EU: benefits from the application of EU directives and challenges for the future, 03/02/2004, p. 20.

[35] Ramboll and HTW Chur (2011), p. 95.

3.2 Addressing Impediments to Market Integration

The preceding section identified several determinants that strengthen or obstruct procurement market integration. This section examines how the above determinants could be addressed by the legislator or by the tendering authority to improve cross border public procurement to facilitate the realisation of the economic benefits associated with higher competition and market integration. First issues that cannot be addressed easily by procurement rules are examined while subsequently issues that can more readily be addressed are treated. It bears express mentioning that this treatment does not examine the question of whether market integration *should* be advanced, nor does it closely consider the costs for procuring entities as this would require good understanding of the magnitudes of the expected costs and benefits.

Increasing financing by the EU was shown to have a significantly positive impact on cross-border public procurement competition. Having the European Commission organise public procurements on behalf of the Member States is, however, unlikely to be perceived favourably by Member States nor by economists that are critical of unlimited centralisation. It is therefore unlikely to have an extension of EU tenders beyond what would generally fall within the sphere of EU competences.

Similarly a 'common language' or a 'common currency' has been shown to have a positive effect on cross-border public procurement but it is not something that can be addressed within the framework of public procurement rules. General information about the procurement process and the procurement tender itself that is made available in a relevant foreign language or a reduction in the language requirements for official documents could nevertheless enhance transparency and reduce information and tender participation costs for prospective bidders. Lowering costs of taking part in tenders could help to attract cross border bidders.

There are, however, also several areas that were identified above that can be influenced by the legislator or directly by the tendering authorities. For example, the use of negotiated procedures vis-à-vis open tendering can be achieved through a change in the procurement rules. The extent to which negotiated procedures may be used will, however, be co-determined by the actual object of the tender. The underlying intuition is of course that standardised products can more effectively be procured via open procedures rather than by negotiations.

It has been suggested that larger contract values have strongly positive effects upon cross-border public procurements. Contract values are of course dependent upon the object of the procurement, but public procurement authorities could employ their margin of discretion to combine independent procurement tenders into larger ones. In the alternative, procurement authorities could also cooperate and organise joint procurement tenders that are likely to attract more foreign competition. Organising such joint procurements at a more centralised level of government or in a collaborative tender of several local tender authorities may also mitigate the domestic bias in local tenders and contribute to higher contract values at the same time. It bears mentioning, however, that larger procurement tenders may discourage small and medium sized firms to participate, leading perhaps to fewer serious bidders and potentially less competition.

There are also a number of factors that impede cross-border competition and hence market integration.

The above section indicated that a high level of competition and a large number of bidders participating in a procurement tender discourages competition from other EU Member States. As one of the motivations for attracting cross-border competition is to benefit from more competitive prices it would not be sensible to discourage local competition and local bidders to attract bidders from other Member States.

The study by Ramboll and HTW Chur (2011) identified 'lack of experience in doing business abroad' as an obstacle to take part in cross-border procurements. Government authorities could establish a 'one-stop-shop' desk that supports large and in particular small and medium size enterprises in preparing for businesses and to offer them an information service for interesting procurements in their respective line of businesses. Such measures may be conducive to incentivize SMEs to engage more strongly in cross-border public procurement and trade. Such measures are believed to reduce the information costs for undertakings and hence make it easier for them to cross the border. In practice, support structures do already exist in various Member States to help foreign companies. It may therefore be wondered if inclusion of support structures within the framework of procurements would be desirable.

Similarly legal requirements that are perceived as barriers to entry can be addressed. A further harmonisation of required documents and translation requirements can reduce procurement costs for bidders and lower the threshold for participation. If horizontal harmonisation of relevant documents across Member States is not a feasible option, perhaps acceptance of equivalence would still be possible for procurement authorities. Some flexibility here may help to reduce the costs of participating in a procurement tender.

Corruption deters cross-border participation in tenders because competitors as bidders may shy away from taking part in procurement tenders that are not competitive. From a public procurement perspective, tender processes and winner selection criteria should be open and transparent to prevent corruption. Increasing the level of transparency beyond what is optimal may, however, give rise to other malpractices such as bid-riggings. Procurement laws cannot only be used to ensure an optimal transparency but can also address other aspects facilitating corruption. They can for example regulate bidder screening to prevent repeat offences, the storage and evaluation of procurement data, and introduce independent audits and evaluation standards.[36]

In light of the preceding, the legislator as well as public procurement authorities can address some of the obstacles identified to obstruct market integration in the area of public procurement.

[36] PWC (2013), p. 10.

The section above suggested that elements supporting market integration such as a common currency, common language and EU financing are beyond the scope of procurement rules. Other elements that affect cross border procurements such as negotiated procedures, contract values, SMEs, local tenders, language requirements as well as legal obstacles and corruption can be addressed in various degrees and through different measures by procurement rules to enhance cross-border competition in public procurement markets and thus facilitate market integration. Regarding lack of experience, duplication with existing structures should be avoided.

4 The 2014 EU Public Procurement Reform and Market Integration

This section of the chapter examines the 2014 EU Public procurement reform in the areas identified above to assess the likely implications for market integration. As described above public procurement was deemed instrumental to achieve the Europe 2020 strategy by increasing the efficiency of public spending, to allow small and medium-sized enterprises (SMEs) to take part in public procurement, and to enable procurers to make better use of public procurement in support of common societal goals. The approach towards market integration in the area of procurement markets has therefore shifted under the 2020 strategy from fostering competition to other areas. This section examines the possible effects of the legislative changes in light of the market integration insights gained in the preceding section.

The 2014 reform affords procuring entities greater freedom to choose procurement procedures. Under the former procurement rules, open procedures had priority over *negotiated procedures* or the competitive dialogue.[37] Under the new rules the constraints to use negotiation procedures have been relaxed and the former negotiation procedure is replaced by the competitive procedure with negotiation.[38] Any bidder can request to participate in response to a call for participating in a competition but only those economic operators invited by the contracting authority may submit an initial tender which constitutes the basis for the subsequent negotiations. Tender participation costs are thus reduced, which also encourages foreign bidders to take part in cross-border procurements.

It has been shown that *local tenders* attract less cross-border public procurements, entailing that tenders organised at higher levels of governments have a stronger impact on cross border competition and hence market integration. The administrative level at which public procurements are held are thus relevant for market integration. The 2014 public procurement regulation bears tribute to this insight by facilitating procurements through central purchasing bodies or joint procurements through national and cross-border procurements. The new rules

[37] Bovis (2007), p. 229.

[38] See Article 29 of 2014/24/EU.

contain a clarification of the existing legal rules on this issue and thus are expected to have a positive effect on cross border competition and market integration through mitigating the negative impact of local tenders on cross-border public procurements and by increasing the size of contracts.

Higher *contract values* lead to more cross-border procurement and hence to better market integration. Under the new procurement rules, however, it appears that the lot size may get smaller, not bigger. The new Directive provides the possibility for tendering authorities to subdivide a contract into smaller lots.[39] In case the authority decides not to subdivide the contract, it must give an indication of the main reasons for its decision. The implicit incentive seems thus to be that lots will be subdivided, which should allow small firms to compete for contracts as well. On one side this possibility allows for more competition because more SMEs are likely to be able to participate while it still allows large companies to take advantage of their economies of scale.[40]

While the lowering of contract values may be creating the possibilities for more competition because the number of serious bidders may increase, this development may have a negative effect on cross-border public procurement. *SMEs* are not the companies that are frequently engaging in cross-border public procurements and increased competition in a particular procurement market works to shy away foreign competitors. It may therefore be expected that although domestic competition is likely to increase, market integration may not.

The new Directive strives to facilitate SME participation in procurements. Tendering authorities may limit the number of lots that may be awarded to one bidder.[41] An explanation requirement safeguards that this provision is not used in a competitively restricting manner. This provision is intended to prevent that large bidders win all the tenders. This could make it more interesting for smaller bidders to take part in the tender. Also the turnover requirement that can be asked for is restricted to a maximum of twice the contract value size, except in duly justified cases.[42] These provisions help SMEs to take part in procurement tenders. It may also help to deepen market integration if foreign companies are attracted to take part in domestic public procurements. It may, however, be wondered if SMEs are likely to be the decisive driving force behind market integration in Europe given that presently they are often times refraining from engaging in cross-border public procurements.

Another element that was identified as an obstacle for public procurement are *language requirements*. Addressing language barriers through public procurement law is only possible in an indirect way, i.e., through trying to reduce information and translation costs for bidders. Improving information and lowering costs of participating in a tender can also help to reduce legal requirements for cross-border

[39] See Article 46(1) of Directive 2014/24/EU.

[40] Dimitri et al. (2006), p. 215.

[41] See Article 46(2), Directive 2014/24/EU.

[42] See Article 58(3), Directive 2014/24/EU.

procurement—another element discussed above. In general, lower bidder costs should reduce the administrative burden on participating in public tenders and give rise to more competition. The 2014 public procurement reform addresses these issues in several ways.

The introduction of the European Single Procurement Document,[43] for example, allows bidders to take part in a tender without obliging them to present all required documents proving that they meet the tender criteria. A declaration made by bidders replaces such certificates relating to *inter alia* grounds of exclusion (Article 57) and selection criteria (Article 58). Only the bidder winning the tender will actually have to furnish the relevant documents, thus avoiding all other bidders the costs of attaining and translating documents.

Furthermore, the online information system E-Certis[44] will provide an up to date list of certificates and other forms of documentary evidence that tendering authorities shall primarily rely upon. This online repository will reduce the information costs for bidders and help thereby facilitate their participation in a domestic as well as cross-border tender. The European Single Procurement Document and the E-Ceteris will thus both help to stimulate bidder participation in public procurement tenders and thereby support market integration.

Also *corruption* negatively impacts cross border public procurement and thus market integration. As was the case under the former public procurement rules, also under the 2014 Directive a tenderer who has been convicted by final judgment for corruption of which the contracting authority is aware shall be excluded from participation in a public contract.[45] The definitions of corruption were also broadened to expressly include legal definitions of the contracting authority's or the economic operator's Member States.[46] Moreover, corruption plays a more prominent role in the Directive because it is frequently referred to and procuring entities are reminded that traceability and transparency of decision-making procedures are essential for fighting corruption and that they should keep adequate documentation of essential elements and decisions of individual procurement procedures and provide access to interested parties.[47] Moreover, Member States must regularly submit a monitoring report on the frequent sources of wrong application or of legal uncertainty, the possible structural or recurring problems or other serious irregularities such as corruption.[48]

The above shows that the 2014 public procurement reform does address several impediments to procurement market integration in the EU. It is, however, also apparent that the recent public procurement rules, particularly in the area of small

[43] Article 59, Directive 2014/24/EU of the European Parliament and of the Council of 26 February 2014 on public procurement and repealing Directive 2004/18/EC [2014] OJ L 94/65.

[44] Article 61, Directive 2014/24/EU.

[45] Article 57, Directive 2014/24/EU.

[46] Article 57(3), Directive 2014/24/EU.

[47] Recital 126 Directive 2014/24/EU.

[48] Article 83, Directive 2014/24/EU.

and medium enterprises and contract values may have a positive effect on intra-national competition but may not have a strong impact on cross-border competition and hence market integration. The overall finding is therefore that the improvements in the 2014 public procurement directive 2014/24/EU is likely to have only a limited effect on market integration. In some areas the EU legislator has therefore made a trade-off between intra-national and inter-national competition and favoured the former rather than the latter. This is of course in conformity with the objective of the 2014 reform in light of the Europe 2020 goals, but clearly indicates that enhancing competition in public procurement markets does not directly lead to more market integration.

5 The Chinese Government Procurement Law and Market Integration

Before the introduction of the Government Procurement Law in 2003 China had a Bidding Law adopted in 2000 and directed towards public works, and local 'tendering' rules that generated legal ambiguity.[49] The recognition of local protectionism and increasing public spending as well as corruption problems provided strong motivation for the introduction of the Government Procurement law.[50] Since 2003 the GPL provides the national legal framework for procurements.

This section of the chapter examines the Chinese GPL in light of the market integration determinants identified in the EU context. It bears mentioning of course that the European experience is derived from integrating the markets of different nation states while China is a single nation state. Insights gained in the European context may therefore not be directly applicable to China.

Language requirements that are identified in the EU context to help market integration are not problematic in China that benefits from one official language. Also legal obstacles should not be problematic given that the same laws are applicable in the country after the Bidding Law and the Government Procurement Law were introduced.[51] Local implementation rules of the GPL are few but may occasionally differ.[52] Procurement markets should therefore be strongly integrated and yet the Chinese procurement markets remains obstructed by local protectionism.[53]

---

[49] Tian (2001), p. 218.

[50] Wang and Zhang (2010), p. 26.

[51] For an account on the state of various procurement rules and associated problems see Tian (2001), p. 207.

[52] Cao (2013), p. 212.

[53] Intergovernmental Group of Experts on Competition Law and Policy, Geneva, 9–11 July 2012, Roundtable on 'Competition Policy and Public Procurement' Written contribution by China, p. 9,

The European experience suggests that *local tenders* inhibit procurement market integration. Encouraging joint procurements may therefore help to break up local biases in tenders and help to attract more cross-regional competition in public procurements. Joint procurements are likely to be having larger *contract values* and hence help to attract more large bidders.

Addressing the issue of local or regional biases, the Chinese Government Procurement law provides not only for a decentralised but also for a centralised procurement possibility. All goods, services and works listed on the centralised procurement catalogue must be procured by a 'Centralized Procurement Institution' while those items not enlisted may be entrusted as well.[54] Centralized Procurement Institutions are non-profit organisations that can be established by cities with districts or people's governments at the level of autonomous prefectures or above. These institutions are non-profit making and are not subject to any kind of subordination by procurement agencies or administrative organs[55] although in practice they are established by or attached to local financial departments and are under budgetary control,[56] calling into doubt their effective independence. Moreover, Wang and Zhang (2010) point out that no attempt has been made in the GPL to unify the approval of the qualification of procuring agencies but have left these issues to be decided upon by the existing administrative authorities.[57] On the other side, however, the GPL specifies that purchasers are to select their procurement agency in full independence.[58]

The system of centralised procurements has a number of other deficiencies. It is for example submitted that the centralised procurement system may actually enable provincial governments to erect obstacles to trade (1) because the provincial level governments can exempt procurement contracts from the centralised procurement system,[59] (2) because provincial governments participate in composing the centralised procurement catalogue,[60] and (3) because the centralised procurement institutions are affiliated with sub-provincial governments.[61] Discretion may also enter the centralised procurement system in relation to the poor drafting of Article 18 GPL. This Article specifies that in case an entity has 'special requirements' for the item to be purchased, the entity may be allowed by the provincial government (or above) to conduct the procurement by itself. Given the absence of a definition of 'special requirements' the obligation to rely on central procurement may be

---

http://unctad.org/meetings/en/Contribution/ciclp2012_RT_PP_China_en.pdf. Last accessed 16 April 2015.

[54] Article 18 Government Public Procurement Law (GPL).

[55] Article 16 and 60 GPL.

[56] Wang and Zhang (2010), p. 47.

[57] Wang and Zhang (2010), p. 45.

[58] Article 19 GPL.

[59] Article 18 GPL.

[60] Article 7 GPL.

[61] Wang and Zhang (2010), p. 46.

circumvented in practice. Another element that may undermine the effective working of the system of centralised procurements is related to the qualification of its staff. While procuring agencies have played an important role in China,[62] centralised procurement institutions are viewed to be less effective in hiring well trained experts because in practice the salary of the employees is comparable to that of civil servants.[63] Last but by no means least, the scope of what is subject to centralised procurement is likely to vary from province to province because both the Centralized Procurement Catalogue and the Prescribed Procurement Thresholds of procurement projects funded by central and provincial budgets are to be determined by central government and provincial governments respectively.[64]

Another issue identified in the EU context to strengthen market integration are *small and medium-sized enterprises*. The Government Procurement Law provides that procurements shall facilitate national economic and social development policy objectives including environmental protection, assistance to minority regions, the promotion of small and medium-sized enterprises, etc.[65] Until a few years ago, however, there were few implementation measures at local level that actually would have led to SME support.[66] In the aftermath of the 2009 financial crisis the Ministry of Finance and Information Technology issued an Interim Measure on Facilitating the Development of SMEs in Government Procurement to support SMEs.[67]

Support measures include earmarking part of the budget for SMEs, encouraging sub-contracting, preferential treatment in the bid evaluation stage, better payment terms, support schemes regarding contract finance, bid security and performance bonds, and capacity training and advisory as well as measures directed towards reducing information costs of bidders. Perhaps most direct and hence noteworthy are the first three measures. In accordance with Article 4 of the Interim Measure authorities must earmark at least 30 % of their annual budget for contracts to SMEs and 60 % thereof should go to small and micro-sized enterprises. Participation of SMEs as subcontractors is encouraged by the Interim Measures by including the share awarded to SMEs in the statistical data of procurement projects targeted at SMEs.[68] Small and micro-sized firms or consortia exclusively composed of these firms enjoy preferential treatment in the bid evaluation stage by having their submitted prices reduced by 6–10 % in comparison with medium- and large sized

[62] See Tian (2001), pp. 209–210.

[63] Wang and Zhang (2010), p. 47.

[64] Wang and Zhang (2010), p. 46.

[65] Article 9 GPL.

[66] See Cao (2013), pp. 211–224, for a critical assessment.

[67] The following treatment is based Cao (2013), pp. 211–224.

[68] Article 8(2) Interim Measure The Interim Measure on Facilitating the Development of SMEs in Government Procurement (Treasury document No. [2011]), jointly issued by Ministry of Finance and Ministry of Industry and Information Technology, on December 29, 2011 and effective on January 1, 2012.

firms. If the share of small and micro-sized enterprises in a consortium reaches 30 %, the consortium enjoys a preferential treatment of 2–3 % at the bid evaluation.

There are a number of critiques potentially endangering the efficacy of the introduced measures. The merging of earmarking the budget for individual SMEs and for subcontracting may undermine the impact of this support measure and as SMEs are already forming part of tendering consortia.[69] Another critical element regards the classification of companies. The classification system of companies is based on a system of self-declaration which is supplemented by a system of government supervision by the local competent authorities and a bid challenging system under the Interim Measures. Local supervision may entail that different standards may apply in different parts of China, especially because a clear definition and guidance on how to assess affiliate companies of SMEs are not included in the interim rules. This could create the danger that larger companies set up subsidiaries that would qualify as SMEs so as to benefit from the preferential treatment schemes.

Overall, it can thus be observed that the Chinese SME rules that were recently introduced are in particular focusing on small and micro-sized firms while medium sized enterprises are not enjoying most of the support measures.

Corruption was one of the most important concerns that led to the introduction of the Government Public Procurement Law[70] and is still an important concern in China.[71] Transparency is deemed to mitigate corruption. The Chinese public procurement legislation therefore places a strong emphasis on transparency that also includes the collective opening of tender submissions.[72] While this is laudable in terms fighting corruption, this facilitates bid rigging conspiracies, i.e., cartel formation. From a market integration perspective, however, it may be expected that fighting corruption will have a positive effect on inter-regional public procurement.

China has been employing public procurement rules to address local or provincial protectionism. Examining the market integration determinants in the GPL, it appears that China does not need to address issues such as language requirements and also legal requirements are less of a problem because China is a nation state. China in particular has been focusing on local tenders and contract values, supporting SMEs and by addressing corruption. Importantly China established a system of centralised procurements, addressed in particular small and micro-sized firms. The impact of the centralised procurement system on market integration is believed to be impeded by the degree of discretion afforded to local governments because of lack of precision in drafting and the difficulty to attract expert staff members. Similarly the effectiveness of the SME support scheme is undermined by clarity regarding subcontracting and the benefiting of budget lines earmarked for

---

[69] See also Cao (2013), pp. 218 and 220.

[70] Tian (2001), p. 215.

[71] See also the chapter by Shen and Philipsen contained in this book.

[72] Weishaar (2013), Chapters 7 and 8.

SMEs. Moreover it may be wondered if small and micro-sized firms are the best target to enhance inter-regional market integration.

6 Comparison and Concluding Remarks

This chapter examined the EU's and China's approach to procurement market integration without—as stated above—examining whether market integration is beneficial or desirable. The chapter has shown that in both cases the measures taken under Directive 2014/24/EU and the GPL were directed towards fostering competition and help to use public funds more effectively. Comparing both experiences it can be observed that there are important differences between the applied approaches. Clearly it must be borne in mind that China as a nation state does not encounter all challenges found in the European context but is also able to employ potentially promising solutions that would not be easily applied in the EU.

European public procurement laws have been striving to foster more competition and thereby to harvest the benefits associated with market integration. So far the market has been strongly resisting cross-border competition. The recent reform of the procurement rules does take some steps to deepen market integration, particularly in the area of E-procurements, the E-ceteris information system and the European Single Procurement Document. The EU's revisions in the area of contract values and SME support may, however, not be helping market integration as such and could potentially work against further integration. This is related to the fact that SMEs are refraining from crossing the border, and targeting larger companies may thus be more effective for the procurement market. It is therefore apparent that the legislator follows a multi-objective approach trying to find a balance between more intra-regional and inter-regional trade and competition at the same time.

Also in the Chinese context it can be observed that not every advancement in fostering competition within a province is likely to lead to more cross-border market integration. In the area of SMEs the strong focus on small and micro-sized enterprises may strengthen local competition but may not lead to the reduction of local barriers to trade. By contrast to the EU, China is employing a centralised procurement system that has its own challenges and may not be as effective to overcome local protectionism as it could have been. The EU is strengthening its regulatory system in this area to facilitate that tendering entities cooperate in their purchases. The system is, however, not as comprehensive as the Chinese one in the sense that it is not mandatory. It may therefore be worthwhile for the European legislator and Member States to take a close look at the Chinese experience in this area and to consider if they would like to make advances in the area of market integration.

References

Bird and Bird (2008) Verhältnis zwischen Binnenmarktwirkung der EU -Vergaberegeln und den durch die Anwendung des europäischen Vergaberechts verursachten Transaktionskosten für deutsche öffentliche Auftraggeber as cited in Ramboll, Chur HTW (2011) Final report cross-border procurement above EU thresholds http://ec.europa.eu/internal_market/publicprocurement/docs/modernising_rules/cross-border-procurement_en.pdf. Last accessed 16 Apr 2015

Bovis CH (2007) EU public procurement law. Edward Elgar, Cheltenham

Bovis CH (2012) EU public procurement law, 2nd edn. Edward Elgar, Cheltenham

Cao F (2013) Building up SME programmes in government procurement in China: legal structure, recent developments and the way forward towards the WTO-GPA. Public Procurement Law Rev 6:211–224

COM (2010) 2020, Commission Communication Europe 2020, a strategy for smart, sustainable and inclusive growth. European Commission, Brussels, 3 March 2010

Commission of the European Communities (1988) Europe 1992, the overall challenge. SEC (88) 524 final, Brussels, 13 April 1988

COWI (2003a) European Commission, DG Internal Market, Study on Monitoring of Public, Procurement in the European Union Using Panel Data, Lot 1. Final Report, July 2003. http://ec.europa.eu/dgs/internal_market/docs/calls/2004/2004-10-d/2004-09-15-study200307-1_en.pdf. Last accessed 16 Apr 2015

COWI (2003b) European Commission, DG Internal Market Study on Monitoring of Public Procurement in the European Union Using Panel Data Lot 2. Final Report, July 2003. http://ec.europa.eu/dgs/internal_market/docs/calls/2004/2004-10-d/2004-09-15-study200307-2_en.pdf. Last accessed 16 Apr 2015

Dimitri N, Pacini R, Pagnozzi M, Spagnolo G (2006) Multi-contract tendering procedures and package bidding in procurement. In: Dimitri N, Pacini R, Pagnozzi M, Spagnolo G (eds) Handbook of procurement. Cambridge University Press, Cambridge

EIM/KMU Forschung Austria (2004) The access of SMEs to public procurement contracts. http://ec.europa.eu/enterprise/newsroom/cf/_getdocument.cfm?doc_id=3687

European Commission (1996a) Green Paper. Public procurement in the European Union: exploring the way forward. COM (96) 583 final. 27 November 1996

European Commission (1996b) The 1996 Single Market Review Commission Staff Working Paper. SEC (96) 2378, Brussels

European Commission (1998) Public procurement in the European Union. COM (98) 143 final. 11 March 1998

European Commission (2000) Proposal for a Directive of the European Parliament and of the Council on coordination of procedures for the award of public supply contracts, public service contracts and public works contracts. COM (2000)275 final/2. 30 August 2000, replacing COM (2000)275 final. 10 May 2000

European Commission (2004) A report on the functioning of public procurement markets in the EU: benefits from the application of EU directives and challenges for the future. Brussels, 3 February 2004

Eurostrategy consultants (1999) as cited by European Commission (2004) A report on the functioning of public procurement markets in the EU: benefits from the application of EU Directives and challenges for the future. http://ec.europa.eu/internal_market/publicprocurement/docs/public-proc-market-final-report_en.pdf

GHK and Technopolis (2007) SMEs access to public procurement. http://ec.europa.eu/enterprise/dg/files/evaluation/pme_marches_publics_report_en.pdf. Last accessed 16 Apr 2015

Griffiths RT (2004) History of the European Union, an audio course on the origins and developments of the EU. Home Academy, www.home-academy.nl. Last accessed 16 Apr 2015

ICLEI (2003) Study contract to survey the state of play of green public procurement in the European Union final report. Freiburg, July 2003. http://ec.europa.eu/environment/gpp/pdf/iceisstudy.pdf. Last accessed 16 Apr 2015

Intergovernmental Group of Experts on Competition Law and Policy Roundtable on 'Competition Policy and Public Procurement'. Written contribution by China, Geneva, 9–11 July 2012. http://unctad.org/meetings/en/Contribution/ciclp2012_RT_PP_China_en.pdf. Last accessed 16 Apr 2015

Poncet SA (2005) Fragmented China: measure and determinants of Chinese domestic market disintegration. Rev Int Econ 13(3):409–430

PWC (2013) Public procurement: costs we pay for corruption identifying and reducing corruption in public procurement in the EU. http://ec.europa.eu/anti_fraud/documents/anti-fraud-policy/research-and-studies/pwc_olaf_study_en.pdf. Last accessed 16 Apr 2015

Ramboll and Chur HTW (2011) Cross-border procurement above EU thresholds. Final report. http://ec.europa.eu/internal_market/publicprocurement/docs/modernising_rules/cross-border-procurement_en.pdf. Last accessed 16 Apr 2015

Schumann RA (1990) Europe – a fresh start: The Schuman Declaration, 1950–1990. I office for official publications of the European Union. In: Nelsen BF, Stubb A (2003) The European Union readings on the theory and practice of integration, 3rd edn. Palgrave Macmillan, Basingstoke

Tian J (2001) Public procurement in China: the way forward. Public Procurement Law Rev 10:207–228

Wang P, Zhang X (2010) Chinese Public procurement law: an introductory textbook. Publication by the EU Asia Inter University Network for Teaching and Research in Public Procurement Regulation. https://www.nottingham.ac.uk/pprg/documentsarchive/asialinkmaterials/chinese publicpocurementlawintroduction.pdf. Last accessed 16 Apr 2015

Weishaar SE (2013) Cartels, competition and public procurement: law and economics approaches to bid rigging. Edward Elgar, Cheltenham

Part II
Financial Regulation

Lessons from the European Sovereign Debt Crisis for China

Jiye Hu and Shouji Sun

JEL Classification G11 • G15 • K23

1 Introduction

Although China's economic development is currently healthy and stable, plenty of analysts worldwide warn that, following the US subprime mortgage crisis and the European countries' sovereign debt crisis, the next financial crisis may take place in China.[1] What China could learn from the lessons of the international financial crisis, especially from the European sovereign debt crisis, is quickly becoming an important issue for Chinese policy makers, scholars and the public at large.

From a legal perspective, sovereign debt has fewer available avenues of legal enforcement, compared to corporate debt. Panizza et al. (2009) find limited support for theories that explain the feasibility of sovereign debt based on either external sanctions or exclusion from the international capital market, and more support for

We received very helpful comments on earlier versions of this paper from Michael Faure and Niels Philipsen (Maastricht University), Stefan Weishaar (Groningen University), and Prof. Xi Tao and Xu Guangdong (China University of Political Science and Law). None of the above should be held responsible for any errors or omissions.

[1] Wolf (2012) and Friedman (2013).

J. Hu (✉)
Center for Law and Economics at the China University of Political Science and Law, Beijing, China
e-mail: hujiye@sina.com

S. Sun
University of International Business and Economics, Beijing, China
e-mail: sunvssun@gmail.com

N. Philipsen et al. (eds.), *Market Integration: The EU Experience and Implications for Regulatory Reform in China*, China-EU Law Series 2,
DOI 10.1007/978-3-662-48273-5_5

explanations that emphasise domestic costs of default. As such, we must look for the institutional reasons for the European countries' sovereign debt crisis.

In a report to the US Congress, Nelson et al. (2011) argued that although Greece only accounted for 2.4 % of the total Eurozone GDP, the implications of its crisis are far-reaching. Furthermore, the Greek crisis has sparked larger discussions about how to resolve the tensions among the Eurozone's united monetary policy and multi-national fiscal policies.

Arghyrou and Tsoukalas (2010) find that the escalating nature of the Greek crisis is very likely to be the result of: (a) the steady deterioration of Greek macroeconomic fundamentals over the period 2001–2009, and (b) a double shift in market expectations from a regime of credible commitment. Even today, Greece has not solved these problems.

On the debt's impact, Alesina and Tabellini (1990) consider a theoretical case where domestic debt is honoured ahead of external debt. According to the results of their model, the equilibrium level of government debt is larger. Consequently, the larger the degree of polarisation between alternating governments, the more likely it is that the current government will not be re-elected.

Some scholars believe that European countries might seek a deeper level of fiscal union as the prescription for preventing similar crises. Consistent fiscal and monetary policies among EU Member States are good for market integration. Both the direct fiscal costs and the indirect ones should be considered because GDP and tax revenues tend to remain low for a sustained period in the aftermath of a banking crisis.[2] The European Council of 24–25 March 2011 adopted a comprehensive package for strengthening the preventive and corrective mechanisms to address internal and external imbalances. In addition, the package included the establishment of a permanent crisis management mechanism—the new European Stability Mechanism (ESM)—which entered into force on 1 July 2013.[3]

Other scholars believed that the financial crisis is similar to a bacterial infection: as global capital markets increasingly embrace sovereign bonds, the potential for a nation's debt default to trigger a larger systemic collapse increases as these relationships become more tightly linked. Hence, the European debt crisis followed the US subprime mortgage crisis and the wider international ramifications of that financial crisis. As to the lesson for China, Yu (2010) believes that in Greece the labour costs increased rapidly, economic growth slowed down and, at the same time, the inflation rate kept rising while the fiscal situation deteriorated significantly. Moreover, joining the European Community and the Eurozone allowed Greece to receive a large number of transfer payments from other EU countries. When Greece committed to bringing its economy into order and meeting the Maastricht Criteria, inflation lowered and interest rates improved significantly and, as a consequence, was lending to default.[4] Schwarcz (2012) analyses and compares debt restructuring

[2] Reinhart and Rogoff (2009).

[3] The European Central Bank (ECB) (2011), pp. 71–84.

[4] Wolf (2015).

alternatives to bailouts. Under a free-market option, sovereign debtors and their creditors attempt to consensually negotiate a debt restructuring, aided by collective-action clauses and by exchange offers with exit consents. Similar to the problem of "too big to fail" of large banks, nations—even those as small as Greece—can be seen as too big to fail if their default could trigger a wider economic collapse. With the casting off of the capital constraints, the Greek government had no incentive to reduce the fiscal deficit, eventually resulting in a debt crisis.

Zheng (2011a) holds that the welfare system was the major escalating factor of the European debt crisis. In the countries in crisis, the ageing population was increasing, while economic growth was slow; and in combination with government's actions to please the voters, this inevitably led to a growing pension deficit. Additionally, the higher pension replacement rate indicated that the intergenerational burden was not sustainable. However, Zheng (2011b) believes that the European debt crisis is not because of the welfare system: rather it is the inevitable result of the economic crisis, the financial crisis and the political crisis. Hence he claims that the idea that the welfare crisis has led to the debt crisis is incorrect.

From the above views we could find that in reviewing the same European debt crisis, different scholars presented different conclusions through their own research. However, only few scholars looked deeply into the private pension system, more specifically the relationship between the development of pension finance and the European debt crisis. Although the European Union has promoted market integration in the past decades, in this contribution we find that there are obvious differences in financial systems among the debt crises that occurred in Portugal, Italy, Greece, Spain (the PIGS) and other European countries like the Netherlands, Switzerland and the UK (the NSU). This paper aims to analyse the internal reasons for the disintegration of the above seven EU members using the latest data provided by the EU, the OECD and other organisations.

The structure of this chapter is as follows: Section 2 analyses the European debt crisis of the PIGS to explain the institutional reasons related to private pensions. Section 3 presents empirical results to find the key reasons for the European debt crisis. Section 4 proposes recommendations concerning the development of private pensions and the pension finance framework for China.

2 One of the Institutional Reasons for the European Debt Crisis

Many scholars believe that the European debt crisis is mainly caused by the PIGS's overly generous spending on social welfare.[5] To verify the relationship among social welfare spending and debt, we use the ratio of social welfare expenditure to

[5] Zheng (2011a).

GDP as an index to verify this hypothesis. In the meantime, we also use the pension expenditure and projection indicator, which includes gross public pensions (i.e., before taxes and compulsory social security contributions) as a percentage of GDP. There are different categories of pension benefits, some of which (for example, disability pensions) may be paid to people who have not reached the standard retiring age. The projections are made based on Eurostat's population projection and commonly agreed underlying economic assumptions that have been prepared by the European Commission and the Economic Policy Committee of the EU.

From the data in Table 1 we find that the ratios of social welfare spending to GDP in Greece, Italy and Portugal have ranked in the top 3, compared with other countries in 2012 at the outbreak of the debt crisis. All are close to 20 % and are higher than the EU's average ratio of 16.9 %. In NSU, however, especially in the Netherlands and Switzerland, the ratio of social welfare spending to GDP was significantly lower than in the PIGS, indicating that social welfare spending pressure in these countries is relatively low. Many domestic and foreign scholars had reached the same conclusion, which is supported by the data presented in Table 1.

However, with further analysis of the data we also find that the PIGS's social welfare expenditure was in fact only slightly higher than the EU-27 countries' average. In other words, the gap is not so significant. This may be because the level of economic and social development in OECD countries is relatively close, so the level of social welfare is also marginally different. Moreover, with the accelerated process of EU integration and increased mobility, there is an increasing homogeneity of social welfare. While there are some differences in social welfare projects and the amount of payments among the states, there is no huge gap overall. Take the ratio of Greece, the most seriously affected country in the sovereign debt crisis, as an example. When comparing the Netherlands and Switzerland to Greece, we find that the ratio of social welfare spending to GDP is much smaller than in Greece. That being said, the per capita GDP in these three countries was €32,700, €39,500

Table 1 Public social expenditure and pension expenditure to GDP

	Public social expenditure to GDP (%)			Pension expenditure and projections to GDP (%)		
Year	2001	2005	2012	2010	2015	2030
Aver. of EU-27	*15.4*	*15.5*	*16.9*	*11.3*	*11.2*	*11.9*
Portugal	11.5	14.4	18.0	12.5	13.3	13.2
Italy	16.1	16.9	19.9	15.3	14.9	14.5
Greece	15.4	14.1	20.0	13.6	14.1	14.1
Spain	11.7	11.6	16.1	10.1	10.4	10.6
Aver. of PIGS	*13.7*	*14.3*	*18.5*	*12.9*	*13.2*	*13.1*
Netherlands	11.1	10.9	12.2	6.8	6.8	9.1
Switzerland	10.5	11.5	–	–	–	–
UK	12.8	12.6	15.4	7.7	7.4	7.7
Aver. of NSU	*11.5*	*11.7*	*13.8*	*7.3*	*7.1*	*8.4*

Source: Eurostat official website: http://epp.eurostat.ec.europa.eu

and €19,900 respectively in 2011; therefore, in absolute figures, per capita social welfare expenditures in the three countries were, respectively, €3859, €4306, and €3861. Considering the living costs are also different, the gap among them was very small. While the PIGS' ratio of social welfare spending to GDP is higher than the NSU's ratio, the gap is not particularly significant, and the absolute data of the social welfare spending among EU countries is insignificant. As a result of the well-developed nature of the overwhelming majority of EU countries, as well as the extent of market integration in the EU, the level of social welfare as a whole is higher in the EU than in other countries. Therefore, social welfare spending alone could not be defined as the main reason for the debt crisis and we need to consider other causes.

From the data we also find that the pension expenditure and projection indicators of PIGS are significantly higher than that of NSU. Public pensions are one of the most significant liabilities of governments; as such, PIGS are required to plough a much higher proportion of their fiscal revenue into their pension systems than NSU. This endangers the sustainability of their pension systems and worsens their debt situation. Taking Greece as an example: up to 2014, the GDP was 26 % below its pre-crisis peak. Spending by the Greeks on goods and services has in fact fallen by at least 40 %.[6] We can see that NSU's Pension expenditure and projections for GDP are much lower than for PIGS. Significantly, this indicates that NSU have considerably more room to manoeuvre with regard to their treasuries meeting the challenges posed by a debt crisis.

In almost all countries under review, the public pension has occupied the most important position in the social welfare system. Pension spending has become an important welfare indicator in Europe and in the United States. Differences among the pension systems of European countries are numerous, so to facilitate a comparison every country's pension system is regarded as a public Pay-As-You-Go (PAYG) pension system and a private accumulated pension funds system which is contributed to by both employer and employee. Now we will move from the EU to the OECD. We use Allianz's Pension Sustainability Index (PSI), which combines the various characteristics of pension systems with the factors that influence them to help track and evaluate policy changes made in a total of 50 large-population countries around the world, as a composite index of pension systems. The PSI is able to evaluate the long-term financial sustainability of national pension systems and the consequent pressure on governments to reform them. In the PSI, Australia, Sweden, New Zealand and Norway ranked in the top 4 and Thailand ranked 50th.

From Table 2 we can see that, compared to welfare spending levels in Table 1, the differences between the pension structure can explain the institutional reason of the PIGS' debt crisis more powerfully. The pension replacement rate is the rate of retirement pension income compared to last month's salary income, and reflects the level of pension benefits for retirees. The total pension that an individual gets after retirement usually relates to the level of the country's social welfare. The total

[6] Wolf (2015).

pension gap of the EU, as with social welfare, is not very large. The core difference lies in the structure of the pensions. From Table 2 we can see that the PIGS mainly rely on public pensions, and the total replacement rate is higher than the average of the OECD-34 countries (only 50 %). For example, in Greece, the public pension replacement rate went up to 70.5 %, making it one of the highest among OECD countries, meaning Greece has a higher retirement income. PIGS countries, most especially Greece, all have underdeveloped private pensions. They mainly depend on the public pension which is only the first of "three pillars" the World Bank recommends, and their pension deficit can rely on financial subsidies. With the growing elderly population, the pension debt has become an increasingly heavy financial burden. One pillar could not hold the debt and may have led to the debt crisis. However, NSU's public pension replacement rates are only 30–40 %, much lower than PIGS, thus the NSU governments' financial burdens are lighter. As NSU all have mandatory or voluntary private pensions as an important supplement, they could avoid the crisis that happened in Greece, because they established truly multi-pillar pension systems in the past decades. As NSU have other pillars, in addition to public pensions, their overall pension replacement rate is quite high: the replacement rate in the Netherlands is close to 100 %.

There appear to be huge gaps of the occupational pension coverage among PIGS and NSU. The occupational pension coverage rate for the whole working population was only 0.3–7.6 % in PIGS. In Greece the rate is only 0.3 %. As such, almost all retirees rely on public pensions which worsened the debt crisis. However, the proportion in NSU is much higher: take the Netherlands and Switzerland as examples, the occupational pension coverage rate for the working population was between 70 and 116 %. The UK's coverage rate in 2011 was only 43.6 %, but, according to its 2008 pension act, from October 2012 all employees must "auto-enrol" into an occupational pension system in the next few years which is semi-mandatory, so the occupational pension coverage rate will increase significantly. The UK should soon be able to reach the level of Switzerland and the Netherlands. As such, the occupational pensions, as the second pillar, will play a more important role in the UK's pension system.

From Table 2 we can also deduce that private pension assets are another important indicator. Private pension assets in the PIGS represented a very small ratio to their GDP. In Greece, the amount was only $6 per capita, the ratio is only 0.9 %. Pension assets per capita in Portugal, Italy and Spain all are less $3000, and such pitiful amounts of private pension assets are obviously inadequate in developed European countries. Because the average rate of OECD-34 countries is 72.4 %, the PIGS' private pension assets are not only much lower than NSU, but also lower than all OECD-34 countries. So when the debt crisis attacked, large public pension deficits inevitably appeared. As the private pension system was unable to make up an independent pillar in PIGS's fiscal system, the depth and breadth of the debt crisis were exacerbated. In NSU, however, per capita private pension assets were up to tens of thousands of dollars, which was 20–30 times that of PIGS. When they were faced with similarly insufficient public pensions, the private pensions could constitute a significant proportion of the income of retirees.

Table 2 Pension structure's gap among PIGS and NSU

Items	Public pension replacement rate (%)	Private pension replacement rate (%)	Occupational pension coverage rate (%)	Per capita of private pension assets (dollars)	Private pension assets/GDP (%)	Pension sustainability index
Year	2011	2011	2011	2010	2011	2013
OECD	50.0	–	–	–	72.4	–
Portugal	54.7	–	8.4	2633	8.3	34
Italy	71.2	–	14.0	1865	2.1	39
Greece	70.5	–	0.3	6	0.9	43
Spain	73.9	–	18.6	2858	11.1	40
Netherlands	33.1	66.7	116.3	60,741	149.3	5
Switzerland	32.0	23.1	70.5	76,523	103.2	7
UK	32.6	34.5	43.3	32,098	95.0	10

Data sources: OECD (2013), OECD (2014) and Allianz (2014); Allianz International Pensions Country Factsheets 2013; Population data of per capita from the Eurostat website: http://epp.eurostat.ec.europa.eu

Moreover, this part of the private pension system was completely market-oriented and fully independent from government. Employers and employees shared responsibility in the field of the respective pensions, and greatly reduced the government's financial burden. In this sense, the European debt crisis, to some extent, was a crisis of pension system defects. Without private pensions, the public pensions in the PIGS could not support the overall situation and, eventually, this absence both led to and further exacerbated the debt crisis.

PIGS rank significantly lower on the PSI than NSU and we credit the lack of private pensions for this. The Netherlands is ranked 5th, which is the highest in all seven specimen countries. Switzerland and the UK ranked 7th and 10th, respectively, because of their well-developed private pension funds. PIGS ranked towards the bottom of the list from 34th to 43rd. As a reference, China ranked 45th of the list, very near to Greece. The index likely indicates that the pension systems of NSU are more sustainable. So, during the process of market integration among EU Member States, one of the most important fields may be the development of their private pension system, and it is clear that PIGS have a long way to go.

Arguably, the lack of private pensions has also caused the underdevelopment of pension finance. The pension finance theory is formed from pension investment practices in the EU and North America. In 1974, the US Congress enacted the "Employee Retirement Income Security Act", which laid a solid foundation for security and large-scale development of the US's private pension plans. In 1978, by the revised tax act, 401 (k) and 403(b) plans paved the way for the development of private pension. To that end, employers and employees could take a certain percentage from their salary and put it into pension accounts. Contributions within those prescribed limits are free from income tax, and investment income is not subject to capital gains tax. Private pension funds could be on a tax-deferred basis, and became fundamental and institutional factors of pension finances. As Bodie (1990) pointed out, pension funds in the US play a significant role in asset securitisation, derivatives, debt and other financial innovations. With the pension funds as long-term capital, the US not only achieved a great development in the real economy, but also prosperity in financial markets. Private pensions have become the most important institutional investors in the capital market of the US. By the end of 2013, US pension fund assets were up to $16.89 trillion, accounting for 100.7 % of its GDP, and the proportion invested in the stock market was up to 50.7 % (OECD 2014).

Besides the US, some European countries also have well-developed pension finance. Using NSU as an example, private pensions were gradually playing an increasingly important role in economic life. The decision-makers in these countries had to examine pension finance from a deeper level, and establish effective regulation for pension finance to promote the stability of the entire financial system. In recent years, large-scale riots occurred in Western countries, for example in Spain, Greece, and France (whose private pension assets are similar to Greece's), and all were linked to widespread public dissatisfaction with the pension systems. There is no doubt that sound pension systems, especially via private pension funds, have become the key to stabilising the capital market.

3 Reasons for the European Debt Crisis: Empirical Results

The above analysis focused on the impact of private pension assets on the sovereign debt crisis. From the previous data we only got a sampling of seven countries, which begs the question: if we enlarge the samples to more countries would we get similar results?

3.1 Variables Description and Data Source

The fundamental characteristics of a debt crisis are vast debt and fiscal deficit, so we are going to look into the reasons for a debt crisis from the perspectives of expenditure rather than revenue. In an ageing society, the dependency ratio is used to measure the pressure on the productive population. This ratio is made up of the number of people aged 65 and over compared to the number of people aged 15–64. The aged dependency ratio is positively correlated with government debt and fiscal deficit.

The immediate impact of an ageing population is the increasing social security expenditure. In this chapter, we use the ratio of expenditure on social protection to GDP to measure the social expenditure. This ratio is also positively correlated with government debt and fiscal deficit (Table 3).

Expenditure on social protection (ESP) is the index used to measure social welfare expenditure overall. In researching the reasons for the debt crisis, it is necessary to analyse the specific factors of the social welfare system. In this chapter, we use two variables to present the internal structure of the social welfare system. The first one is the ratio of general government contributions to GDP (GGC). The second one is the ratio of private pension assets to GDP (PPA). The first variable relates to the difference between contributory social insurance and non-contributory social welfare. The non-contributory social welfare includes social assistance schemes and universal benefit schemes. The former provides a safety net for those who cannot support themselves financially with means test,

Table 3 Variables description and data source

Variables	Abbreviation	Time	Data resource
Debt/GDP	Debt	2001–2010	Eurostat
Fiscal deficit/GDP	Deficit	2001–2010	Eurostat
GDP per capita	GDPP	2001–2010	Eurostat
Expenditure on social protection/GDP	ESP	2001–2010	Eurostat
General government contributions/GDP	GGC	2001–2010	Eurostat
Private pension assets/GDP	PPA	2001–2010	OECD
The aged dependency ratio	ADR	2001–2010	OECD
Inflation rate	INFLA	2001–2010	Eurostat

Source: Eurostat yearbook and OECD: Pension Markets in Focus, 2014

while the latter provides universal benefit for all the eligible people without means test. The expenditure for the non-contributory scheme comes from fiscal revenue. The second variable relates to the difference between public pension expenditure responsibility and private expenditure responsibility.

The variables of aged dependency ratio, general government contributions and expenditure on social protection have a positive impact on government debt and fiscal deficit (i.e., reducing both) and the variable of private pension assets has a negative effect (i.e., increasing both). Besides the above four variables, this paper uses GDP per capita and the inflation rate as control variables.

The empirical research for this paper included data from 2001 to 2010, and information from 13 countries, including Belgium, Germany, Portugal, Denmark, Finland, Iceland, Ireland, Italy, Netherlands, Norway, Spain, Sweden, and the United Kingdom. In this paper, we use the ratio of government debt to GDP and the ratio of deficit to GDP as dependent variables. The data concerning aged dependency ratio and private pension asset came from OECD (Pension Markets in Focus 2014) and the data for the other four variables came from Eurostat.

3.2 Descriptive Statistics

Table 4 contains the descriptive statistics of the six variables. From the table, we can find that there is a sizeable difference in fiscal deficit and government debt between those 13 countries. The maximum fiscal deficit is 30.90 % of GDP, while some countries have a fiscal surplus. The maximum government debt is 119.20 % of GDP, the minimum is 0, and the mean of debt is 56.54 %.

Amongst the independent variables, beside GDP per capita, the standard deviation of private pension assets (PPA) is the biggest. For expenditure on social protection (ESP), the maximum data is 33.26 %, the minimum data is 14.79 %, and the mean is 26.22 %. The maximum of government contribution (GGC) is 23.68 %, the minimum is 4.95 %, and the mean is 12.40 %. The maximum of aged dependency ratio (ADR) is 33.70 %, the minimum is 17.40 %, and the mean is 26.25 %

Table 4 Descriptive statistics

Variables	Mean	Maximum	Minimum	Std. dev.	Obs.	Cross-section
Deficit	0.66	30.90	−18.80	6.29	130	13
Debt	56.54	119.20	0.00	25.46	130	13
GDPP	33,980	51,792	19,574	6710	130	13
ESP	26.22	33.26	14.79	3.85	130	13
GGC	12.40	23.68	4.95	3.90	130	13
PPA	37.54	138.05	2.24	40.35	130	13
ADR	26.25	33.70	17.40	3.99	130	13
INFLA	2.41	16.30	−1.70	2.03	130	13

3.3 Results

This is short panel data because the number of countries is less than the number of years considered. According to the F ratio, it rejects the hypothesis of mixed effect models but accepts that it should be applied to fix effect models. Furthermore, the Hausman test shows that the model should be applied to fix effect. In the estimate of fix effect, considering the differences in expenditure on social welfare across countries, the GLS method (cross-section weights) is used.

Because the variable of GDP per capita and the inflation rate affect the dependent variable, we should eliminate the influence and control two independent variables. First, after controlling GDP per capita and the inflation rate, the variables of aged dependency ratio, expenditure on social protection and government contribution are significant in the first three models with dependent variable deficit (Table 5) or debt (Table 6). For example, after controlling GDP per capita and inflation rate, when the aged dependency ratio increases 1 %, the ratio of deficit to GDP will increase 0.69 %. In the same way, when expenditure on social protection increase 1 %, the ratio of deficit and debt to GDP will increase 1.59 % and 3.26 % respectively. When government contributions increase 1 %, the ratio of deficit to GDP will increase 2.36 % and the ratio of debt to GDP will increase 4.92 %. The results indicate that aged dependency ratio is the key factor to influence fiscal deficit and debt. When there are increasing numbers of ageing people the government has to spend more money on the elderly and, consequently, has to contribute more money to social welfare schemes.

Second, after controlling GDP per capita and inflation rate, the private pension assets variable is significant, but the sign of the variable is inconsistent with the theory prediction. In theory, the private pension assets have profound influence on the fiscal deficit and debt. However, the regression results conflict with the theory prediction. There are two explanations for the contradiction. The first explanation is that the sample includes 13 countries and the most typical countries which have little private pension assets and huge fiscal deficits, such as Greece and France, are not included. Because the private pension assets are minuscule in those countries, in some years there are no relevant statistics so those countries are not included in the sample. The second reason is that the value of private pension assets fluctuates and is easy influenced by financial market. The descriptive statistics presented in Table 4 indicated that the standard deviation of private pension assets is the biggest in those independent variables.

Lastly, GDP per capita is significant in all the models and its sign is consistent with theory prediction. This indicates that economic development is the key variable influencing fiscal deficit and debt. The aged dependency ratio, expenditure on social protection and government contribution all influence the expenditure side of government finance and the GDP per capita influences the revenue side of government finance. Therefore, the debt crisis is the compounded effect of the expenditure side and the revenue side.

Table 5 Estimation results (cross-section weights)

Dependent variable: deficit	Model 1	Model 2	Model 3	Model 4	Model 5	Model 6
ADR	0.69*** (4.09)					−0.08 (−0.67)
ESP		1.59*** (18.64)			1.67*** (18.519)	1.63*** (7.90)
GGC			2.36*** (15.48)			0.08 (0.26)
PPA				0.15*** (4.15)	−0.04** (−2.14)	−0.04** (−2.17)
GDPP	−0.0007*** (−5.67)	−0.0003*** (−4.10)	−0.0005*** (−6.36)	−0.0009*** (6.51)	−0.0002*** (−2.73)	−0.0002* (−2.34)
INFLA	−0.22 (−1.17)	0.42*** (3.45)	0.42*** (3.07)	−0.22 (−1.22)	0.41*** (3.42)	0.43*** (3.51)
Constant	9.08* (1.79)	−31.88*** (−8.75)	−11.17*** (−3.34)	24.79*** (−5.96)	−34.85*** (−8.85)	−32.92*** (−7.23)
Adjusted R^2	0.77	0.94	0.85	0.81	0.94	0.93
Obs	130	130	130	130	130	130

***, **, * indicate the significance at 1 %, 5 % or 10 % confidence level, the *t* value is shown in the brackets

Table 6 Estimation results (cross-section weights)

Dependent variable: debt	Model 1	Model 2	Model 3	Model 4	Model 5	Model 6
ADR	2.61*** (5.69)					−0.39 (−0.54)
ESP		3.26*** (8.05)			3.10*** (7.24)	2.62** (2.13)
GGC			4.92*** (8.12)			1.42 (0.89)
PPA				0.45*** (4.16)	0.25** (2.19)	0.27** (2.29)
GDPP	−0.0023*** (−6.33)	−0.0011*** (−2.92)	−0.0014*** (−3.69)	−0.0026*** (−7.34)	−0.0018*** (−4.14)	−0.0020*** (−4.03)
INFLA	−1.01* (−1.88)	1.01 (1.59)	0.79 (1.28)	−0.07 (−0.12)	1.66*** (2.57)	1.65*** (2.57)
Constant	69.69*** (5.55)	6.84*** (0.37)	41.39*** (2.74)	129.91*** (11.39)	−24.32 (−1.21)	43.08* (1.76)
Adjusted R^2	0.95	0.93	0.94	0.95	0.94	0.95
Obs	130	130	130	130	130	130

***, **, * indicate the significance at 1 %, 5 % or 10 % confidence level, the *t* value is shown in the brackets

4 Lessons to Learn for China: Developing Pension Finance

From the above data and the statistics of the European debt crisis, several lessons can be learned by China for its own pension finance development. According to Huang's research report (Huang et al. 2013), there will be serious structural problems in China's pension system. For a long time, the Chinese government's largest financial risk was the pension deficit, and the total pension liability was 62–97 % of GDP. With a rapid increase in pension expenditure, the liability may even exceed the total amount of state-owned assets. Moreover, an ageing population will further expand the pension gap. Consequently, if it is not reformed, the current pension system will seriously damage financial sustainability.

The data from China's sixth census (2010) shows that: China is the only country in the world where the elderly population is more than 100 million, and that number is growing by 3.2 % annually. Considering the globally-unique, rigid "one family one child" policy, in the coming decades China will only face increasing pressure on the pension system. Facing the reality that China has the largest ageing population in the world and the pension system is far from perfect, the possibility for accumulation of pension funds is seriously limited. Based on the current fiscal regime, the public pension system will be incapable of supporting the fallout; it is not possible to meet the crisis of future's pension payments. Once China encounters a debt crisis like Greece's, it is likely to trigger a pension crisis. There is no doubt that China should take precautions to avoid the nightmare of the debt crisis occurring in China. To that end, China should institute a major national strategy for social security by developing personal accounts for pensions, investing properly and developing a pension system based on enterprise annuity and occupational pensions.

China's economic growth has been thriving since the reform, and the basic status of the market in allocating resources is increasingly strengthened. From the perspective of law and economics, the institutional reform of the pension should pay more attention to market forces, especially to the rise of personal pensions, which must be invested in the capital market throughout the career for value preservation. The pension assets of China are lower than in developed countries. Hence, the enormous ageing pressure forces China to seriously reflect on the pension financial development and to understand the necessity of the development of pension finance fully. Taking steps to develop pension finance, particularly by deepening financial reform, promoting financial innovation and maintaining financial stability, can reduce the question of over-reliance on indirect financing in China's financial system. On 6 December 2013, China's Ministry of Treasury, the State Administration of Taxation and Ministry of Human Resources and Social Security issued the No. 103 document to guide the investment of enterprise annuity and occupational pension. The employer's contribution to enterprise annuity and occupational pension will get income tax free; at the same time the employees also face zero personal income tax on contributions of less than 4 % of their salary. This kind of preferential policies will benefit future private pension development in China.

At present, China has placed too much reliance on an indirect financing system. In 2012, financial institutions made RMB 8.2 trillion of new loans in the calendar-year, but equity financing was RMB 321 billion and bond financing of listed companies was RMB 272.3 billion. We can calculate the percentage of the three kinds of financing: 93.3, 3.6, 3.1 % (People's Bank of China 2013). In the US, with the well-developed financial markets, these three types of financing accounted for 56, 11 and 32 % in the period 1970–2000 (Mishkin 2009). Compared with the US, China has a serious lack of direct financing, and more depend on indirect financing by banks. The structure of the financial market in China is not reasonable because it has not yet formed a pension plan with institutional investors similar to the US 401 (k) and 403(b). As stocks in Europe and America hit a new high since the financial crisis, the composite Index of the Shanghai Stock Exchange hit its lowest point, 1849, in June 2013. The lack of real long-term investments by institutional investors is one of the most important reasons for the downturn of the stock market and in turn has further affected direct financing. The issue of new shares was completely stopped during the first half of 2013, contributing to a vicious cycle.

The best way to overcome the predicament of the capital market is to let pension funds invest in capital markets. China's experience shows that their pension investments can get a good return in capital markets. Although the stock market has not been reliably upward-moving in recent years, the latest report of the National Social Security Fund—a strategic reserve fund—shows that the investment income for 2013 was 6.2 %, and the average annual investment return rate since its inception in 2000 is as high as 8.13 %.[7] For example, the enterprise annuity can invest in capital markets, and has reached an overall yield of 8.35 % in 2007–2012.[8] Therefore, although the stock market fluctuated frequently and the stock index hit a recorded low, the national social security fund and the enterprise annuity investment still made an extraordinary performance. This proves that China's private pensions can achieve both preservation and appreciation by investing in the capital market and that pension finance has favourable prospects in China. Because of its nature as a long-term accumulation, the pension system is compatible with capital market realities, which require long-term strategic investors. Both the historical experience of developed countries in the area of pensions finance and the recent experience in China indicate that the healthy development of the capital market requires pension investments. To eliminate the public concern of uncertainty for the future, China urgently needs to establish a systematic and reliable pension system so that pensions can increase their value by investing in the capital market.

How to create a basic framework for the pension financial system is becoming increasingly important by learning the lessons of PIGS for China.

---

[7] National Social Security Fund Annually Report of 2013, June 2014. See at its official website at (in Chinese): http://www.ssf.gov.cn/cwsj/ndbg/201406/t20140627_6063.html.

[8] Hu Xiaoyi (Deputy Minister, Ministry of Human Resource and Social Security), speech on Xinhua press conference, see: http://news.xinhuanet.com/fortune/2013-04/25/c_124629338.htm.

First, China should truly make the individual accounts have real money. "Social pooling and individual accounts" which were designed and implemented at the beginning of the establishment of the social security system in 1997, are institutional innovations in the world. The employer contributes 20 % to a social pooling account, while employees contribute 8 % of their salary to their individual accounts. In this combined system, the social pool is a Pay-As-You-Go system, while the individual accounts constitute an accumulated funding system. However, a large number of the current retirees, more specifically those who were working during the time of the centrally planned economy, did not sufficiently contribute to the social pool. After all, before the establishment of the social security system in 1997, China only had retirement payments paid out by employers. Consequently, to pay the retirees' benefits money has to be borrowed from the individual accounts of workers who are currently working; the current workers' personal accounts are de facto partly empty. It is therefore very important now to pursue individual accounts and to make proper investments. Taking the RMB 9.3 trillion (the total wage in 2013) as the base; if the pensions of the individual accounts can reach 8 % of total wages, then there will be nearly RMB 744 billion that can be invested each year.[9] At present, China should focus on separating the accumulated pensions of individual accounts from the social pooling, and introduce individual accounts to capital markets under regulation and let them participate in corporate stocks and bonds which were issued in the financial market. In this way, on the one hand, China can solve the problem of the financing structure that depended too much on indirect financing. On the other hand, China can create conditions for increasing the value of the individual accounts pensions.

Second, China should strive to expand the coverage of the enterprise annuity, which is the second pillar of the pension system. If conditions permit, it can study the British system and move towards being mandatory in the future. Up to the end of the third quarter of 2014, there were only 72,171 enterprises which had established an enterprise annuity in the entire country, accounting for about 0.6 %, and covering only 22 million workers. Most of these enterprises are State-owned enterprises of central and local governments; transportation, communications, energy, financial and other monopolistic enterprises, while SMEs are basically excluded. Even so, the total assets of enterprise annuities amounted to only RMB 685.6 billion.[10] This small amount cannot be compared to international private pension assets, which are tens of trillions of dollars. However, the good news is that the occupational pension system of civil servants and employees of public institutions were implemented on 1 October 2014: employers must contribute 8 % and employees 4 % to employees' occupational pension accounts, which can invest in the capital market like an enterprise annuity. There is no doubt that the coverage of the occupational pension and enterprise annuity must be extended in

[9] National Bureau of Statistics Official website: http://www.stats.gov.cn/english/.

[10] Ministry of Human Recourses and Social Security, Statistics Report of 2014, See: (in Chinese) http://www.mohrss.gov.cn/shbxjjjds/SHBXJDSgongzuodongtai/201412/W020141211410761720514.pdf.

the future, so that the total assets of China's private pension system can improve significantly, and truly form the second pillar of pensions, preventing the problem of a single pillar failing to support the overall situation.

Third, China should promote the reform of its capital market, and promote the development of pension finance. Finance is the core of the modern economy, while the capital markets are an important part of the financial markets. China's capital market has completed the share reform and introduced Share Price Index Futures. Thus, the legal system and the capital market regulatory system will be improved, and mechanisms of a sound, transparent, efficient, safely operated market system will be completed. This will provide necessary institutional safeguards for the safety, profitability and liquidity of the pension system. China must establish and improve the financial supervision of the new pension system, and it should learn from the foreign experience of the pension financial regulatory system. In addition, China should concentrate on the regulation of pensions from the current, decentralised financial departments to eliminate regulatory gaps and overlaps. Considering the significant development of future pension finance and the requirements for comprehensive operation and supervision, a Pension Financial Supervisory Authority should be built into the "National Financial Supervision Commission" in the department system reform in the future. This authority should be responsible for the organisation, coordination and supervision of the pension financial system, and promote the development of pension finance, so as to deal with the challenges of an ageing crisis.

References

Alesina A, Tabellini G (1990) A positive theory of fiscal deficits and government debt. Rev Econ Stud 57:403–414

Allianz (2014) Pension sustainability index. Allianz International Pension Papers 1/2014

Arghyrou MG, Tsoukalas JD (2010) The Greek debt crisis: likely causes, mechanics and outcomes. Cardiff economics working papers, ISSN 1749-6101, April 2010

Bodie Z (1990) Pension funds and financial innovation. Financ Manag 19(3):11–22

Friedman G (2013) Recognizing the end of the Chinese economic miracle. Geopolitical Weekly, 23 July 2013. http://www.stratfor.com/weekly/recognizing-end-chinese-economic-miracle

Huang Y, Chang J, Yang SL (2013) China: beyond the miracle (Part 8 – Can China manage its fiscal risks?). Barclays Emerging Markets Research, 28 January 2013

Mishkin FS (2009) The economics of money, banking, and financial markets, 9th edn. Pearson

Nelson RM, Belkin P, Mix DE (2011) Greece's debt crisis: overview, policy responses, and implications. Congressional Research Service Report for Congress, Prepared for Members and Committees of Congress, 18 August 2011

OECD (2013) Pensions at a glance 2013: retirement-income systems in OECD and G20 countries. OECD, Paris

OECD (2014) OECD Institutional Investors Statistics 2014. OECD, Paris

Panizza U, Sturzenegger F, Zettelmeyer J (2009) The economics and law of sovereign debt and default. J Econ Lit 47(3):651–698

People's Bank of China (2013) China financial stability report 2013, China Finance Press

Reinhart CM, Rogoff KS (2009) This time is different: eight centuries of financial folly. Princeton University Press

Schwarcz SL (2012) Sovereign debt restructuring options: an analytical comparison. Harv Bus Law Rev 2:95–121

The European Central Bank (ECB) (2011) The European stability mechanism. ECB Monthly Bulletin, July

Wolf M (2012) The next big financial crisis will be made in China. Financial Times, 28 February 2012. http://www.cnbc.com/id/46564626

Wolf M (2015) Greek debt and a default of statesmanship. Financial Times, 27 January 2015. http://www.ft.com/intl/cms/s/0/44c56806-a556-11e4-ad35-00144feab7de.html#axzz3RIeNjWTW

Yu Y (2010) From European sovereign debt crisis to global sovereign debt crisis. Int Econ Rev 6 (余永定:"从欧洲主权债危机到全球主权债危机",《国际经济评论》,2010 年第6 期)

Zheng B (2011a) Too generous pension in Greece is the important precipitating factor of its sovereign debt crisis. Chinese Soc Secur 12 (郑秉文:"养老金过度慷慨是希腊主权债务危机的重要诱因",《中国社会保障》, 2011年第12期)

Zheng G (2011b) Lessons from European sovereign debt crisis: how to complete China's pension system. Chinese Labor Security News, 27 December 2011, p 3 (郑功成:"从欧债危机看中国养老金制度的完善",《中国劳动保障报》2011年12月27日第3版)

Why Are China's State-Owned Enterprises so Profitable? A Financial Repression Perspective

Guangdong Xu and Binwei Gui

1 Introduction

In mainstream economics, the justification for state-owned enterprises (SOEs) in a market economy is that such enterprises correct market failures that arise in the provision of public goods, i.e., goods whose consumption is characterised by non-rivalry and non-exclusivity.[1] The social need for public goods cannot adequately be met by private suppliers because of the free-rider problem, i.e., when people who cannot be excluded from enjoying the benefits of a public good may withhold payment for it in the hopes that others will pay their share. In other words, public goods can be systematically undersupplied by the market. However, the government can provide public goods with financing derived from tax revenues rather than from the proceeds of sales, which can eliminate the free rider problem and improve social welfare by guaranteeing sufficient supplies of public goods.

SOEs may also be understood as an efficient tool of social control. Djankov et al. (2003) argue that if certain social problems in some situations (such as disorder[2]) are too big for other social arrangements, such as courts or regulatory

[1] Non-rivalry means that consumption of the good by one individual does not reduce the availability of the good for consumption by others, whereas non-excludability implies that no one can be effectively excluded from consumption of the good.

[2] Disorder refers to the risk of private expropriation that individuals face with respect to their persons and their property that might result from banditry, murder, theft, violation of agreements, torts, and/or monopoly pricing, among other misdeeds. Disorder is also reflected in the private subversion of public institutions (such as courts) through bribes and threats, which allows private violators of laws, regulations and standards to escape penalties.

G. Xu (✉) • B. Gui
Center for Law and Economics at the China University of Political Science and Law, Beijing, China
e-mail: guangdongx@cupl.edu.cn; guibinwei@163.com

N. Philipsen et al. (eds.), *Market Integration: The EU Experience and Implications for Regulatory Reform in China*, China-EU Law Series 2,
DOI 10.1007/978-3-662-48273-5_6

agencies, to address successfully, government ownership can be relied upon as the last resort (although government ownership may increase the risk that dictatorship will ensue[3]). For example, Hart et al. (1997) argue that prisons should be publicly owned because the risk of private jailers mistreating inmates is too high. Compared with a government institution, a private prison owner has a stronger incentive to engage in cost reductions, which might—at least in principle—lead to substantially reduced quality in certain important dimensions, such as prison violence and the quality of prison personnel.

Even in most situations in which state ownership seems desirable, private ownership is typically superior for several reasons, including the incentives that private entrepreneurs have to innovate.[4] After all, there is an inherent flaw in state ownership: bureaucrats who control the enterprises and other assets have no incentive to make good decisions because their personal income and wealth is not connected with the income and profit of the SOEs they manage. In other words, there is a mismatch between residual claims and residual control.[5]

In Kornai's words, "whatever state-owned firm one takes as an example, there is no individual, family, or small group of partners to whom one can point as owners. As no one can pocket the profits and no one need pay out of his own pocket for the losses, property in this sense is not only depersonalized but eliminated. State property belongs to all and to none".[6]

Numerous empirical studies that compare the performance of SOEs with the performance of private enterprises have revealed the inefficiencies of SOEs and hence their limitations in addressing social problems.[7] In general, "research now supports the proposition that privately owned firms are more efficient and more profitable than otherwise-comparable state-owned firms"[8]; moreover, in transition economies, "privatization is strongly associated with more enterprise

[3] Dictatorship refers to the risk of expropriation that individuals face with respect to their persons and their property from the state and its agents in such forms as murder, taxation, and/or multiple types of violations of property rights. Dictatorship is also embodied in other types of more subtle expropriation, such as when state regulators restrict firms' competitive entry.

[4] Shleifer (1998).

[5] These two terms have been used extensively in firm theory under the influence of Grossman and Hart (1986) and Hart and Moore (1990). Equity investors of a corporation have the "residual claim" in the sense that they receive whatever is left in the corporation after all outstanding debts (or "fixed claims") are paid. Residual rights of control result from the impossibility of designing and enforcing complete contracts, particularly with respect to complex and dynamic transactions. Because all contracts are unavoidably incomplete and someone must thus be authorised to fill in the gaps, residual rights of control can be defined as the right to determine the uses of assets under circumstances that are not specified under a contract. The basic principle is that "control rights and income rights are highly complementary and so . . .it makes sense to allocate them to the same person" (Hart 1995, pp. 64–65).

[6] Kornai (1992), p. 75.

[7] Megginson and Netter (2001) and Djankov and Murrell (2002).

[8] Megginson and Netter (2001), p. 380.

restructuring",[9] which in turn improves these economies' overall economic performance.

China does not appear to be an exception to the "bad SOE" story for most of its reform period. For example, after reviewing the relevant empirical literature, Hovey and Naughton (2007) conclude that the "ownership structure does significantly influence the performance and value of Chinese firms" and that "state ownership is generally negatively correlated to performance".[10] Similarly, in a review of state-enterprise reform in China beginning in the early 1980s, Yusuf et al. (2006) posit that "studies extending back into the latter half of the 1980s have repeatedly shown that the efficiency and productivity of SOEs lag behind COEs [collectively owned enterprise], TVEs [township and village enterprises], and joint ventures".[11] Indeed, China's SOEs were so inefficient that almost half were running losses in the 1990s. Subsequent divestment and/or closure of thousands of small and medium-size SOEs improved the situation, although 30 % of the surviving SOEs remained in the red in 2002.[12]

However, the situation has changed drastically during the last decade, and the profitability of China's SOEs has increased impressively. The reported average return on equity (ROE) of an SOE in China jumped from only 2.2 % in 1996 to 15.7 % in 2007, before sliding back to 10.9 % in 2009 (World Bank and DRC 2013). From 2003 to 2011, the net profits of China's SOEs increased from CNY 320 billion to CNY 1.9 trillion, based on average annual growth of 25.2 %.[13] A report issued by the China Enterprise Confederation/China Enterprise Directors Association in 2012 showed that 310 of the 500 top enterprises in China were SOEs, with total assets of CNY 116.7 trillion and total profits of 2.1 trillion. The remaining 190 enterprises were privately owned, with profits of only CNY 0.3 trillion, which is equal to one-seventh of the profits earned by SOEs.[14]

Why are China's SOEs so profitable in recent years, despite the inefficiencies inherent in their corporate governance structure? Certainly, the revitalisation of China's SOEs can be attributed at least in part to the reform strategies adopted by the Chinese government to improve their performance, such as corporatisation, reorganisation, and market openness.[15] However, an increasing amount of evidence shows that the major driving force behind the profitability of China's SOEs consists of certain distorted economic policies that favour SOEs at the expense of private

[9] Djankov and Murrell (2002), p. 740.

[10] Hovey and Naughton (2007), p. 138.

[11] Yusuf et al. (2006), p. 14.

[12] Yusuf et al. (2006), p. 14.

[13] "China SOEs report surge in profits", China Daily, 24 October 2012. Available at http://www.chinadaily.com.cn/china/2012-10/24/content_15843885.htm (accessed 9 August 2014).

[14] "Zhongguo qiye 500 qiang guoqi zhan juedui youshi, lirun shi minqi 7 bei" (SOEs dominate private enterprises in the 500 top enterprises in China, with a sevenfold gap in profits". Available at http://finance.china.com.cn/news/gnjj/20120903/992916.shtml (accessed 9 August 2014).

[15] Nolan and Wang (1999), Zhang (2004), Aivazian et al. (2005) and Lin and Rowe (2006).

enterprise development and the greater social welfare. For example, Li et al. (2012) and Du and Wang (2013) argue that Chinese SOEs have been highly profitable over the past decade because they enjoy monopolies in upstream industries such as energy, raw materials, banks, and telecommunications, whereas the downstream industries such as manufacturing and other tradable sectors are largely liberalised. As a consequence, in this vertical structure, upstream SOEs are able to accumulate profits by extracting monopoly rents from the downstream private sector businesses. Similarly, a joint report issued by the World Bank and the Development Research Centre of the State Council of China (DRC) also claim that "a disproportionate share of SOE profits comes from a few monopolies that earn artificially high rates of return because of restrictions on competition, while SOEs as a class have enjoyed access to cheaper capital, land and natural resources".[16]

In this chapter, we will elucidate the understanding of the high profitability of China's SOEs by empirically examining how SOEs profit from one such economic policy: financial distortion (or financial repression). Economically, China exhibits typical symptoms of a financially repressed economy, such as regulated interest rates, dominance of state ownership, and managed credit allocation. Consequently, scarce financial resources have been systematically allocated to SOEs at a price that is far lower than it would have been in a more liberalised financial environment. In other words, SOEs in China are profitable simply because they are supported by financial rents created by distorted financial policies, without which it would be difficult or impossible for China's SOEs to survive, not to mention develop or profit.

The remainder of this chapter is organised as follows. Section 2 describes the historical development of China's SOEs. Section 3 discusses the nature of China's financial system. Section 4 empirically examines the connections between financial repression and the profitability of China's SOEs. Finally, Section 5 concludes.

2 SOE Reform in China: Past and Present

Compared with a market economy in which private enterprises play a key role in the provision of goods and services, a planned economy, such as that of pre-reform China, mainly relies on SOEs to transform economic resources into products. Indeed, as Naughton (2007) notes, "state-owned industry was the core of the command economy".[17] During the pre-reform period, Chinese central planners exerted tight control over almost every aspect of industrial production, and SOEs were left with little autonomy to make decisions regarding financing, investment,

[16] World Bank and DRC (2013), p. 105.

[17] Naughton (2007), p. 298.

production, sales, and profit distribution.[18] In addition, SOEs acted as mini-societies, providing lifetime employment and even certain basic services, such as hospitals, schools, pensions, etc., for their employees and their employees' families.

Pre-reform SOEs were highly inefficient because managers and workers operated under distorted incentives.[19] First, with jobs guaranteed and wages untethered from productivity, management had difficulty in motivating workers to work hard. Second, one of the main goals of management was not to maximise profits, but to meet the production targets set by the planning authority, which meant that management had little incentive to increase output beyond targeted amounts; even worse, management was sometimes incentivised to lower production targets by underreporting the enterprise's productive capacity. Third, because management received materials and other required inputs from the planning authority, it had little incentive to manage the use of the inputs economically. Finally, policy burdens, such as generous social welfare benefits to staff, were also blamed for the problems of pre-reform SOEs.[20]

The inefficiencies of the pre-reform system of SOE management and governance stifled improvements in quality and productivity, which stagnated at low levels throughout the 1960s and 1970s.[21] Beginning in the late 1970s, China embarked on a process of SOE reform that was designed to tackle the inefficiencies inherent in SOEs. The reform can be roughly divided into three phases. During the first phase (1979–1992), China attempted to transform SOEs from "work units" integrated in the government bureaucracy into autonomous and profit-oriented commercial entities. Two important experiments were implemented during this period (Li and Brødsgaard 2013). The first was to adopt the policy of "fang quan rang li" (granting power and relinquishing parts of profits) from 1979 to 1986, which aimed at delegating more power to—and leave more profits for—the enterprises. The other was to implement the "chengbao zeranzhi" (contract responsibility system) from 1987 to 1992, which gave managers autonomy and incentivised them to improve efficiency, while holding them accountable for the results. Unfortunately, the contract responsibility system failed to induce increased profitability or efficiency because many of the targets specified in contracts were inadequate or based on flawed measures of economic performance. In general, reform strategies adopted in

[18] As Lin et al. (2003, p. 55) generalise, "[a]ll production materials used by SOEs were supplied by the government through planning, and all their output was sold to and allocated by the state. All revenue was remitted to the state, and all expenditures were approved and allocated by the state...Investments in basic construction, funds for renovating fixed assets and for technological upgrading, expenses for pre-production tests, and funds for miscellaneous capital acquisition were all appropriated by the state...Both workers' recruitment and their wages were arranged by the state according to plan".

[19] Chow (2007), p. 36.

[20] Lin et al. (1998).

[21] Brandt et al. (2008).

this period "appear to have had only a limited effect on the technical efficiency of state enterprises".[22]

During the second phase (1992–2002), China attempted to transform SOEs into modern corporations characterised by clearly defined property rights, clear-cut responsibility and authority, and separation of the functions of government and enterprises. A milestone in this period was the adoption of the Company Law in 1994, which provided a framework for corporatizing SOEs. Over time, a growing number of the (mainly smaller) SOEs were converted into limited liability companies, while other (mainly larger) SOEs became shareholding corporations, all featuring modern corporate governance structures, such as boards of directors that were responsible to shareholders and that supervised the management of enterprise operations. The "zhua da fang xiao" strategy was implemented in 1997—which led to the government retaining control mainly of the large SOEs and letting go of the smaller SOEs—in response to the dire situation described above in which more than 60 % of China's large SOEs were operating at a loss during the mid-1990s. The privatisation of small and unprofitable SOEs occurred on a substantial scale, leading to a massive downsizing of the state sector. Thus, during this period, commentators indicated that "there have been real reforms of the ownership, management, and organization of SOEs that have affected productivity in the state-owned industrial enterprise sector, but these reforms have fallen well short of transforming these enterprises into independent market-oriented firms that behave much like their counterparts in the private or collective sectors".[23]

After Hu Jintao and Wen Jiabao assumed leadership of the government in 2003, Chinese SOE reform entered its third phase with the establishment of the State-owned Assets Supervision and Administration Commission (SASAC), an authority that was established by the State Council in 2003 to undertake the government's functions as investor and owner of state assets. In practice, the SASAC is only charged with the responsibility of supervising the operation of the 113 central SOEs (CSOEs),[24] whereas the other SOEs are supervised by local SASACs. The reform theme of this period can be termed "concentration".[25] In 2006, the SASAC identified seven strategic sectors—defence, electric generation and distribution, petroleum and petrochemicals, telecommunications, coal, civil aviation and waterway transport—in which the state would keep "absolute control". In addition it identified certain "basic" or "pillar" industries—including machinery, automobile

[22] Yusuf et al. (2006), p. 76.

[23] Yusuf et al. (2006), p. 113.

[24] For the complicated role played by the SASAC, see Lin and Milhaupt (2013), who conclude that the SASAC is "simultaneously weaker and more powerful than a typical controlling shareholder in other regimes. It is weaker because it lacks the exclusive power to appoint top management of the most important enterprises whose shares it controls and defers to other agencies – and even to the SOEs themselves – on substantive issues outside its realm of expertise. It is more powerful because of the vast scope of its holdings over the most important firms in the national economy and because of its super control rights, which trump standard corporate law norms, in state enterprise assets".

[25] Li and Brødsgaard (2013).

manufacturing, information technology, construction, steel, base metals, and chemicals—in which the state would retain a "strong influence".[26] China's SOEs are thus concentrated in these strategic and pillar industries in which they enjoy protection from private competition through entry barriers and/or other constraints. The weak and unfair competition resulting from such an administrative monopoly has been deemed one of the most serious problems facing private enterprise in China and the major source of monopolies in China's economy.[27]

SOEs are currently significantly different from what they were 30 years ago when the reforms were first introduced. In particular, the importance of SOEs in the economy has been in constant decline since the mid-1990s. The state sector's share in the total number of industrial enterprises (with annual sales over CNY 5 million) fell from 39.2 % in 1998 to 4.5 % in 2010; during this same period, SOEs' share of total industrial assets dropped from 68.8 to 42.4 %, while their share of total employment decreased from 60.5 to 19.4 %.[28] In addition, the share of SOEs in total national industrial output dropped to 26.2 % in 2011 from 77.6 % in 1978.[29]

Despite these declines, SOEs—and CSOEs, in particular—continue to play a vital role in China's economic development. CSOEs continue to dominate the so-called "strategic" and "pillar" industries, which are regarded as the backbone of the national economy. The power of these CSOEs has been growing in terms of total assets, sales revenue and profits.[30] The total assets of the CSOEs jumped to CNY 28 trillion in 2011 from CNY 7.1 trillion in 2002 on annual growth of 16.4 % during this period. Total revenue earned by these companies increased from CNY 3.4 trillion in 2002 to CNY 22.5 trillion in 2012, with annual growth of 20.9 % during this period. More importantly, the CSOEs have become the most profitable firms in China. The CSOEs generated total profits of up to CNY 1.3 trillion in 2012 compared with CNY 240.6 billion in 2002, based on an average annual growth rate for profits of approximately 18.4 % during this period.

Nevertheless, the impressive performance of CSOES is, in fact, illusory. More accurately speaking, SOEs, particularly CSOEs, are profitable simply because they enjoy a number of subsidies and other forms of preferential treatment from the Chinese government, which has been confirmed by recent studies. For example, a report submitted to the U.S.-China Economic and Security Review Commission in 2009 finds that China's government subsidies to absolute control (i.e. strategic) industries (including armaments, power generation and distribution, oil and petrochemicals, telecommunications, coal, civil aviation, and shipping) and heavyweight (i.e. pillar) industries (including machinery, automobiles, information technology, construction, and iron & steel and non-ferrous metals) in which SOEs dominate are

[26] "Absolute control" is generally understood to be majority ownership, whereas "strong influence" reflects an ownership share of between 30 and 50 %. See Szamosszegi and Kyle (2011).

[27] World Bank and DRC (2013).

[28] World Bank and DRC (2013).

[29] Yu (2014).

[30] Yu (2014).

meaningful: the range of subsidy rates (equal to the total value of the subsidies enjoyed by a firm divided by its sales) is 0.57–44.93 %, the average subsidy rate is 18.6 %, and the median subsidy rate is 14 % (Capital Trade Incorporated 2009).

In 2011, the Unirule Institute of Economics, a Beijing-based independent think tank, issued a report systematically examining the subsidies enjoyed by SOEs during the 2001–2009 period.[31] According to this report, the following four major factors have contributed to huge SOE profits: (1) unpaid rents for nationally owned lands given to SOEs at no cost or very low prices, (2) unpaid rents for nationally owned natural resources (such as oil, natural gas and coal) that were extracted by SOEs at very low prices, (3) cheap loans and credit from state-owned banks, and (4) direct governmental fiscal subsidies. Table 1 shows that from 2001 to 2009, SOEs paid CNY 682.7 billion less, on average, than what they should have paid out as expenses annually. In total, for the 9 years from 2001 to 2009, CNY 6144.3 billion was not paid out as expenses but was instead appropriated by SOEs and included in their nominal profits.[32] If the benefits derived from governmental policies favouring SOEs were deducted from their nominal profits, the real profits of Chinese SOEs were in fact negative in 5 years from 2001 to 2009 (Table 2).

Chinese citizens, who are the nominal owners of these SOEs, can hardly benefit from these profits, whether they are real or nominal.[33] The Chinese government collected low or no dividends from SOEs before 2007, when the State Council began requiring CSOEs to begin paying dividends that ranged from 0 to 10 % of net profits. In 2011, SOE dividend rates were increased by 5 % across the board and now range from 5 to 15 %. These rates, however, remain far below average dividend rates paid by established industrial firms in the United States (50–60 %) and the average dividend rates paid by SOEs in a group of five developed economies (33 %). Moreover, the dividend rates paid by CSOEs to the government in its capacity as shareholder are lower than those paid to private shareholders by Chinese SOEs that are listed in Hong Kong. Most importantly, virtually all the dividends paid by SOEs to the government are eventually recycled back to the SOEs: more than 92 % of the dividends paid by CSOEs to the government in 2012 were remitted back to SOEs as subsidies.

[31] Unirule Institute of Economics (2011).

[32] It is notable that this figure does not include the unpaid rents for other natural resources such as ferrous and nonferrous metals as well as license fees for telecommunication resources such as 3G networks.

[33] World Bank (2009) and Milhaupt and Zheng (2014).

Table 1 Benefits accruing to Chinese SOEs because of government favouritism, 2001–2009 (CNY millions)

	2001	2002	2003	2004	2005	2006	2007	2008	2009
Unpaid land rents	291,689	275,570	272,736	265,916	258,466	257,433	289,022	295,382	372,528
Unpaid resource rents (oil)	16,519	16,143	18,896	24,994	40,969	30,538	28,897	25,084	41,633
Unpaid resource rents (gas)	873	974	1073	1321	1755	2061	2503	3334	3676
Unpaid resource rents (coal)	11,527	13,795	15,062	18,393	25,483	28,595	34,974	42,354	46,201
Lower bank interest rates	217,983	220,101	208,670	309,186	235,078	275,565	350,914	482,184	454,169
Fiscal subsidies	26,176	21,401	19,404	18,198	16,657	18,022	17,757	95,551	80,957
Total	564,767	547,984	535,841	638,008	578,408	612,214	724,067	943,889	999,164

Source: Unirule Institute of Economics (2011)

Table 2 Nominal and real profits of Chinese SOEs (CNY million)

	2001	2002	2003	2004	2005	2006	2007	2008	2009
Nominal profits	238,856	263,294	383,620	545,310	651,975	848,546	1,079,519	906,359	928,703
Real profits	−325,934	−284,726	−152,244	−92,657	73,967	248,197	365,402	82,625	−207,480

Source: Unirule Institute of Economics (2011)

3 China's Financial Repression

Financial repression, according to Ito (2008), refers to "the notion that a set of government regulations, laws, and other non-market restrictions prevent the financial intermediaries of an economy from functioning at their full capacity". Policies that result in financial repression include interest rate ceilings, liquidity ratio requirements, high bank reserve requirements, capital controls, restrictions on market entry into the financial sector, credit ceilings or restrictions on the direction of credit allocation, and government ownership or control of banks.

Financial repression theory has its origins in the work of McKinnon (1973) and Shaw (1973), who argue that many countries—primarily developing countries but also some developed countries—have historically restricted competition in the financial sector through government intervention and regulation. Thus, these authors maintain that a repressed financial sector discourages both savings and investment because the rates of return are lower than what might otherwise be obtained in a competitive market. In such a system, financial intermediaries do not function at full capacity and fail to channel savings efficiently into investments, thereby impeding overall economic development.

China's financial system conforms to the stereotype described by financial repression theory. For example, Huang and Wang (2011) argue that "despite more than 30 years' economic reform, the Chinese economy still possesses the typical characteristics of financial repression: heavily regulated interest rates, state-influenced credit allocation, frequently adjusted reserve requirements and tightly controlled capital accounts".[34] Johansson (2012) also claims that repressive financial policies constitute a central problem in the Chinese economic system.

Interest rate controls stand out as the most salient component of the Chinese version of financial repression. China's central bank, the People's Bank of China (PBOC), maintains a cap on deposit rates for all financial institutions and, until 20 July 2013, also maintained a floor on loan rates. More importantly, the central bank appears to adjust the benchmark interest rates asymmetrically in response to inflation and is thus quicker to adjust deposit and lending rates downward than upward.[35] When inflation rises, interest rate rigidity leads to lower or even negative real interest rates, and this trend has become more pronounced since 2004.[36]

The direct result of the central bank's approach to setting nominal interest rates is that household interest earnings, on average, have been far lower than they would have been in a more liberalised financial environment in which market forces play a major role in determining interest rates. By contrast, enterprises—particularly SOEs—appear to be the major beneficiaries of interest rate controls. Ma and Yi (2010) find that net interest payments as a share of GDP by the non-financial corporate sector dropped by 50 % between 1992 and 2007. The low cost of

[34] Huang and Wang (2011), p. 834.

[35] Liu et al. (2009).

[36] Lardy (2012).

financing has led to a significant increase in the profitability of enterprises since the early 1990s. The ratio of profits to industrial value added rose from an average of 22.6 % during the 1995–1999 period to 34.4 % in 2008; similarly, the share of enterprise income in GDP rose from 14.2 % in the second half of the 1990s to 22.9 % in 2008.[37] SOEs, in particular, benefit disproportionately from such financial repression. For example, Ferri and Liu (2010) show that the costs of financing for SOEs are significantly lower than for other companies, particularly than for private enterprises; if SOEs had to pay the same interest rates as private enterprises, their current profits would be wiped out entirely.

In addition to interest rate controls, China's economy suffers from other financial repression policies, namely, credit misallocation, the dominance of state ownership, and exchange rate distortion. Credit misallocation means that scarce financial resources have been systematically and continually allocated to less profitable but more politically preferable ventures, particularly SOEs, whereas private firms—which have become the driving force behind China's economic growth—are forced to rely on informal and even underground credit channels to finance their survival.

After several decades of economic reform, China's non-state sector has replaced SOEs as the key driver of China's economic growth.[38] However, entities in the non-state sector, private enterprises in particular, have been intentionally discriminated against in terms of credit access and availability. For example, Huang (2006) shows that domestic private firms in China are among the most financially constrained in the world. In addition, Brandt and Zhu (2007) find that over the 1998–2003 period, the state sector, which is defined to include companies in which governments have significant ownership shares, continued to absorb between one-half and two-thirds of new bank lending. According to the Report on the Development of Private Economy in China 2008–2009, the narrow private sector (i.e., domestic privately owned and individual businesses) accounted for only 7.4–13.5 % of the total bank loans issued from 2002 to 2008.[39]

The argument that the private sector is financially disfavoured in China is further supported by empirical studies. For example, based on the set covering more than 20,000 Chinese firms over the 1998–2005 period, Poncet et al. (2010) find that private firms, in contrast to SOEs, relied significantly on cash flow to finance their investments, which is evidence of credit constraints. Guo et al. (2014) find that private firms continue to face serious difficulties in securing bank loans, even after the Communist Party of China (CPC) changed its attitude from anti-capitalist to pro-capitalist in 2002.

Internal and informal finance, such as retained earnings, trade credit, and private loans, have played a disproportionately important role in financing the growth of private firms.[40] Whereas internal financing and informal lending might be expected

[37] Yang (2012).

[38] World Bank and DRC (2013).

[39] http://www.china.com.cn/news/zhuanti/09myjjlps/2009-09/28/content_18621412.htm.

[40] Huang (2003), Allen et al. (2005), Héricourt and Poncet (2009) and Poncet et al. (2010).

to help private entrepreneurs start their businesses, the continued growth of private firms will finally outstrip the support offered by these informal financial mechanisms. Without access to formal financing, private firms will inevitably be trapped in an inefficient state of small size, simple and outmoded technologies, and short life spans.[41] Given the importance of private firms in driving China's economic growth, their uncertain future might endanger the long-term sustainability of the economy.

China has the highest level of bank ownership by the state of any major economy in the world. According to Barth et al. (2006), 87 countries had some level of governmental bank ownership at the end of 2001.[42] However, in only 15 of these 87 countries did the percentage of bank-owned assets at government-owned banks exceed 50 %, and China was identified as having the highest level of government ownership with 98 % of total bank assets held by state-owned banks. China's state domination of the banking sector also stands in contrast to the experience of Eastern European transitional economies and other emerging markets. The McKinsey Global Institute (2006) shows that state-controlled banks accounted for 83 % of bank assets in China in 2004, compared with 33 % in Brazil, 18 % in South Korea, 20 % in Poland, and 16 % in Chile. Similarly, Deng et al. (2011) claim that 18 of the 20 largest banks in China are directly state-controlled and accounted for CNY 58.58 trillion—approximately 73 % of total bank assets—at the end of 2009.

State ownership has long been argued to be detrimental to financial development, and the China seems to be no exception to this proposition.[43] For example, using Chinese provincial data from 1991 to 1997, Park and Sehrt (2001) find that economic fundamentals such as industrial growth, agricultural growth, and GDP per capita have had little effect on total lending by state banks, whereas the responsiveness of lending to policy concerns, such as SOE output, is significant. Based on data from 1997 to 2004, Podpiera (2006) reports that the pricing of credit risk by state-owned banks remains undifferentiated and that bank lending decisions continue to be driven by the availability of funds and do not appear to consider enterprise profitability. In addition, compared with joint-stock banks, state-owned banks are less profitable,[44] less prudent in their lending,[45] and less X-efficient.[46]

In fact, at one time, China's state-owned banks accumulated huge amounts of non-performing loans (NPLs), which drove the banking sector to the verge of bankruptcy by the end of 1990s. Using officially published data, Allen et al. (2008) compare NPLs in China, the United States, and other major Asian economies from 1998 to 2006 and report that, measured as a fraction of GDP, China's NPLs are the largest in the group from 2000 to 2006, reaching levels as high as

[41] Huang (2006).

[42] Barth et al. (2006), pp. 148–149.

[43] World Bank (2001) and La Porta et al. (2002).

[44] Ferri (2008).

[45] Jia (2008).

[46] Fu and Heffernan (2007).

20.0–22.5 % of GDP (in 2000 and 2001). The NPL problem appears to have been mitigated since that time, and China's banking sector has thus been strengthened since 2006, at least according to officially reported figures. However, this improvement should primarily be attributed to government aid in the form of recapitalisation of bad loans, the transfer of bad loans from banks to asset management companies, and rapid expansion in bank lending as a response to recent economic prosperity. However, without fundamental changes, the NPL problem faced by state-owned banks may recur and even worsen if economic conditions deteriorate.

Finally, China's currency policy has regularly been criticised for pursuing a type of mercantile advantage by devaluing the RMB and stimulating exports. For example, Goldstein and Lardy (2008) conclude that "any methodology that defines the equilibrium exchange rate for the renminbi as the real effective exchange rate that would produce 'balance' in China's global current account position, or in its basic balance, or in its overall balance-of-payment position, yields the qualitative conclusion that the renminbi is significantly undervalued and most likely by an increasing margin over time". Similarly, a report issued by the International Monetary Fund (IMF) claims that "the renminbi remains moderately undervalued against a broad basket of currencies".[47]

Maintaining an inflexible exchange rate over long periods requires a large set of distortionary policies. For example, Prasad (2009) shows that China's monetary policy independence has been severely weakened by its undervalued currency strategy. More specifically, because of this currency undervaluation, the volume of exports continually increases, capital inflows steadily grow, and there has been a dramatic accumulation of foreign exchange reserves. To sterilise the liquidity generated by this growth pattern (and to address the corresponding inflation problem), the PBOC must set interest rates administratively at very low levels such that its sterilisation costs can be minimised and speculative capital inflows discouraged. Distorted interest rates will lead, in turn, to inefficient consequences.

The influence of financial repression, particularly interest rate distortion, has been tested by numerous empirical studies, and many of these have identified a negative association between interest rate repression and certain fundamental macroeconomic variables, such as savings rates, investment, and economic growth.[48] Other financial repression policies, such as entry restrictions and state ownership in the banking sector, have also proven harmful to financial development.[49]

Several empirical studies show that financial repression has also been harmful to China's economic growth. For example, Boyreau-Debray (2003) finds that the ratio of state-owned bank credit to GDP has a negative impact on provincial economic growth and that this negative impact is largely a consequence of the burden of supporting the state-owned sector. Similarly, Guariglia and Poncet (2008) report

[47] IMF (2013).

[48] Fry (1978, 1997) and Roubini and Sala-i-Martin (1992).

[49] Barth et al. (2006) and World Bank (2001).

that the indicators measuring the level of state interventionism in China's finance sector—such as the share of state-owned banks in total bank credit or the ratio of total state-owned bank credit to GDP—are negatively associated with GDP growth, physical capital accumulation, and productivity growth. However, other studies find that the role of financial repression is more complicated. Huang and Wang (2011) show that the connection between financial repression and economic growth is changeable: financial repression initially promoted economic growth in the 1980s and 1990s but has inhibited economic growth over the past decade. Xu and Gui (2013) demonstrate that China's repressed financial system acts as a double-edged sword: on the one hand, the system helps China accomplish extraordinary economic growth by subsidising investment and production, while on the other hand, it endangers China's economic health by hindering efficiency, slowing job creation, and distorting the country's economic structure.

4 Financial Repression and the Profitability of SOEs: An Empirical Examination

4.1 A Rough Estimate of Rents from Financial Repression

We will first estimate the rents that SOEs obtain from financial repression. As we have discussed above, interest rates are lowered intentionally as part of the policies of financial repression, and cheap credit is allocated to SOEs and other entities favoured by the Chinese government; consequently, rents are created and then distributed to the beneficiaries of such financial repression policies. The rents from financial repression can be expressed as the volume of credit multiplied by the difference between the loan cost that firms should pay under a normal market environment and the loan cost that firms actually pay under financial repression, which thus leads to the following equation:

$$\begin{aligned}\text{Rents} &= \text{balance of bank loans} \times \text{interest spread} \\ &= \text{balance of bank loans} \\ &\quad \times (\text{market interest rate} - \text{statutory interest rate})\end{aligned} \tag{1}$$

Because the China Statistical Yearbook does not classify loan data according to the ownership of enterprises, we cannot directly obtain the data regarding the balance of bank loans extended to SOEs. We therefore must use a method similar to that used by Yin and Xu (2011) to estimate the ratio of loans extended to SOEs to total loans made:

$$\begin{aligned}&\text{the ratio of loans extended to SOEs to the overall loans}\\&\quad=\big(\text{short-term loans} - \text{loans extended to agriculture}\\&\qquad-\text{loans extended to Township and Village Enterprises}(TVEs)\\&\qquad-\text{loans extended to foreign-funded enterprises}\\&\qquad-\text{loans extended to private enterprises and self-employed individuals}\big)/\\&\qquad\;(\text{short-term loans}).\end{aligned}\tag{2}$$

Because the China Statistical Yearbook no longer reports disaggregated data on short-term loans after 2010, we use the moving average method to estimate the ratio of loans extended to SOEs to total loans made from 2010 to 2012. The one-year lending rate is calculated according to the PBOC's benchmark lending rates.[50] If there were interest rate adjustments in a given year, the mean value of the interest rate during that year will be calculated and accepted as the interest rate for that year. We use the GDP deflator to measure overall price changes (inflation rate). The GDP deflator is calculated from nominal and real GDP data, which can be obtained from the China Statistical Yearbook. The real statutory interest rate equals the nominal interest rate (one-year lending rate) minus the inflation rate.

It is a considerably difficult task to estimate the real market interest rate, which is typically assumed to be 10 %.[51] However, according to Caprio et al. (1996), financial repression would most likely drive down interest rates by two percentage points. We define the difference between 10 % and the real statutory interest rate as spread 1 and 2 % as spread 2, respectively. The basic data are shown in Tables 3 and 4.

If we assume that the real market interest rate is 10 %, it is obvious that the rents from financial repression are greater than the profits earned by SOEs in most years. The financial repression rents remain more than 30 % of the profits earned by SOEs when 2 % is taken as the interest rate spread in most years.

4.2 The Regression Model

Given the availability of the data, we use the data of "state owned and state holding industrial enterprises" as an alternative to the data of overall SOEs.[52] The time span of our analysis is from 1999 to 2011 because the China Statistical Yearbook did not report economic indicators of each industry according to registration type (state-owned and state-holding industrial enterprises, foreign-funded enterprises, etc.) until 1999.

There are 39 industries in the industrial sector. After excluding three industries in which the data are incomplete (Mining of Other Ores, Manufacture of Artwork

[50] See "benchmark lending rates of financial institutions", available at: http://www.pbc.gov.cn/publish/zhengcehuobisi/631/2012/20120706181352694274852/20120706181352694274852_.html.

[51] Gu et al. (2006).

[52] A similar method is used by Unirule Institute of Economics in its 2011 report.

Table 3 Balance of bank loans, interest rates, and inflation rate in China from 1997 to 2012

Year	Balance of bank loans	Ratio of loans extended to SOEs to total loans	Balance of bank loans extended to SOEs	Nominal interest rate	Inflation rate	Real statutory interest rate	Real market interest rate
1997	74,914.1	81.5	61,055	9.36	1.52	7.84	10
1998	86,524.1	79.3	68,613.6	7.47	−0.89	8.36	10
1999	93,734.3	78.1	73,206.5	6.12	−1.27	7.39	10
2000	99,371.1	78.7	78,205	5.85	2.03	3.82	10
2001	112,314.7	77.1	86,594.6	5.85	2.05	3.8	10
2002	131,293.9	77.9	102,278	5.58	0.6	4.98	10
2003	158,996.2	77.7	123,540.1	5.31	2.59	2.72	10
2004	178,197.8	76.8	136,855.9	5.45	6.93	−1.48	10
2005	194,690.4	75.5	146,991.2	5.58	3.92	1.66	10
2006	225,347.2	78.4	176,672.2	5.85	3.81	2.04	10
2007	261,690.9	78.5	205,427.3	6.81	7.64	−0.82	10
2008	303,394.6	78.1	236,951.2	6.53	7.76	−1.24	10
2009	399,685	77.6	310,155.6	5.31	−0.61	5.92	10
2010	479,196	77.1	369,460.1	5.56	6.64	−1.08	10
2011	547,947	76.6	419,727.4	6.19	7.8	−1.62	10
2012	629,947	76.1	479,389.7	6.29	1.89	4.4	10

Source: China Statistical Yearbook

and Other Manufacturing, and Recycling and Disposal of Waste), we construct a panel data set that consists of 36 industries over 13 years.

The specification of the model is as follows:

$$s\_profit_{i,t} = \beta_0 + \beta_1 reali_t + \beta_2 dloan_t + \beta_3 markup_{i,t} + \beta_4 output_{i,t} + \beta_5 growth_t + \beta_6 crisis_t + u_i + \varepsilon_{i,t} \quad (3)$$

In this model, $i = 1, 2 \ldots 36$, representing each of the 36 industries that will be examined in this study. Variable $t = 1, 2 \ldots 13$, representing each year from 1999 to 2011. s_profit indicates the profits of SOEs and is calculated in terms of fixed 1999 prices. The variables we employ are as follows, where the first two are explanatory variables, and the remainder are control variables (Table 5).

1. The real statutory interest rate for each year (*reali*) is the first explanatory variable. Because we assume that real market interest rates remain unchanged, the interest spread (which equals the real market interest rate minus the real statutory interest rate) can be measured by the level of *reali*. The lower that *reali* is, the more severe the financial repression and the higher the financial repression rents. We expect that *reali* will be inversely proportional to SOEs' profits.
2. The annual increment of credit (*dloan*) is the second explanatory variable. Because most of the cheap credit is extended to SOEs, a higher increment of

Table 4 Interest rate spread, financial repression rents, and profits of SOEs in China from 1997 to 2012

Year	Spread (1)	Spread (2)	Financial repression rents (1)	Financial repression rents (2)	Profits of SOEs	Ratio of financial repression rents to profits of SOEs (10 %) (1)	Ratio of financial repression rents to profits of SOEs (2 %) (2)
1997	2.16	2	1316.17	1221.1	791.2	166.35	154.34
1998	1.64	2	1126.01	1372.27	213.7	526.91	642.15
1999	2.61	2	1908.31	1464.13	1145.8	166.55	127.78
2000	6.18	2	4835.2	1564.1	2833.8	170.63	55.19
2001	6.2	2	5371.1	1731.89	2811.2	191.06	61.61
2002	5.02	2	5135.1	2045.56	3786.3	135.62	54.03
2003	7.28	2	8991.09	2470.8	4769.4	188.52	51.81
2004	11.48	2	15,714.27	2737.12	7368.8	213.25	37.14
2005	8.34	2	12,259.63	2939.82	9579.9	127.97	30.69
2006	7.96	2	14,058.1	3533.44	12,193.5	115.29	28.98
2007	10.82	2	22,233.67	4108.55	17,441.8	127.47	23.56
2008	11.24	2	26,630.38	4739.02	13,335.2	199.7	35.54
2009	4.08	2	12,665.93	6203.11	15,606.8	81.16	39.75
2010	11.08	2	40,931.45	7389.2	21,428.2	191.02	34.48
2011	11.62	2	48,770.93	8394.55	24,669.8	197.69	34.03
2012	5.6	2	26,853.5	9587.79	24,277.3	110.61	39.49

Source: China Statistical Yearbook

credit means that SOEs will receive more subsidies. We use the GDP deflator to convert the annual increment of credit into values expressed in constant 1999 prices. We expect that this indicator will be positively proportional to SOEs' profits.

3. Our first control variable is the price mark-up indicator (*markup*), which is a ratio with a numerator that is the "producer price indices for industrial products by sector" and a denominator that is the "purchasing price indices for industrial producers". This ratio reflects a firm's pricing power and is used to characterise the degree of monopoly in certain industries. We expect this indicator to be positively proportional to firms' profits, regardless of whether they are SOEs.
4. The gross industrial output value (output) variable is used to describe certain industries' scale of output. In general, the larger the scale of a firm's production, the lower its average costs will be. We also use the "producer price indices for industrial products by sector" to convert this indicator into values expressed in constant 1999 prices. We expect that this indicator will be positively proportional to firms' profits, regardless of whether they are SOEs.
5. The nationwide annual GDP growth rate (*gdp*) is the next control variable. The profits of enterprises are influenced by the economy and will increase with GDP

growth and decrease during recessions. Therefore, we expect this indicator to be positively proportional to firms' profits, regardless of whether they are SOEs.

6. We employ a dummy variable for the financial crisis of 2008 (*crisis*), which hit China's economy seriously. Thus, we need a dummy variable to capture its exogenous shock. The variable is set to 1 in 2008 and 0 in other years. We expect this indicator to be inversely proportional to firms' profits, regardless of whether they are SOEs.

Before conducting a panel regression, we run stationarity tests on the variables. The approach of Maddala and Wu (1999) is used to perform an augmented Dickey-Fuller (ADF) unit root test on the variables. We choose a maximum lag of 6 years and use the Schwarz information criterion (SIC) to choose the optimal lag items. A model with an intercept and trend is employed. The results show that the variables are stationary, and the *p*-values of the Chi-square statistics are less than 0.01.

Moreover, to avoid endogeneity, we include a one-period lag of *dloan* as the instrumental variable. Given the large differences that may exist among different industries, we integrate the individual effects into the model and perform a Hausman test to determine whether to choose random effects or fixed effects for the analysis. The Hausman test rejects the null hypothesis that the regressors are exogenous, and we thus choose the fixed effects model.

The regression results are shown in "Model 1: s_profit" of Table 6.

The results from model 1 in Table 6 show that the profits of SOEs tend to decrease when the real statutory interest rates increase (which can be argued to reflect the relaxation of financial repression), and this effect is significant at the 5 % level. By contrast, although the expansion of credit has a positive impact on the profits of SOEs, the impact is not statistically significant. The reason for this result may be explained by the following: although the expansion of credit leads to more financial repression rents granted to SOEs, their general level of profits may be driven down by projects with low yields that are attracted to the credit market by the easy credit.

As expected, the price markup indicator, the gross industrial output value, and overall GDP growth all contribute to increased SOE profits. The financial crisis of 2008 negatively affected SOE profits, but the impact is not statistically significant.

To further reveal the impact of financial repression on SOE profits, we construct the following model (model 2):

$$diff_{i,t} = \beta_0 + \beta_1 reali_t + \beta_2 dloan_t + \beta_5 growth_t + \beta_6 crisis_t + u_i + \varepsilon_{i,t} \quad (4)$$

In this model, *diff* is the difference between the profits of SOEs and those of foreign-funded enterprises in the 36 industries from 1999 to 2011. In general, an increase in interest rates will decrease the profits of enterprises, but this effect will be more significant for SOEs who benefit disproportionately from financial repression policies. Therefore, the difference between the profits of SOEs and those of foreign-funded enterprises should be narrowed with increased interest rates. SOEs

Table 5 Description of variables

Variables	Variable definition	Mean	Median	S.D.	Min	Max	Obs.
s_profit	Profits of SOEs	147.84	21.56	375.02	−933.24	3123.92	468
f_profit	Profits of foreign-funded enterprises	119.18	48.85	204.14	−65.99	1895.1	468
diff	Profits of SOEs minus profits of foreign-funded enterprises	28.66	−19.2	365.65	−918.17	2824.35	468
reali	The real statutory interest rates	2.01	2.04	2.96	−1.62	7.39	13
dloan	Annual increment of credit	26,304.09	24,731.44	17,366.93	5524.49	67,376.81	13
markup	Price markup indicator	0.99	0.97	0.07	0.72	1.52	468
output	Gross industrial output value	2597.11	820.23	4909.57	22.12	40,566.62	468
growth	Annual GDP growth rate	10.02	9.63	1.75	7.62	14.16	13

Source: China Statistical Yearbook

Table 6 Panel regression results

Explanatory variables	Model 1:s_profit		Model 2:diff	
reali	−9.41** (4.15)	−7.64** (3.65)	−0.35* (0.20)	−0.25* (0.13)
dloan	0.001 (0.001)		0.001* (0.0006)	0.001* (0.0006)
markup	267.44* (150.61)	229.88* (139.69)		
output	0.03*** (0.003)	0.03*** (0.003)		
growth	10.53* (5.89)	12.25** (5.76)	10.53* (6.21)	10.92* (5.97)
crisis	−28.31 (34.44)		−7.54 (36.32)	
adj. R^2	0.25	0.26	0.15	0.17
obs.	468	468	468	468

Notes: the numbers in parentheses are standard errors. ***, ** and * indicate 1 %, 5 % and 10 % levels of significance, respectively. For each regression model, we report two types of results: the first contains the initial regression results with all the explanatory variables included, and the second contains the regression results with significant explanatory variables

benefit much more from credit expansion than foreign-funded enterprises, and the difference between the profits of SOEs and those of foreign-funded enterprises should thus be enlarged with expanded credit. The price markup indicator and the gross industrial output value are not included in the model because they are industry-level indicators and should not influence the profits of various types of enterprises differently. Given the inherent inefficiencies of SOEs, we assume that SOEs are more susceptible to the macroeconomic climate and to external shocks. We therefore include the GDP growth indicator and the dummy variable of the financial crisis in the regression equation, and we expect that GDP growth contributes to firm profitability whereas the financial crisis damages SOE profitability.

The variable *differ* passes the unit root test, and the Hausman test rejects the null hypothesis that the regressors are exogenous. We therefore choose the fixed effects model. The regression results are shown in "Model 2: differ" in Table 6.

Model 2 in Table 6 shows that when the real statutory interest rates increase (a sign of relaxing financial repression), SOE profits decrease more than those of foreign-funded enterprises, leading to a narrowed gap between the former and the latter. By contrast, SOE profits increase more than those of foreign-funded enterprises with expanded credit, leading to a wider gap between the former and the latter.

As expected, SOEs are more susceptible to the macroeconomic climate and to external shocks. Economic prosperity is more likely to lead to a greater increase in SOE profits and therefore a wider gap between the profits of SOEs and those of foreign-funded enterprises. Similarly, the financial crisis has a stronger negative influence on SOE profits.

5 Concluding Remarks

China's SOEs have become extraordinarily profitable in recent years. Unfortunately, this development cannot be relied on as evidence to show that SOEs in China have been successfully transformed into commercial entities that are as vigorous, competitive, and efficient as private enterprises. The truth is simple. As we have demonstrated in this chapter, most of the profits earned by Chinese SOEs result from distorted economic policies, such as financial repression policies, that generate enormous economic rents that only SOEs (or other politically favoured entities) enjoy. Without the support of these policies and the subsequent economic rents, China's SOEs may already be insolvent or even bankrupt in the process of marketisation.

Distorted economic policies, such as financial repression policies, are therefore key to understanding the unusual profitability of China's SOEs. However, as we have previously shown elsewhere, these policies are harmful to China's economic health in the long run: they damage economic efficiency, slow job creation, and distort the country's economic structure.[53] In addition, private enterprises, which have become the driving force of China's economic growth, are intentionally discriminated against in an environment characterised by financial repression and must rely on internal financing and informal lending to support their development. Therefore, it might be argued that the profits of Chinese SOEs are earned at the expense of the development of private enterprises, and the continuous high profitability of China's SOEs can be understood as a symptom of a distorted level playing field in China.

A market-oriented financial reform is called for to pave the way for China to transform its economy to become more sustainable by such means as liberalising interest rates and eliminating credit discrimination against private enterprise. Such policies, however, will inevitably face political obstacles from powerful interest groups, such as SOEs, who benefit disproportionately from the current distorted financial environment. SOEs, particularly those CSOEs who act as "national champions" in sectors of strategic importance, play an important role in shaping China's economic policies and regulations.[54] The prospects for China's financial reform (liberalisation) are therefore not promising. Unless the Chinese government changes its attitude toward SOEs, and SOEs thus lose their influence in the political arena, it seems unlikely that the SOE-friendly but efficiency-damaging financial system will be changed in the near future.

[53] Xu (2014) and Xu and Gui (2013).

[54] Brødsgaard (2012) and Wang (2014).

References

Aivazian VA, Ge Y, Qiu J (2005) Can corporatization improve the performance of state-owned enterprises even without privatization? J Corporate Finance 11:791–808

Allen F, Qian J, Qian M (2008) China's financial system: past, present, and future. In: Brandt L, Rawski TG (eds) China's great economic transformation. Cambridge University Press, Cambridge

Allen F, Qian J, Qian M (2005) Law, finance, and economic growth in China. J Financial Econ 77:57–116

Barth JR, Caprio G Jr, Ross L (2006) Rethinking bank regulation: till Angles govern. Cambridge University Press, New York

Boyreau-Debray G (2003) Financial intermediation and growth: Chinese style. World Bank Policy Research working paper no. 3027

Brandt L, Zhu X (2007) China's banking sector and economic growth. In: Calomiris C (ed) China's financial transition at a crossroads. Columbia University Press, New York

Brandt L, Rawski TG, Sutton J (2008) China's industrial development. In: Brandt L, Rawski GT (eds) China's great economic transformation. Cambridge University Press, Cambridge

Brødsgaard KE (2012) Politics and business group formation in China: the party in control? China Q 211:624–648

Capital Trade Incorporated (2009) An assessment of China's subsidies to strategic and heavy-weight industries. Report prepared for the U.S.-China Economic and Security Review Commission. http://origin.www.uscc.gov/sites/default/files/Research/AnAssessmentofChina%27sSubsidiestoStrategicandHeavyweightIndustries.pdf. Accessed 18 Aug 2014

Caprio G Jr, Atiyas I, Hanson JA (1996) Financial reform: theory and experience. Cambridge University Press, New York

Chow GC (2007) China's economic transformation, 2nd edn. Blackwell, Malden

Deng Y, Morck R, Wu J, Bernard Y (2011) Monetary and fiscal stimuli, ownership structure, and China's housing market. NBER working paper, 16871

Djankov S, Murrell P (2002) Enterprise restructuring in transition: a quantitative survey. J Econ Lit 40:739–792

Djankov S, Glaeser E, La Porta R, Lopez-de-Silanes F, Shleifer A (2003) The new comparative economics. J Comp Econ 31:595–619

Du J, Wang Y (2013) Reforming SOEs under China's state capitalism. In: Zhang J (ed) Unfinished reforms in the Chinese economy. World Scientific, Singapore

Ferri G (2008) Are new tigers supplanting old mammoths in China's banking system? Evidence from a sample of city commercial banks. J Bank Finance 33(1):131–140

Ferri G, Liu L (2010) Honor Thy creditors Beforan Thy shareholders: are the profits of Chinese state-owned enterprises real. Asian Econ Pap 9(3):50–71

Fry MJ (1978) Money and capital or financial deepening in economic development. J Money Credit Bank 10(4):464–475

Fry MJ (1997) In favour of financial liberalisation. Econ J 107:754–770

Fu X, Heffernan S (2007) Cost X-efficiency in China's banking sector. China Econ Rev 18:35–53

Goldstein M, Lardy NR (2008) China's exchange rate policy: an overview of some key issues. In: Goldstein M, Lardy NR (eds) Debating China's Exchange Rate Policy. Peterson Institute for International Economics, Washington

Grossman SJ, Hart O (1986) The costs and benefits of ownership: a theory of vertical and lateral integration. J Polit Econ 94:691–719

Gu H, Shi H, Liu W (2006) woguo yinhang daikuan lilv de jiegouxing fenxi (A structural analysis of the banks' lending rates in China). xueshu yanjiu (Acad Res) 3:62–65

Guariglia A, Poncet S (2008) Could financial distortions be no impediment to economic growth after all? Evidence from China. J Comp Econ 36:633–657

Guo D, Jiang K, Kim B-Y, Xu C (2014) Political economy of private firms in China. J Comp Econ 42:286–303

Hart O (1995) Firm, contracts, and financial structure. Oxford University Press, Oxford
Hart O, Moore J (1990) Property rights and the nature of the firm. J Polit Econ 98:1119–1158
Hart O, Shleifer A, Vishny R (1997) The proper scope of government: theory and an application to prisons. Q J Econ 112:1127–1161
Héricourt J, Poncet S (2009) FDI and credit constraints: firm-level evidence from China. Econ Syst 33:1–21
Hovey M, Naughton T (2007) A survey of enterprise reforms in China: the way forward. Econ Syst 31:138–156
Huang Y (2003) Selling China: foreign direct investment during the reform era. Cambridge University Press, New York
Huang Y (2006) Do financing biases matter for the Chinese economy? Cato J 26(2):287–306
Huang Y, Wang X (2011) Does financial repression inhibit or facilitate economic growth? A case study of Chinese reform experience. Oxf Bull Econ Stat 73(6):833–855
IMF (2013) People's Republic of China: staff report for the 2013 Article IV consultation. IMF Country report no. 13/211. http://www.imf.org/external/pubs/ft/scr/2013/cr13211.pdf. Accessed 28 Jan 2014
Ito H (2008) Financial repression. In: Reinert K, Ramkishen R (eds) The Princeton encyclopedia of the world economy. Princeton University Press, Princeton
Jia C (2008) The effect of ownership on the prudential behavior of banks-the case of China. J Bank Finance 38(1):77–87
Johansson AC (2012) Financial repression and China's economic imbalances. In: Mckay H, Song L (eds) Rebalancing and sustaining growth in China. ANU E-Press, Canberra
Kornai J (1992) The socialist system: the political economy of communism. Princeton University Press, Princeton
La Porta R, Lopez-de-Silanes F, Shleifer A (2002) Government ownership of banks. J Finance 57:265–301
Lardy NR (2012) Sustaining China's economic growth after the global financial crisis. Peterson Institute for International Economics, Washington
Li X, Brødsgaard KE (2013) SOE reform in China: past, present, and future. Copenhagen J Asian Stud 31(2):54–78
Li X, Liu X, Wang Y (2012) A model of China's state capitalism. Hong Kong University of Science and Technology Working Paper. http://papers.ssrn.com/sol3/papers.cfm?abstract_id=2061521. Accessed 20 May 2014
Lin L-W, Milhaupt CJ (2013) We are the (national) champions: understanding the mechanisms of state capitalism in China. Stanford Law Rev 65(4):697–759
Lin S, Rowe W (2006) Determinants of the profitability of China's regional SOEs. China Econ Rev 17:120–141
Lin JY, Cai F, Li Z (1998) Competition, policy burdens, and state-owned enterprise reform. Am Econ Rev 88(2):422–427 (Papers and Proceedings)
Lin JY, Cai F, Li Z (2003) The China miracle: development strategy and economic reform. The Chinese University Press, Hong Kong
Liu M-H, Margaritis D, Tourani-Rad A (2009) Monetary policy and interest rate rigidity in China. Appl Financial Econ 19:647–657
Ma G, Yi W (2010) China's high saving rate: myth and reality. Int Econ 122:5–39
Maddala GS, Wu S (1999) A comparative study of unit root tests with panel data and a new simple test. Oxf Bull Econ Stat 61:631–652
McKinnon RI (1973) Money and capital in economic development. Brookings Institution, Washington
McKinsey Global Institute (2006) Putting China's capital to work: the value of financial system reform. http://www.mckinsey.com/Insights/MGI/Research/Financial_Markets/Putting_Chinas_capital_to_work. Accessed 28 Jan 2014
Megginson WL, Netter JM (2001) From state to market: a survey of empirical studies on privatization. J Econ Lit 39:321–389

Milhaupt CJ, Zheng W (2014) Beyond ownership: state capitalism and the Chinese firm. ECGI working paper series in law 251:2014. http://papers.ssrn.com/sol3/papers.cfm?abstract_id=2413019. Accessed 21 July 2014

Naughton B (2007) The Chinese economy: transitions and growth. The MIT Press, Cambridge

Nolan P, Wang X (1999) Beyond privatization: institutional innovation and growth in China's large state-owned enterprises. World Dev 27(1):169–200

Park A, Sehrt K (2001) Tests of financial intermediation and banking reform in China. J Comp Econ 29:608–644

Podpiera R (2006) Progress in China's banking sector reform: has bank behavior changed? IMF working paper, WP/06/71

Poncet S, Steingress W, Vandenbussche H (2010) Financial constraints in China: firm-level evidence. China Econ Rev 21:411–422

Prasad ES (2009) Is the Chinese growth miracle built to last? China Econ Rev 20:103–123

Roubini N, Sala-i-Martin X (1992) Financial repression and economic growth. J Dev Econ 39:5–30

Shaw ES (1973) Financial deepening in economic development. Oxford University Press, New York

Shleifer A (1998) State versus private ownership. J Econ Perspect 12(4):133–150

Szamosszegi A, Kyle C (2011) An analysis of state-owned enterprises and state capitalism in China. U.S.-China Economic and Security Review Commission Report. http://origin.www.uscc.gov/sites/default/files/Research/10_26_11_CapitalTradeSOEStudy.pdf. Accessed 16 Aug 2014

Unirule Institute of Economics (2011) guoyou qiye de xingzhi, biaoxian, yu gaige (The nature, performance, and reform of the state owned enterprises). http://www.unirule.org.cn/xiazai/2011/20110412.pdf. Accessed 15 July 2014

Wang H (2014) China's long march toward economic rebalancing. Policy brief 38, Center for International Governance Innovation. http://www.cigionline.org/sites/default/files/cigi_pb_38.pdf

World Bank (2009) Effective discipline with adequate autonomy: the direction for further reform of China's SOE dividend policy. World Bank Policy Note, No. 53254. http://www-wds.worldbank.org/external/default/WDSContentServer/WDSP/IB/2010/03/02/000333038_20100302031054/Rendered/PDF/532540ESW0P11310final0Nov27020090En.pdf. Accessed 18 Aug 2014

World Bank (2001) Finance for growth: policy choices in a volatile world. Oxford University Press, New York

World Bank, and DRC (Development Research Center of the State Council of China) (2013) China 2030: building a modern, harmonious, and creative high-income society. The World Bank, Washington

Xu G (2014) Is China an anomaly for the 'Law Matters' hypothesis? Asian J Law Soc 1:339–365

Xu G, Gui B (2013) The connection between financial repression and economic growth: the case of China. J Comp Asian Dev 12(3):385–410

Yang DT (2012) Aggregate savings and external imbalances in China. J Econ Perspect 26 (4):125–146

Yin X, Xu Y (2011) zhongguo jinrong yizhi wenti de zhengzhijingjixue (The political economy of China's financial repression). dangdai jingji kexue (Mod Econ Sci) 5:10–17

Yu H (2014) The ascendency of state-owned enterprises in China: development, controversy and problems. J Contemp China 23(85):161–182

Yusuf S, Nabeshima K, Perkins DH (2006) Under new ownership: privatizing China's state-owned enterprises. The World Bank, Washington

Zhang L-Y (2004) The roles of corporatization and stock market listing in reforming China's state industry. World Dev 32(12):2031–2047

Is There a Level Playing Field in China's Capital Markets? An Analysis of Public and Private Enforcement

Wenjing Li and Tianshu Zhou

1 Introduction

In Chinese capital markets, listed companies can be divided into two groups according to their identity: listed State-owned enterprises (SOEs) and private background (PB) listed companies. As of the end of January 2013, there were 2443 listed companies on China's capital markets, of which 953 are SOEs. These companies account for nearly 51.4 % of the total share value of all listed companies. Because of this condition, there is an argument that China's stock markets are driven by policy or certain political targets rather than normal market mechanisms. Two points support this argument. First, the role of the capital markets has been to raise money for reforming SOEs rather than to allocate capital to the most efficient enterprises. Second, the market regulators have been both regulators and supporters, with the mission of keeping share prices high to promote the financing of SOEs.[1] In addition, the court system is perhaps substantially influenced by the political system in China, which may give rise to the preferential treatment of SOEs in private litigation.[2] Given the origin of the capital markets in China, the background of the market regulators, and the preferences of the court system, an important question arises: in terms of private and public enforcement of laws, is China's securities market a fair playing field?

This chapter is organized as follows. Section 2 provides a brief introduction to the public regulators in China. Section 3 provides empirical evidence and case

[1] Clarke (2008), p. 41.

[2] Young et al. (2007).

W. Li (✉) • T. Zhou
Center for Law and Economics at the China University of Political Science and Law, Beijing, China
e-mail: 18600039134@163.com; tianshu0214@hotmail.com

N. Philipsen et al. (eds.), *Market Integration: The EU Experience and Implications for Regulatory Reform in China*, China-EU Law Series 2,
DOI 10.1007/978-3-662-48273-5_7

studies of China's public enforcement of misrepresentation cases. Section 4 introduces the empirical evidence of private enforcement in China. Finally, a short conclusion is made.

2 A Brief Introduction of the China Securities Regulatory Commission

Administrative regulation undoubtedly plays the most important role in China's regulatory regime. As Hutchens (2003) argued, "rather than existing to provide clear notice to private parties of legal rights and duties, PRC legal enactments exist to facilitate management of a complex society by an administrative state".[3] Notably, even until 1988, no formal legislation had been enacted to govern State-owned enterprises in China. The functions of formal legislation—for example, the protection of creditors and accountability of managers—were managed through the State's administrative procedure.[4] This culture of strong administrative regulation has been inherited by the current regulatory regime. The China Securities Regulatory Commission (CSRC) is the public regulator of the equity markets in China. Unlike many regulators in developed nations, the CSRC is not a quasi-governmental organization, it is an administrative organ controlled by the government. In accordance with China's Securities Law 2005, the CSRC's powers are divided into three parts: (1) formulating regulation; (2) investigation and supervision; and (3) legal enforcement. Its powers range from proactive to reactive, and it plays an important role in promoting compliance with securities market regulations. The CSRC contributes considerably to the increasing legal certainty surrounding corporate governance issues. It does so by enacting quasi-legislation, including regulations and guidelines, to implement the principles of the Company Law 2005 and Securities Law 2005. In general, these regulations and guidelines are legally binding, and all listed companies must comply with them. The CSRC actively performs its supervisory and legal enforcement powers. In terms of proactive enforcement, it is entitled to verify the Articles of Association of companies seeking listing in mainland China and is responsible for ensuring that all companies on China's securities market meet the required corporate governance standards. In terms of reactive enforcement, the CSRC has enforcement power against market participants. In accordance with Article 193 of the Securities Law 2005, the CSRC is authorized to impose a fine on issuers and public companies that are engaged in misrepresentation (including disclosing misleading or false information or conducting a major omission in information disclosure). The range of this fine is between RMB 300,000 and RMB 600,000 for public companies. The executives

[3] Hutchens (2003), p. 625.

[4] Clarke (2003), p. 496.

and any other person directly responsible for misrepresentation shall be given a warning and a fine ranging from RMB 30,000 up to RMB 300,000.

3 Is the CSRC Protecting a Level Playing Field: Case Studies of Misrepresentation

3.1 Why Misrepresentation Cases?

Information asymmetry is a core problem of securities markets. As argued by Cearns and Ferran (2014), enhancing public confidence in the credibility of the financial statements of listed companies is a key element of an effective system of securities regulation. Consequently, public enforcement against information asymmetry problems (e.g., false disclosure or delayed disclosure) is important. Insider trading, the other major category of enforcement cases in China, provides little information about the issue being investigated in this paper. The CSRC's enforcement actions against insider trading usually only impose fines and disgorgements on the insiders, whistle blowers, brokers and governmental officers. In other words, punishments rarely extend to the listed company in general, regardless of its identity. It therefore provides little evidence to distinguish the CSRC's enforcement actions against SOEs and PB public companies. In contrast, the CSRC usually punishes both public companies and their senior executives in misrepresentation cases, which provides a general basis for comparing public enforcement actions against listed companies with different identities. An important question remains: are listed SOEs frequently engaging in misrepresentation? If they are not, the investigation is meaningless. Research has indicated that undisclosed intercorporate loans and other undisclosed related-party transactions are the most important strategies for controlling shareholders to exact funds from listed SOEs.[5] As Howson insightfully indicates, State-owned controlling shareholders have a virtual habit of directing those listed companies to provide undisclosed financial guarantees for the obligations of other controlled subsidiaries of the controlling shareholder.[6]

[5] Huyghebaet and Wang (2012); Berkman et al. (2009).

[6] Howson (2014), p. 692.

3.2 Public Enforcement Actions Against Listed SOEs and Listed PB Companies: Empirical Evidence and Case Studies

3.2.1 Empirical Evidence

Our research methodology is simple: The CSRC publishes its enforcement actions on its website and so we reviewed all public enforcement actions from 2008 to 2013, and selected the misrepresentation cases. We then gathered the following key information: (1) amount of fines on public companies, (2) amount of fines on executives or independent directors, and (3) public companies' backgrounds.[7]

With respect to the misrepresentation cases, the CSRC performed more enforcement actions and imposed heavier fines against PB listed companies (see Figs. 1 and 2). The data for 2008 is not difficult to explain. Generally, the enforcement

Fig. 1 Number of enforcement actions against listed SOEs and private background listed companies

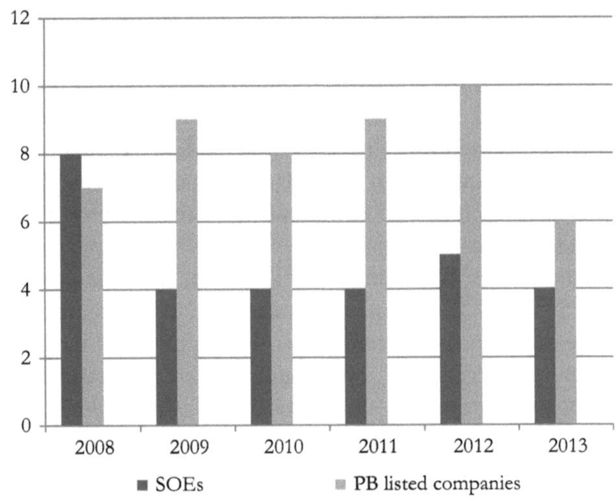

[7] It is difficult to identify who the SOEs are in China's capital markets because the boundary between SOEs and PB companies has been blurred. Many listed companies have both state and private investment. For this point see Milhaupt and Zheng (2015). This paper sets out general criteria for distinguishing SOEs from PB listed companies: 1. listed company's majority shareholder should be an SOE or a governmental authority (e.g., SASAC), 2. State shareholding exceeds 10 % of the company's total shareholding. The 10 % of shareholding not only represents considerable economic interests but significant managerial power. In accordance with China's Company Law, shareholders with 10 % of shares can call extraordinary shareholders' meetings. Based on these criteria, the SOEs only include companies with substantial state-control and state-interests, which could potentially influence the CSRC's judgment, but do not include companies with a small proportion of state-ownership. Furthermore, note that the listed SOEs are not defined in a narrow sense by these criteria. The companies in which state-shareholding is less than 10 % only occupied a small proportion.

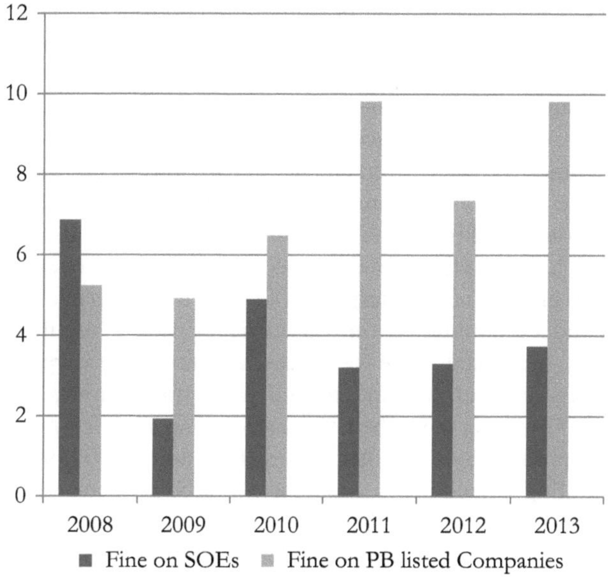

Fig. 2 Administrative fines imposed on listed SOEs and private background listed companies on the basis of breaching disclosure rules from 2008 to 2013 (million RMB) (There is no constructive way to collect the number of listed SOEs or PB listed companies in each year. Therefore, it is very difficult, if not impossible, to compare enforcement actions against SOEs and private companies. However, the official authority indicates that PB listed companies occupied nearly half of the market capitalization (around 49 %) of the two securities markets in early 2013. Although it may define SOEs in a different way, e.g. including all listed companies with state-shareholding without considering its proportion, this tells us there are no considerable differences between the total numbers in Fig. 1 and this figure and the average number per market capitalization before 2013. If we consider the increase of private shareholding in the capital markets in recent years, the gap of the average figures between SOEs and PB listed companies per capitalization should be even larger than that of the total figures in the years before 2013.)

actions in 2008 concerned misrepresentation cases that occurred before 2005. During that period, PB companies only comprised a small proportion of all listed companies. However, from this rudimentary data, we conclude that China's securities markets are unfair. There are two possible explanations for this: 1. Listed SOEs are perhaps better market participants who have stronger incentives to comply with the law and regulations. 2. Even if listed SOEs are engaged in an equal amount of violations, the CSRC may employ different regulatory tools to constrain listed SOEs' problems. This regulatory tool is either as severe as (or even more severe than) the general *ex post* enforcement approach, or it can be less severe. If the latter is the case, the CSRC gives preference to SOEs. The answer to the above possibilities can be found in CSRC's annual report.

The CSRC tends to adopt the *ex ante* cooperative approach to regulate Central Government Owned (CGO) listed companies. For example, in 2009, the CSRC disclosed that it formulated a unique regulatory model for CGO listed companies, namely "improving effective regulation on central government owned listed companies by enhancing regulation of substantial controller".[8] This is a regulatory model under which the complicated relationship between listed companies and their parent company are carefully investigated and regulated. In this model, the CSRC intends to maintain listed SOEs' independent positions and minimize the substantial controllers' excessive influence on listed SOEs' operations and assets. This model is not characterized by enforcement but by cooperation between CGO listed companies or their parent companies and the CSRC. It can be divided into two substantial approaches. First, on-site visits and investigation—as of November 2009, the CSRC has completed investigations of 62 central government controlled corporate groups and financial enterprises (42 % of the companies in this particular category). Second, combining administrative licensing with regulation—the CSRC comprehensively examined some key areas, including the corporate governance structure, industry competition and related party transactions, by gathering and exploiting the information from the CGO listed companies' corporate issues under administrative approval by the CSRC. As of the end of 2009, 90 violations were found in controlling shareholders and substantial controllers' operations through this particular regulatory approach. However, the CSRC did not impose fines or other types of penalties. Instead, it provided 78 suggestions for these problems.[9] This regulatory model was further improved in 2010. According to CSRC's 2010 annual report, the CGO listed companies have serious problems with majority shareholder embezzlement, industry competition and related-party transactions. The CSRC performed on-site investigations at 46 CGO corporate groups. Nearly 200 CGO listed companies were involved in these investigations, and 71 violations by majority shareholders or substantial controllers were found. Similar to the previous year, the CSRC did not impose any enforcement action against these violations. Instead, it cooperated with the State-owned Assets Supervision and Administration Commission (SASAC) and Stock Exchanges to train nearly 400 executives in 73 CGO listed companies.[10]

Two important insights can be drawn from the above information: 1. CGO listed companies are equally engaged in illegal activities: many substantial problems were found during the CSRC's on-site investigations. 2. The CSRC adopts a less severe approach to regulate CGO listed companies: suggestions and training but no enforcement actions. Other data from the CSRC's annual report provide some useful information related to this regulatory model. In 2011, listed SOEs accounted for 51 % of all public companies violating the insider trading regulations. In 2012, this figure dropped to 28 %.[11] In its 2012 report, the CSRC declared that the number of listed SOEs that were engaged in insider trading decreased dramatically. Nonetheless, improvement of listed SOEs' compliance to regulation was a product of the

[8] See CSRC Annual Report 2009, 33 available at: http://www.csrc.gov.cn/pub/newsite/zjhjs/zjhnb/. Accessed 28 Sept 2014.

[9] Ibid.

[10] CSRC Annual Report 2010, p. 30. Accessed on 28 Sept 2014.

[11] CSRC Annual Report 2012, p. 28. Accessed on 28 Sept 2014.

CSRC's preferential regulatory approach. The CSRC contributed extensive resources to identifying emerging problems and risks of CGO listed companies at an earlier stage and took appropriate steps to mitigate and cure the discovered problems. They made great efforts to investigate the root causes of misbehaviour, e.g., the controlling shareholder and substantial controller of the corporate group. In contrast, no evidence indicates that the CSRC offers similar *ex ante* service to PB listed companies. Consequently, preferential treatment has been granted by the CSRC to CGO listed companies.

3.2.2 Case Studies

Setting Out General and Specified Standards

Besides adopting a cooperative regulatory model, does the CSRC apply identical standards to listing SOEs and listed PB companies without bias when it enforces rules? Some representative cases are examined in this part. The legal grounds for the CSRC's enforcement are Articles 68, 193 and 213 of the Securities Law 2005,[12] which stipulate the liabilities of listed companies and their executives when they breach disclosure rules. Based on the statutory rules, the CSRC has developed a general regulatory approach to misrepresentation cases in practice. In the first stage, it clarified some important notions that are ambiguous in the statutes. In the Hailong Keji case,[13] it held that every executive of a listed company, whether director or independent director, is liable for any forgery, misleading or omitted information. They should perform their duties in the best interests of the company and its shareholders as a whole and in accordance with the laws, regulations and articles of association. Furthermore, the UK style standards of duty of care, skill and

[12] Article 68 states: The directors and senior managers of a listed company shall approve the periodic report of their company in written form. The board of supervisors of a listed company shall carry out an examination of the periodic report of the company as formulated by the board of directors and produce the relevant examination opinions in writing. The directors, supervisors and senior managers of a listed company shall guarantee the authenticity, accuracy and integrity of the information as disclosed by their listed company.

Article 193 states: [w]here an issuer, a listed company or any other obligor of information disclosure fails to disclose information according to the relevant provisions or where there is any false record, misleading or major omission in the information as disclosed, the securities regulatory body shall order it to be corrected, give a warning and impose a fine of 300,000 yuan up to 600,000 yuan. The person in charge and any other person directly responsible shall be given a warning and imposed a fine of 30,000 yuan up to 300,000 yuan.

Article 213 states: [w]here an acquirer fails to discharge its obligations of announcing its acquisition of a listed company, tendering an acquisition offer, submitting a report on its acquisition of the listed company, etc., as is required by the provisions of this Law, or amends the tendered acquisition offer without approval, it shall be ordered to rectify, be given a warning, and shall, in addition, be fined not less than 100,000 yuan but not more than 300,000.

[13] (2008) No. 1.

diligence are adopted in a piece-meal approach.[14] The LanGuang Keji case[15] launched an objective standard of duty of diligence. Directors should work with the general knowledge, skill and diligence that may reasonably be expected of a person in a similar position. If this standard is not achieved, he or she breaches the duty of diligence. The subjective standard was likewise integrated into the CSRC's regulatory practice. In the Datang Dianxin case,[16] one of the independent directors, Ms. Li, was a senior accountant. The CSRC held that Ms. Li was liable for the company's misrepresentation because of a breach of the duty of diligence. Although she noted some of the accounting problems in board meetings, she did not perform due diligence toward other more serious accounting problems.

Furthermore, the CSRC sets out more specific standards. Executives or independent directors who sign documents marred by false or omitted information are penalized based on a breach of the duty of loyalty or the duty of diligence. Independent directors or executives who only "rubber stamp" cannot escape administrative penalties. They need to prove that they have actively taken the necessary steps to require insiders or substantial controllers to fix the problems. For example, in the Xichang Dianli case,[17] the company was seriously engaged in misrepresentation. During the CSRC's investigation, one of the company's independent directors, Mr. Tan, claimed that he only participated in a board meeting once and that all of his signatures were made by other executives with his permission. He claimed he was badly informed and should not be liable for the violation. This claim was dismissed by the CSRC. In contrast, the other executive, Mr. Wang, who actively challenged the company's illegal transactions and voluntarily cooperated with the CSRC and other authorities, was not held liable for the violation. Furthermore, similar to section 173 of the U.K. Company Act, the CSRC places great emphasis on a director's duty of independent decision making. In a case in 2008, the CSRC clarified that "signature under duress, badly informed decision or working without payment" cannot constitute a valid legal basis for avoiding punishment.[18] Granting "carte blanche" between board members is prohibited by the CSRC as well.[19] The CSRC clarified its position: a director who gives other board member carte blanche in all corporate matters breaches duties of loyalty and facilitates insider control problems. Shareholders appoint a particular individual to be the director of a company based on their trust in his or her professional skills and personal integrity. "Carte blanche" in all corporate matters breaches this relationship of trust between shareholders and directors. The CSRC further elaborates that a director should review corporate proposals and make an independent decision with a clear judgment, either to approve or reject. With this

[14] For general information, see Sealy and Worthington (2010), p. 330.

[15] (2008) No. 50.

[16] (2008) No. 28.

[17] (2008) No. 24.

[18] (2008) No. 34.

[19] (2010) No. 13.

decision, the director can authorize other board member to vote on her behalf. A director who grants an authorization should perform supervisory tasks of his or her delegate. Moreover, a director who is blindly reliant on an external audit report also runs the risk of being held liable for a company's violations. In the Haixing Keji case, an executive claimed that he relied on the unreserved external auditor's report when he signed documents which included forged information. The CSRC held that executives should perform their duties based on their own knowledge and professional skills with a diligent attitude. They should work in accordance with the laws and regulations and without influence from shareholders or other insiders. They should make their independent decisions based on their professional judgments and comprehensively understand the potential legal consequence of their behaviour.[20] The executive's defence was dismissed.

In addition to personal liability, the CSRC confirmed that although misrepresentation was generally conducted by corporate insiders or majority shareholders, the liability should extend to the listed companies. In the Nanjing Zhongbei case,[21] the listed SOE claimed that the company's misrepresentation of related party transactions was conducted by individual persons without authority from the board of directors. In this case, the company was likewise a victim of the violation. Additionally, the company took several steps to mitigate the negative influences of the illegal, related-party transactions and misrepresentations after it become aware of the violations. It informed administrative authorities and the public security organization in time, made complementary disclosures, positively cooperated with official authorities during the investigation, and enhanced its inner self-governance. The company therefore claimed that it should not be held liable for the misbehaviour. The CSRC dismissed this claim. It held that in accordance with the mandatory rules of securities law, the regulatory body has the authority to impose administrative liability on listed companies that breach disclosure rules. Although administrative fines exert a negative influence on a company's interests, they are not only justified, but necessary, especially in a case where violations of disclosure rules are caused by "insider control" because of majority shareholders' negligence or insufficient supervision. The CSRC dismissed the second claim as well. It held that in this case, the company's subjective motivation and its objective of fixing the negative influence of the violation were important factors that should be taken into consideration in allocating liabilities. However, the seriousness of the violation and the degree to which misrepresentation damaged investors' interests, market credibility and confidence should be carefully evaluated. In the Wu Liang Ye case,[22] the CSRC insisted on its regulatory standards. Wu Liang Ye was a listed SOE that operated a famous Chinese wine brand. It omitted major information about its investment in a financial entity in its annual report. Furthermore, the CSRC identified several major problems with Wu Liang Ye's 2007 annual report

[20] (2012) No. 25.
[21] (2010) No. 10.
[22] (2011) No. 17.

during its on-site visit and urged Wu Liang Ye to issue a complementary public statement to correct this information. However, Wu Liang Ye did not perform this duty in a timely manner. The CSRC held that Wu Liang Ye's violation had "serious negative social influences"; accordingly, a 600,000 RMB fine was imposed on the Wu Liang Ye Company. In short, the CSRC has developed a general regulatory model with several important standards for dealing with misrepresentation cases. Under this model, the CSRC imposes monetary penalties on both executives and companies after it gathers sufficient evidence of violation. Nevertheless, a few exceptions can be found; these are presented below.

Lenient Standards Toward Listed SOEs with Powerful Controllers

CSRC's *ex post* enforcement becomes lenient in situations where the wrongdoers' substantial controller is powerful. In the Shanxi Jingmi case,[23] the listed company was engaged in serious misrepresentation. From 2000 to 2004, Shanxi Jingmi's forged profit reached 69,623,683 USD in its financial reports. Additionally, its financial reports fraudulently recorded the company as having 47,951,885 USD in bank deposits. Furthermore, a large quantity of internal corporate loans was not properly disclosed by the company. From 2002 to 2004, it had 16 undisclosed corporate loans valued at 79,738,296 USD. In this case, the CSRC should have evaluated the seriousness of the violation and its negative market influences, as it had in the Nanjing Zhongbei case. However, the fine imposed by the CSRC hardly matched the seriousness of the violations: 50,000 RMB fine on one executive, 30,000 RMB fines on four executives and no fine on the public company. The decision was inconsistent with its standard decisions in other cases: liability must extend to the company. In this case, the CSRC reserved its statutory power. The reason can be found in Shanxi Jingmi's 2009 annual report. Shanxi Jingmi's controlling shareholder was Shenzhen Tianhua Electronic Power Investment Company (Tianhua Company). However, Tianhua Company acquired Shanxi Jingmi's shares from the SASAC of Shanxi Province by fraudulent market strategies in 1998. The executives of Tianhua Company were punished by criminal law, Tianhua Company's shareholder's position was disqualified, and its shareholdings were disgorged to the SASAC of Shanxi Province. In this case, Shanxi Jingmi's substantial shareholder was the SASAC of Shanxi Province when it engaged in misrepresentation. The CSRC was reluctant to damage the SASAC of Shanxi Province's interests and reputation.

Similarly, Longchang Company disclosed forged assets valued at 25,668,130 USD and forged income valued at 10,414,836 USD from 2002 to 2004.[24] It also had a large amount of undisclosed corporate loans and litigations, which can be directly attributed to the instructions from the majority shareholder. The CSRC allocated all

[23] (2008) No. 36.

[24] (2008) No. 10.

liabilities to the executives and no liability to the public company. Again, the substantial owner of Longchuan Company was a powerful entity. It was controlled by the China National Petroleum Company (CNPC), a central government-owned enterprise, and ranked 4th according to Fortune's Global 500 in 2014. In the Yueyang Xingchang Company case,[25] the CSRC adopted an even softer enforcement approach on the China Petrochemical Corporation (Sinopec) subsidiary. Sinopec, similar to CNPC, is a central government-owned enterprise operating in the energy-related industry and ranked 3rd in Fortune's Global 500, 2014. In 2007, Sinopec acquired 24 % of Yueyang Xingchang Company's shares. In accordance with the law and regulations, any acquisition equal to or exceeding 5 % of a company's shares should be disclosed promptly. Xingchang Company did not disclose any information to the general public in a timely manner and even stayed quiet in its annual report. The CSRC only issued a warning and no substantial monetary penalty on the company and its executives. In the above cases, the enforcement approach breaks the bottom-line of the CSRC's standards: imposing fines on both listed companies and executives. Furthermore, the CSRC may not even be authorized to reserve monetary penalties in misrepresentation cases. Article 193 of the Securities Law clearly states that "the securities regulatory body shall order it to be corrected, give a warning and impose a fine of 300,000 yuan up to 600,000 yuan" when a public company is engaged in misrepresentation. The requirements of this mandatory rule are simple and clear. In a literal sense, any order of correction and public warning should be combined with a monetary penalty in a misrepresentation case. Imposing a monetary fine on wrongdoers is not only an authority but a duty for the CSRC. The CSRC has the authority to decide the amount of the fine within a certain range but does not have the authority to reserve the monetary penalty when it issues a warning against a violation of disclosure rules. The other important fact that deserves to be noticed is that both the Shanxi Jingmi and Tianhua Company cases were decided by the CSRC in 2008. After the CSRC launched its *ex ante* cooperative approach toward CGO listed companies in 2009, this type of case became rare. From 2009 to 2013, only 1 case can be found. The preference for *ex post* enforcement was largely replaced by *ex ante* cooperation.

Consequently, this section presented both empirical data and case law analysis to investigate the important question of whether the CSRC enforces regulations against listed SOEs and PB listed companies without bias. To provide an accurate answer to this question, a clear distinction between local government-owned (LGO) listed companies and CGO listed companies should be made. In accordance with the empirical results and the cases studied the CSRC endeavours to control market participants' behaviour by issuing warnings and fines. It uses *ex post* enforcement power to fight against LGO, SOEs and PB listed companies' misbehaviour. However, toward powerful CGO listed companies, it adopts a cooperative model of regulation with occasionally soft enforcement.

[25] (2012) No. 45.

4 Private Enforcement

The Chinese Security Law was enacted in 1998, and the private enforcement of the law was boosted in 2002 when the Supreme Court issued a Notice which constituted a new milestone.[26] The Supreme Court confirmed that local intermediate courts were capable to hear securities litigations against misrepresentation. The Notice provided a workable legal regime for the private enforcement of securities law. In some respects, it was enacted in a plaintiff-friendly way. For example, it gives plaintiffs an autonomous position from which to choose the eligible parties they would like to sue. This means plaintiffs could pursue their interests by bringing litigation action against a "deep pocket" defendant. Additionally, the provision applied a statute of limitations of 2 years to private securities litigations rather than the standard 1-year special statute of limitations (Xi 2006, p. 495). Nonetheless, private enforcement is subject to administrative and criminal sanctions (public enforcement). In other words, aggrieved investors can only file a lawsuit against a party who has received an administrative fine from the CSRC or another administrative organization, such as the Ministry of Finance, based on fraudulent disclosure, or parties convicted for misrepresentation by a court. The private enforcement regime has been integrated into Securities Law 2005. However, the pre-trail condition is still not removed under the formal legislation.

Although private enforcement can be applied in cases of misrepresentation in China, it is hard to find all of the private enforcement cases because there is no available official data. Information about private enforcement mainly comes from second-hand material, such as news reports and journal articles.[27] The data have been collected by the following method: a keyword search was performed, including the terms "company's name (company which had been punished by the CSRC because of misrepresentation)",[28] "misrepresentation" (*Xujia Chenshu*), and

[26] "Zuigao Renmin Fayuan Guanyu Shouli Zhengquan Shichang Yin Sujia Chengshu Yinfa De Minshi Qinquan Jiufen Anjian Youguan Wenti De Tongzhi" [The Notice on Relevant Issues Concerning Accepting Civil Tort Dispute Cases Caused by Misrepresentation on Securities and Several Provisions on Hearing Civil Compensation Caused by Misrepresentation on the Securities Markets] issued by China's Supreme Court on 15th January 2002, Article 17 which states "misrepresentation indicates the market participants breach relevant law and regulation during their IPO or securities transactions in the secondary market by disclosing false information, misleading information, omitting material information, or not appropriately disclosing information".

[27] Alternative approaches that provide first-hand materials were sought. While using the largest case law system organized by Peking University, i.e. the *Beida Fabao* system, unfortunately, only 2 cases of private enforcement against misrepresentation were found. One is the *Daqing Lianyi* case, the other is the *Huawen Keji* case.

[28] As mentioned above, there is a pre-trial condition stating that shareholders can only sue a public company after an administrative or criminal punishment by the regulatory authorities or court was administered. Therefore, searching for the name of companies that have been punished by the CSRC using terms such as "misrepresentation" (*Xujia Chenshu*) and "private compensation" (*Minshi Peichang*) on the internet is reasonable and possibly the only method to search for these types of cases.

"private compensation" (*Minshi Peichang*) via the Google Chinese website and Baidu, a Chinese search engine for websites, news and journal articles. At least 37 private enforcement cases were found from 2008 to 2013. All of these cases were related to public punishment decisions on misrepresentation of the CSRC or Ministry of Finance. Because the information was collected via an indirect way, some major omissions and inaccuracies remain. First, it is possible that some private litigation cases against misrepresentation were not captured by the data collection method used. This can be attributed to a lack of media attention given to cases where, e.g., the claimed compensation is minuscule, the number of plaintiffs is very small, or media are corrupted by the defendant. Second, the data collected might not always be complete in all cases, particularly when settlements between plaintiffs and defendants were not publicised because of confidentiality agreements underlying the settlements. The defendant sometimes requires the plaintiffs and their lawyers to sign a confidentiality agreement, which removes their right to disclose key information about the settlement to the general public. Third, while conducting cross-checks, ambiguity of data found in different sources may have contributed to the inaccuracy of the findings. Some cross-checks showed that different news reports published different figures. In cases of conflicting data in news reports, the source with the higher reputation was given preference, e.g., newspapers or journals on securities markets were viewed as more reliable than internet media. Another problem is that news reports and even some journal articles are not academic products: they widely used terms including "approximately" (*Dayue*), "nearly" (*Jiangjin*), or "more than a certain number" (*Da yu mouyi shuzi*) in their descriptions. As a result of the shortage of first-hand material, we keep these terms (which indicate the ambiguity of the data) in this chapter. After having transparently addressed the problems encountered during data collection and evaluation, an objective presentation of the data is still viewed as viable based on the accessible materials. However, the data on the intensity of private enforcement might still be considered under-representative, considering the above-mentioned problems.

With respect to the private enforcement of misrepresentation cases, it is difficult to find out whether the court supported more claims against PB listed companies or SOEs. The data indicate that the results vary across different years, as we can see in Figs. 3 and 4[29]; however, from 2008 to 2013, taking account of the total amount, SOEs faced more enforcement actions and had to pay more compensation than PB listed companies.[30] Considering that in the Chinese stock market the total share

[29] Figure 3 demonstrates that in 2008, 2009 and 2011, more private actions were taken against SOEs. In 2012 and 2013 more litigation was directed at PB listed companies, whereas in 2010, the number of private actions against SOEs and PB listed companies was equal. Figure 4 shows that in 2008, 2009, 2010, 2011 and 2013, more compensation had to be paid by SOEs, and PB listed companies paid more compensation only in 2012.

[30] From 2008 to 2013, there were 22 litigations against SOEs and 15 cases against PB listed companies, and in those 6 years, the SOEs paid more than 97.67 million RMB in compensation, and PB listed companies 20.34 million RMB.

Fig. 3 Number of private enforcement actions against listed SOEs and private background listed companies from 2008 to 2013

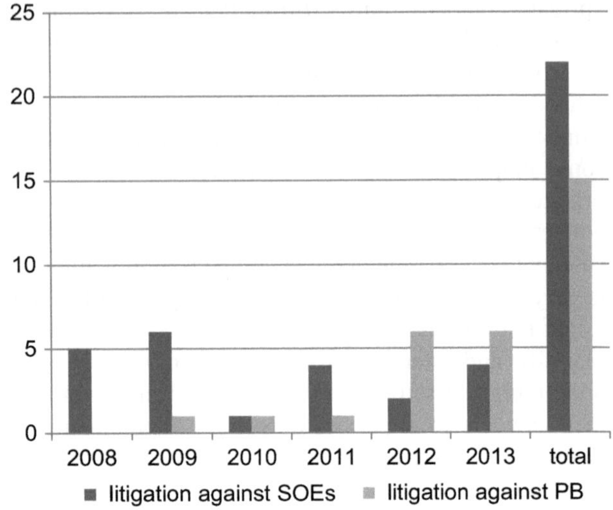

Fig. 4 Compensation (private enforcement) from listed SOEs and private background listed companies on the basis of breaching disclosure rules from 2008 to 2013 (million RMB)

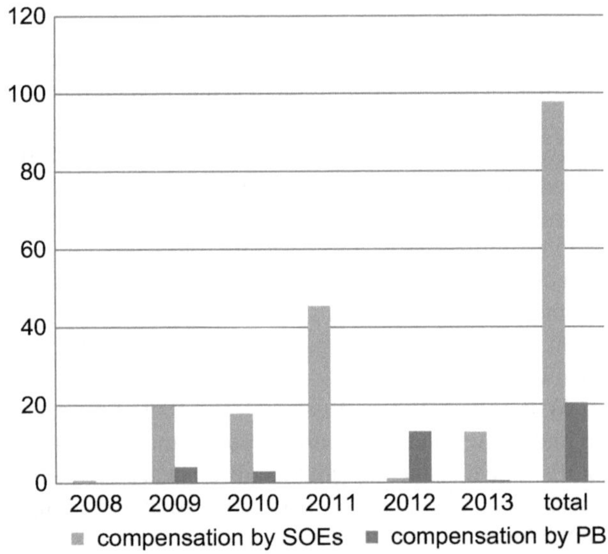

value of SOEs is higher than that of PB listed companies, more private enforcement directed at SOEs may be a natural result. Furthermore, we cannot ignore the following facts:

1. Because many dispersed investors are possibly involved in the misrepresentation cases, the judicial proceedings are often complicated and can take considerable time for courts to make judgments or for the parties to reach settlements.

Therefore, some litigation is still in process, and the statistics of compensation may be incomplete.

2. Although we found that SOEs were more involved in private enforcement, all such SOEs are LGO listed companies, we cannot find any CGO involvement. From the data of public enforcement, we also found a similar phenomenon because public enforcement is required as a precondition for investors to file litigation according to the Supreme Court Notice in 2002. Therefore, private enforcement is affected by public enforcement.
3. Some compensation can be paid even without litigation, for example, Ping An Security (the sponsor of Wanfu Shengke Public Company) created a fund of 300 million RMB to compensate the investor losses caused by the misrepresentation of Wanfu Shengke before litigation. The compensation fund created by Ping An Security is a milestone in the Chinese capital market.[31] In this case, Ping An Security was the sponsor for the IPO of Wanfu Shengke, but it failed to find the financial fraud conducted by Wanfu Shengke. The CSRC issued punishments for both Wanfu Shengke and Ping An Security. On the same date that the punishments were issued, Ping An Security created a compensation fund to compensate the loss of investors; therefore, lawyers and investors can negotiate under the framework of the funds before starting litigation, which can improve the efficiency of the compensation and provide an alternative to litigation. Compensation funds can be regarded as a better choice for many investors, for example, in another famous case, the Everbright insider trading case, the investors and lawyers required Everbright to establish a fund such as Ping An.

5 Conclusion

This research achieved important findings on the public and private enforcement of Chinese securities law. With reference to public enforcement, the CSRC enforces mandatory rules against both LGO and PB listed companies. The "central power versus local power" mechanism works well in practice. The CSRC makes great efforts to fight against misbehaviour by LGO enterprises. However, this does not mean that the "ownership bias" is eliminated in China. The CSRC does provide regulatory subsidies to CGO listed companies. The subsidies can be divided into two parts: one is contributing more resources to engagement in *ex ante* cooperation with CGO listed companies, e.g., providing corrective solutions and suggestions to problematic or illegal business activities and providing professional training to executives; the other is enforcing regulation with looser standards. With reference

[31] http://finance.sina.com.cn/stock/quanshang/thyj/20130510/145915421372.shtml, according to the report, Ping An Security claimed that as the sponsor of the IPO, it was responsible for the misrepresentation of Wanfu Shengke, which was punished by the CSRC. Hence, it announced that it would create a special fund to compensate the investors who suffered loss in the Wanfu Shengke case. The scale of the fund was approximately 300 million RMB.

to private enforcement, although the data demonstrated that the courts have heard more cases against LGO listed companies and have granted more compensation from LGO than PB listed companies, these results could be consistent with the market structure. We realize that the compensation we refer to is perhaps incomplete. Moreover, as we noticed in the public enforcement cases, it is difficult to find CGO listed companies in private enforcement cases. Hence, because private enforcement is based on public enforcement, the subsidies to CGO listed companies can also affect private enforcement.

References

Berkman H, Cole R, Fu L (2009) Expropriation through loan guarantees to related parties. J Bank Finance 33:141–156

Cearns K, Ferran E (2014) Non-enforcement led public oversight of financial and corporate governance disclosures and of auditors. ECGI Law working paper 101/2008 March 2008. Available via SSRN. http://papers.ssrn.com/sol3/papers.cfm?abstract_id=1111779. Accessed 16 Mar 2015

Clarke D (2003) Corporate governance in China: an overview. China Econ Rev 14:496–507

Clarke D (2008) The ecology of corporate governance in China. GWU Legal Studies Research Paper No. 433. Available via SSRN. http://ssrn.com/abstract=1245803. Accessed 16 Mar 2015

CSRC Annual Report 2009. http://www.csrc.gov.cn/pub/newsite/zjhjs/zjhnb/

CSRC Annual Report 2010. http://www.csrc.gov.cn/pub/newsite/zjhjs/zjhnb/

CSRC Annual Report 2012. http://www.csrc.gov.cn/pub/newsite/zjhjs/zjhnb/

Howson N (2014) Quack corporate governance as traditional Chinese medicine – the securities regulation cannibalization of China's corporate law and a state regulator's battle against party state political economic power. Seattle Univ Law Rev 37:667–716

Hutchens W (2003) Private security litigation in China: material disclosure about China's legal system. Univ Pa J Int Econ Law 24:599–689

Huyghebaet N, Wang LH (2012) Expropriation of minority investor in Chinese listed firms: the role of internal and external corporate governance mechanism. Corporate Governance Int Rev 20:308–332

Milhaupt C, Zheng WT (2015) Beyond ownership: state capitalism and the Chinese firm. Available via SSRN. http://ssrn.com/abstract=2413019. Accessed 16 Mar 2015.

Sealy L, Worthington S (2010) Cases and materials in company law, 9th edn. Oxford University Press, Oxford

Xi C (2006) Case note: private enforcement of securities law in China: Daqing Lianyi co v. Zhong Weida and others, Heilongjiang High Court. J Comp Law 2:492–495

Young A, Li G, Lau A (2007) Corporate governance in China: the role of the state and ideology in shaping reforms. Company Lawyer 28:204–211

Part III
Freedom of Establishment, Professional Regulation and Self-Regulation

Regulation of the Inter-Provincial Establishment of Companies: Applying the Private Interest Approach to China

Guang Shen and Niels Philipsen

1 Introduction

As stated in an IMF Working Paper from 2004, enterprises in China usually encounter barriers when they invest across provinces.[1] According to another (more recent) study, protectionist measures are taken by local authorities, which lead to restrictions on the inter-provincial establishment of companies and market segmentation.[2] Nevertheless, these statements are not backed by strong empirical evidence. Moreover, there appears to be limited research on how, in practice, rules on the inter-provincial establishment of companies are applied. That being said, the impact of regulation on the inter-provincial establishment should not be underestimated. In 2013, the Communist Party of China announced that it would "tidy up and annul all sorts of regulations and methods that impede the national unified market and fair competition".[3]

The question that is addressed in this chapter is whether the private interest approach to regulation (as part of the economic theory of regulation, and different from the public interest approach)[4] can provide explanations for the existing

Guang Shen is receiving a scholarship from the China Scholarship Council for his research.

[1] Boyreau-Debray and Wei (2014), p. 6.

[2] 夏立军、陆铭、余为政, 政企纽带与跨省投资—来自中国上市公司的经验证据,《管理世界》(月刊), 2011年第7期。Xia et al. (2011), p. 139.

[3] 中共中央关于全面深化改革若干重大问题的决定(全文), Decision of the Central Committee of the Communist Party of China (CCCPC) on Some Major Issues Concerning Comprehensively Deepening the Reform. The document can be obtained in English from http://www.china.org.cn/chinese/2014-01/17/content_31226494_3.htm, accessed 8 October 2014.

[4] For details see Philipsen (2003), pp. 9–27.

G. Shen (✉) • N. Philipsen
Faculty of Law, Maastricht University, Maastricht, The Netherlands
e-mail: guang.shen@maastrichtuniversity.nl; niels.philipsen@maastrichtuniversity.nl

N. Philipsen et al. (eds.), *Market Integration: The EU Experience and Implications for Regulatory Reform in China*, China-EU Law Series 2,
DOI 10.1007/978-3-662-48273-5_8

regulation of the inter-provincial establishment of companies and its enforcement. To explore the hypothesis that private interests are served by controlling entry into the market, we will investigate which benefits officials and incumbent firms can gain from regulation of establishment.

We begin in Sect. 2 by discussing the regulation of inter-provincial establishment of companies in China, with a focus on the question of whether entry barriers can be erected from these legal provisions. Section 3 presents existing empirical evidence on establishment in practice, aiming to examine whether in China the application (i.e. enforcement) of the regulation leads to entry barriers. The public interest approach to regulation and the private interest approach to regulation are summarized in Sect. 4. Further exploring the private interest hypothesis, in Sect. 5 we address the question of which private interests may be pursued through regulating inter-provincial establishment. The focus will be on how the traditional private interest approach may need to be adapted to better fit the more specific (legal, cultural and political) context of China. Section 6 provides an analysis of our own qualitative empirical analysis (interviews conducted by Shen Guang) on the formation of companies across provinces, with the aim of finding out whether the private interest approach can be backed. Conclusions are presented in Sect. 7.

2 Regulation of the Inter-Provincial Establishment of Companies in China

2.1 Rules on the Cross-Provincial Establishment of Companies[5]

If Chinese firms want to establish businesses across provincial borders, they can either form subsidiaries or branches. Minimum capital requirements have been defined for subsidiaries, but not for branches. Of all the conditions required for inter-provincial establishment, licensing requirements appear to be most important. There is a registration requirement that applies both for the inter-provincial establishment of subsidiaries and for the inter-provincial establishment of branches.

[5] The regulation of the inter-provincial establishment presented here is necessarily brief. Both Foreign Invested Enterprises (FIEs) and domestic companies constitute Chinese companies. Expansion of FIEs is governed by the Law on Wholly Foreign-owned Enterprises (外资企业法) (Amended 2000), the Law on Contractual Joint Ventures (中外合作经营企业法) (Amended 2000), the Law on Equity Joint Ventures (中外合资经营企业法) (Amended 2001), the Provisional Regulations Governing Investment within the Territory by FIEs (外商投资企业境内投资的暂行规定) (2000) (hereinafter the Regulations for Reinvestment) and other laws. The Company Law (公司法) (Amended 2005) and related provisions regulate the cross-border establishment by domestic companies. In 2014, the Company Law was amended significantly. Because of this amendment, the regulation of the establishment of companies in the People's Republic of China has undergone some major changes. This chapter does not take into account these changes. The English versions of most of the above laws are available on www.fdi.gov.cn.

Other licensing obligations for the inter-provincial establishment are presented in the following paragraphs.

According to the Company Law, domestic firms that want to form branches or subsidiaries in another province need to acquire permission "if the business scope of these branches and subsidiaries contains any matter subject to approval".[6] Moreover, if the incorporation of the branches and subsidiaries invested in is subject to approval, it is necessary to complete the relevant approval formalities before registering the establishment.[7]

In terms of the inter-provincial establishment by Foreign Invested Enterprises (FIEs), FIEs opening subsidiaries in designated "restricted investment fields" shall also obtain approvals from commercial agencies, apart from (i.e. in addition to) the registration of establishment.[8] Before permitting establishment, commercial authorities should ask for the opinions of authorities administrating the fields these subsidiaries operate in.[9] When subsidiaries are established in "permitted and encouraged fields", such establishment only needs to go through the registration procedure.[10] FIEs forming branches in any of the "restricted, permitted or allowed fields" are asked to obtain project approval from the Development and Reform Commissions (DRCs) prior to registering their establishment.[11]

As shown above, in terms of governing inter-provincial establishment, licensing systems can be created for business scope, registration of establishment, and incorporation. Whether, or not, a particular type of business scope can be subject to licensing is provided by Article 12 of the Administrative License Law of 2003 (ALL).[12] The next section elaborates on the contents of this article.

2.2 *Rules That Constrain Business Licensing*

Article 12 of the ALL provides a list of matters for which "an administrative license may be established", including e.g. "special activities that directly bear on the state security, public security, macro-economic control, ecological environment

[6] Articles 12 and 14 of the Company Law. The State Administration of Industry and Commerce (SAIC), Materials for the Establishment Registration of Branches, 国家工商总局, 分公司设立登记提交材料, http://www.saic.gov.cn/ywbl/bszn/nzdjzn/200902/t20090224_11945.html, accessed 8 October 2014.

[7] Articles 6 and 14 of the Company Law and Materials for the Establishment Registration of Branches.

[8] Article 9 of the Regulations for Reinvestment. According to the Catalogue for the Guidance of Foreign Investment Industries (Amended 2011) (hereinafter the Catalogue), foreign investment fields are divided into encouraged, restricted and prohibited categories.

[9] Article 10 Regulations for Reinvestment.

[10] Article 7 Regulations for Reinvestment.

[11] US Chamber of Commerce (2012), p. 36.

[12] 行政许可法 (2003).

protection, and those directly relating to human health, safety of life and property", and professional services.[13] Nevertheless, paragraph (6) of this article leaves open the possibility to establish a licensing regime in any situation, even if none of the other criteria have been fulfilled. Moreover, there is no judicial review of (problems that arise from) the enforcement of administrative rules in relation to the establishment of companies. Together, these two problems can cause barriers to inter-provincial establishment by companies.

2.2.1 Possibility to Extend Licensing Regimes to Every Matter

Article 12 of the ALL provides a list of activities, vocations and products that may be regulated through licensing, Article 12 (5) governs business licensing and provides that licensing may be adopted for the establishment of enterprises or other institutions, which needs to address the question of their capacity to be a subject of law.[14] However, for matters other than those mentioned in paragraphs (1) to (5), administrative licenses may be established in accordance with laws and regulations, as provided in Article 12 (6). Thus, it seems possible to use licensing for almost every matter, regardless of the provisions included in Article 12 (1) to (5).

2.2.2 Lack of Judicial Review

Courts in China do not have the power of judicial review of general rules. This implies that, if local authorities create licensing systems by means of local legislations, businesses cannot challenge these laws in courts.

Article 12 (2) of the Administrative Procedure Law (the APL) (1989) and relevant interpretations exclude general rules from the scope of judicial review.[15] According to Article 12 (2), courts are not entitled to deal with suits against administrative regulations, the rules of local governments, the rules of the departments under the State Council or decisions and orders with general binding force promulgated by administrative organs.

Article 3 of the Judicial Interpretation for the APL (2000)[16] explains what is meant by "decisions and orders" as referred to in Article 12 (2). Administrative normative documents with the following characteristics fall into the definition:

[13] See on the latter Philipsen (2010), pp. 216–218.

[14] The translation of the ALL is mostly based on http://www.fdi.gov.cn, accessed 11 February 2013, although we made some changes in the translation of Article 12 (5). Its official translation is "the establishment of the enterprises or other institutions, which needs to determine a subject qualification". (企业或其他组织的设立等, 需要确定主体资格的事项).

[15] 行政诉讼法(1989)The English version of the APL referred to in this chapter is available online, at: http://www.npc.gov.cn/englishnpc/Law/2007-12/11/content_1383562.htm, accessed 8 October 2014.

[16] 最高人民法院关于执行《中华人民共和国行政诉讼法》若干问题的解释 (2000).

(1) those created by administrative authorities; (2) those regulating unspecified objects of laws; and (3) those that can be used repeatedly.

The absence of judicial review leads to various negative effects.[17] One of the adverse impacts, according to Xiong and Zhang (2013), is the creation of excessive entry barriers. In the process of formulating macroeconomic policies, certain administrative agencies tend to extend their licensing authority and impose duplicate and multiple licensing obligations.[18]

3 The Reality of Inter-Provincial Establishment

Chinese companies, either foreign-funded or domestic-invested, which want to expand across provincial borders, may encounter barriers to market entry that have been erected by local licensing authorities. This will be illustrated by some examples.[19]

Licensing restrictions often appear in relation to the inter-provincial establishment of pharmacies. The general manager of a large pharmacy chain stated in 2013 that local protectionism is a severe problem. Pharmacy chains usually encounter problems in their applications for certificates and licenses, imposed on them by agencies for industry and commerce, tax, drug administration, etc. Non-local pharmacies often face much more restricted market entry conditions than local rivals and there are unfair and irregular practices involved in the licensing process.[20] Some regions even refuse to process non-local companies' applications for opening shops by publicly stating that "our local retailers cannot do business and survive, if your stores are set up here".[21]

---

[17] Liu and Huang (2000), p. 57.

[18] 熊文钊、张伟, 防止国家政策部门化, 来源: 瞭望新闻周刊, Xiong and Zhang (2013). China's then-premier Wen Jiabao attached great importance to this paper and gave an impetus. (李蒙、程遥, 熊文钊: "大部门制"的吹鼓手, Li and Cheng (2013).

[19] Many of the sources quoted in this section are (Chinese) magazines, newspapers and websites. Academic sources on the topic of practical barriers to entry in China are rather difficult to find. We realize of course that these non-academic sources should be interpreted with some caution.

[20] 中国经济周刊, 大型连锁药店拼命扩张, 难跨"定点"关, 2013-04-03, China Economic Weekly (2014). It should be noted here that the services provided by a pharmacy consist not only of professional services (pharmaceutical services, e.g. providing advice to patients and doctors and controlling for drug interaction), but also of business activities (selling prescription and OTC drugs). That is why it is relevant to discuss the establishment of pharmacies also in the context of business licensing. See further Philipsen (2013), pp. 226–227.

[21] 连锁还是封锁?国家药监局负责人痛斥地方保护主义(新华社供稿),《南方日报》, 2001年9月03日, 参见人民网, Chain operation or Blockade? Official in Charge of the State Food and Drug Administration Severely Criticized Local Protectionism (sources: Xinhua News Agency), Nan Fang Daily, 03/09/2001, People's Daily Online, http://www.people.com.cn/GB/other4789/20010903/550686.html, accessed 8 November 2012.

According to the Beijing Morning Post, many drugstore chains are subject to interference from local governments when setting up their inter-regional shops. In the process of establishing its branch in a southern city, a domestic drugstore chain received a notice from the local drug administrative bureau, indicating that its application for establishment could not be approved even after all the requirements regarding capital, personnel and shop site were met. The reason was that there was already a pharmacy within 500 m of the potential location for the branch. Therefore, the establishment of a branch did not meet the requirements for the planning of pharmacy sites. However, within less than half a month after that decision was taken, a local company successfully set up its pharmacy on the same site.[22]

As reported by Nanfengchuang, the company 999, registered in Guangdong province and one of the biggest pharmaceutical corporations in China, was denied the opening of a branch in Nanchang, although it seemed to have satisfied all requirements. The explanation given was that the local Food and Drug Administration (FDA) refused to deal with 999's license application promptly. The authority explained that it turned out to be very time-consuming to process the application. It planned to study 999's situation and discuss it first with the Chamber of Commerce, the local pharmaceutical company and related pharmaceutical stores. Only after these steps were taken, a decision could be made.[23]

Another case in point is the establishment of café chains. Here, non-local chains often face additional licensing requirements imposed by local authorities. For example, the Beijing Youth Daily has indicated that the development of café chains is obstructed by local protectionism. One manager of a café chain complains that even if licenses for national application are used to open cafés in local regions, there are still many key issues that need to be considered and solved. As a result, opportunities are lost in many cases. Because of the seriousness of the protectionism, companies from outside have to meet additional thresholds, which causes difficulties when they attempt to set up new businesses in a local market.[24]

According to an article published in the 21st Century Business Herald, many formalities imposed by various administrative agencies, ranging from ministries to local governmental cultural departments and cultural inspection teams at county level, are involved in the setting up of café chains.[25] Furthermore, as argued by the Zhongguancun Online, local protectionism takes various forms. Café chains have to deal with endless reviews, inspections and approvals of the authorities for public security, industry and commerce, health, etc. In addition, there are many competent authorities. The owners of these cafés have to cope with "interim measures" and

---

[22] 鄢晨, 走好, 连锁药店!,千京晨报, 2001年11月8日, Ye (2001).

[23] 袁卫东、毛译敏, 谁在阻击药业连锁, 南风窗 2001.11下, 页7. Yuan and Mao (2001), p. 7.

[24] 千京青年报,《连锁网吧"鸡肋"式生存文化部欲靠免税救场》, 2005-01-17, Beijing Youth Daily (2005).

[25] 21 世纪经济报 (记者: 雷中辉), 连锁网吧鸡肋式生存文化部救场三年免税, 2005 年01月16日, 21st Century Business Herald (2005).

"provisional regulations" of governments at all levels, besides the remaining red-tape documents.[26]

Shifting our attention to barriers to the expansion of FIEs, several cases indicate that additional unlawful licensing requirements are applied in the retail industry. According to China Business, to increase local tax revenues, conditions for local market entry require foreign invested retailers to pay a tax to the regions where their shops operate.[27] Thus, local authorities usually require these firms to take the form of subsidiaries or to move their headquarters to regions administrated by these agencies. In other instances, these departments ask for the building of distribution centres in their areas, as additional strings attached to the establishment of FIEs.

The Guangzhou government offered such terms to Wal-Mart China's expansion in its region, although Wal-Mart China's investment was welcomed, according to a former commercial official. More specifically, this FIE had to relocate either its headquarters or accounting centre to Guangzhou, or it had to create an independent management system for all of its branches in Guangzhou. Without meeting these conditions, Wal-Mart China would not be allowed to set up supermarkets in the city of Guangzhou.[28] The Guangzhou authorities imposed the relocation requirement for tax reasons.

According to a renowned financial professional, Wal-Mart China set up an accounting centre for all its branches and located it in Shenzhen, the municipality where Wal-Mart China's headquarters are situated. Therefore, the financial flows of all the outlets are calculated in Shenzhen.[29] Moreover, the local shops only pay sales tax (the amount of which is rather small) to the local tax authorities where their business is located. Other taxes, such as the corporate income tax and the value added tax (VAT), are paid to the Shenzhen region.[30]

One provincial governmental officer stated that his region was tricked into stimulating Wal-Mart China's investment, as revealed by an insider. This is because the tax contribution made by one Wal-Mart shop to "his" area only amounted to about 1 million RMB.[31] Apparently, the region may have offered preferential terms to attract Wal-Mart China's establishment, with an expectation of increasing tax revenues. Nevertheless, the real tax contribution disappointed him, which explains why he made the above statement.

---

[26] 中关村在线, 网吧连锁: 前途有些光明道路绝对曲折, 2006年09月06日, Zhongguancun Online (2012).

[27] 进入中国12年终辗转进广州, 沃尔玛区域突围, 2007年12月17日, 来源: 中国经营报, With Twists and Turns for 12 Years After its Entry into China, Wal-Mart Finally Opens up Markets in Guangzhou, 17th Dec. 2007, sources: *China Business*, http://bj.house.sina.com.cn/mansion/2007-12-17/1008229736.html, accessed 21 November 2013.

[28] 周芳, 被拒13年, 沃尔玛终以妥协得进广州, 经理日报, 2009-11-08, Zhou (2009).

[29] 刘林鹏, 重庆释放沃尔玛被捕员工, 绿色猪肉导致损失近亿, 每日经济新闻, 2012年05月02日, Liu (2012).

[30] 黄清燕, 迎合地方政府, 沃尔玛设数十子公司加速扩张, 2010-03-18, 来源: 每日经济新闻, Huang (2010).

[31] 孙欣, 沃尔玛的羁绊, 中国企业家, 2008 (21), Sun (2008).

According to Zhou (2009), Wal-Mart China's corporate structure implied that, in establishing shops in Guangzhou, Wal-Mart China would profit from these outlets, whereas the city of Guangzhou would not benefit from tax receipts.[32] However, Wal-Mart China refused to move its headquarters. As reported by China Business, this attitude put the firm in real difficulties with the Guangzhou municipality. As a result, Wal-Mart China had difficulties establishing branches in the city. As a result of the twists and turns of the administrative process, Wal-Mart did not open a store in Guangzhou until its 12th year in China.[33] As reported by Zhou, an agreement was finally reached for the establishment of Wal-Mart China's Guangzhou outlets, which allowed the municipality of Guangzhou to receive business tax revenues. To realize this aim, Wal-Mart China's supermarkets in Guangzhou had to be established as corporations whose capital is subscribed by Wal-Mart and local firms together. In other words, Wal-Mart China is prevented from setting up branches in Guangzhou.[34]

In fact, Guangzhou is not the only place where Wal-Mart China's expansion is restricted.[35] Because of the location of its headquarters, regions apart from Shenzhen firmly opposed Wal-Mart's establishment of branches in these areas.[36] For instance, in both Shanghai and Hangzhou, Wal-Mart experienced difficulties when adding a distribution centre.[37] In the process of establishing its first store in Shanghai, the company faced significant hurdles. In addition to the normal establishment conditions, the Shanghai authority also requested Wal-Mart to set up a distribution centre. Wal-Mart China stopped its expansion in Shanghai after stating that such a requirement was unacceptable.[38] In 2003, the Shanghai municipality

[32] 周芳, 被拒 13 年, 沃尔玛终以妥协得进广州, 经理日报, Zhou (2009).

[33] 进入中国 12 年终辗转进广州, 沃尔玛区域突围, 2007年 12月17日, 来源: 中国经营报, With Twists and Turns for 12 Years After its Entry into China, Wal-Mart Finally Opens up Markets in Guangzhou, 17 December 2007, sources: China Business, http://bj.house.sina.com.cn/mansion/2007-12-17/1008229736.html, accessed 21 November 2013.

[34] 周芳, 被拒 13 年, 沃尔玛终以妥协得进广州, 经理日报, 2009-11-08, Zhou (2009).

[35] 进入中国 12 年终辗转进广州, 沃尔玛区域突围, 2007年12月17日, 来源: 中国经营报, With Twists and Turns for 12 Years After its Entry into China, Wal-Mart Finally Opens up Markets in Guangzhou, 17 December 2007, sources: China Business, http://bj.house.sina.com.cn/mansion/2007-12-17/1008229736.html, accessed 21 November 2013.

[36] 刘林鹏, 重庆释放沃尔玛被捕员工, 绿色猪肉导致损失近亿, 每日经济新闻, 2012 年 05月02日,Liu (2012).

[37] 李纬娜, 沃尔玛、家乐福谁赢得中国市场?, 财经, 2007-7-22, Li (2007). The Asia Case Research Centre, University of Hong Kong, Wal-Mart Stores: "Every Day Low Prices" in China, http://www.scribd.com/doc/51421286/WalMart-China-Strategy, accessed 27 October 2012 (link has been removed).

[38] The Asia Case Research Centre, University of Hong Kong, Wal-Mart Stores: "Every Day Low Prices" in China, http://www.scribd.com/doc/51421286/WalMart-China-Strategy, 27 October 2012 (link has been removed).

denied this firm's investment project for the reason that no hypermarket building was allowed within the city's outer-ring road.[39]

A study from Hong Kong University demonstrates that the Shanghai authority clearly wanted to increase its tax revenues generated from the operation of a distribution centre there, Based on this experience, Wal-Mart China lists local protectionism as one of the most serious problems for expanding its business in China. An analysis from Hong Kong University also holds that local administrative agencies usually create difficulties for the establishment of companies in their regions for their own gain.[40] Moreover, according to a domestic commercial venture's manager, some regions not only became less eager to attract Wal-Mart, but also supported local enterprises more in building shops. The reason is that these outlets contribute all their tax revenues to regional authorities.[41]

Other foreign-funded retailers are also likely to encounter entry barriers for tax reasons, similar to Wal-Mart China. For instance, METRO China could not enter certain regional markets because of tax payment issues, as confirmed by one of its former staff members.[42]

Sun (2008) concludes that Wal-Mart China may end up in conflict with local governments that cannot be easily resolved. This type of conflict is the third element restricting the expansion of this FIE, in addition to the influence of the Ministry of Commerce (MOFCOM) and local retailers.[43] According to the National Business Daily, these conflicts are caused by the fact that local regions cannot profit from Wal-Mart China's operation in terms of tax receipts.[44] This is because most of this FIE's tax is paid at its headquarters, as shown by China Business. Thus, local

[39] 进入中国 12 年终辗转进广州, 沃尔玛区域突围, 2007 年 12月17日, 来源: 中国经营报, With Twists and Turns for 12 Years After its Entry into China, Wal-Mart Finally Opens up Markets in Guangzhou, 17 December 2007, sources: China Business, http://bj.house.sina.com.cn/mansion/2007-12-17/1008229736.html, accessed 21 November 2013.

[40] The Asia Case Research Centre, University of Hong Kong, Wal-Mart Stores: "Every Day Low Prices" in China, http://www.scribd.com/doc/51421286/WalMart-China-Strategy, accessed 27 October 2012 (link has been removed). Because Wal-Mart China is an FIE, local protectionism here may also refer to the obstacles faced in relation to Foreign Direct Investment more generally. For example, see the MOFCOM, Overview of FDI in China, http://english.mofcom.gov.cn/aarticle/topic/bizchina/fdiinchina/200406/20040600233643.html, 14 June 2004, accessed 21 February 2013.

[41] 孙欣, 沃尔玛的羁绊, 中国企业家, 2008 (21), Sun (2008).

[42] 进入中国 12 年终辗转进广州, 沃尔玛区域突围, 2007 年 12 月 17日, 来源: 中国经营报, With Twists and Turns for 12 Years After its Entry into China, Wal-Mart Finally Opens up Markets in Guangzhou, 17 December 2007, sources: China Business, http://bj.house.sina.com.cn/mansion/2007-12-17/1008229736.html, accessed 21 November 2013.

[43] 孙欣, 沃尔玛的羁绊, 中国企业家, 2008 (21), Sun (2008).

[44] 沃尔玛: 妥协于中国消费模式?每日经济新闻, Wal-Mart: Compromising itself by Accepting the Chinese Consumption Model? National Business Daily, http://news.yipu.com.cn/shAngye/cs/229423.html, accessed 22 November 2013.

governments refuse to grant certain licenses to Wal-Mart China, thereby effectively keeping it from opening outlets in many Chinese cities.[45]

It follows from the above that companies, at least in certain sectors (particularly in services sectors), have faced entry barriers when attempting to expand into local markets outside their headquarters' area. According to Tang (2013), the barriers created by administrative agencies constitute an important interference with market competition, restricting the entry of new enterprises.[46] Since 2013, the emphasis of the "deepening reform" in China has been placed on combating regional protection.[47]

4 The Theory of Regulation

This section briefly addresses the public interest approach and the private interest approach to regulation.[48] In subsequent sections we will address the question whether the private interest approach can provide explanations for the regulation of the inter-provincial establishment and its enforcement, different from (or in addition to) public interest explanations.

4.1 The Public Interest Approach

A public interest approach to regulation starts from the assumption that regulation is always aimed at increasing social welfare. Applying this (optimistic) view to the regulation of market entry, this approach demonstrates that entry regulation of new ventures can cut inferior products from unreliable providers out of the market, therefore increasing the average quality of products. As a result, entry regulation has the potential to increase consumer welfare. However, whether excluding certain products from the market increases social welfare, depends crucially on (the heterogeneity of) actual consumer preferences.[49]

---

45 进入中国 12 年终辗转进广州, 沃尔玛区域突围, 2007 年 12 月 17 日, 来源: 中国经营报, With Twists and Turns for 12 Years After its Entry into China, Wal-Mart Finally Opens up Markets in Guangzhou, 17 December 2007, sources: China Business, http://bj.house.sina.com.cn/mansion/2007-12-17/1008229736.html, accessed 21 November 2013.

46 唐开康, 公平竞争的市场体系是改革最大红利, 光明日报, 2013 年 12 月 03 日, Tang (2013).

47 中共中央关于全面深化改革若干重大问题的决定 (全文), Decision of the CCCPC on Some Major Issues Concerning Comprehensively Deepening the Reform, http://www.china.org.cn/chinese/2014-01/17/content_31226494_3.htm, accessed 5 February 2014.

48 For a recapitulation of private and public interest theory, see also the contribution to this volume by Philipsen and Zhou. For a longer review, see Philipsen (2003), Chapter 2.

49 See more particularly Shapiro (1986).

Theoretically, if there is a market failure in the form of externalities, information problems, market power or public goods, regulation may be justified on the ground of public interests. However, this of course does not imply that *licensing* needs to be introduced. Public interest theory suggests that a proportional cure for the market failure at hand needs to be chosen, and the less a particular regulatory instrument intervenes in a market, the better. Rules on mandatory information provision, labelling, certification or performance standards may be (better) alternatives for licensing, depending on the seriousness of the market failure and the specific context.[50]

The first market failure that may justify regulation on public interest grounds is the existence of externalities.[51] Externalities arise if the effects of the actions performed by subject A partially influence subject B. According to Ogus and Zhang (2005), in many developing countries, licensing systems have been introduced in relation to construction safety, waste disposal and other aims. Some goods and services subject to these regimes can potentially cause externalities. For instance, the use of nuclear materials can have a significant adverse impact on third parties. If left unregulated, badly designed buildings may collapse (calling for licensing of architects and engineers); food and medicines can have a negative health impact, etc. Nevertheless, it follows from the economic literature that negative externalities may explain operation licensing, but do not necessarily justify entry licensing.[52]

The presence of information problems can be another public interest reason for regulation. Issues of information asymmetry appear more particularly in the provision of experience goods and trust goods.[53] The qualities of experience goods cannot be tested before purchasing.[54] Trust goods are characterized by the fact that consumers cannot judge their quality even after consumption.[55] Professional services are examples of experience or trust goods (think of, for example, the pharmaceutical services we referred to earlier), but products provided by companies can also be experience goods or trust goods. Registration procedures provide companies with some kind of government approval, signifying that they are reliable enough to trade with citizens and other ventures.[56]

---

[50] For further details on instrument choice, see Ogus (1994) and Philipsen (2003).

[51] Of course, government intervention is only necessary when transaction costs prevent efficient bargaining from taking place, according to the well-known Coase theorem.

[52] Ogus and Zhang (2005), p. 139. The failure to obtain an entry license results in companies not being able to conduct business in any sector. However, the failure to acquire an operation license, does not prevent a company from being formed, nor does it prevent a company from operating in unregulated fields, as long as it does not engage in the industries governed by the operation licensing regime (Ogus and Zhang 2005, p. 126).

[53] Den Hertog (2003), pp. 13–14.

[54] Nelson (1970), p. 312.

[55] Darby and Karni (1973), pp. 68–69.

[56] See also Djankov et al. (2002), p. 2.

In addition to externalities and information problems, a third public interest justification for regulation is (abuse of) market power. This type of market failure is more particularly the subject of competition law.[57] The fourth public interest justification for regulatory intervention is the presence of public goods: those being goods that are characterized by non-rivalrous consumption and non-excludability.[58] These last two types of market failure will not be further addressed here.

It is important to remember that the existence of market failure does not necessarily require regulation.[59] Sometimes liability rules, taxation or subsidies, or market-based instruments (such as emissions trading) may solve the problem. Moreover, there may be regulatory failures if added transaction costs or misallocations in other economic sectors outweigh the increased value in efficiency arising from regulation.[60]

4.2 The Private Interest Approach

The private interest approach to regulation stresses the influence of interest groups (such as industry lobby groups and professional associations) in the formation of regulation. The basic assumption is that there is a demand and supply for regulation; and interest groups (the demand side) try to influence the political decision-making process with the aim of seeking rents for themselves. The fact that resources are used to capture wealth transfers from the general public to specific interest groups is unproductive from a social welfare point of view.[61] Olson found that interest groups, such as industry lobby groups, are more likely to be successful in their lobbying activities if they are relatively small, well organized and focused on a clear common goal; especially when there are high information costs for the public at large of finding out that regulation is not in the public interest.[62]

According to Stigler's "theory of economic regulation" (1971), regulation originates where the benefits are concentrated (the industry) and the costs can be divided over a large group. Industry lobbies for restrictive entry regulation, for

---

[57] A related issue is the presence of natural monopolies. Regulation in the form of e.g. price regulation or government supervision over market deregulation (such as the "services of general economic interest" regime in the EU) may be required. Philipsen (2003), pp. 12–13; Boehm (2007), pp. 1-2. See also the contributions to Part I of this book.

[58] Den Hertog (2000), p. 230.

[59] Den Hertog (2003), p. 42.

[60] Ogus (1994), p. 30.

[61] Philipsen (2007), p. 116.

[62] Olson (1965), Chapters 1–3. The concept of "rent seeking", introduced by Anne Krueger in the Political Economy of the Rent-Seeking Society, refers to the political activity of citizens and groups using scarce resources to pursue monopoly rights granted by authorities (see Den Hertog 2000, p. 243).

example in the form of licensing, as this restricts competition and increases profits of the insiders in the market.[63] *Legal* entry barriers (i.e. in the form of protective regulation) according to Stigler are more effective against competitive pressure than "traditional" entry barriers discussed in economic literature, such as limit pricing strategies, collusion, vertical integration and product differentiation. Peltzman (1976), who extended Stigler's model, Posner (1974, 1975) and Becker (1983) all later pointed to the fact that different interest groups are often in competition with each other for political favours.[64] The political outcome will reflect concessions to all interest groups, and depends on the respective strengths and efficiency (in lobbying) of each interest group in the lobbying process. In Becker's model, the view that governments correct market failures (public interest approach) and the view that governments favour the politically powerful (private interest approach) are to some extent unified.[65]

Different from the Chicago theory of regulation, the Virginia (Public Choice) school emphasizes the costs of the lobbying process—a process famously termed "rent seeking" by Krueger (1974). The fact that resources are only used to obtain or maintain legal protection or other political favours is a clear cost to society.[66] A starting point of any Public Choice analysis, as found e.g. in Buchanan and Tullock (1962), is that in essence there is no difference between the behaviour of politicians and the behaviour of market actors; both groups are pursuing the maximization of utility.[67] Politicians may want to be re-elected, or they may want to increase the size of their bureaucracy or power, and in the process they are likely to provide inefficient regulation (serving particular lobbying groups) in exchange for obtaining votes.[68] Because of the "vote motive" for being re-elected, politicians will especially have incentives to meet the needs of small and tightly organized groups.[69]

In the Chicago and Public Choice theories described above, public agents play a relatively passive role as a broker between the different interest groups. Boehm (2007) explains that the so-called "tollbooth theory" goes one step further, as it claims that public agents play a much more active role. Scholars such as De Soto (1989) and Shleifer and Vishny (1994) have pointed out that politicians and bureaucrats enjoying a monopolistic position are able to formulate inefficient

---

[63] Stigler (1971), pp. 3–4. He famously stated that; "as a rule, regulation is acquired by the industry and is designed and operated primarily for its benefits". It should be emphasized that Stigler's work has a strong empirical basis.

[64] Together these contributions are usually referred to as the "Chicago theory of regulation". See e.g. Philipsen (2003), pp. 25–26, and Boehm (2007), pp. 4–7.

[65] Becker (1983), p. 383.

[66] See also the work by Bhagwati (1982).

[67] Buchanan and Tullock (1962), pp. 17–39.

[68] Philipsen (2003), p. 24. See also Buchanan et al. (1980) and Boehm (2007), pp. 7–8.

[69] Shughart II (2008).

regulations (red tape), which enable them to obtain rents through bribes and campaign contributions.[70] The regulatory control that politicians have over firms provides opportunities for officials to seek rents through corruption.[71] Shleifer and Vishny (1994) refer in that respect to the situation in Italy and the Philippines.[72] The authors hold that an important reason for the existence of many permits and regulations is that it allows officials to take bribes, since they are entitled to decide whether or not permits will be granted.[73] The creation of more extensive regulation in their view is connected with producing socially inferior results.[74]

5 Interests of the Actors Involved in the Regulation of Inter-Provincial Establishment

In this section we will investigate what the private interests are that may be served by regulating the inter-provincial establishment of companies. We will focus on the interests of local officials, local firms, and other companies, respectively.

5.1 *Local Officials*

As stated by Mehra and Meng (2008), "barriers to external competition that bolster the income of local enterprises translate into higher levels of employment for the local population and more tax revenues for local government".[75] Local governments hence clearly face incentives to protect local industry to generate market demand for local products and labour. While this may sounds good in itself, destructive competition between provinces or regions is the likely end result.[76] Moreover, from a private interest perspective, local officials have additional reasons to protect local industry. In the following we will focus on two of these

[70] Boehm (2007), p. 9.

[71] For a brief overview of the economic literature on corruption, see Boehm (2007), pp. 11–15. Corruption differs from lobbying in that it is illegal, secret and non transparent and reflects narrow interests (e.g. of one firm), whereas lobbying is legal, relatively transparent and reflects broader interests (e.g. of one industry). The main forms in which corruption presents itself are defined by Boehm as bribery, embezzlement, fraud, extortion, favouritism and nepotism. See also Andvig et al. (2000).

[72] Shleifer and Vishny (1994), p. 1007.

[73] Shleifer and Vishny (1993), p. 601.

[74] Djankov et al. (2002), p. 3.

[75] Mehra and Meng (2008), pp. 399–400.

[76] This chapter is not the place to discuss this issue in detail, but applying the economics of federalism to the issue of cross-provincial establishment in China will be subject of future work. See also Mehra and Meng (2008), p. 400.

reasons: the quest for promotion (Sect. 5.1.1) and the problem of corruption (Sect. 5.1.2).

5.1.1 Promotion

One explanation for local protectionist practices in China may be that local officers are striving for promotion within the Communist Party of China (CPC).[77] When entry barriers are created for companies from other jurisdictions, this can serve as a shield that protects local economies. Moreover, local protectionism may negatively affect the economic development of other regions. As a result, local officials are more likely to receive promotion. To grasp this causal relationship, one needs to consider how local governors can obtain career advancement in China.

According to Zhou (2004), the growth rate of GDP is the most important criterion for promoting officials in China. Local officials from different regions not only compete with each other in terms of GDP growth and taxation; they also compete for advancement in their official careers.[78] In reality, getting a promotion is likely to be more important to officers.[79] Pi (2008) demonstrates that, currently, local officeholders attach high importance to winning the competition for advancement.[80] Moreover, only a limited number of local officers can obtain a promotion.[81] This results in a situation in which local governors are motivated to promote the economic development of their own areas at the expense of other regions, as pointed out by Zhou.[82]

Local protectionism can boost local economic development in the short term, according to Pan (2009).[83] Moreover, since a local governor's term of office is usually short, welcoming the investment of non-local firms may not be helpful in the search for promotion. In practice, more than half of all local officeholders serve for only 2 years, as reported by the 21st Century Business Herald (2014b). The average tenure in office for governors at county levels is 3 years.[84] According to the Legal Daily (2013), it can be learnt from press reports that the term of a local public servant in a particular job is often very short.[85] If the actual term of office is only 2 or 3 years, start-ups funded by businesses from other regions would not generate much tax revenues in this period of time.

---

[77] Zhou (2004), p. 37.

[78] Zhou (2004), p. 34.

[79] Zhou (2007), p. 38.

[80] Pi (2008), p. 122.

[81] Zhou (2004), p. 34.

[82] Zhou (2004), p. 34.

[83] 潘勇, “保增长” 别纵容了地方保护主义, 齐鲁晚报, Pan (2009).

[84] 21 世纪经济报道, 地方债治本之道: 地方官员向当地百姓负责, 2014 年 1月3日, 21st Century Business Herald (2014a).

[85] 法制日报, 严格任期制, 避免官员成 “临时工”, 2013 年 7月15日, Legal Daily (2013).

Creating barriers to market access can be profitable for local economies. The development of locally important industries is immediately connected with the revenue of local governments.[86] Moreover, State-owned enterprises (SOEs) pay taxes according to their administrative subordination, as pointed out by Mao. For example, SOEs administrated by a provincial government have tax obligations to this particular provincial authority.[87] If administrative power is used to shield local enterprises, local enterprises can squeeze out any competition, make more profits and pay more taxes.[88]

According to Guo and Hu (2002), if locally owned companies are not competitive and suffer from shrinking profits, local agencies usually exercise their administrative powers to restrict or prohibit the entry of non-local firms rather than increasing the local companies' competitive abilities. This type of behaviour may result in the presence of administrative monopolies.[89]

Furthermore, obstructing the establishment of non-local firms can harm the economy of other regions. If companies headquartered in province A open branches in another region B, these branches pay a bulk of its enterprise income tax to province A.[90] The enterprise income tax, the consumption tax and the VAT are the main taxes imposed on enterprises; together accounting for the lion's share of tax revenues.[91] Entry barriers may also cause additional negative effects on the economic growth of other areas: for example, firms from other jurisdictions may not be able to provide services in regions outside their headquarters without establishing branches in these regions. Pan (2009) concludes that local officials can take protectionist measures in the name of promoting economic development, benefiting the public, etc., and rather than being punished for this, they gain prestige and wealth.[92]

A conclusion that we can draw from this is that in China, local officeholders' incentives to seek promotion seem to differ to some extent from the incentives discussed in traditional public choice theory. Promotion rather than the "vote motive" drives local officials to introduce entry barriers.

---

[86] Guo and Hu (2002).

[87] Zhongguowang (2014).

[88] 潘勇, "保增长" 别纵容了地方保护主义, 齐鲁晚报, Pan (2009).

[89] Guo and Hu (2002). The notion of administrative monopolies refers to a situation in which an administrative agency abuses its administrative power to restrict or eliminate competition. See Huang (2008), p. 92.

[90] This information is obtained from two civil servants of tax authorities in Beijing and Chengdu.

[91] Deng (2003), p. 16.

[92] 潘勇, "保增长" 别纵容了地方保护主义, 齐鲁晚报, Pan (2009).

5.1.2 Corruption

In a global study from 2002, Djankov et al. found that more intensive regulation of entry is generally related to higher corruption.[93] In the context of inter-provincial establishment of companies, rent seeking by officials through the creation of market entry barriers can be understood from two perspectives.

First, local officeholders may erect entry barriers in exchange for personal gains provided to them by market incumbents. Existing producers may try to exclude competitors from other jurisdictions from the market; entry barriers, such as licensing, serve that purpose well. As demonstrated by Xin, there is a tendency to impose additional licensing requirements on non-local firms to protect local industries.[94] Also, a study by Deng reports that local protectionist measures often result from "an improper use of administrative power", i.e. corruption.[95]

According to Hu and Guo (2013), corruption by local officers and rent seeking by local companies have caused severe regional market disintegration in China. The authors back up this statement with convincing empirical evidence: based on panel data concerning 28 provinces in the period 1988–2010, they conclude that the more corrupt local public officials are, the greater the regional market fragmentation, and vice versa. Creating entry barriers for non-local ventures allows local officials to take bribes from local enterprises and increase tax revenues. These incentives drive officeholders to implement local protectionist measures.[96]

Second, local officials may want to create entry barriers, as this provides them with the opportunity to take bribes from *non-local* firms. If businesses from other jurisdictions want to enter local markets, they may have to offer bribes to local officers. For example, in Jilin province some officials in charge of the establishment by non-local firms "used every opportunity to make personal gains", and were strongly criticized for their behaviour by the CPC provincial chief of Jilin. These officials were seeking rents, whenever non-local businesses applied for an approval of their investment plans or had to complete other procedures necessary for establishment in Jilin. The officeholders concerned even claimed that it is "the custom of Jilin officers to gain benefits in the process of non-local firms' investment".[97]

---

[93] Djankov et al. (2002), pp. 26–27.

[94] 新望, "地方保护主义" 该收场了, Xin (2014).

[95] Deng (2003), p. 15.

[96] Hu and Guo (2013), p. 45.

[97] 常旭， 吉林省委书记批少数部门对外来企业雁过拔毛， 城市晚报， 2008 年 04月17日, Chang (2008).

5.2 Local Industries

According to Zhang et al. (2013), firms tend to rely on local governments in regions where local protectionism is severe. When encountering difficulties, local firms often seek help from local governments.[98] For example, when faced with the expansion plans of non-local rivals, local leading supermarkets have repeatedly used their influence over regional governments, creating numerous difficulties to retailers from other areas.[99]

Guo and Hu (2004) state that favoured firms and industries can develop cosy relationships with local office holders. This provides tremendous opportunities for rent seeking, since administrative authorities are able to use their administrative power to reward local business.[100]

According to the empirical research of Jun Hu and Feng Guo mentioned above, companies tend to bribe local officials to exercise protectionism in the regions in which they are headquartered. Local enterprises prompt authorities to create impediments for market entry, thus avoiding competition with ventures from other regions. Rent seeking by local firms leads to market fragmentation.[101]

5.3 Other Industries

Also other industries are likely to cater to local authorities that are responsible for managing entry into local markets. As pointed out in a workshop organized by the American Chamber of Commerce in China (hereinafter AmCham China), it is necessary for FIEs to show their definite contribution to the market and industry sites they want to operate in. Drawing support from regional governments can accelerate the granting of licenses because of their ability to facilitate the application procedure. Local authorities are often willing to provide such assistance since they might want to increase employment and attract capital, whereas the central government might not.[102]

For instance, foreign invested retailers, including Carrefour China and Wal-Mart China, make use of public media to show that they contribute substantially to the Chinese (local) economy, e.g. by increasing local tax revenues or creating jobs. A

[98] Zhang et al. (2013), p. 85.

[99] 潘沩, 本土超市卖场为何难出苏宁国美, 21 世纪经济报道, Pan (2011).

[100] Guo and Hu (2004), pp. 265 and 279; Mehra and Meng (2008), p. 400.

[101] Hu and Guo (2013), p. 45.

[102] AmCham China, License to Expand—A 2012 Business Climate Survey Event 25 April 2012, http://www.amchamchina.org/article/9560, accessed 8 October 2014. AmCham China points out that some of the key problems for FIEs in obtaining licenses include the inconsistency of Chinese licensing requirements, the uneven enforcement of licensing rules, lengthy procedures, and the fact that licenses are not granted equally to Chinese and foreign firms.

senior PR officer from a renowned FIE once made the humorous remark that his venture can easily win more government favours if it would advertise the company's contribution to administrative achievement.[103]

Moreover, since officers can arbitrarily decide to implement local protectionist measures, firms may have to bribe officials when entering into regional markets.[104] The 21st Century Business Herald reports that rent seeking is more likely when there is local protectionism. The cost of PR increases if non-local companies want to enter into local markets or provide market access opportunities for their products.[105] The China Business (2013) reveals that Wal-Mart China might have offered bribes to acquire licenses for new shops, to finish establishment procedures and deal with government inquiries. However, Wal-Mart could not comment on these statements, as an investigation was being conducted under the Foreign Corrupt Practices Act (US).[106]

6 Interview Results

A number of interviews have been conducted by Guang Shen to provide further insights into the reality of the inter-provincial establishment of companies. The information obtained from these interviews offers some support for the assumption that promotion is a significant incentive (as presented in Sect. 5.1 above), although hard conclusions could not be reached. All interviews were held on a semi-structured basis, i.e. interviewees conveyed their opinions on specific issues of establishment based on a questionnaire.

6.1 Access Barriers Erected by Local Licensing Authorities

Strict licensing requirements are imposed to create market entry barriers in certain fields, according to Z, a local licensing official. In these industries, monopolies or SOEs have occupied a significant market share and have gained huge profits. To impose obstacles for potential competitors, authorities usually set very harsh terms for businesses to obtain licenses. The establishment of these licensing systems can block the expansion of non-local companies.[107]

---

[103] 黄霞, 洋零售的 "讨好" 术, 羊城晚报, Huang and Yangcheng Evening News (2014).

[104] Deng (2003), p. 15.

[105] 21 世纪经济报导, 警惕国内地方保护主义复苏, 21st Century Business Herald (2014b).

[106] 中国经营报, 沃尔玛反腐调查波及中国, 或关闭 100 家亏损门店, China Business (2012).

[107] Interview with Z, a local licensing official, 20 August 2013 (interview transcript on file with the authors). With more than 17 years of experience, Z is a licensing official of a local Administration of Industry and Commerce in Shandong Province.

Z provides an example concerning the difficulties of entering the market for public transport. Currently, mainly local SOEs provide public transportation services and they make good profits doing so. To prevent (or restrict) competition, local authorities have established licensing regimes that regulate market access. Ordinary individuals or businesses can hardly form companies for passenger transport, because of the strict requirements that need to be fulfilled to obtain a license.[108]

According to N, a local licensing officer, it is likely that local protectionism is the norm in the café industry. The same is true of the coal mining, highway construction, and town and village bank establishment industries. Local ventures are more likely to obtain licenses and to do business in these industries than companies that have been incorporated in other regions.[109]

According to a recent report; in the logistics industry, when non-local companies try to form branches, local Administrations of Industry and Commerce (AICs) in some cases refuse to deal with business license applications,. These authorities have given various reasons for their refusal. In other cases, additional licensing requirements have been defined for non-local entrepreneurs that need to be carried out before a company can be registered.[110]

The expansion of café chains is hindered significantly by local cultural authorities, as C, a national café chain manager, demonstrated. Although C's company has a permit for opening cafés nationwide, as a result of the behaviour of local cultural agencies, it still encounters tremendous difficulties in the process of establishing branches. These licensing authorities require C's firm to obtain their permission prior to opening shops in their regions. Local protectionism can be noticed here in the approval process. In some cases, enterprises meeting certain conditions have been granted licenses, whereas non-local firms meeting the same conditions were not.[111]

C provided us with several examples demonstrating the difficulties in the expansion of his company. For example, one requirement made in a particular district provides that a license for an additional cyber café will be given only if a firm can open five such branches in this area. This provision most certainly benefits local companies only. This is because these businesses have already established numerous internet cafés and therefore can easily obtain a new permission. By

[108] Interview with Z, a local licensing official, 20 August 2013 (interview transcript on file with the authors).

[109] Interview with N, a local licensing official, 6 August 2013 (interview transcript on file with the authors).

[110] 中国物流与采购联合会， 物流业消除地区封锁、打破行业垄断的政策建议 （内部资料），页1。 CFLP, Policy Suggestions for the Logistics Industry to Erase Regional Blockades and Break Industrial Monopolies (unpublished), p. 1. In our interview with a senior researcher from the CFLP, the interviewee indicated that AICs and local governments make it difficult for logistics companies to set up businesses.

[111] Interview with C, a national café chain's manager, July 2013 (interview transcript on file with the authors).

contrast, most non-local enterprises are only starting their business in this region and hence by no means are able to meet these requirements.[112]

6.2 *Interests of Officials in Creating Entry Barriers*

6.2.1 Promotion

According to X, apart from legal restrictions on business scope, other elements that can influence the inter-provincial establishment of companies include tax revenues, employment and social stability. Governments usually expect that benefits in the form of taxation, employment and stability can be derived from the establishment of companies in their local areas.[113]

First, with respect to taxation, when new factories are opened, local governments always consider the ability of such factories to make profits and generate tax revenues, as pointed out by X. For tax reasons, local governments usually prefer the establishment of subsidiaries to the establishment of branches. As mentioned before, subsidiaries pay a large share of their taxes in local regions, whereas branches do not. To attract subsidiaries, local authorities often apply favourable conditions to this business form.[114]

A case in point is X's own corporate group. Most businesses established by this group are subsidiaries rather than branches, because the conditions attached to this particular business form are more favourable. For example, governments are usually willing to provide land so that subsidiaries can be formed in the logistics industry. In addition, attractive terms can be given in terms of land prices and locations, and land is highly valuable to the establishment in the logistics trade. Moreover, subsidiaries can get tax refunds. In contrast, it is very uncommon for branches to receive such advantageous treatment.[115] Recent empirical research has indicated that, for tax reasons, only the establishment of subsidiaries is allowed in the logistics industry.[116]

[112] Interview with C, a national café chain's manager, July 2013 (interview transcript on file with the authors).

[113] Interview with X, an enterprise manager, 13 August 2013 (interview transcript on file with the authors). Mr X works on company registration and investment in the logistics industry. His employer is a Fortune 500 enterprise and SOE in a coastal province, which has opened hundreds of subsidiaries across China.

[114] Interview with X, an enterprise manager, 13 August 2013 (interview transcript on file with the authors).

[115] Interview with X, an enterprise manager, 13 August 2013 (interview transcript on file with the authors).

[116] 中国物流与采购联合会，物流业消除地区封锁、打破行业垄断的政策建议（内部资料），页1。CFLP, Policy Suggestions for the Logistics Industry to Erase Regional Blockades and Break Industrial Monopolies (unpublished), p. 1.

Some firms establish branches rather than subsidiaries, but it was noted that this business form is used in special situations only. For instance, enterprises owned by the central government sometimes choose to establish branches in Zhejiang province. These SOEs are usually large firms in monopolistic industries, such as petrochemicals, telecoms and banking. In addition, they own advanced technology in these fields that local authorities do not have. As a result, it is difficult for local governments to influence the investment intentions of these firms.[117] There may also be other cases in which branches are opened rather than subsidiaries. However, this may be possible only when tax agreements are reached. Such contracts are signed between local governments and enterprises, requiring the latter to pay a certain amount of taxes.[118]

Local licensing official N notes that in some cases both subsidiaries and branches can be opened. In other cases, the establishment can only be in the form of subsidiaries. A case in point is the formation of project ventures in the real estate/property industry. When real estate businesses bid for a vacant lot in areas other than their places of incorporation, they are usually asked to establish subsidiaries rather than branches. This is because companies formed for land development projects often need to pay up to 30 % of their investment as tax. Moreover, such investments often have an enormous scale amounting to billions of RMB. This means that the tax contributions of such plans can be considerable. Therefore, for tax reasons local governments usually require the incorporation of subsidiaries in that trade.[119]

Local protectionism in the café industry can also be explained by tax reasons. According to C, local firms usually share common benefits with local authorities via tax payments. Moreover, some local cafés are funded by regional cultural companies, which in turn are funded by local authorities governing the café industry.[120]

Second, local authorities usually hope that the establishment of non-local firms can benefit existing local firms that are in financial difficulties. For example, local governments may require non-local firms to explore new markets for local ventures.[121]

Corporations that can bring these advantages are more likely to (be allowed to) form businesses in local markets. SOEs tend to accept the local governments' terms because of their social commitment. Thus, these enterprises do not experience any difficulties when establishing across provincial borders, although their operating

[117] Interview with X, an enterprise manager, 13 August 2013 (interview transcript on file with the authors).

[118] Interview with X, an enterprise manager, 13 August 2013 (interview transcript on file with the authors).

[119] Interview with N, a local licensing official, 6 August 2013 (interview transcript on file with the authors).

[120] Interview with C, a national café chain's manager, July 2013 (interview transcript on file with the authors).

[121] Interview with X, an enterprise manager, 13 August 2013 (interview transcript on file with the authors).

costs may be high.[122] Because of the SOE's contribution to local welfare, local governments often offer attractive conditions to the incorporation of SOEs in their areas. For example, as mentioned above, they can supply land with high economic value to these companies, which is essential to the formation in certain fields.[123]

As for Mr X's business, it usually employs local workers. Moreover, it can promote the sales of local products in other provinces. For example, his company assists in the marketing of steel produced in the province where his business opened a steel plant. In return, the corporation receives generous treatment in terms of land use.[124]

Also the foreign invested giants such as Wal-Mart China can establish their companies in different provinces rather easily. The explanation provided by Mr X is that they can ensure a high employment rate because of their commercial strength. Being competitive and dynamic corporations, they are better able to deal with certain business risks, and to grow rapidly and stably. This reduces the risk that their employees are laid off.[125] In contrast, private holding companies tend to downsize their staff. With an aim of pursuing economic efficiency, they are usually reluctant to recruit and maintain a large work force. Moreover, they lack the motivation to promote the development of related industries and local economies. Thus, it is likely that local authorities do not applaud the establishment by private enterprises.[126]

6.2.2 Corruption

Not surprisingly, we were unable to obtain hard evidence of corruption from our interviews. Nevertheless, we found that licensing agencies sometimes deal with licensing applications "with strings attached". Furthermore, it is rather common that personal connections are used in license applications.

According to N, some licenses with high market values are hard to obtain, such as licenses for the opening of cafés. As a result, elements other than those provided for in law play a role in the license approval procedure. For example, enterprises affiliated with governments are more likely to obtain approval. Also, personal connections are sought. It is not uncommon for companies to ask their acquaintances in licensing authorities for help. Furthermore, companies may offer bribes to

[122] Interview with X, an enterprise manager, 13 August 2013 (interview transcript on file with the authors).

[123] Interview with X, an enterprise manager, 13 August 2013 (interview transcript on file with the authors).

[124] Interview with X, an enterprise manager, 13 August 2013 (interview transcript on file with the authors).

[125] Interview with X, an enterprise manager, 13 August 2013 (interview transcript on file with the authors).

[126] Interview with X, an enterprise manager, 13 August 2013 (interview transcript on file with the authors).

licensing officials with the profits they can earn from their investment projects. However, such practices take place only in highly profitable or competitive markets. In other markets, license applications are likely to be approved according to law.[127]

To acquire licenses in backward regions, businesses usually have to pay additional fees to licensing authorities, as H remarks. License applications that appear to satisfy all requirements can still be denied by licensing officials in these areas who deliberately create difficulties for applicants. For example, private holding companies from Wenzhou, a city renowned for its private economy, first had to establish connections with licensing officers before they could invest in certain underdeveloped areas. Only after having established such connections could they obtain the necessary licenses. It should be noted that these licensing barriers do not necessarily imply that there is a prevalence of local protectionism in these places; local officials usually want to attract investment.[128]

As demonstrated by C, in a northern province, local cultural agencies set a precondition for his firm to obtain licenses. The authorities ask his business to fund them by contributing 0.8 million RMB, to support local cultural activities.[129]

7 Conclusions

The principal aim of this chapter was to find out whether the regulation of the inter-provincial establishment of companies in China can be explained by private interest considerations. In the preceding sections, we examined the rules on company formation, the enforcement of these rules, and the interests that may be served by controlling market entry.

Looking at the prevailing laws in relation to the inter-provincial establishment of companies, we highlighted two problems in Sect. 2 of this chapter. First, we noted that Article 12 (6) of the ALL seems to leave open the possibility of establishing licensing regimes for every matter. Second, the absence of judicial review means that licensing cannot be constrained effectively. In practice, multiple cases can be identified in which licensing authorities used their administrative powers to cause difficulties for companies wanting to establish across provincial borders. We presented a number of examples—taken both from existing sources (journals,

[127] Interview with N, a local licensing official, 6 August 2013 (interview transcript on file with the authors). Mr N is a licensing official of a local Administration of Industry and Commerce in Zhejiang Province.

[128] Interview with H, a corporation lawyer, 26 August 2013 (interview transcript on file with the authors). Mr H works at the legal department of an SOE and has also dealt with the legal affairs of other private companies. One of his duties is to complete registration procedures and obtain licenses for the expansion of these businesses.

[129] Interview with C, a national café chain's manager, July 2013 (interview transcript on file with the authors).

newspapers, websites), as analysed in Sect. 3, and from our own interviews with stakeholders, as presented in Sect. 5—which suggest that local governments strive to increase tax revenues, thereby showing a preference for the establishment of subsidiaries over the establishment of branches. Furthermore, we found that generating local employment is another goal, which sometimes results in officials imposing special conditions on non-local companies, such as a requirement to help local firms in financial difficulties. Both the existing literature and our interviews confirmed that administrative agencies are able to use their powers to their own (or to the local economy's) advantage, sometimes requesting additional licensing fees from non-local applicants. Of course, whether they in fact use these powers depends on the specific context, e.g. whether the market concerned is competitive or profitable,[130] to what extent local lobbying groups are active, whether an area is a "backward region", etc.

The findings we presented in this paper, taken from existing sources and from the interviews we conducted, provide some support for Stigler's hypothesis that regulation is used as a barrier to entry, serving the interests of local companies. It also provided some support for the hypothesis that public officials do not (only) take into account social interests, but private interests as well, including their own. Nevertheless, the explanations for existing licensing barriers in China do not seem to be entirely consistent with those suggested by the traditional public choice theory. Although corruption, a central element in the "tollbooth view" presented in Sect. 4, explains some of the entry barriers experienced by non-local firms and FIEs, the "vote motive" for re-election does not seem to be relevant in the Chinese context. A much more likely explanation for entry control is that it affects the behaviour of local officers seeking promotion considering that career advancement within the CPC is to some extent linked to (local) GDP growth. This career advancement motive creates a level of competition between local areas that has the potential to become destructive. Moreover, in combination with the often short-term tenure of local officials, and the goal of creating strong local industries (who in turn become strong lobbying groups), it provides incentives to create barriers to cross-provincial establishment.

The evidence we collected from existing sources, as well as the interviews we conducted with stakeholders, provides some evidence for the view that companies seeking to expand across provincial borders face licensing barriers created by local officeholders. However, we are unable to make a strong *general* statement regarding the importance of the promotion seeking argument or corruption as being main drivers for licensing barriers. The importance of these factors is likely to vary between industries and provinces. There remain many situations, where investment by FIEs and non-local industries is welcomed, as it enhances local economic growth and employment. However, it is the persistent nature of the licensing

---

[130] In that respect it may also be relevant whether it concerns service enterprises or industrial enterprises. Most of our examples indicating the presence of licensing barriers related to the former category.

barriers in certain industries and certain areas that remains highly problematic, preventing real market integration from occurring.

References

21st Century Business Herald (2005) Café Chains Have Difficulties to Survive, but Businesses Are Hard to Abandon Their Operations. The Ministry of Culture Wants to Supports the Market by Cutting Tax, 16 January 2005. http://finance.sina.com.cn/g/20050116/13541297608.shtml. Accessed 27 Oct 2012

21st Century Business Herald (2014a) A fundamental way to solve local-government debt: local officials should be responsible to local inhabitants, 3 January 2014. http://henan.sina.com.cn/news/finance/2014-01-03/0759-118650.html. Accessed 6 Apr 2014

21st Century Business Herald (2014b) Being aware of a revival of local protectionism. http://news.sohu.com/20090217/n262288107.shtml. Accessed 6 Feb 2014

Andvig JC, Fjeldstad O-H, Amundsen I, Sissner T, Soreide T (2000) Research on corruption: a policy oriented survey. Chr. Michelsen Institute, Bergen

Becker GS (1983) A theory of competition among pressure groups for political influence. Q J Econ 98(3):371–400

Beijing Youth Daily (2005) Café chains have difficulties to survive, but businesses are hard to abandon their operations. The Ministry of Culture Wants to Cut Tax to Support the Market, 17 January 2005. http://www.ccm.gov.cn/wlpd/wlpdwbsc/201105/t20110520_109908.htm. Accessed 27 Oct 2012

Bhagwati J (1982) Directly unproductive, profit-seeking (DUP) activities. J Polit Econ 90 (5):988–1002

Boehm F (2007) Regulatory capture revisited – lessons from economics of corruption. http://www.icgg.org/downloads/Boehm%20-%20Regulatory%20Capture%20Revisited.pdf. Accessed 8 Oct 2014

Boyreau-Debray G, Wei S-J (2014) Can China grow faster? A diagnosis of the fragmentation of its domestic capital market. IMF Working Paper. www.imf.org/external/pubs/ft/wp/2004/wp0476.pdf. Accessed 5 Feb 2014

Buchanan JM, Tullock G (1962) The calculus of consent: logical foundations of constitutional democracy. University of Michigan Press, Ann Arbor

Buchanan JM, Tollison RD, Tullock G (eds) (1980) Toward a theory of the rent-seeking society. A&M University Press, College Station

Chang X (2008) The Jilin Provincial CPC chief criticizes some departments for making personal gains through governing non-local companies. Chenshiwanbao, 17 April 2008. http://news.sina.com.cn/c/2008-04-17/005315370056.shtml. Accessed 20 Feb 2014

China Business (2012) Wal-Mart's Anti-Corruption Inquiry Spreads to China, 100 Shops at Loss Position may be Closed. http://finance.qq.com/a/20121124/001799.htm?pgv_ref=aio2012&ptlang=2052. Accessed 22 Sept 2013

China Economic Weekly (2014) Big drugstore chains try every means to expand, but certain stores have exclusive access to consumers with social medical insurance. http://www.21cbh.com/HTML/2013-4-3/3ONDE4XzY1NDU3OQ.html. Accessed 15 Feb 2014

Darby M, Karni E (1973) Free competition and the optimal amount of fraud. J Law Econ 16:67–88

De Soto H (1989) The other path. Basic Books, New York

Den Hertog JA (2000) General theories of regulation. In: Bouckaert B, De Geest G (eds) Encyclopedia of law and economics, vol III, The regulation of contracts. Edward Elgar, Cheltenham, pp 223–270

Den Hertog JA (2003) Public and private interests in regulation: essays in the law and economics of regulation. http://igitur-archive.library.uu.nl/dissertations/2003-0207-165004/full.pdf. Accessed 8 Oct 2014

Deng D (2003) Research on regional protectionism in the period of institutional reform. J Guangdong Bus Coll 2003(1):13-20 (邓大才, 体制转轨时期的地方保护主义研究, 广东商学院学报, 2003 年第 1 期)

Djankov S, La Porta R, Lopez-de-Silanes F, Shleifer A (2002) The regulation of entry. Q J Econ 117(1):1–37

Guo Y, Hu A (2002) Administrative Monopoly in Economy Transition in China. http://www.chinareform.org/publications/reports/200206/t20020618_111297.htm. Accessed 5 Jan 2014

Guo Y, Hu A (2004) The administrative monopoly in China's economic transition. Communist Post-Communist Stud 37:265–280

Hu J, Guo F (2013) Rent-seeking, bureaucratic corruption and market segmentation. Econ Manag 2013(11):36–47 (胡军, 郭峰, 企业寻租、官员腐败与市场分割, 经济管理, 2013 第11期)

Huang Y (2008) When administrative monopolies meet legal challenges. China Rep 2008 (8):92–93 (黄勇, 当行政垄断遭遇法律"挑战", 中国报道, 2008 年第 08 期)

Huang Q (2010) By winning the acceptance of local governments, Wal-Mart accelerates its expansion for dozens of branches, 18 March 2010, sources: National Business Daily, http://money.163.com/10/0318/04/621FQG5L00253B0H.html. Accessed 21 Nov 2013

Huang X, Yangcheng Evening News (2014) "Foreign invested retailers" ways to win favours. http://www.ycwb.com/gb/content/2002-08/21/content_408528.htm. Accessed 2 Feb 2014

Krueger A (1974) The political economy of the rent-seeking society. Am Econ Rev 64:291–303

Legal Daily (2013) The provision on the term of office should be implemented strictly, 15 July 2013. http://epaper.legaldaily.com.cn/fzrb/content/20130715/Articel07002GN.htm. Accessed 6 Apr 2014

Li W (2007) Who will win the Chinese market: Carrefour or Wal-Mart? Caijing, 22 July 2007. http://www.17pr.com/viewnews-11472.html. Accessed 17 Nov 2013

Li M, Cheng Y (2013) Zhaowen Xiong: A promoter of super-ministry system. http://www.mzyfz.com/news/mag/m/20080505/102622.shtml. Accessed 12 Nov 2013

Liu P (2012) Chongqing authority releases Wal-Mart's employees arrested. organic pork causes almost 01 billion RMB losses National Business Daily(2 May 2012), Accessed 21 Nov 2013

Liu X, Huang J (2000) Administrative actions should be brought into the jurisdiction of administrative procedures. Mod Law Sci 22(3):56–59

Mehra S, Meng Y (2008) Against antitrust functionalism: reconsidering China's Antimonopoly Law. V J Int Law 49(2):380–429

Nelson P (1970) Information and consumer behavior. J Polit Econ 78(2):311–329

Ogus AI (1994) Regulation: legal form and economic theory. Clarendon, Oxford

Ogus A, Zhang Q (2005) Licensing regimes east and west. Int Rev Law Econ 25:124–142

Olson M (1965) The logic of collective action: public goods and the theory of groups. Harvard University Press, Cambridge

Pan Y (2009) Do not allow local protectionism in the name of increasing economic growth. Qiluwanbao, http://news.sohu.com/20090217/n262287832.shtml. Accessed 6 Feb 2014

Pan W (2011) Why domestic supermarkets cannot grow to giants like Gome and Suning. 21st Century Business Herald, http://finance.sina.com.cn/leadership/20111009/033210584730.shtml. Accessed 2 Feb 2014

Peltzman S (1976) Toward a more general theory of regulation. J Law Econ 19:211–240

Philipsen NJ (2003) Regulation of and by pharmacists in the Netherlands and Belgium: an economic approach. Intersentia, Antwerpen-Groningen

Philipsen NJ (2007) The law and economics of professional regulation: what does the theory teach China? In: Eger T, Faure M, Zhang N (eds) Economic analysis of law in China. Edward Elgar, Cheltenham, pp 112–150

Philipsen NJ (2010) Regulation of liberal professions and competition policy: developments in the EU and China. J Competition Law Econ 6(2):203–231

Philipsen NJ (2013) Regulation of pharmacists: a comparative law and economics analysis. Eur J Comp Econ 10(2):225–241
Pi J (2008) Regional market integration under inter-jurisdictional competition in China: on the role of the Chinese central government in regional market integration. Econ Res J 2008(3):115–124 (皮建才, 中国地方政府间竞争下的区域市场整合, 经济研究, 2008 年第 3 期)
Posner RA (1974) Theories of economic regulation. Bell J Econ Manag Sci 5(2):335–358
Posner RA (1975) The social costs of monopoly and regulation. J Polit Econ 83(4):807–827
Shapiro C (1986) Investment, moral hazard and occupational licensing. Rev Econ Stud 53:843–862
Shleifer A, Vishny RW (1993) Corruption. Q J Econ 108(3):599–617
Shleifer A, Vishny R (1994) Politicians and firms. Q J Econ 109(4):995–1025
Shughart II WF (2008) Public choice. http://www.econlib.org/library/Enc/PublicChoice.html. Accessed 8 Oct 2014
Stigler GJ (1971) The theory of economic regulation. Bell J Econ Manag Sci 2:3–21
Sun X (2008) The barriers for Wal-Mart. China Entrepreneurs (21). http://www.iceo.com.cn/renwu/34/1999/1130/174785.shtml. Accessed 20 Nov 2013
Tang K (2013) The biggest profit of the reform is a market system for fair competition. Guangming Daily, 3 December 2013. http://opinion.haiwainet.cn/n/2013/1203/c232601-19993178.html. Accessed 16 Feb 2014
US Chamber of Commerce (2012) China's approval process for inbound foreign direct investment: impact on market access, National Treatment and Transparency. http://www.uschamber.com/sites/default/files/reports/020021_China_InvestmentPaper_hires.pdf. Accessed 8 Oct 2014
Xia L, Lu M, Yu W (2011) Political relations and inter-provincial investment-empirical evidence from Chinese listed companies. Manag World 7:139
Xin W (2014) Local protectionism should be stopped. http://www.china-review.com/sao.asp?id=5707. Accessed 15 Oct 2014
Xiong W, Zhang W (2013) Protecting state policies from being used for sector interests. Sources: Liaowang News Weekly, http://news.sohu.com/20060521/n243333237.shtml. Accessed 12 Nov 2013
Ye C (2001) Wish a good development to drugstore chains. Beijing Morning Post, 8 November 2001. http://www.china.com.cn/chinese/health/73872.htm. Accessed 25 Oct 2012
Yuan W, Mao Y (2001) Who is blocking the pharmaceutical chain. Nanfengchuang 11:7
Zhang G, Wang Y, Liu Z (2013) Local protection, corporate investment and corporate competitive advantage: evidence from Chinese manufacturing listed companies. Econ Survey 2013 (5):84–89 (张功富、王永强、刘振, 地方保护、企业投资与竞争优势——基于中国制造业上市公司面板数据的实证研究, 经济经纬, 2013 年第 5 期)
Zhongguancun Online (2012) Café chains: a cautiously optimistic future, but absolutely difficult to develop. http://netbar.txwm.com/wbchain/v14143.html. Accessed 30 Oct 2012
Zhongguowang (2014) Regional protectionism weakening state capacity. http://www.china.org.cn/english/2001/Mar/9673.htm. Accessed 7 Feb 2014
Zhou L (2004) The incentive and cooperation of government officials in political tournaments. An interpretation of prolonged local protectionism and duplicative investments in China. Econ Res J 2004(6):30–40. http://wenku.baidu.com/view/05704cd5b9f3f90f76c61b74.html (周黎安, 晋升博弈中政府官员的激励与合作: 兼论我国地方保护主义和重复建设问题长期存在的原因, 经济研究, 2004 年第 6 期)
Zhou L (2007) Governing China's local officials: an analysis of the promotion tournament model. Econ Res J 2007(7):36–50 (周黎安, 中国地方官员的晋升锦标赛模式研究, 经济研究, 2007 年第7期)
Zhou F (2009) After being kept out of Guangzhou for 13 years, Wal-Mart China finally enters into this market through compromising, JingLiRibao, 8 November 2009. http://cjb.newssc.org/html/2009-11/08/content_735222.htm. Accessed 22 Nov 2013

Business Restrictions in the Legal Professions: Do We Need More Market Integration?

Niels Philipsen and Qi Zhou

1 Introduction

In some countries lawyers are not allowed to form multi-disciplinary partnerships (MDPs)[1] with other professionals, such as accountants and notaries.[2] This prohibition is sometimes incorporated in public regulation, but in some jurisdictions it follows from self-regulation formulated by the Bar, aimed at the protection of lawyers' independence and respect for ethical values.[3] Competition authorities have generally been sceptical of a ban on MDPs, because such a ban would restrict

An early version of this paper was presented at the workshop 'The Professions between Competition and Regulation: Interdisciplinary Perspectives', Paris, 27–28 September 2013, University Paris Ouest Nanterre La Défense. Disclaimer: parts of this the paper are based on contract research that Niels Philipsen (with colleagues) has conducted for the European Commission/DG MARKT and for the International Bar Association. In the framework of these studies, interviews were held with professional associations and professionals, legal inventories were made, and economic analyses were carried out. One of the studies is under embargo and not all of its results can be published here.

[1] According to Mullerat (2000, p. 481), MDPs are characterized by the following: they provide more than one professional service; they include lawyers as partners, directors or share owners; and there is profit sharing between members of more than one profession.

[2] See with respect to Europe, e.g. Paterson et al. (2003), pp. 49 and 56.

[3] European Commission (2003a), pp. 12–13.

N. Philipsen (✉)
Faculty of Law, Maastricht University, Maastricht, The Netherlands
e-mail: niels.philipsen@maastrichtuniversity.nl

Q. Zhou
University of Leeds, School of Law, Leeds, UK
e-mail: Q.Zhou@leeds.ac.uk

N. Philipsen et al. (eds.), *Market Integration: The EU Experience and Implications for Regulatory Reform in China*, China-EU Law Series 2,
DOI 10.1007/978-3-662-48273-5_9

competition.[4] The European Court of Justice (ECJ) also showed some scepticism in its judgement in the *Wouters* case of 2002, which dealt with a prohibition of MDPs between members of the Bar and accountants in the Netherlands. The ECJ held that 'a prohibition of multi-disciplinary partnerships of members of the Bar and accountants [is] liable to limit production and technical development'.[5] Also from the perspective of free movement of persons and services, differences in regulation of MDPs may lead to barriers for cross-border activities.[6]

Besides a prohibition on MDPs, other restrictions on business form may exist, such as rules that prohibit the formation of a limited liability company or more directly prescribe a specific legal form, or rules that prohibit the involvement of outside capital. In this chapter such 'legal form and shareholding requirements' are referred to as rules on alternative business structures (ABSs).[7] For example, a study by Panteia and Maastricht University (2012) concluded that, while ordinary partnerships are allowed in all EU Member States, in some countries (such as Latvia, Lithuania and Luxembourg) lawyers are not allowed to organize in the form of a company; in the UK and Ireland this form is prohibited for barristers and advocates, respectively.[8]

In the following sections, restrictions on MDPs and ABSs related to the legal professions are evaluated from an economic perspective, but also in relation to the EU legal framework on free movement of legal professions. A central question in this paper is whether there is a case for EU intervention. This chapter is structured as follows. Section 2 provides an overview of existing economic literature on professional regulation and multi-disciplinary partnerships. Section 3 presents the views of profession members, based on interviews that were held in the context of research projects conducted for the European Commission. Section 4 considers restrictions on MDPs and ABSs in the light of the freedom of services and freedom of establishment. The question of whether *European* intervention (rather than national law) is needed is addressed in Sect. 5, by applying the economics of federalism. Subsequently, Sect. 6 provides some implications for China, by focusing on the question of whether ABSs and MDPs should be allowed in China considering its current regulatory framework and the analysis presented in earlier sections of this chapter. Finally, Sect. 7 provides some concluding remarks.

---

[4] Examples are the OFT in the UK and the Canadian Competition Bureau. See Philipsen and Olaerts (2010), Chapter 3.

[5] Case C-309/99, *J.C.J. Wouters, J.W. Savelbergh and Price Waterhouse Belastingadviseurs BV v Algemene Raad van de Nederlandse Orde van Advocaten*, 19 February 2002, paras 86–90. Eventually the ECJ decided that the regulation concerned did not infringe European competition rules, since the ban on MDPs could have reasonably been considered necessary for the proper practice of the legal profession as organized in the Netherlands (para. 110).

[6] See Panteia and Maastricht University (2012).

[7] This is in line with the terminology used e.g., in Panteia and Maastricht University (2012).

[8] Panteia and Maastricht University (2012), pp. 196–198. The report includes a table with the rules on ABSs and MDPs per jurisdiction.

2 An Economic Approach to Business Restrictions

There is a large body of literature that presents justifications for the regulation of professional services. Section 2.1 reviews the two major economic approaches to regulation; subsequent sections critically evaluate the theoretical (Sect. 2.2) and empirical (Sect. 2.3) literature that discusses the effects of restrictions on ABSs and MDPs involving lawyers.

2.1 Economic Theories of Regulation

Two main economic approaches to the study of regulation exist in literature, viz. the public interest approach and the private interest approach. The *public interest approach* perceives regulation as a possible remedy for various forms of market failure.[9] It assumes that regulation is always designed to serve the public interest.[10] With regard to the market for legal services, the most distinctive form of market failure is caused by information asymmetry between legal professionals (lawyers) and their customers (actual or potential clients, notably when these are not business clients but individual consumers). Legal services are experience goods, the quality of which can only be observed after clients receive the service.[11] Where the quality of legal services differs between lawyers, higher-quality lawyers are unable to distinguish themselves from lower-quality lawyers through signalling the true quality of their services. The information asymmetry between legal professionals and customers, if unregulated, will result in a deterioration of the quality of legal services. At the extreme, it may give rise to the well-known 'market for lemons' problem.[12] Lawyers may also exploit the information deficiency of their clients. Because of their lack of legal knowledge, many customers (with the exception of business clients and repeat users) are unable to evaluate the service or the package of services offered by their lawyers. This may create an opportunity and a perverse incentive for the lawyer to provide the client with unnecessary services.[13] Scholars of public interest theory propose that regulation should be used to tackle these

[9] The term 'market failure' refers to perceived shortcomings of the market system itself to deal with certain problems that prevent an economically efficient outcome in a market.

[10] Economists would say that regulation is directed towards an improvement in social welfare. For details, see Philipsen (2003), pp. 10–18.

[11] Some professional services can be considered as 'trust goods', which are characterized by the fact that consumers cannot judge their qualities even after consumption. See on this also the contribution to this book by Shen and Philipsen, Sect. 4.1.

[12] See Akerlof (1970).

[13] These are the well-known problems of adverse selection and moral hazard. For further details and a discussion of the practical relevance of adverse selection and moral hazard in the market for legal services, see Van den Bergh (2007), pp. 20–22; Garoupa (2008), pp. 467–468; and Philipsen (2010), pp. 205–206.

problems. Possible regulatory solutions to the problem of information asymmetry include mandatory disclosure of information, licensing or certification.

Other forms of market failure may be prevalent in legal services markets in addition to information asymmetry. On the one hand, there may be *negative* externalities, i.e. poor quality legal services inflicting costs on third parties. For example, inappropriate legal advice can harm not only the direct buyer of legal services, but also the buyer's contracting partners in later stages of the production and distribution chain.[14] On the other hand, there may be *positive* externalities, equally affecting the functioning of legal service markets. Some legal services can be considered as 'public goods', in the sense that they do not only benefit the direct buyer of the service, but society as a whole, by playing a role in constructing and facilitating a well-functioning judicial system. Following this line of reasoning, in an unregulated market, there may be an underproduction of legal services that generate such positive externalities and an overproduction of legal services that generate negative externalities.[15] From a public interest perspective, some government intervention may be justified to deal with externalities. This intervention may take the form of regulation, liability rules, or a market-based instrument such as taxation.

It is important to note that the costs of correcting market failure by means of regulation always need to be smaller than the efficiency gains derived from the regulation. Moreover, regulation should not limit market entry or restrict competition more than is necessary to cure the prevailing market failure. Finally, it should be noted that governments may have other public interest justifications for regulation of legal services besides correcting market failures, for example related to goals of distributive justice (e.g. access to legal services for the poor) and paternalistic goals (e.g. forcing laymen to get legal assistance when they engage in important transactions).

The *private interest approach* explains the existence of regulation because of the pursuit of private gains by powerful interest groups in society, such as professional associations.[16] The basic idea is that interest groups are continually influencing political decisions to seek rents for themselves, which is unproductive from a social welfare point of view. For example, professional associations might lobby for regulation that restricts competition between professionals, or regulation that makes entry into the profession more difficult. Because professional associations are small relative to the public as a whole, single issue oriented and well-organized, they are likely to be successful in obtaining wealth transfers at the expense of the public through lobbying.[17]

[14] Van den Bergh (2007), p. 22; Philipsen (2003), pp. 17–19.

[15] Van den Bergh (2007), p. 24; Philipsen (2010), pp. 206–207.

[16] This approach has developed from different theories, such as public choice, capture theory and the 'Chicago' theory of regulation. For descriptions and references, see Philipsen (2003), pp. 23–27.

[17] Economists would say that the transaction costs of professional associations are low, while the information costs of the public at large of finding out about the detrimental effects of (too) restrictive regulation are high. Olson (1965). See also Van den Bergh (2007), pp. 25–26; and Garoupa (2008), p. 470.

Which theory provides a more correct account of the existence of regulation? The answer, as always, lies in empirical research. Although there are certainly some empirical studies (mainly from the US) in support of private interest theory and its rent-seeking hypothesis, there is no real consensus in the literature on the actual incidence and consequences of rent-seeking activities in the legal professions.[18]

2.2 *Restrictions on MDPs and ABSs: Theoretical Perspectives*[19]

2.2.1 Alternative Business Structures

The prohibition of the use of limited liability partnerships in legal service markets is usually defended by the argument that unlimited liability has a strong disciplinary function towards the professionals in a partnership. Moreover, unlimited liability may nurture trust in legal professionals. A limited financial liability would reduce the sanction costs of a law firm for misconduct of its partners because of which the professional duty to clients may be compromised. An unlimited financial liability, however, increases the sanction costs of all partners for a wrongdoing of one partner, giving them incentives to monitor the quality of services provided by their partners.[20] This theoretical proposition has not been empirically proven. In fact, a number of corporate and accounting scandals, such as the well-known Arthur Andersen/Enron case, can be considered as serious challenges to this proposition.[21] According to Van den Bergh a ban on limited liability partnerships is unnecessary, as 'the interest of consumers may be adequately protected by imposing mandatory liability insurance or by measures which ensure an adequate capitalisation of the partnership'.[22]

Similar arguments apply to rules that restrict the ownership and management of law firms. The rule that only permits qualified lawyers to own and manage law firms does not necessarily improve the quality of legal services. Nonetheless, it has been argued in the literature that restricting the outside ownership and management of law firms can protect the professional integrity of lawyers. The removal of this restriction may put lawyers in a dilemma, having to choose between maximizing the (external) owner's commercial profits and acting in the best interests of their clients. This argument, however, is dubious. Obviously, lawyers themselves also

---

[18] Philipsen (2010), pp. 207–208. Attempts at an empirical analysis of regulation in the legal services markets include Faure (2003), Paterson et al. (2003), Pagliero (2005), and the studies mentioned in Stephen and Love (2000).

[19] This subsection draws heavily from Philipsen (2014b), Section 6.4.1.

[20] OECD (2000), p. 26; Van den Bergh (2007), p. 50.

[21] For more details, see Philipsen (2009).

[22] Van den Bergh (2007), p. 50.

have an incentive to seek profits. It does not seem to be the case that the removal of ownership restrictions, particularly by allowing other professionals such as accountants to participate in the management of law firms, exacerbates the above-mentioned dilemma.[23] Furthermore, ownership restrictions may cause inefficiencies. Not only do they limit the possibilities of achieving economies of scale, but they also limit the possibilities to attract financial and human capital. Ownership restrictions may undermine the development and expansion of law firms. In addition, the prohibition on hiring non-lawyers as managers may discourage innovation in the management of law firms and legal services.[24]

The OECD in an early study argued that '[t]hese constraints limit the creation of new and possibly more cost-efficient business structures. In considering whether to permit limited-liability corporate forms, it may be necessary to balance the risk of diluting those protections against the benefits of access to capital or management flexibility'.[25] Similarly, Garoupa (2008) argues that restrictions on organizational forms are '*difficult to justify by reference to the public interest. If some aspects of professional services may favour partnerships over corporations, the market and not the professional body should be expected to solve this tendency*'.[26] Considerations should also be given to the globalization movement in the legal professions and the internalization of legal services markets. If some countries impose legal restrictions on ownership structure, they will impair competition in the international legal service market by limiting the entry to the domestic market to foreign law firms.[27]

However, the benefit from internationalization of legal service markets is not always large. Copenhagen Economics (2006) argued that the removal of ownership restrictions would only generate small gains. Because law firms are not heavily capital dependent, access to capital is probably not a real obstacle to law firms, so it is argued.[28] Moreover, outside ownership could damage the independence of lawyers and 'there is a real risk that other types of owners (e.g. banks) would want to own their own law firms to increase the price towards their loyal clients'.[29] Lawyer independence and client confidentiality should always be observed.

[23] Van den Bergh (2007), p. 50. See also Grout (2005), who finds it difficult to understand the assumption that there is a distinction between the incentives of lawyers working together and their incentives when they are owned or majority managed by non-lawyers.

[24] See also Copenhagen Economics (2006, p. 15), where it is mentioned that outside owners might have better access to capital, are better at reducing costs or better at developing new business ideas.

[25] OECD (2000), pp. 26–27.

[26] Garoupa (2008), p. 483, referring to Hansmann (1990).

[27] See also Garoupa (2008), p. 484. A related issue put forward by Garoupa is that of in-house lawyers, as found in large companies and banks. Because in-house counsel improves business compliance and reduces information asymmetry between corporations and external lawyers, there is no obvious public interest argument to restrict the legal activity of in-house lawyers.

[28] Copenhagen Economics (2006), p. 49.

[29] Copenhagen Economics (2006), p. 15. However, this particular statement is not backed by any arguments based on economic theory or empirical evidence.

Because this may conflict with the interests of non-lawyer owners, regulation that covers all owners should be designed, if outside ownership is to be allowed at all. An example of such regulation mentioned by the authors is 'letting employees who are not lawyers own part of the firm'.[30]

Grout (2005), in a study for the UK's Department of Constitutional Affairs, evaluates the potential risks associated with the introduction of outside ownership in greater detail. He makes a distinction between small and large partnerships (including MDPs). In small partnerships some restrictions on non-lawyer management composition would make sense according to Grout, whereas for large partnerships this was not the case. In any partnership the return of each partner comprises of two parts, namely a lawyer-specific part based on human capital used within the partnership, and a business-specific part consisting of a share of the return to the partnership. The human capital component makes up a significant portion of an individual partner's return and therefore directly steers his or her behaviour. The fact that a regulatory body such as a Bar can impose heavy sanctions (e.g. disbarring) on lawyers in case of inappropriate behaviour, and thereby affect that lawyer's human capital, implies that such a body would have more 'bite' on a lawyer partner than a non-lawyer partner. Of course, a non-lawyer partner's human capital may also be damaged if found guilty of a serious misdemeanour, but not to the same extent. In small partnerships or MDPs, one might therefore consider to opt for the 'majority lawyer' rule, or (as this is a slightly arbitrary rule) a similar minor restriction to management composition.[31]

In large partnerships, the aggregate value of the company's shares can be large. '*This can create a strong incentive to monitor the behaviour of the professionals in the firm, particularly if there is a broader corporate reputation at risk.* [... Customers] *may be willing to pay more for their legal services as a result if this effect is strong. However, if equity is concentrated in a few hands then* [...] *the human capital at risk for a lawyer owner will be almost insignificant in comparison to the value of his/her equity at risk. Since the lawyer owner's human capital at risk is an insignificant part of their total risk, when it comes to calculus as to whether to risk an inappropriate act or not it should be almost irrelevant whether a combined owner/manager is a lawyer or not*'.[32] Whereas lawyers have often put forward that non-lawyer owners may benefit from distorting the behaviour of a lawyer manager, Grout emphasizes exactly the opposite view. Because the human capital of the lawyer manager is the major part of a lawyer's assets at risk where there is a non-lawyer owner, the regulatory structure 'bites' significantly on the behaviour of the lawyer manager. Any equity value that is saved by protecting a major client goes to the outside owner, so the lawyer will be less inclined to take risks in the light of the (expected) gains to losses ratio. The author therefore concludes that regulation should be focused on the underlying incentives rather than on the business

[30] Copenhagen Economics (2006), p. 15.

[31] Grout (2005), p. 2.

[32] Grout (2005), p. 2.

structure, by looking at the size of the firm and the concentration of ownership.[33] This also implies, for example, that it may be appropriate for large firms to impose restrictions on management incentive schemes (irrespective of whether the management consists mainly of lawyers or non-lawyers), to prevent too risky strategies and to minimize the chances of misconduct.

2.2.2 Multi-Disciplinary Partnerships

In a paper prepared for the OECD, Roger van den Bergh presents an overview of the arguments in favour of and against a ban on MDPs.[34] The two main arguments *in favour of* a restriction on MDPs mainly come from legal professionals themselves and concern professional secrecy and conflicts of interest, respectively. With regard to the former, it is argued that partnerships with other professionals threaten the confidence in the lawyer-client relationship, if non-legal professionals do not owe a duty of professional secrecy (the 'attorney-client privilege').[35] With regard to the latter, the co-operation between lawyers and accountants may generate conflicts of interest that are detrimental for consumers. Mullerat (2000) notes that '*both the accountant and the lawyer must be independent. But the accountant must also be impartial* [. . .] *while the lawyer in essence is partial (a defender of one party). The two of them working in association, becoming a single-adviser entity, could not carry out such conflicting functions*'.[36]

The main justification for the prohibition on legal disciplinary partnerships (LDPs) in common law countries, e.g. between barristers and solicitors, is that barristers ought to provide independent advice. Barristers' independence and impartiality would be compromised by a partnership with solicitors. Another justification is that LDPs would give rise to the risk of market concentration. LLPs encourage mergers between solicitor firms and barristers' chambers. Consequently, there would be fewer barristers who provide services to smaller solicitor firms.[37]

Similarly, the risk of market concentration and compromise of professional independence would exist if MDPs consisting of lawyers and accountants were permitted.[38] Lawrence J. Fox criticized MPDs in the US. Before the Enron scandal,

[33] Grout (2005), pp. 2–3. In the paper some empirical evidence is presented to back the distinction between small and large firms. This evidence according to the author shows that 'misconduct and poor quality is heavily focused on small businesses' (see pp. 31–32).

[34] Van den Bergh (2007), pp. 49–50.

[35] See also Mullerat (2000), p. 482.

[36] Mullerat (2000), pp. 482–483. The author (p. 492) furthermore argues that MDPs represent 'a new step in the deprofessionalization' and commercialization of the legal profession.

[37] For an extensive analysis of LDPs, see Clementi (2004), pp. 108–128.

[38] See for example the analysis of the *Wouters* case in Sect. 3 below, where it is pointed out the accountancy market is much more concentrated than the legal services market. See also Mullerat (2000).

he wrote an article criticizing the practice of the big accounting firms. Fox argued that the Big 5 accounting firms (currently Big 4), by hiring thousands of lawyers, 'have mounted a frontal assault on the legal profession that threatens to destroy the foundation of professional independence, loyalty and confidentiality'.[39] He stated that these firms had violated the legal profession's rules on governing conflicts of interest and confidentiality, and rules prohibiting a limitation of lawyer liability and direct solicitation of clients. The shift in activities from (mainly) auditing to other services, such as consulting, data processing, and legal services, thus not only threatens the independence of the accounting firms in conducting the auditing function, but also the independence of legal professionals. Furthermore, referring to empirical evidence of noncompliance with auditor independence rules by employees of these firms who were investing in audit clients, Fox did not believe in the 'firewalls [...] which separate those who work on an audit from those who want to invest in companies being audited'.[40]

Justifications for the restriction of MDPs can also be found in the economic literature. The major economic justification is the argument of 'agency costs'. According to Carr and Matthewson (1990) and Matthews (1991), sole practitioners and professional partnerships are the most likely form of organization, because it is least costly for professionals to monitor the quality of services themselves. Efforts in production and quality of professional services cannot be judged properly by non-professionals.[41]

There are several economic arguments *against* restrictions on MDPs. First, as argued by Van den Bergh (2007), MDPs would be able to offer 'full service' to consumers by bringing together the expertise of different professions. Second, a restriction on MDPs undermines the realization of economies of scope. It would prohibit the exchange of information between different professionals on specific problems from a multidisciplinary perspective. This is inefficient: MDPs would save transaction costs and reduce the number of individual contacts between consumers and professionals.[42] In relation to both ABSs and MDPs, Stephen and Love (2000) also refer to 'economies of specialization'. They note that '[*i*]*n a multi-lawyer firm it is, perhaps, more likely that there will be a specialist within the firm who is the least-cost provider of the service function. The probability of this being so may increase the more lawyers there are in the firm. [...] the fewer the number of partners and the more specialized the service function required the more likely that the firm will not be the least-cost supplier. This may even be the more so if the firm is an MDP*'.[43] A similar point is made by Garoupa (2008). He argues that '*by banning other organisational forms* [i.e. corporations, MDPs], *the specialisation of*

[39] Fox (2000), p. 1097.

[40] Fox (2000), pp. 1100–1101.

[41] Garoupa (2008), p. 483. Furthermore, Carr and Matthewson (1990, p. 328) found that partnerships dominate sole practitioners when client cases are large and the detection of chiselling is low.

[42] Van den Bergh (2007), p. 49.

[43] Stephen and Love (2000), p. 1005.

professionals beyond particular aspects of their service (thus lowering the cost of providing services) and economies of scope (by providing a 'one-stop shop' service including lawyers, accountants, surveyors and tax advisers) are lost'.[44] Thirdly, different professions may face different business cycles and fluctuations in income. A restriction of MDPs would then take away the possibility to spread related risks among the partners.[45] All of these benefits of MDPs can lead to lower prices for consumers. Finally, innovation may be promoted: MDPs would facilitate access to capital for investments in equipment and infrastructure to improve consumer services.[46]

The core question on the regulation of MDPs seems to be whether a less restrictive regulatory control would be effective to achieve the aims of protecting professional secrecy and preventing conflicts of interest.[47] Van den Bergh made three suggestions.[48] The first and least restrictive option is to introduce information remedies, which simply require *informing the client* that the duty of confidentiality of one MDP member conflicts with the duty of disclosure of another MDP member. The second option is to prohibit certain information exchanges between members of different professions in the same partnership. So-called 'Chinese walls' could be introduced, preventing information flows from professionals in the partnership who are bound by professional secrecy to other members in the partnership who are not. However, the problem with Chinese walls is that they 'are often a deceptive concept used to avoid an insurmountable obstacle' (i.e. the legal privilege).[49] The third option suggested by Van den Bergh is a general duty of secrecy, imposing this duty *on all partners* in an MDP.[50]

2.3 *Restrictions on ABSs and MDPs: Empirical Evidence*[51]

The theoretical propositions presented above are not always backed by empirical studies. In fact, some of the theoretical propositions are difficult to test in practice. For example, how should economies of scope be measured? How should the impact

44 Garoupa (2008), p. 483. Fox (2000, pp. 1105–1106) is not optimistic about the concept of one-stop shopping, claiming that it (and lawyers working for nonlawyers) reduces the legal profession to yet 'another profit center at a department store for consulting services'.

45 Van den Bergh (2007), p. 49.

46 Van den Bergh (2007), p. 49.

47 It should be noted with respect to MDPs consisting of lawyers and accountants, that there have been many changes in the (now *stricter*) regulation of the latter profession, in particular with regard to audit services. This includes rules on auditors' independence, auditor rotation and quality of accounting services. See Philipsen (2009, 2012).

48 Van den Bergh (2007), pp. 49–50.

49 Mullerat (2000). See also Scott and Konsta (1999).

50 See also Deards (2002).

51 This subsection draws heavily from Philipsen (2014b), Section 6.4.2.

of MDPs on the duty of professional secrecy be evaluated? And how can different business models, including those involving outside owners, be analysed empirically? Nonetheless, empirical studies can provide answers to some (other) important questions such as what are business clients' preferences for professional services. Questionnaires can be used to find out whether there is a demand from business clients for one-stop shopping, or what their views and worries about professional values of lawyers and auditors working for the same firm are.[52] In addition, it is also possible to test empirically the effects of MDPs and relaxations in ownership and management rules on concentration in the legal service markets.[53] However, there has been scant empirical literature on the specific arguments mentioned in the previous section, apart from the Clementi report in the U.K., which suggested that indeed there appears to be some consumer interest in the convenience and accessibility of 'one stop shopping' provided by MDPs.[54] Results of the (limited) empirical research undertaken by Philipsen and colleagues in the framework of research projects for DG MARKT, consisting inter alia of interviews of professionals, will be presented in Sect. 3.

There are some empirical studies that deal with different but related questions. Stephen and Gillanders (1993) conducted a study of law firms in the UK. They found that that the mutual control within law firms is usually characterized by an *ex ante* screening of prospective partners; an *ex post* monitoring by professionals in the partnership is rarely used. This challenges the main argument that the unlimited liability partnership is better to maintain the quality of professional service than the limited liability partnership.[55] Carr and Matthewson (1990) showed, that in the U. S., the average size of a law firm was larger in states that allowed limited liability partnerships than in states where this was prohibited. This could be presented as tentative evidence for efficiency gains deriving from limited liability partnerships. A similar conclusion was reached in a study of the UK architectural professions in the 1980s by Button and Fleming (1992). The authors suggested that the abolition of the rule preventing practice under limited liability led to a considerable growth in limited liability companies, almost entirely at the expense of 'sole principal' architectural practices.[56]

[52] See also Fox (2000), pp. 1104–1108, who mentions a lack of empirical evidence, but also (implicitly) suggests that the information asymmetry between business clients and professionals is too large to generate reliable results.

[53] Studies on the effects of ownership rules, mergers and accountancy scandals on concentration in the *audit* market have been performed by GAO (2003) for the U.S., and Oxera (2006, 2007) for the U.K. See also Philipsen (2009) in a report for the OECD.

[54] Clementi (2004, pp. 133–134). Clementi also suggests, without quoting specific research, that e.g. in the context of claims arising out of motor accidents, MDPs could offer an integrated service, dealing with property damage, health, rehabilitation and compensation. Another example are affinity groups such as trade unions, which provide a range of legal services to their members, including legal advice.

[55] Stephen and Love (2000), p. 1009; Van den Bergh (2007), p. 50.

[56] See also Indecon and London Economics (2003), p. 48.

Indecon (2003) refers to a U.S. FTC study on the effects of MDPs between dentists and dental auxiliaries (i.e. hygienists and assistants).[57] In this study, States with and without a rule restricting the use of dental auxiliaries were compared. In the States without such a restriction, costs of individual treatments were 6–30 % lower, while the quality of services provided by auxiliaries (for the dental procedures studied) was found to be equal to that provided by dentists. The authors concluded that 'relaxation of restrictions on the number of hygienists that a dentist may employ would benefit consumers by providing the same quality of service at a lower price'.[58]

Stephen (2002) undertook an empirical study of European jurisdictions. He found that commercial law practices in the states permitting MDPs are dominated by the legal branch of the major international accounting firms. The author provides an explanation of this in terms of the internal efficiency of law firms in various jurisdictions. As a result of EU legislation that aims for a Single European Market in legal services,[59] '*differences in efficiency of law firms arising from differences in competitive pressure across jurisdictions are likely to lead to cross-border mergers involving law firms from 'efficient' and 'inefficient'*[i.e. those where competition is restricted, leading to higher fee levels] *jurisdictions. Such mergers are likely to lead to pressure building up in the more regulated jurisdictions for further liberalisation of legal service markets*'.[60] Therefore, so Stephen argues, EU legislation may indirectly increase efficiency, although it does not directly reduce the power of national bar associations.[61]

2.4 Concluding Remarks

As we have shown so far, it is difficult to provide a conclusive answer to the question if ABSs and MDPs should be permitted. Various theoretical propositions supporting and opposing a legal prohibition of ABSs and MDPs have been documented in the literature. Empirical studies, which largely are lacking, unfortunately do not provide us with sufficiently strong evidence in relation to the specific theoretical propositions. However, it appears that the arguments in favour

[57] Indecon and London Economics (2003), p. 47. See also Van den Bergh (2007), p. 51.

[58] Liang and Ogur (1987), p. 3.

[59] The author mentions the Establishment Directive (98/5/EC) and (to a lesser extent) the Mutual Recognition Directive (89/48/EEC). Citizens of a Member State refused entry to the legal profession could qualify in another Member State and thereafter practice in the restrictive state, as long as the costs of this procedure are compensated by the gains from practicing in the restrictive state. Any practice rules designed to restrict competition between lawyers in one jurisdiction, thereby raising fee levels, will attract lawyers from other jurisdictions where fees are lower, according to Stephen (2002), p. 118.

[60] Stephen (2002), p. 115.

[61] Stephen (2002), p. 124.

of ABSs and MDPs are often based on economic theory. Despite lacking empirical evidence, we can safely argue that ABSs and MDPs potentially lead to a number of efficient outcomes, based on economic theory as well as on the input from stakeholders (interview results) presented above. These business forms are likely to improve competition in legal service markets, reduce transaction costs, enhance the quality of legal services and facilitate the internationalization of legal services markets and the globalization of the legal profession. Obviously, we should certainly not underestimate the possible risk associated with ABSs and MDPs. The differences in professional ethics and legal duties do pose new challenges to the regulation of ABSs and MDPs. However, it would be reasonable to say that these risks do not justify a full prohibition of ABSs and MDPs, because either the risks also existed in 'traditional' law firms (i.e. the trade-off between professional values and profit making) or they can be properly addressed by other, less strict forms of regulation. A full prohibition of ABSs and MDPs cannot be justified from an economic perspective.

3 Views of Professionals

This section shows the views of (legal and other) professionals on MDPs and ABSs. Section 3.1 summarizes some results from an earlier study on professional regulation commissioned by DG Competition, and Sect. 3.2 present the results of interviews held with stakeholders, as part of research carried out by Philipsen and colleagues for a DG MARKT study.

3.1 Responses to 2003 Questionnaire (DG Competition): MDPs

Around the time of the *Wouters* and *Arduino* judgements,[62] the European Commission (DG Competition) started an extensive investigation into competition and regulation in professional services markets, focusing inter alia on legal and accountancy services.[63] In the framework of this project, the Commission in 2003 invited interested parties—such as professional associations and consumer representatives—to respond to a questionnaire and an earlier study[64] conducted by the Austrian *Institut für Höhere Studien* for DG Competition. One of the topics under discussion was the extent to which MDPs between lawyers and accountants need to

[62] Cases C-35/99 (*Arduino*) and C-309/99 (*Wouters*), both decided on 19 February 2002 and dealing with competition issues in the legal services market.

[63] For details, see Terry (2009) and Philipsen (2010).

[64] Paterson et al. (2003).

be regulated. The Commission noted that: *'[t]here are rules governing co-operation between members of the legal profession and other groups in the majority of Member States. Legal practitioners are generally free to hire non-lawyers as employees in their companies. However, there are often severe restrictions on the scope for lawyers who work in companies other than law firms to provide legal advice to third parties or other legal services'*.[65] The study then pointed at the many differences in regulation between EU Member States, and asked whether the legal prohibition on MDPs was justified. In some countries (e.g. Austria, Denmark, Estonia,[66] Ireland, Italy and Greece) MDPs were totally prohibited. Legal practitioners were forbidden from forming any type of MDP, which enables lawyers and other professionals to work jointly within the same firm. However, in others (e.g. France and Germany) lawyers were permitted to participate in MDPs under certain circumstances. For example, in Germany, lawyers were permitted to form co-operations with other comparable professionals such as chartered accountants and tax advisors. However, inter-professional co-operation was made very difficult by the rules governing formation of private limited companies.[67]

The far majority of respondents to the questionnaire sent out by the EC consisted of professionals and professional associations. Some respondents from the accounting profession suggested that there is a need for some regulation of MDPs involving accountants. The *Fédération des Experts Comptables Européens* argued that regulation should be deployed to organize relationships between professionals who are subject to different ethical rules on confidentiality, independence, and conflicts of interest. Nonetheless, a full prohibition of inter-professional co-operation would reduce competition too much.[68]

Many associations of legal practitioners held the view that regulation of co-operation between lawyers and other professionals was necessary to protect lawyers' independence and respect for ethical values such as professional secrecy and avoidance of conflicts of interest. Further, the *Council of Bars and Law Societies of Europe* (CCBE) argued in favour of regulation limiting MDPs, suggesting that such rules protect the core values of the legal profession by ensuring that practitioners are subject to a single consistent code of conduct enforced by the local bar. Others argued that it is increasingly important for lawyers and other professionals to be able to provide a range of services within a single company as long as it does not endanger lawyers' ethical values. For example, the law firm *Clifford Chance* stated that different rules on inter-professional co-operation in the EU cause significant obstacles for international legal services companies.[69]

[65] European Commission (2003b), p. 9.

[66] European Commission (2004).

[67] European Commission (2004).

[68] European Commission (2003a), p. 7.

[69] European Commission (2003a), pp. 12–13.

3.2 *Interview Results DG MARKT Study (2012): MDPs and ABSs*

For a case study on MDPs involving lawyers and other professions, a number of short interviews was held in Summer 2012 with representatives from (predominantly) Dutch organizations of notaries, tax advisers and accountants, and with the *Fédération des Experts Comptables Européens.*[70] The Netherlands was chosen because in that country, contrary to for example Belgium and Luxemburg,[71] there is no prohibition on MDPs consisting of lawyers and notaries or tax advisers. MDPs between notaries and accountants, however, are not allowed.

Interviews with representatives from the Dutch associations of notaries and tax advisers, respectively, confirmed that Dutch professionals working in the big law firms sometimes encounter practical problems abroad.[72] For example, Dutch MDPs consisting of notaries and lawyers are not allowed in (*inter alia*) Belgium and Luxembourg, while MDPs consisting of tax advisers and lawyers are not allowed in France and Slovakia. In these cases, 'in-house' provision of services is not possible and external relationships with profession members in the Member States concerned need to be established. As a result, there are less opportunities to come up with creative solutions for clients (*cf.* the argument pro MDPs from the economic literature, on innovation of consumer services) and, of course, also prevents a one-stop shop from being created in those countries.[73] Moreover, it prevents risk spreading between professions from taking place. This is a lost opportunity in times of crisis given that, as it was suggested by one of the interviewees, the legal profession to a large extent is 'anti-cyclical' and the notary profession 'cyclical'.[74] With respect to tax advisers, it was also noted, however, that regulation of the profession differs widely across the EU, so decisions on whether to allow MDPs or not can better be taken at the national level.[75]

With respect to the need for harmonization of professional regulation across the EU, it was stressed that the degree of regulation differs widely across different EU countries, which makes harmonization of law unlikely and unnecessary. For the same reason, it also seems wise to leave the decision of whether to allow

---

[70] This case study was part of a wider study on free movement of lawyers: see Panteia and Maastricht University (2012). The idea of this case study was to involve professionals who are not lawyers. In other parts of the research, interviews were held with lawyers themselves.

[71] Attempts were made also to contact professional organizations in Luxemburg, but these attempts were unsuccessful.

[72] The interview with two anonymous respondents from the CFE (held 12 July 2012) made clear that German MDPs face similar problems.

[73] Interview with anonymous respondent working as a notary in a big Dutch law firm, 23 August 2012. It was noted furthermore that lawyers in Luxemburg (and to a lesser extent in Belgium) operate almost like a cartel. They are not interested in co-operation with notaries.

[74] Interview with anonymous respondent from the Royal Netherlands Notarial Organisation KNB, 16 July 2012.

[75] Interview with two anonymous respondents from the CFE (held 12 July 2012).

co-operation with other professions or not to the discretion of the Member States. With regard to notaries, interviewees pointed out the importance of an objective knowledge test before allowing someone to work as a notary in another EU Member State. However, it was also argued that a prohibition on MDPs with lawyers is neither necessary nor beneficial for clients.[76]

The situation regarding integrated services provided by accountants and lawyers is different, as these MDPs are also not allowed in the Netherlands. From an interview with the Netherlands Association of Accountants, as well as from the earlier response by the Fédération des Experts Comptables Européens to a DG Competition survey, it followed that the arguments generally put forward by lawyers (independence, conflicts of interest, legal privilege) are shared by a number of accountants.

In a separate case study on ABSs, professionals were asked whether there are reasons to regulate business structures. Opinions varied widely among the individual lawyers that were interviewed. However, the CCBE has taken a strong position against non-lawyer owned firms, considering them a threat to core values of the profession such as independence, avoidance of conflicts of interest and confidentiality, especially when there are no safeguards in place. Furthermore, interviewees (lawyers and law firms) argued, from a 'free movement' perspective, that allowing firms that potentially involve non-lawyers in another (more strict) EU Member State would constitute a considerable burden for bars in such state, especially if the bar is structured in a decentralized manner. Each (local) bar would have to be able to check for the safeguards for ABSs that have been implemented in the less regulated jurisdiction (e.g. England and Wales).[77]

4 Free Movement of Lawyers

The economic analysis of business restrictions, as presented in Sect. 2 above, is focused on efficiency and is therefore directly linked to the goals of any competition law (although European competition law, of course, also serves a specific goal of market integration[78]). It is therefore not surprising that competition authorities, including the European Commission and several national competition authorities,

[76] Interview with two anonymous respondents from the CFE (held 12 July 2012).

[77] Panteia and Maastricht University (2012), pp. 199–200. The authors, however, do not consider the 'free movement' argument very convincing, as it is for the country of origin to supervise whether the structural requirements are met which are imposed upon the ABS under home country law; bars in other Member States, where the ABS is active temporarily or in established form, are faced with the supervision of such activities only from the point of view of host country regulation, which is not different from the supervision of host country law firms.

[78] And it is well-known that the goals of efficiency and market integration may conflict. See e.g. Bishop and Walker (2010).

have critically reviewed all kinds of restrictions to competition in professional services markets, including restrictions on the formation of ABSs and/or MDPs.[79]

In this section, however, we will consider restrictions on ABSs and MDPs from the perspective of EU rules on free movement of lawyers. From this perspective, market integration (creating a 'level playing field') is the main policy goal, rather than efficiency. An economic rationale can be found in the enhancement of cross-border trade and indicators such as GDP and labour productivity, which is expected to result from this market integration. Furthermore, consumers can benefit from a wider variety of legal services offered, e.g. Greek people living in Germany may prefer to contact a Greek lawyer established in Germany, or business clients established anywhere in the EU may have a demand for, for example, lawyers specialized in UK law.[80] Section 4.1 recapitulates the relevant EU rules on free movement; subsequently, in Sect. 4.2 we will present some findings from the Panteia/Maastricht University study (2012) for DG MARKT on free movement of lawyers, to the extent that the findings relate to rules on ABSs and MDPs.[81]

4.1 EU Directives on Free Movement

Lawyers take up a unique position when it comes to the legal regime for free movement applicable to them in the EU, as the profession of lawyer is the only (liberal) profession that is covered by a separate system of Directives: the Lawyers' Services Directive and the Lawyers' Establishment Directive. The system applicable to lawyers employs a unique mechanism of mutual recognition, without (immediate) integration into the profession of the receiving Member State.[82]

The Lawyers' Services Directive is aimed at individual lawyers and does not address firm structure. Article 11 of the Lawyers' Establishment Directive,

---

[79] E.g. OFT (2001), Competition Authority (2006), NMa (2006) and Competition Bureau (2007).

[80] See on the market integration rationale also other contributions to this book, including the chapter 'Introduction'.

[81] The study consisted of country studies in all (then) 27 EU Member States (including legal desk research and interviews with national organizations), interviews with representative organizations at the EU level, interviews with law firms, 21 qualitative case studies, and a web survey among lawyers. The focus of the study was on implementation of the Lawyers' Directives, evaluating these directives (also in relation to the Services Directive and the Qualifications Directive), and on identifying any remaining barriers to free movement of lawyers across the EU.

[82] Panteia and Maastricht University (2012), p. 5. Besides these two Lawyers' Directives, lawyers can also make use of the general system of Directive 2005/36 (on the recognition of professional qualifications), which leads to full integration in the profession of the receiving Member State, if the lawyer concerned successfully completes an aptitude test. The Lawyers' Establishment Directive also offers a possibility to integrate fully in the legal profession, without the need to do an aptitude test, but only after the lawyer concerned has practiced for 3 years in the receiving country under the system of the Establishment Directive.

however, explicitly deals with the rules on joint practice by lawyers.[83] It is articulated in the preamble of the Lawyers' Establishment Directive that it aims to prevent that the fact that lawyers belong to a grouping in their home Member State would be used as a pretext to deter them from establishing themselves in the host Member State. It also recognizes that Member States should be allowed to take appropriate measures with the legitimate aim of 'safeguarding the profession's independence'.[84]

It follows from the foregoing that the Lawyers' Establishment Directive recognizes the right of Member States to impose requirements limiting shareholdership of law firms to members of the profession, as well as prohibiting the decision-making power in law firms from being exercised, de facto or de jure, by persons who do not have the status of lawyer. Moreover, it is recognized that these requirements may not only be imposed on 'national' groupings, but, insofar as they apply to national groupings, they may also be imposed on 'foreign' groupings seeking to establish a branch or subsidiary within their territory. Other legal form and shareholder requirements may only be imposed insofar as compliance therewith is justified by the public interest in protecting clients and third parties. In other words, despite the fact that restrictions on ABSs and MDPs may limit the free movement of professionals, EU law recognizes that there can be justifications for such restrictions.

4.2 *Findings Study on Barriers to Free Movement*

One of the objectives of the 2012 study for DG MARKT referred to in the previous subsection, was to identify (remaining) barriers and difficulties for the free movement of lawyers.

A web survey among 2365 lawyers across the EU showed that almost a third of the lawyers that have established in another country did not experience difficulties related to practicing the legal profession while being established in another country. However, one third of these lawyers has experienced difficulties related to *professional indemnity insurance* (e.g. because they had to take out insurance in both their home and home country). One quarter experienced difficulties because of *continuing requirements of the Bar in the home state*, resulting from the requirement to stay registered with the home bar. Difficulties related to *double deontology* (i.e. that the Directive requires lawyers to comply with deontological rules of both the home and

[83] The rather difficult drafting of Article 11 has led to considerable problems of implementation in the Member States. A violation observed in many Member States is the need to objectively justify application of the host Member State's professional rules with regard to branch offices and agencies. Member States either completely ignore the requirement or explicitly state that their own professional rules shall apply. A possible reason for this is the unclear wording of Article 11 (5) and its complex relationship with Article 11 (1). See Claessens (2008), p. 238.

[84] Maastricht University and Panteia (2014), p. 96.

the host Member State) were encountered by one-fifth of the lawyers. Furthermore, one of the 'case studies'[85] carried out in the framework of our research shows that lawyers who are employed as in-house counsel may experience difficulties carrying out cross-border activities because *in-house employment* is not permitted for lawyers in many Member States.[86]

Lawyers that have provided cross-border temporary services have encountered fewer difficulties than those that have established in another country. The survey shows that half of the lawyers that have provided temporary services did not encounter any difficulties related to the practice of their profession at all. The difficulties that have been most commonly encountered by the others are a lack of professional expertise in the law of another Member State and difficulties related to *language*. About one out of every ten lawyers have encountered difficulties related to *double deontology* and a *lack of understanding and acceptance* by other professionals, such as judges and local lawyers.

Strikingly, barriers to free movement related to restrictions on ABSs or MDPs were not or rarely identified by the lawyers who participated in the survey. This would suggest that the differences between Member States' regulations of business form, pointed out in Sect. 1 above,[87] do not constitute an important barrier to free movement of lawyers in the EU. However, according to Maastricht University/Panteia (2014), the application of legal form and shareholding requirements to cross-border provision of services and cross-border establishment is an area with many legal uncertainties. These uncertainties as such may already be a cause of restriction to cross-border activity.[88] Finally, an alternative (private interest) explanation could be that lawyers (or law firms) who benefit from restrictions to competition do not have an incentive to report that business restrictions are a barrier to free movement. It is hence difficult to draw hard conclusions regarding the question of whether legal form and shareholding requirements restrict free movement of professionals solely based on these stakeholder opinions.

5 Is There a Need for European Intervention?

From the previous sections we can conclude that the theoretical economic literature provides many arguments against restrictions on ABSs and MDPs involving lawyers. Additionally, from a competition law[89] and free movement perspective, it is

[85] Twenty-one of such qualitative case studies were conducted on specific topics (including those on MDPs and ABSs: see Sect. 3.2 above). In the context of these case studies, 76 interviews were held.

[86] Panteia and Maastricht University (2012).

[87] See also Maastricht University and Panteia (2014), Chapter 3.

[88] Maastricht University and Panteia (2014), p. 136.

[89] For more information on the competition law perspective, see e.g. Philipsen (2012).

clear that disproportional and unnecessary restrictions to ABSs and MDPs will not be allowed. Arguments that support restrictions on ABSs and MDPs primarily come from lawyers themselves (and in case of MDPs involving accountants, other professions back up these arguments) and relate to possible conflicts of interest between lawyers and managers or members of other professions, the fear that commercial interests may prevail over the interest of the client, and the public good character of legal services.[90] However, these arguments are formulated in a rather general way and are not supported by strong empirical evidence. As shown in Sect. 4 above, in the Panteia/Maastricht University study for DG MARKT on free movement of lawyers,[91] restrictions on ABSs and MDPs were not identified by stakeholders as one of the most important barriers to cross-border establishment or cross-border provision of legal services. Furthermore, one may wonder if business form restrictions are a proportional cure for the market failures of information asymmetry and externalities caused by low-quality services. After all, to a large extent these market failures can be addressed by qualification requirements and rules on entry into the profession.

However, we can also conclude that some professions—including notably the legal, notary and tax advisory professions—are regulated rather differently in each Member State, with different professional monopolies and exclusive tasks being assigned to the particular profession members. This is a strong argument for leaving regulation of these professions, especially on the (still sensitive) issue of multidisciplinary cooperation and alternative business structures, in the hands of the Member States, provided of course that such regulation is proportional, necessary and non-discriminatory.[92] This would also be in line with Article 11 of the Lawyers' Establishment Directive (98/5/EC)[93]; and with some of the economic literature,[94] which argues that if there is a demand for ABSs and MDPs, the market rather than EU regulation will lead Member States into re-assessing their rules on business structure. If there would be economic evidence of negative effects of business restrictions on trade, sectorial productivity and GDP, our conclusion would be different. However, the Maastricht University/Panteia study from 2014, which precisely dealt with this topic in the economic part of the study, found very limited effects in this regard.[95]

---

[90] In Maastricht University and Panteia (2014), we again held interviews with various professional associations (including those for legal professions), asking them for justifications with regard to legal form requirements and shareholding requirements, respectively. The justifications mentioned are very similar to those found in previous reports, as far as the legal professions are concerned. See Maastricht University and Panteia (2014), pp. 113–114.

[91] Panteia and Maastricht University (2012).

[92] See also Articles 15 and 16 of the Services Directive (2006/123/EC).

[93] And more generally with the subsidiarity principle.

[94] See also Sect. 2.3 above.

[95] UM and Panteia (2014), Chapter 8. The report is still under embargo; more details cannot be provided here.

European intervention in the form of a general prohibition on business form restrictions would clearly go too far. According to the economic theory of federalism, moving to the European level rather than regulating at national (or regional) level is recommended (from an efficiency perspective[96]) only if there are significant transboundary externalities, if transaction costs of having many different national (or regional) laws are higher than the costs of harmonizing these different laws; or when there is a 'race to the bottom' between Member States setting lenient (safety, quality, environmental, etc.) standards to attract industry.[97] If these scenarios do not apply, a decentralized approach is preferred to harmonization, because preferences of people are best represented at local or national level.[98] Hence, differences between Member States (e.g. in terms of legal services markets that are organized differently, with different reserved activities) should not necessarily be regarded as something bad, as these differences can represent different preferences. With regard to legal services, the argument of transboundary externalities makes sense, as indeed the effects of low-quality legal services easily cross country borders. The other two criteria do not seem to be relevant.

Hence, unless there is strong empirical evidence showing the negative effects of restrictions on ABSs or MDPs on trade, sectoral productivity, or GDP,[99] no regulatory action at the European level seems warranted. Nevertheless, the 'values' of competition can be promoted by the European Commission (competition advocacy) so that Member States can act individually to the fullest possible extent. Alternatively, a Commission Recommendation, as in the case of auditor liability (Recommendation 2008/437/EC),[100] could be an optional strategy for the European Commission.

6 Implications for China

In this section, we draw a number of implications for China from the analysis in the previous sections. Two questions will be answered. First, should any form of limited liability such as a corporation or limited liability partnership be permitted as an alternative business structure (ABS) of law firms in China? Second, should

[96] It should be stressed that in the EU the 'internal market goal' exists alongside the goal of economic efficiency and other goals such as non-discrimination and consumer protection, which provides the EU with another theoretical argument to intervene in the legal services market. This 'internal market goal', however, may conflict with economic efficiency.

[97] See generally Van den Bergh (2000), Faure (2003), and Van Boom (2011). See also the work by Bruno Frey on functionally overlapping and competing jurisdictions—FOCJ: e.g. Frey (2009).

[98] Moreover, people have the options of voice or exit to influence decision making. See Tiebout (1956) and Faure (2003). Furthermore, having different laws rather than one allows for regulatory competition.

[99] Which, as stated earlier, is the topic of our current study for DG MARKT.

[100] See Philipsen (2014a).

Chinese law permit multi-disciplinary partnerships (MDSs)? The case study of China is of particular value for both future regulatory reform in China and the general study of regulation of the legal professions. The Chinese legal services market differs from European markets in a number of ways. Therefore, the propositions in the previous sections cannot apply equally to China without qualification.

Should a law firm in China be permitted to form in an arrangement of limited liability such as a corporation or limited liability partnership? To answer this question, we first briefly review the current law in China. Under the current legal rules, there are four types of business structure for a law firm. First, a law firm can be formed as an unlimited-liability partnership, which requires a minimum capital of 300,000 RMB and at least three partners with 5-year experiences in legal practice.[101] Second, a law firm can be formed as an individual-owned firm, which requires only one qualified lawyer-owner with 5-year experiences in legal practice and a minimum capital of 100,000 RMB.[102] The owner of the law firm owes an unlimited personal liability to the firm. Thirdly, a law firm can be formed as a state-invested firm, which must have at least two full-time lawyers, but no minimum capital requirement.[103] Finally, a law firm can be formed as a special partnership, which is a type of qualified limited-liability partnership. It requires a minimum capital of 10 million RMB and at least 20 partners.[104] In this arrangement, if one or more partners commit intentional or reckless misconduct, they will be held jointly unlimitedly liable, but other partners will have limited liability, i.e. only to the extent of their investment shares in the firm. However, all of the partners will owe a joint unlimited-liability for other misconduct.

The current regulatory regime in China strictly controls business structures of law firms. No law firm can be established as a company. The form of limited-liability partnership is only permitted as an exception where either the law firm has a large capital (10 million RMB) or the law firm is invested in by the state. In the latter case, the legal liability of the firm is eventually shouldered by the local government. In the reform of the last 5 years, most state-invested law firms have been restructured to an unlimited-liability partnership. Local governments have sold their shares in law firms to individual lawyers. It seems that state-invested law firms will disappear in the future.

Our analysis in the previous sections suggests that prohibiting ABSs may generate efficiency losses. Economic justifications for the prohibition can hardly be found in the European or American context. The regulatory prohibition of ABSs in EU Member States may undermine both competition in the European legal services markets and the idea of the freedom of establishment in the EU. The choice

[101] Article 7 of The Regulatory Method of Law Firms (2008) *Si Fa Bu Lv Shi Shi Wu Shuo Guan Li Ban Fa*.

[102] Article 9.

[103] Article 10.

[104] Article 8.

of the organizational structure of a law firm could be left for the market to decide: if any alternative structures to the form of unlimited-liability partnerships turn out to be more efficient, they are likely to emerge from the market themselves. And, although ABSs may give rise to some new regulatory challenges such as the challenge to the independence of legal profession or the privilege of legal professionals, these new problems can be solved effectively by a proper regulatory reform, albeit (so we argued) on Member State level rather than at the EU level.

We do not suggest that the above propositions apply unconditionally to China. The current regulatory restriction on ABSs in China should be retained in the foreseeable future. The merit of a limited liability partnership is that it helps law firms to raise financial capital. In a limited liability partnership, people, in particular risk-cautious people, are more willing to make an investment. If the limited liability partnership were allowed, law firms would raise capital much more easily than under the current regulatory regime. Yet, this merit may be exaggerated. Legal services are very much a type of knowledge-intensive business, relying (more) on human capital rather than financial capital. The prosperity and development of a law firm are more dependent upon its success in attracting talented lawyers than in garnering financial investors. A need for a large capital for a law firm is not as crucial a condition as for other types of capital-intensive business. It does not seem to be that the improved access to financial capital through ABSs would add too much value to the legal service market.

But as we discussed above, ABSs may give rise to a risk that consumers of legal services may not be adequately compensated for the misconduct of their lawyers. Of course, this problem can be solved at least in theory by the imposition of a legal duty to purchase mandatory insurance on law firms. This option is not viable in China at the moment. Under the current law, there is no legal duty to force law firms or lawyers to insure themselves against their professional negligence. By 2013, there were about 13,835 law firms in China, mostly ‘high street’ firms in a small or medium size without insured against their legal liabilities.[105] They charge relatively lower prices for their services and compete for the volume of business. Only a minority of them are large law firms offering services to the ‘top-end’ consumers such as big companies. The imposition of mandatory insurance will imply a significant cost for medium or small size law firms. In addition, the insurance industry in China is still under-developed; the types of professional negligence insurances available are quite limited.[106] The premiums for such insurances are unaffordable for many medium and small size law firms. The prohibition of ABSs in China also reflects the fact of the undeveloped insurance market for professional negligence.

If ABSs were permitted without a well-developed insurance market, it would put consumers of legal service at risk. There would be a new regulatory challenge for

[105] Report on Social Responsibilities of Chinese Legal Practitioners (中国律师行业社会责任报告), at http://www.acla.org.cn/html/xinwen/20130827/11102.html. Accessed 10 Mar 2015.
[106] Ibid.

the protection of consumers. The level of risk generated by ABSs for the Chinese legal services market is disproportionate to their benefits. Thus, it seems proper for China to retain the current regulatory control until its insurance market can accommodate the risk of professional negligence more effectively and efficiently.

Now, we turn our discussion to the question of if MPSs should be permitted in China, limiting our discussion to MDPs consisting of different legal professions. The arguments we presented in earlier sections in relation to the European context equally apply to China. MPSs can improve efficiency by reducing transaction costs in the legal service market. MPSs can offer a package of professional services to consumers saving their time and costs to shopping round. At the same time, MPSs also create new regulatory challenges.

However, the need for MDPs consisting of different legal professions in China is not as urgent as in the EU because of the different characteristics of its legal services market. In the EU, the market integration objective and the freedom of movement of goods and services are important drivers for such MDPs. The co-existence of different legal traditions represents a unique European characteristic of its legal services markets. The EU comprises of not only both common law and civil law traditions, but also post-communist legal systems. However, the idea of market integration, and social and commercial interactions among the European jurisdictions give rise to an inevitable trend that the demand for cross-jurisdiction legal services is higher. This offers business opportunities for legal professionals in one Member State to invest in law firms in other Member States. In Europe, the majority of potential investors in law firms are foreign lawyers who do not hold a legal qualification in the given state.

Furthermore, the range of legal services in the European market is more diverse. A large number of non-contentious legal services occupy a significant proportion of services offered in the market. From property conveyance between individuals, to mergers and acquisitions between the giant commercial enterprises, lawyers play an important role in both social and commercial lives. Arguably, these non-contentious legal practices are the real motivation for lawyers in one European jurisdiction to invest in a law firm in another jurisdiction.[107]

In contrast, the situation is quite different in China. There will be fewer lucrative business opportunities for foreign lawyers or law firms to explore. China is a united single jurisdiction where there is one legal system in the mainland. A lawyer can offer legal services to the whole country. Law firms, subject to certain regulatory requirements, are able to open branches or representative offices in other cities. Unlike the EU, where there are different national laws that may impede cross-jurisdiction legal services, in China there is no such legal barrier. Once a person is qualified as a legal professional, he can practice law nationwide.

In addition, the range of legal services in the Chinese market is not as diverse as in Europe. This confines business opportunities for foreign lawyers. Property

[107] See also Panteia and Maastricht University (2012) for an explanation of why lawyers want to provide services abroad or establish in another Member State.

conveyance between individuals in China barely involves lawyers. It is conducted by the vendor, the purchaser, the estate agency and the bank. The drafting of wills is often undertaken by individuals themselves with the aid of a notary. Even in the case of mergers and acquisitions, or the drafting of commercial contracts by small and medium size firms, lawyers are not usually hired.[108] Only the minority of large firms use legal services in non-contentious business such as issuing bonds or shares, listing the company in the stock market, and mergers and acquisitions between large companies. In brief, non-contentious legal services do not occupy the major share of the legal practice by Chinese lawyers. The main demand for legal services in the Chinese market is of contentious nature with a focus on Chinese national law, such as litigation, arbitration, and mediation. Given the language barriers and the required level of Chinese legal knowledge, it is not very attractive for foreign lawyers to invest in Chinese law firms. Therefore, although there is no economic justification for prohibiting cooperation between different legal professions in China, the need for such MPDs in China is not as urgent and necessary as in Europe.

7 Conclusions

The above discussion shows that there is no easy answer to the question if MDPs and ABSs are efficient from the law and economic perspective. On the one hand, it can be argued that prohibition of MDPs and ABSs undermines competition, generates inefficiency losses and increases transaction costs for (potential) clients. On the other hand, both MDPs and ABSs give rise to a number of potential problems, such as conflicts of interest and insufficient protection of the legal privilege. Proper regulatory mechanisms should be used to tackle these problems.

In addition, there are different views among professionals. In the UK especially, the idea of competition and a free market for lawyers (at least solicitors) seems to be shared by policymakers and regulators, although legal professionals may to some extent still hold an opposite view. To the extent that this is so, this may be explained by the private interest theory of regulation, which argues that the key players in a regulated industry prefer to protect their monopolistic position and control over the entry to the market. In some other EU Member States, such as Germany, regulators and legal professionals do not (yet?) fully embrace the idea of allowing ABSs involving lawyers. It remains to be seen whether the innovations in the legal services market in the UK, where different business models have been introduced, will transfer to other jurisdictions.[109] As we indicated in Sect. 3 of this contribution, opinions from profession members differ with respect to the need to regulate MDPs involving lawyers and other professions: notaries and tax advisers confirm many of

[108] Liu (2012), Chapter 1.

[109] For a detailed analysis of developments in the UK legal services market, see Stephen (2013).

the benefits of such MDPs, but with regard to MDPs consisting of accountants and lawyers, most professionals seem to support restrictions.

Concerning the question of whether in the EU regulation on ABSs and MDPs needs to be harmonized, we pointed out that full harmonization of law is both unlikely and unnecessary. The degree of regulation of the legal (and related) professions differs widely across EU Member States, especially in how professional monopolies (i.e. exclusive tasks) of different professions are defined. Although restrictions on ABSs and MDPs may limit the free movement of professionals between Member States and may affect trade or economic growth, we did not find any empirical evidence for this in the studies presented in this chapter. Furthermore, EU law recognizes that there can be justifications for such restrictions, as provided by Article 11 of the Lawyers' Establishment Directive. In our view, the best way to achieve market integration is therefore to rely on the market mechanism rather than EU intervention to lead Member States into re-assessing their rules on business structure, where this is necessary and efficient. This view is supported by several economic papers presented in this chapter as well as by the economic theory of federalism.

Finally, we presented some implications for China, arguing that—despite the many benefits of ABSs—China's current regulatory restrictions on ABSs may have to be retained for some time, at least until its (underdeveloped) insurance market can accommodate the risk of professional negligence more effectively. With regard to MDPs consisting of different legal professions, we concluded that the need for this business form in China today is not as urgent and necessary as in Europe. However, as the EU is slowly moving towards more integrated and less regulated legal services markets, it would be wise for China to follow these developments closely.

References

Akerlof G (1970) The market for lemons: quality, uncertainty and the market mechanism. Q J Econ 85:488–500

Bishop S, Walker M (2010) The economics of EC competition law: concepts, application and measurement, 3rd edn. Sweet & Maxwell, London

Button K, Fleming M (1992) The effects of regulatory reform on the architectural profession in the United Kingdom. Int Rev Law Econ 12:95–112

Carr J, Matthewson F (1990) The economics of law firms: a study in the legal organization of firms. J Law Econ 33:307–330

Claessens S (2008) Free movement of lawyers in the European Union. PhD dissertation, Maastricht University, Maastricht

Clementi D (2004) Review of the regulatory framework for legal services in England and Wales. Final report. http://www.avocatsparis.org/Presence_Internationale/Droit_homme/PDF/Rapport_Clementi.pdf. Accessed 12 Jan 2015

Competition Authority (2006) Competition in professional services: solicitors & barristers. Dublin

Competition Bureau (2007) Self-regulated professions: balancing competition and regulation. Gatineau, QC

Copenhagen Economics (2006) The legal profession: competition and liberalisation. Copenhagen, January

Deards E (2002) Closed shop versus one stop shop: the battle goes on. Eur Law Rev 27:618–627

European Commission (2003a) Invitation to comment. Regulation in liberal professions and its effects: summary of responses. Competition DG, Brussels

European Commission (2003b) Stocktaking exercise on regulation of professional services: overview of regulation in the EU Member States. Competition DG, Brussels

European Commission (2004) Stocktaking exercise on regulation of professional services: overview of regulation in the new EU Member States. Competition DG, Brussels

Faure M (2003) How law and economics may contribute to the harmonisation of tort law in Europe. In: Zimmerman R (ed) Grundstrukturen des Europäischen Deliktsrechts. Nomos, Baden-Baden, pp 31–82

Fox LJ (2000) Accountants, the hawks of the professional world: they foul our nest and theirs too, plus other ruminations on the issue of MDPs. Minnesota Law Rev 84:1097–1113

Frey BS (2009) A new concept of European federalism. LSE 'Europe in Question' discussion paper series, LEQS paper no. 03/2009, London School of Economics and Political Science, London

GAO (2003) Public accounting firms: mandated study on consolidation and competition. GAO-03-864, Report to the Senate Committee on Banking, Housing, and Urban Affairs and the House Committee on Financial Services. United States Government Accountability Office, Washington, DC, July

Garoupa N (2008) Providing a framework for reforming the legal profession: insights from the European experience. Eur Bus Organ Law Rev 9:463–495

Grout PA (2005) The Clementi report: potential risks of external ownership and regulatory responses: a report to the Department of Constitutional Affairs. CPMO working paper series no. 05/135, University of Bristol, July

Hansmann H (1990) When does worker ownership work? ESOPs, law firms, codetermination and economic democracy. Yale Law J 99:1749–1816

Indecon, London Economics (2003) Indecon's assessment of restrictions in the supply of professional services, prepared for the Competition Authority. Indecon International Economic Consultants and London Economics, Dublin/London, March

Liang N, Ogur JD (1987) Restrictions on dental auxiliaries: an economic policy analysis. Federal Trade Commission, Washington, DC

Liu YP (2012) The regulation of legal practitioners. Chinese University of Law and Politics Press, Bei Jing (刘宇平《律师法学》中国政法大学出版社:千京, 2012。)

Maastricht University, Panteia (2014) Inventory of legal form and shareholding requirements in the EU services sector and their economic assessment. Report for European Commission/DG Internal Market and Services. Maastricht-Zoetermeer, 29 January

Matthews RCO (1991) The economics of professional ethics: should the professions be more like business? Econ J 101:737–750

Mullerat R (2000) The multidisciplinary practice of law in Europe. J Legal Educ 50(4):481–493

NMa (2006) Inventarisatie vrije beroepen: Advocatuur. Nederlandse Mededingingsautoriteit, Den Haag, October

OECD (2000) Competition in professional services, DAFFE/CLP/(2000)2. Directorate for Financial, Fiscal and Enterprise Affairs, Committee on Competition Law and Policy, Paris

OFT (2001) Competition in professions. Report by the Director General of Fair Trading. Office of Fair Trading, March

Olson M (1965) The logic of collective action. Harvard University Press, Cambridge

Oxera (2006) Competition and choice in the UK audit market. Prepared for Department of Trade and Industry and Financial Reporting Council. Oxera Consulting Ltd, Oxford, April

Oxera (2007) Ownership rules of audit firms and their consequences for audit market concentration. Final Report prepared for DG Internal Market and Services. Oxera Consulting Ltd, Oxford, October. http://ec.europa.eu/internal_market/auditing/docs/market/oxera_report_en.pdf. Accessed 12 Jan 2015

Pagliero M (2005) What is the objective of professional licensing? Evidence from the US market for lawyers. Job Market Paper. London Business School, London, and University of Turin, Turin

Panteia, UM (2012) Evaluation of the legal framework for the free movement of lawyers. Report for European Commission/DG Internal Market and Services. Zoetermeer – Maastricht, 28 November. http://ec.europa.eu/internal_market/qualifications/docs/studies/2013-lawyers/report_en.pdf. Accessed 12 Jan 2015

Paterson I, Fink M, Ogus A et al (2003) Economic impact of regulation in the field of liberal professions in different Member States: regulation of professional services. Study for the European Commission. Institute for Advanced Studies, Vienna

Philipsen NJ (2003) Regulation of and by pharmacists in the Netherlands and Belgium: an economic approach. Intersentia, Antwerpen-Groningen

Philipsen NJ (2009) Competition and regulation in auditing and related professions, DAF/COMP (2009)19. OECD, Directorate for Financial and Enterprise Affairs, Competition Committee, Paris. http://www.oecd.org/dataoecd/8/8/44762253.pdf. Accessed 12 Jan 2015

Philipsen NJ (2010) Regulation and competition in the legal profession: developments in the EU and China. J Competition Law Econ 6(2):203–231. doi:10.1093/joclec/nhp009

Philipsen NJ (2012) Regulation of accountants. In: Van den Bergh R, Pacces AM (eds) Encyclopedia of law and economics: regulation and economics. Edward Elgar, Cheltenham, pp 715–742

Philipsen NJ (2014a) Limiting auditors' liability: the case for (and against) EU intervention. Geneva Papers 39:585–597

Philipsen NJ (2014b) Recent developments in the regulation of auditors: an economic perspective. In: Philipsen NJ, Xu G (eds) The role of law and regulation in sustaining financial markets. Routledge, Oxon/New York, pp 127–149

Philipsen NJ, Olaerts M (2010) Restrictions on MDPs and business organization in the legal professions: a literature survey. Report for the MDP committee of the International Bar Association. Maastricht University, ICGI/Metro, Maastricht

Scott A, Konsta S (1999) Chinese walls. Accountancy 123:92–93

Stephen FH (2002) The European Single Market and the regulation of the legal profession: an economic analysis. Managerial Decis Econ 23:115–125

Stephen FH (2013) Lawyers, markets and regulation. Edward Elgar, Cheltenham/Northampton

Stephen FH, Gillanders DD (1993) Ex post monitoring versus ex ante screening in the new institutional economics. J Inst Theor Econ 149:725–730

Stephen FH, Love JH (2000) Regulation of the legal profession. In: Bouckaert B, De Geest G (eds) Encyclopedia of law and economics, vol III, The regulation of contracts. Edward Elgar, Cheltenham, pp 987–1017

Terry LS (2009) The European Commission project regarding competition in professional services. Northwestern J Int Law Bus 29(1); Penn State Legal Studies Research Paper No. 10-2009. Available at SSRN: http://ssrn.com/abstract=1374855. Accessed 12 Jan 2015

Tiebout CM (1956) A pure theory of local expenditures. J Polit Econ 56:416–424

Van Boom W (2011) Harmonizing tort law: a comparative tort law and economics analysis. In: Faure M (ed) Tort law and economics, Encyclopedia of law and economics, 2nd edn. Edward Elgar, Cheltenham/Northampton, pp 435–449

Van den Bergh R (2000) Towards an institutional legal framework for regulatory competition in Europe. Kyklos 53:435–466

Van den Bergh R (2007) Towards better regulation of the legal professions. In: OECD, Competitive restrictions in legal professions, DAF/COMP(2007)39, OECD: Directorate for Financial and Enterprise Affairs, Competition Committee, Paris, pp 17–71

The Regulation of Corporate Environmental Responsibility

Mengxing Lu and Michael Faure

1 Introduction

In this chapter, we wish to address a relatively new, but increasingly popular phenomenon,[1] referred to as corporate environmental responsibility (CER). This fits into the much broader notion of corporate social responsibility (CSR).[2] The notion of CER and the corresponding notion of CSR have been developed in response to the traditional economic paradigm in corporate law that the firm should only strive for profit maximisation. More particularly, John Elkington has posited the so-called triple bottom line of people profit and planet (PPP) which should each get equal attention and be balanced within corporate policy.[3]

Mengxing Lu is receiving a scholarship from the China Scholarship Council for her research.

[1] Carroll (1999) held that the concept of corporate social responsibility had a long history, but CSR did not surge in importance until the 1960s and beyond. Vogel (2006) also argued that, although some principles and practices of CSR could date back to more than a century, it was since the early 1990s that CSR had become a considerably important phenomenon.

[2] In some literature, CER is also referred to as environmental CSR.

[3] Elkington (1998).

M. Lu (✉)
Maastricht University, Faculty of Law, Maastricht, The Netherlands
e-mail: mengxing.lu@maastrichtuniversity.nl

M. Faure
Maastricht University, Faculty of Law, Maastricht, The Netherlands

Erasmus School of Law, Rotterdam, The Netherlands
e-mail: michael.faure@maastrichtuniversity.nl

N. Philipsen et al. (eds.), *Market Integration: The EU Experience and Implications for Regulatory Reform in China*, China-EU Law Series 2,
DOI 10.1007/978-3-662-48273-5_10

Although increasingly popular at the policy level,[4] the notions of CSR and as part of this CER were traditionally not popular, neither in the economic approach, nor in law and economics. As far as traditional economics is concerned, the position of Milton Friedman in this respect is well known. He held that the only responsibility of managers in a corporation is to maximise profits.[5] Also from a traditional law and economics perspective, there was little appreciation for corporate social responsibility. Posner held that especially in a competitive market, CSR would not have a bright future for the simple reason that, for example, additional investments in pollution reduction technology would only lead to higher prices, because of which customers would turn away from firms that engage in so-called CSR.[6] The only way in which CSR was viewed from an economic perspective was that it was held that some charitable donations could in some cases be considered as efficient advertising or public relations expenses and thus contributing to profit maximisation.[7]

However, notwithstanding the scepticism of traditional economics as well as law and economics towards CER and CSR, one can notice that these concepts enjoy increasing popularity today. Many firms are engaged in environmental reporting; sustainability indices are published,[8] firms compete to score high on these sustainability indices and instruments are developed to rate corporate social responsibility.[9] Hence, one can in practice notice that the business community appears to consider the notion of CER/CSR more seriously, although form and intensity can obviously differ.[10] There is also an apparent trend towards voluntary measures going beyond mere compliance with mandatory environmental standards (a kind of

[4] See on the increasing popularity of CSR at the government policy level *inter alia* Moon and Vogel (2008), pp. 303–323.

[5] Friedman (1970).

[6] See for example Posner (2003), pp. 435–436.

[7] Engel (1979), p. 1.

[8] See, for example, one of the well-known sustainability indices is the Dow Jones Sustainability Indices (DJSI), which was launched in 1999, as the first global sustainability benchmark. The mission of DJSI is to track the stock performance of the world's leading companies in terms of economic, environmental and social criteria. According to the Annual Review of Dow Jones Sustainability Indices (2013), about 3000 companies around the world were invited to be assessed by DJSI. More information about DJSI can be accessed at: http://www.sustainability-indices.com.

[9] Some scholars observed that in the last decades, CSR rating agencies have experienced a pronounced growth. A CSR rating agency is any organisation that assesses the social and environmental performance of corporations, and its mission is to make corporation's social and environmental effects transparent and available to stakeholders, and corporations attempt to improve their images by publicising positive ratings. The well-known rating agencies include e.g., RobecoSAM, the MSCI KLD 400 Social Index, and Vigeo. However, despite the rapid development of CSR agencies, there are also growing concerns over the transparency and credibility of rating agencies. See on various issues of rating agencies *inter alia* Scalet and Kelly (2010), pp. 69–88; Chatterji et al. (2009), pp. 125–169; and Dommerholt (2012), pp. 45–64.

[10] The forms and intensity of CSR may differ among different sectors, among different districts and nations (like the U.S. and the European Union), and among nations at different development levels (like developed countries and developing countries).

self-regulation) and a tendency towards private environmental standard setting (sometimes referred to as private environmental governance).[11]

The goal of this chapter is not to take a position concerning the question of whether CER is socially desirable or not. Moreover, the goal is certainly also not to argue that CER should become mandatory.[12] This would contradict any definition of CER or CSR which basically assumes that firms are moving voluntarily beyond compliance with the mandatory environmental standards.[13] The goal of our chapter is rather to understand the phenomenon of CER from a law and economics perspective. Hence, we are interested in the question why, differently than the economic logic of profit maximisation at first blush predicts, firms are apparently interested in CER. Moreover, we are equally addressing the relevant law and economics question, being whether there should be any role for regulation (or, more generally, government intervention) to accompany the process of CER which in itself could be regarded as a voluntary mechanism. In this respect, the question obviously arises whether in the emergence of CER there is a risk of market failures (such as information asymmetries) which regulation could potentially remedy.

In the context of this volume addressing market integration, also in China, an examination of the role of CER is interesting in its relationship with formal regulation. CER can clearly be relevant for market integration. For example, if a larger number of different labels would be created, this may make it increasingly difficult to compete in an integrated market. One could equally ask whether formal environmental regulation is perhaps less needed if stakeholders voluntarily regulate via CER. At the same time, the question can arise whether CER can play an important supplementary role in legal systems where, for a variety of reasons, governmental environmental regulation may fail. Latest literature has been relatively critical with respect to the effectiveness of environmental regulation in China.[14] It is especially held that, for a variety of reasons, there are important enforcement deficits which could lead to serious reduction of environmental quality.[15]

Therefore, this chapter first tries to position CER within a broader framework, pointing at the need to internalise environmental externalities via (self-) regulation. The question will hence be addressed to what extent self-regulation could, under

---

[11] Van den Bergh (2013), pp. 129–199.

[12] While some scholars insist on the voluntariness of CSR/CER mechanism, other scholars argue that today CSR/CER consists of both voluntary and mandatory elements. For example, Eijsbouts (2011) holds that "there is no point in debating whether CSR as such should be either voluntary or mandatory" and Kerr et al. (2009) also suggest that both voluntary and mandatory elements can have a "complementary role to play".

[13] Vogel (2006).

[14] Some organisations and scholars pointed out that, although today China has developed a relatively comprehensive framework of environmental laws and regulations, there remain many deficiencies in the enforcement of Chinese environmental law and regulation, such as superficial enforcement, inadequate and weak sanctions, lax investigations and delayed punishment, and so on. See on the various problems with environmental law enforcement in China *inter alia* Wang (2006), pp. 159–194; Ma and Ortolano (2000); and OECD (2006).

[15] See on various problems with the effectiveness of environmental regulation and its enforcement in China *inter alia* Van Rooij (2006), pp. 57–74; and Beyer (2006), pp. 185–211.

circumstances, be an alternative for government regulation in internalising environmental externalities. The reason to focus on self-regulation is obviously related to the fact that CER is, as a voluntary mechanism, also considered as a self-regulatory tool (Sect. 2). Then, we turn to the fundamental question why firms might, under certain circumstances, want to engage in CER and what the business case may be for voluntarily going beyond the formal legal requirements. Is this always, as claimed by Friedman and Posner, in conflict with the goal of profit maximisation (Sect. 3)? A complication which arises within the corporate context where CER is executed is that incentives to engage in CER may be different between shareholders and managers. Thus, in that respect traditional principal-agent problems could equally cause issues where a corporation wishes to engage in CER, but there is disagreement between the shareholders and the management (Sect. 4). The next section (Sect. 5) focuses on the relevant question of whether there is any empirical evidence that CER does pay off for a corporation. Does, as *inter alia* posited by Michael Porter, CER go hand-in-hand with profit maximisation? Next, the question is addressed to what extent CER as a voluntary mechanism may still need accompanying regulation to increase the effectiveness of CER (Sect. 6). This leads then to the question to what extent some form of "conditional self-regulation" is needed for CER. Section 7 concludes.

2 Internalising Externalities via (Self-) Regulation

The traditional law and economics approach to environmental problems, which CER is also supposed to tackle, is that a variety of legal and policy instruments can be needed to internalise (environmental) externalities.[16] Only in the case where transaction costs would be low could this internalisation automatically take place via the Coase theorem, which equally has some relevance for CER (Sect. 2.1). Otherwise, a market failure will remain because of which some form of legal intervention will be necessary (Sect. 2.2). In this regard, the question arises to what extent one could also rely on self-regulation (Sect. 2.3).

2.1 Coase

The traditional starting point for any economic analysis of environmental pollution is the well-known Coase theorem.[17] Coase basically showed that if transaction costs are zero (or low), an optimal allocation of resources (hence, also an internalisation

[16] The traditional instrument for environmental protection is environmental regulation, and governmental officials at various levels are responsible for developing, implementing and enforcing important public environmental regulation. See Van den Bergh (2013), pp. 130–133.

[17] Coase (1960), pp. 1–44.

of an externality) will automatically follow without any necessity for the legal system to intervene. Pointing at the importance of (implicit) negotiations (via the price mechanism) and hence at the importance of the market, the Coase theorem also finds its importance for CER. A lesson from the Coase theorem is that if it were possible to differentiate various consumer groups, corporations could engage in a differentiation whereby e.g., fair trade or organic products would be provided to those consumer groups who would specifically demand it. The assumption in this case is that consumer groups would be willing to reward corporations for CER and would hence be willing to pay a correspondingly higher price in return for corporations meeting the more critical demands of green consumers.[18] Empirical evidence seems to indicate that socially responsible consumption seems to work because consumers, on average, express an incremental willingness to pay for environmentally friendly and socially responsible products.[19] The Body Shop, organic food and the purchase of products with green labels all are examples illustrating this point. However, literature equally indicates that there is large divergence among the different consumer groups. European consumers expressed a willingness to pay for GMO-free organisms that is nearly 30 % higher than US consumers.[20] If environmentally conscious consumers prefer higher environmental standards and have a willingness to pay a corresponding price, the resulting product differentiation perfectly fits into the Coase theorem. Thus, there would as such, as the Coase theorem prescribes, not entail a need for additional regulation. Moreover, in this hypothesis CER also perfectly fits into the profit maximisation rationality because firms would be rewarded for investments in higher environmental standards by consumers who would be willing to pay a corresponding higher price. Going beyond environmental compliance and thus investing more in environmental protection may lead to additional costs which are reflected in higher prices. However, as consumers demand the application of the higher environmental standards, the higher prices do not lead to a loss, but may rather serve as a marketing argument to selectively attract particular green consumers. In this case, we suppose that there is a positive relationship between CER and firms' financial performance in green markets. Although the traditional economic paradigm views CER as a cost, firms with good environmental performance will be rewarded by ethical consumers' willingness to pay a higher price and thus may contribute to the improvement of total welfare. An important condition for this product differentiation to work is, however, that a producer is able to credibly signal his environmental claims to consumers, and that consumers can credibly rely on the claims made by the producer. There is, however, increasing evidence demonstrating that, more particularly as far as eco-labelling is concerned, many of the green claims cannot be substantiated. According to some research, more than 90 % of the environmental claims in eco-labelling would consist of so-called "green washing" (referring to the

[18] Kitzmueller and Shimshack (2012), p. 64.

[19] Kitzmueller and Shimshack (2012), p. 72.

[20] Kitzmueller and Shimshack (2012), p. 73.

fact that the environmental claims made by the label cannot be substantiated).[21] If consumers realise this, it will decrease their willingness to pay additionally for the products with a green claim. In that case, adverse selection may emerge because the producers who truly apply CER will not be rewarded for their environmental investments and will consequently be priced out of the market. This is the famous problem of the market for lemons.[22] In other words, information asymmetry leads to market failure which necessitates regulatory intervention.

Regulation may equally be needed in all other cases where environmental externalities cannot be internalised via the low transaction costs setting as present in the Coase theorem.

2.2 Legal Intervention

In some cases, the Coase theorem will not be applied in practice because of information problems (and hence high transaction costs). In other cases, environmental harm may have a wide-spread nature, latency problems may occur or the number of potential injurers and victims is simply too large, making Coasian bargaining impossible. In that case the market failure constituted by the negative externality will remain and some legal intervention will be indicated.

One possibility is to use the deterrent effect of liability rules, hence of environmental liability.[23] However, it has been indicated that private law solutions (like liability rules) may not be effective when the government holds better information on optimal abatement techniques, when insolvency problems arise, and when for a number of reasons a liability suit for environmental damage can never be brought.[24] Those may all be conditions under which environmental regulation may be more effective than liability rules. Empirical evidence also confirms that the quality of the environment has improved substantially because of regulatory efforts and not so much in response to legal action in tort.[25] Government intervention should, however, not always necessarily take the form of safety standards set by government. The latter is also referred to as command and control regulation. An alternative would consist of so-called economic or market-based instruments.[26] These can consist of either environmental taxes or emission trading.[27] The empirical evidence

---

[21] Martinez Gandara (2013), p. 134.

[22] Akerlof (1970), pp. 488–500.

[23] See *inter alia* Shavell (1980), pp. 1–25.

[24] For example, because the damage can be wide-spread, victims can believe damage has natural causes, victims cannot be identified, and long latency periods and problems of causation may exist (Shavell 1984, pp. 357–370).

[25] Dewees et al. (1996), p. 315.

[26] Johnston (2007), p. 353.

[27] For a comparison see *inter alia* Faure and Weishaar (2012), pp. 399–421.

indicates that the relative effectiveness of either command and control or market-based instruments is totally dependent upon the specific context, type of pollutant regulators, institutional design and other elements.[28]

2.3 *Private or Self-Regulation?*

CER is typically defined as going beyond compliance on a voluntary basis.[29] In that sense, CER could be considered as a form of self-regulation whereby stakeholders, more particularly corporations, would spontaneously take engagements to go beyond compliance with government imposed environmental standards. In some cases, other parties may stimulate corporations to engage in this CER. Of course, many environmental NGOs, in a consultation with corporations, will try to convince corporations to move to CER. In other cases it is more particularly partners in the supply chain that impose high(er) environmental standards upon their business partners. The latter is sometimes referred to as supply chain control or private environmental governance.[30] The latter can equally be important in the context of China: often large retail chains downstream in the supply chain (often situated in Europe and in the US) may impose private environmental (for example food safety) standards on providers upstream in the supply chain, sometimes located in China. Via this supply chain control, private parties (buyers) will impose high standards upon suppliers to be able to correspond to demands of consumer markets in Europe.[31]

Again, the contracting via the supply chain control to a large extent fits into the notion of private contracting and can thus be considered as an application of the Coase theorem. Self-regulation more generally has in some cases been advanced in law and economics literature as an effective tool to regulate externalities at lower costs than via government regulation. Arguments presented in law and economics literature in favour of self-regulation relate *inter alia* to higher expertise of the stakeholders involved (thus leading to lower information costs), lower organisational and administrative costs, and to the fact that business actors may have a larger willingness to apply norms and standards that they would have created themselves.[32] Self-regulation could in that sense lead to a "crowding in" of

---

[28] Faure (2012), pp. 309–310.

[29] Kitzmueller and Shimshack (2012), p. 53.

[30] Van den Bergh (2013), pp. 129–199.

[31] For example, the flower industry of Colombia, as one of the major exporters of cut flowers to Europe, had created the Florverde program to encourage members to adopt a set of environmental friendly standards to satisfy the high standards of the European Union. See Lyon and Maxwell (2008), p. 244.

[32] See for example Cheffins (1997), Chapter 8.

norms.[33] The main advantage of self-regulation from that perspective would be that it could lead to a higher intrinsic motivation of stakeholders to comply, given that they were involved in the creation of the norms and standards. All aforementioned factors are seen as valuable arguments in favour of CER, even as a cost effective alternative for governmental (command and control) regulation.

However, the law and economics literature on self-regulation has equally indicated that there are many problems with self-regulation as well.[34] One problem is that there may be free-riding of particular members. Therefore, some may join the body that would be responsible for self-regulation, thus benefiting from reputational gains with no incentive to comply with the agreed standards. Second, compliance with self-regulation is also based on voluntarism. Enforcement may hence be weak, which can be particularly risky because some emissions can cause substantial environmental harm. Indeed, there are a few typical features of environmental pollution which make it not necessarily a good candidate for self-regulation (only). In this respect, we more particularly refer to the latency problems inherent in environmental pollution.[35] The latency problem states that environmental damage often has a so-called long-tail character. Moreover, environmental damage may be widespread and problems of causal uncertainty may occur. Environmental pollution can also have a transboundary character. All those typical features of environmental pollution may make it substantially more difficult to control, especially emissions, via self-regulation. Consequently, government intervention, either via command and control or market-based instruments, may still be the primary tool needed to control environmental externalities.

Nevertheless, there are some success stories with respect to private environmental governance as well as with environmental branding. For example, consumers tend to reward those traders that engage in CER by paying an "environmental premium". Another case is where buyers are able (via supply chain control) to enforce private safety standards upon suppliers. The empirical evidence of the marketing literature also supports this claim that an increasing number of consumers express their willingness to pay a premium for environmentally friendly and socially responsible products.[36] According to a consumer survey of The Body Shop, their natural and fair trade products are becoming a purchasing trend among consumers. Also, it is assumed that 83 % of their regular customers tend to choose products or services from retailers that take social and environmental issues seriously, and meanwhile 64 % of them are willing to pay a premium for an ethical

[33] Frey (1997), pp. 56–57 and 64; Frey (1999), pp. 395–408.

[34] See *inter alia* Philipsen (2003), pp. 38–39. See also the contribution to this book by Piri Damagh and Faure.

[35] Indicating a potentially long time laps between the moment of the emission and the moment that the damage may occur.

[36] Kitzmueller and Shimshack (2012), p. 52.

product.[37] Moreover, private supply chain standards are becoming a popular business strategy for more and more companies (buyers) who would like to impose private environmental standards on their suppliers. For example, to achieve the target of a safe and responsible supply chain, Wal-Mart imposes high standards on its suppliers regarding their social and environmental conditions.[38] With regard to the environment, besides the mandatory compliance with domestic environmental law, local law and regulation, and international treaties and protocols, Wal-Mart requires its global suppliers to also comply with its specific standards on waste management, air emissions management, water management, energy consumption and greenhouse gas management, land use and biodiversity, environmental management system, hazardous substances management and pollution prevention, noise pollution and nuisance.[39] A similar strategy is implemented by The Body Shop. To manage the sourcing process of natural ingredients, The Body Shop requires new suppliers to comply with its ethical, social and quality criteria, besides the compliance with legal and financial checks.[40] However, as previously stated, many of those cases relate to examples where traders already comply with basic mandatory environmental regulation and CER (in all of its different forms and shapes) mainly resembles an instrument to go beyond compliance with mandatory standards without being a substitute for those standards.

3 Why CER?

As we already stated, CER is defined as going beyond mere compliance with mandatory environmental standards. In law and economics terms it would mean that a corporation goes further, e.g., by moving to apply a higher standard, than the standard which would be merely the result of a marginal cost marginal benefit weighing implicit in the logic of internalising externalities. Moreover, an essential feature of CER is that business would do this on a voluntary basis. The question obviously arises why this would be the case.

[37] The data is from The Body Shop International Values Report 2011. An English version of this report can be accessed at: http://www.thebodyshop.com/content/pdf/global-values_report.pdf. Accessed 16 July 2014.

[38] Wal-Mart publishes and regularly updates *Standards for Suppliers*, which are utilised to evaluate employment practices and environmental compliance in facilities producing merchandises for sale by Wal-Mart. The latest version was adopted in April, 2014 and can be accessed at: http://corporate.walmart.com/global-responsibility/ethical-sourcing/standards-for-suppliers. Accessed 1 August 2014.

[39] See Wal-Mart' *Standards for Suppliers*, which can be accessed at: http://corporate.walmart.com/global-responsibility/ethical-sourcing/standards-for-suppliers. Accessed 1 August 2014.

[40] See *The Body Shop International Values Report 2011*. An English version of this report can be accessed at: http://www.thebodyshop.com/content/pdf/global-values_report.pdf. Accessed 16 July 2014.

3.2 The Porter Hypothesis

The argument that strategic CER could be profit maximising[52] has been hypothesized and developed in further detail by Michael Porter. In contrast to the traditional economic paradigm that environmental regulation imposes additional costs on firms and thus may damage firms' competitiveness in the market,[53] Porter basically argues in many publications that firms that move beyond environmental compliance will automatically not only do more investments in environmental protection, but become more innovative in general. The innovations needed to reach higher environmental standards would, according to Michael Porter, also provide other benefits to the firm. In particular, Porter and Van der Linde believe that regulation can exert substantial influence on firms' environmental innovation in at least six aspects.[54] Consequently, this further innovation would provide strategic gains to the firm because of which those firms that strive for higher standards of environmental protection in the end would also be more profitable.[55] Porter has defended this Porter hypothesis not only with respect to individual corporations, but also with respect to states. He holds that increased environmental performance will lead to increased competitiveness, of both nations and industries.[56]

A new overview of literature shows that the empirical evidence of the Porter hypothesis, although being mixed, to a large extent supports it. Ambec et al. distinguish between a weak and a strong version of the Porter hypothesis. The weak version only indicates that properly designed environmental regulation may spur innovation.[57] The strong version implies a relationship between environmental regulation and the business performance of a firm.[58] The authors conclude that the evidence for the weak version of the Porter hypothesis (that stricter environmental regulation leads to more innovation) is fairly clear and well-established. Empirical evidence concerning the strong version of the Porter hypothesis (that stricter regulation enhances business performance) is mixed: some studies find that environmental regulation has a direct negative effect on business performance,[59] but newer studies also provide clearer support for that hypothesis.[60]

Dan Esty and Michael Porter have also examined the relationship between the stringency of environmental regulation and environmental quality in particular

[52] Kitzmueller and Shimshack (2012), p. 59.

[53] Jaffe et al. (1995), p. 133.

[54] Porter and Van der Linde summarised these six aspects in Porter and Van der Linde (1995), pp. 99–100.

[55] This has *inter alia* been defended in Porter and Van der Linde (1995). For a summary see Faure and Johnston (2009).

[56] Porter (1991).

[57] Ambec et al. (2013), p. 9.

[58] Ambec et al. (2013), p. 9.

[59] Ambec et al. (2013), p. 9.

[60] Ambec et al. (2013), p. 16.

countries. They find that not only the rigor and structure of environmental regulations have a particular impact on environmental performance, but also the enforcement.[61] The empirical evidence hence suggests that a country can benefit environmentally not only from economic growth, but equally from developing the rule of law and strengthening its governance structures.[62] Interestingly, they also found evidence that countries that adopted a stringent environmental regime relative to their income were able to speed up economic growth rather than retarding it.[63] Therefore, the evidence at country level presented by Esty and Porter also confirms that countries adopting a stringent environmental regime do not have to be concerned that this endangers their competitive position. The evidence seems rather to show that it may speed up economic growth instead or retarding it.[64]

3.3 *Product Differentiation and Branding*

The most common case for firms to use CSR is to differentiate their products from other competitors, which is often executed through employing "CSR as a means of product differentiation".[65] Today, product differentiation and branding has become a prevailing business strategy for firms. In practice, some firms specialise via branding in CER and hence, produce green products or services at higher prices. Apparently, consumers are willing to reward particular brands investing in CER (such as fair trade) with their loyalty. Again, as mentioned above, this largely corresponds with the starting point of the Coase theorem: some consumers with higher preferences for environmental services and products may be willing to pay a green "marked up" on the prices corresponding to their preferences. Examples include the Body Shop, organic food, etc. The Body Shop achieved its success in the competing cosmetic industry by creating its ethical brand images: using natural-derived ingredients, against animal testing, treating people well, supporting community fair trade and protecting the planet. It turns out that the ethical business strategies do work and today the Body Shop is well known as one of the worlds' first ethical businesses. Another example is the global booming of organic food. Today more and more people are becoming passionate or even obsessed with organic food, because it is typically advertised as safer, healthier and more nutritious than conventional food. Largely because of consumers' concerns of well-being, health and environmental protection, there has been a sharp increase in organic food sales. For example, the estimated sales of organic products in the U.S. in 2012 amounted

[61] Esty and Porter (2005), p. 424.

[62] Esty and Porter (2005), p. 424.

[63] Esty and Porter (2005), p. 425.

[64] For further details see Faure (2011), p. 393.

[65] Kitzmueller and Shimshack (2012), p. 65.

to $28.4 billion which accounts for over 4 %[66] of total food sales, and it is estimated to reach about $35 billion in 2014,[67] while in Germany—the largest market for organic food in Europe, the organic food sales reached EUR 6.6 billion and the total food sales reached EUR 170 million, accounting for about 4 % of the total food sales in 2011, and in 2013 the organic food sales reached more than EUR 7.6 billion.[68] According to some marketing data,[69] the price for organic food is higher than the price of conventional food, and the premiums for organic food may vary widely. Also, the increasing demand for organic food shows consumers' willingness to pay a premium for purchasing organic food.

One important condition for this case is that firms can signal their environmental attributes to the market and in particularly to the consumers who exactly have the special preference. Eco-labels are one of the most widely employed tools by firms to communicate their products to consumers. In particular, the main purpose of eco-labels is to convey relevant environmental information about a product to the appropriate consumers through the product label.[70] Consequently, it is not a surprise to witness the burgeoning eco-labels during the last couple of years. According to the latest data of the Ecolabel Index,[71] there are 458 eco-labels in 197 countries, and 25 industry sectors.

However, as we indicated above the danger is that this market may only work if consumers can trust the environmental claims that are made. This danger is well known as "green washing", which can be defined as the selective disclosure of positive information about a company's environmental or social performance, while withholding negative information on these dimensions, so as to create an overly positive corporate image.[72] Generally, firms are motivated to engage in green washing, especially when firms are faced with increasingly strong pressure and demands on information closure. Also, more importantly, because eco-labelling is basically a voluntary mechanism with rather limited regulation and weak enforcement, firms can easily get away from punishments. Therefore,

[66] The percentage varies in different food categories. For example, organic products account for larger shares in some categories, such as dairy, fresh fruits and vegetables.

[67] The data is from Economic Research Service, United States Department of Agriculture, which can be accessed at: http://www.ers.usda.gov/topics/natural-resources-environment/organic-agriculture/organic-market-overview.aspx#.U80aJ_mSzts.

[68] The data is from a report *The Food & Beverage Industry in Germany (Issue 2012/2013)* of Germany Trade & Invest (GATI). An English version of this report can be accessed at: http://www.gtai.de/GTAI/Content/EN/Invest/_SharedDocs/Downloads/GTAI/Industry-overviews/industry-overview-food-beverage-industry-en.pdf.

[69] The data is from the United States Department of Agriculture (USDA). More information can be accessed at: http://www.ers.usda.gov/topics/natural-resources-environment/organic-agriculture.aspx#.U9ov2PmSzts.

[70] Martinez Gandara (2013), p. 24.

[71] Ecolabel Index is the largest global directory of eco-labels, currently tracking 458 eco-labels in 197 countries, and 25 industry sectors. More information about the Ecolabel Index can be accessed at: http://www.ecolabelindex.com/. Accessed 7 September 2014.

[72] Lyon and Maxwell (2011), p. 9.

green washing is quite common in the green market, and according to the result of a survey, more than 95 % of consumer products claiming to be green are green washed.[73] As we discussed above (Sect. 2.1), from a law and economics perspective, green washing is a market failure and in particular an adverse selection problem. According to the economic model of green washing established by Lyon and Maxwell, green washing can be utilised as an opportunistic business strategy in which firms will choose whether they will disclose environmental information or withhold, or what information they would like to disclose, positive or negative type, or to what extent they would like to publicise, all or partial, based on the cost-benefit analysis of this strategy.[74] Consequently, it will lead to a market for lemons in which brown products marked by misleading or even false eco-labels will remain in the market while the green products with genuinely good environmental performance may be driven out of the market. In other words, green washing is a significant problem that has negative effects on the eco-labelling mechanism.[75] As the effectiveness of the eco-labelling mechanism largely depends on the consumers' trusts, the risk of green washing can damage consumers' confidence on green products marked by eco-labels and thereby erodes their willingness to pay a premium for green products.

The evidence of green washing indicates the need for accompanying regulation. Also, some researchers argue that controlling it is the only way to ensure that the eco-labelling mechanism runs smoothly.[76] In other words, regulation is not only necessary but also needed to deter green washing, which could take place via a certification, e.g., eco-labelling schemes. Again, also certifications are part of a self-regulatory scheme. However, there are criticisms with respect to certification schemes as well (such as weak standards, ineffective enforcement). The empirical evidence also proves that a certification system alone is not enough to deter green washing.[77] Hence, there may be some role for government intervention in supporting the certification of eco-labelling schemes and it is assumed that the role of government in regulating eco-labelling is critical, because the governmental intervention provides some coercion to consolidate the eco-labelling mechanism.[78]

[73] Martinez Gandara (2013), p. 134.

[74] Lyon and Maxwell (2011).

[75] Terrachoice Part of the Underwriters Laboratories Global Network. The sins of green washing home and family edition. A report on environmental claim made in the North American consumer market (2010). The English version of this report can be found at: http://sinsofgreenwashing.org/index35c6.pdf.

[76] Martinez Gandara (2013), p. 274.

[77] Martinez Gandara (2013), p. 275.

[78] Martinez Gandara (2013), pp. 297–300. See on certification, notably in comparison to licensing, also the contributions to this book by Shen and Philipsen and by Piri Damagh and Faure.

4 Complication: Principal-Agent Problems

So far our analysis of CER assumed that the interests of the managers and the shareholders were aligned. However, it is well-known that within corporate actors the situation may be more complicated. The primary stakeholders that should perform CER are the corporations, but a principal agent problem may arise between the shareholders and the management. It is the well-known problem that there may be a conflict of interest between the shareholder (principal) and the management (agent), which is to be solved in what is now commonly referred to as corporate governance. As long as the interests between shareholders and managers do align, as far as pursuing CER is concerned there is obviously no problem. However, it is possible that there is a divergence of interests between the shareholders and the management which raises the question how to deal with those divergences.

First, it will be indicated why CER could be a shareholder preference (Sect. 4.1); next we will discuss the hypothesis that the shareholders want CER, but the managers do not (Sect. 4.2); finally we address the hypothesis where a manager wants CER, but the shareholder does not (Sect. 4.3).

4.1 *CER as a Shareholder Preference*

The principal-agent problem is one of Friedman's arguments against CSR/CER. Friedman held that a corporate executive, as an employee of shareholders, has a direct responsibility to conduct business in accordance with the maximisation of shareholders' value.[79] The aforementioned argument is generally based on an assumption that shareholders have no other preference but to maximise their own (financial) interests, but in practice there are indeed some cases where shareholders would accept CER. One possibility would be the case of strategic CER. As we already indicated above[80] there are in fact major economic reasons for shareholders to want this, being that to a large extent CER can be in line with profitability of the corporation and hence with the maximisation of shareholders value. This is the case for the three hypotheses defended in the previous section, being strategic CER, CER to stimulate innovation and thus profitability (the Porter hypothesis), and CER as a strategy of product differentiation and branding. In this case, the strategic CER fits into the economic rationale of profit maximisation and thus become desirable for shareholders.

The more interesting hypothesis is hence the one where CER would not be a strategy of profit maximisation, but where shareholders would want CER not for

[79] Friedman (1970) held that mangers' responsibility could be summarised as "making as much money as possible while conforming the basic rules of society, both those embodied in law and those embodied in ethical custom".

[80] See Sect. 3.

reasons of marketing or profit maximisation, but for truly altruistic reasons; this is also referred to as altruistic CER. Some have described the desire for altruism as the preference for a "warm glow".[81] There are quite a few examples of shareholders striving for this warm glow. Some financial institutions[82] focus on CER and CSR and advertise explicitly calling on the feeling good preference on depositors (and presumably shareholders). Also preferences for ecological banking and green finance from not only shareholders, but also customers may fit into this strategy.[83] Of course, to the extent that e.g., green finance corresponds to demands from customers and depositors it is rather a rational response of shareholders to provide this green finance. From that perspective it could again be considered as strategic CER or product differentiation and thus, rather fit into a profit maximising strategy[84] than into a warm glow preference. However, some shareholders explicitly seek CER and even for that reason become shareholders. For example, one can increasingly notice that NGOs purchase shares also within multinational corporations. Even if the amount of shares they own may not give them control of the corporation, it gives them particular rights as shareholders, e.g., to visit and express their voice at the general shareholders meeting. Being a shareholder could therefore be regarded as strategy to attempt to change the policy of a corporation towards CER. Finally, it should be mentioned that some shareholders, more particularly those striving for the warm glow, may demand also other returns on their stock than simply dividends. In sum, there may be a variety of reasons why shareholders would opt for '"doing good".

4.2 Shareholders Want CER While Managers Do Not

A first hypothesis of a conflict between the shareholder and the manager as far as CER is concerned refers to the hypothesis where shareholders would desire that the firm engages in CER (or simply charity) but that the manager refuses. Especially in the case of altruistic CER, shareholders who desire the preference for warm glow, would like to sacrifice some of the firm's profits for doing good, but managers may refuse to enforce this demand, if "they are given a contract in which incentives were

[81] "Utility derived from the mere fact of doing good yourself " (Kitzmueller and Shimshack 2012, p. 60).

[82] An example is the bank Tridos in Belgium, which is one of the world's leading sustainable banks. Its mission is to make money work for positive social, environmental and cultural change. The environmental report of Tridos bank can be accessed at: http://annual-report.triodos.com/en/2013/engagement/environmental-report.html?cat=b. Besides, Deutsche Bank and BNP Paribas also constitute good examples that are devoted to becoming responsible banks, and more information about Deutsche Bank and BNP Paribas in this respect can be accessed at: https://www.db.com/cr/en/responsible-business/index.htm and http://www.bnpparibas.com/en/responsible-bank.

[83] See on green finance *inter alia* Bai et al. (2014), pp. 102–150.

[84] See supra Sects. 3.1 and 3.3.

tied to the financial performance of the firm".[85] This concerns a classic problem of corporate governance where also the traditional remedies available for shareholders to enforce their desires upon the management could be employed. Of course, the possibilities that are at the disposition of a shareholder will largely depend upon the corporation concerned and the applicable legal rules in the specific legal system.[86] However, it is well-known that the traditional remedies provided in corporate governance do not always serve to align interests of shareholders and managers.[87] Hence, shareholders may fail in the sense that they are not able to enforce their preferences upon the management. Of course, the extent to which this problem will arise to a large extent depends upon the size of the corporation, but also upon the question of whether the particular shareholder has a majority or minority position, or more generally, whether the shareholder is able to control corporate policy or not. As the corporate governance literature has indicated, many problems can arise where the management is, more specifically in publicly held companies, not always acting in line with the preferences of the majority of the shareholders.[88] Those principal-agent problems that generally affect corporate policy can therefore also lead to managers not always acting in correspondence with the preferences of the shareholders as far as CER is concerned.

4.3 Managers Want CER While Shareholders Do Not

The second hypothesis concerns the opposite one, being that shareholders do not want managers to act based on the CER, but managers would nevertheless do so. Again, a classic principal-agent problem arises. This is the situation viewed by Friedman where managers who deviate from profit maximisation to practice CSR could be considered cheating their employers, misallocating society's resources, and destroying wealth.[89] It would seem strange to posit a hypothesis where managers rather than shareholders would desire CER. Still, one could imagine a situation where e.g., institutional investors are completely indifferent as far as CER is concerned and where managers for a variety of reasons want to engage in CER. By hypothesis, it is again a situation where the CER does not align with the profit maximising strategy of the firm[90] but where it could be held that the

[85] José and Husted (2008), p. 148.

[86] For a more detailed analysis from a corporate law perspective see *inter alia* Olaerts and Schwarz (2012).

[87] See, for example, Ryan Jr, and Wiggins III (2004).

[88] This can especially be the case where the ownership of shares is widely spread and dispersed because of which a group owning e.g., less than 50 % of share can de facto control corporate policy.

[89] Friedman (1962).

[90] Any of the strategies defended in Sect. 3.

CER is performed at the expense of the shareholders. Charity or other expenses in environmental protection that do not increase profitability thus come at the expense of shareholders' wealth and consequently can decrease their dividend.

In a competitive market, managers would normally not have the possibility to do charitable donations or voluntary corporate reduction of pollution because this could lead to higher prices. Firms will channel the higher pollution control costs by charging higher prices to customers. In a normally competitive market, Posner holds that in the long run this would lead to the bankruptcy of the firm.[91] But even in a monopoly, if firms would incur unanticipated pollution control costs it will lead to losses to the shareholder.[92]

Of course, managers always had discretionary funds at their disposition that they could use to the benefit of the corporation. To the extent that the discretionary use of those funds by the managers would substantially reduce shareholder wealth, the company would become a potential target for a corporate take-over for the simple reason that share prices would drop. In that case the market for corporate control would lead to the replacement of the management that is not maximising shareholder value.[93] But, more generally, shareholders obviously have other remedies at their disposition to align the performance of the managers with their interests. Hence, this does not seem to be a problem that necessarily merits a specific remedy.

5 Does CER Pay Off?

Again, an answer to this question will depend on how one interprets the concept of CER. If CER is merely aimed at internalising externalities it is clearly efficient as it would imply following environmental standards up to the point where marginal costs of pollution control and abatement are equal to marginal benefits in reduced environmental pollution. However, it was indicated that CER is precisely defined as going beyond environmental compliance. In that sense, the question arises to what extent there is empirical evidence that CER does pay off for enterprises that engage in it. This again is clearly and closely related to the Porter hypothesis discussed in Sect. 3.2 above. At that point, we indicated that empirical evidence does seem to support the hypothesis that investments in environmental compliance lead to technological innovations which in turn lead to better performance of firms. It is, however, interesting to look in more detail at some of the empirical evidence concerning the question of whether CER in the end has a positive effect on profitability. Generally speaking the question arises what does empirical evidence indicate that green companies do better than others or, to put it more modestly, can green companies also survive in a competitive environment?

[91] Posner (2003), pp. 435–436.

[92] Posner (2003), p. 436.

[93] Posner (2003), pp. 428–432.

The relationship between corporate social/environmental responsibility and profitability has been one of the most debated issues, considering the increasingly popular and influential belief that there is a business case for CSR. Basically, the business case for CSR refers to the arguments or rationales supporting or documenting why the business community should accept and advance the CSR "cause".[94] According to the business case for CSR, increasing number of corporate executives believe that, if they conduct their businesses in the ways that are more socially and environmentally responsible, it could enhance their competitive advantages.[95] Carroll and Shabana (2010) believe that the first attempt to establish the business case for CSR has been the pursuit of establishing a positive relationship between corporate social performance (CSP) and corporate financial performance (CFP).[96] From a historical perspective, research for exploring and testing the causal link between CSP and CFP have lasted for several decades[97] and it is believed that Bragdon and Marlin conducted "the very first empirical CSP-CFP study" in 1972 (MEW 2007).[98] The major purpose for many of these empirical studies is to find the economic rationale for the business case for CSR and more particularly, whether there exists a positive causal link between corporate responsibility and profitability. The important issues of these empirical studies include "over compliance, voluntary compliance, philanthropy, eco-labelling, productivity, transparency, non-profit labor markets and other subjects".[99] Since then, the empirical evidence regarding the economic justification of CSR has continually accumulated and researchers from different disciplines have examined and tested the empirical relationship between CSP and CFP from different perspectives, including organisational behaviour literature, business and society literature, and social and financial performance literature. Therefore, it is no exaggeration to say that numerous scholars have conducted research aiming at establishing the business case for CSR.

However, as we already indicated when discussing the Porter hypothesis, the empirical evidence in that respect is ambiguous and mixed. A large number of advocates who claim that CSR does pay off have examined and evaluated the business case for CSR empirically from different perspectives. Among the extensive body of CSP-CFP literature, the research by Margolis, Elfenbein and Walsh[100] is one of the most representative and comprehensive empirical studies from an organisational behaviour perspective, conducting a meta-analysis and a comprehensive appraisal of 192 effects revealed in 167 studies from 1972 to 2007. Given the various indicators to measure CSP, MEW sorted the current empirical studies

[94] Carroll and Shabana (2010), p. 86.

[95] Vogel (2006), p. 16.

[96] Carroll and Shabana (2010).

[97] Margolis et al. (2009) point out that: "Scholars have been searching for a link between corporate social performance (CSP) and corporate financial performance (CEP) for thirty-five years".

[98] Margolis et al. (2009), p. 4.

[99] Kitzmueller and Shimshack (2012), p. 70.

[100] Margolis et al. (2009), pp. 5–15.

into nine categories: charitable contributions, corporate policies, environmental performance, revealed misdeeds, transparency, self-reported social performance, observers' perceptions, third-party audits, and screened mutual funds; meanwhile they categorised CFP measures into two broad groups: accounting-based measures of financial returns and market-based measures of financial value. Based on the categorisation of various indicators to measure CSP and CFP, MEW examined each category and they finally found a modest positive average correlation between corporate social and environmental performance[101]: 59 % indicated a non-significant relationship, 28 % a positive relationship, and 2 % a negative relationship between CSP and CFP.[102] Therefore, the authors concluded from their research that the overall effect is positive but small, and moreover, that there is no evidence suggesting companies would suffer financially for CSP.

However, despite the longstanding pursuit of the positive relationship between CSP and CFP, the empirical findings drawn from an extensive body of literature do not establish a solid rationale for the business case of CSR/CER. One of the most important reasons is that the measures of corporate social and financial performance vary widely, just as what Vogel held that it is hard to draw broad conclusions about the relationship between CSR and profits because the studies often measure different things.[103]

Therefore, from an objective point of view, the extensive body of literature in testing the causal link between CSP and CFP does not provide strong support for the claim that firms with good social performance will also perform better in financial aspects than those with bad social performance. But this result does not mean that there is no business case for CSR in practice; instead, the social or environmental performance of firms does have a positive effect on firms' financial performance in some cases, although the overall effect may be not significant. Moreover, the majority of research also proves that at the very least good environmental performance does not lead to poor financial performance.[104]

6 Is Regulation Needed?

Starting point is that an internalisation of environmental externalities should not be voluntary and hence not take place via CER. As we argued above, the market failure caused by the environmental externality should be cured either where possible through bargaining (if transaction costs are low) or through liability rules, command and control or market-based instruments.[105] CER is by definition

[101] Kitzmueller and Shimshack (2012), p. 70.

[102] Margolis et al. (2009), p. 21.

[103] Vogel (2006), p. 30.

[104] Vogel (2006), p. 33.

[105] See supra Sect. 2.

moving beyond compliance with mandatory environmental standards. Given its voluntary nature as such there seems little need to think about a role for law in this respect. However, there may be various ways in which supplementary legal rules could play a role to assist the CER process. We already indicated above that the product differentiation, appealing to a green market, may be problematic to the extent that eco-labelling often leads to green washing. Green washing could lead to an adverse selection, which equals the market for lemons because of which no real green products (which are presumably more costly) would be put on the market. Regulation may be indicated to cure this information asymmetry, for example via certification. However, certification of eco-labels should not necessarily take the form of government regulation as it can equally be based on self-regulation as well. Many of the current certification schemes for eco-labelling are also de facto based on self-regulation. However, also these certification schemes do not go without criticism because of which some have raised questions of whether government regulation should intervene to accompany the certification process.[106]

Market failures resulting from information asymmetry could also occur with respect to all environmental reporting by corporations. Consumers may be overloaded with sustainability reports and reports on CSR performances of a variety of corporations. However, for consumers it may be very difficult to verify the environmental claims that are made for example in sustainability reports. This again raises the question of the need for regulation, but once more to a large extent this has been cured through self-regulation. One can now increasingly notice the emergence of rating indexes whereby a variety of sustainability reports are evaluated and indexed. Moreover, in the literature the value of these various indexes is also compared and rated.[107]

One road where CER may require regulation is in the so-called North-South relationship. Some argue that corporations, especially multinational corporations from the North that do business in developing countries in the South, have to comply with CSR, more particularly as far as respecting environmental norms and human rights is concerned. A problem is that often relocation to developing countries takes place because of lower standards and norms in developing countries which precisely reduces production costs for industry from developing countries. This has led to quite a few conflicts; for example, with indigenous communities for violation of human rights in developing countries by multinational corporations.[108] Consequently, scholars[109] have held that multinational corporations can be held liable under international law or even under national tort law for violations of human rights or environmental pollution which would occur in the South. It is sometimes even held that CER/CSR would require multinational corporations from developed countries to apply the same standards in developing countries as they

[106] Martinez Gandara (2013).

[107] See in this respect *inter alia* Dommerholt (2012).

[108] For an overview of this problem and various examples see Choukroune (2013).

[109] More particularly Van Dam (2011).

apply at home. That, however, raises the question of whether one generally should impose the standards from the North to developing countries as well. Schäfer has rightly indicated that given the different level of development in the South such a requirement may lead to paternalism, forcing developing countries to come to e.g., safety and environmental standards for which they have no need and no preference.[110] However, this is a domain where undoubtedly regulation and more particularly international CSR norms can play an important role.

As far as this North-South relationship is concerned, the question has also been asked to what extent foreign ownership of enterprises in developing countries has resulted in better environmental performance in the South. Interestingly, some studies find a positive relationship, more particularly for Brazil, between foreign investment and environmental performance. For other countries, such as Korea, this relationship could, however, not be confirmed.[111] This hence raises the interesting question to what extent foreign corporations also export their environmental technology and therewith environmental standards when setting up enterprises in the South.

A final point with respect to regulation is obviously how one would have to cure principal-agent problems if they would prevent CER from occurring. As we have argued previously,[112] principal-agent problems may indeed arise concerning the desirability of CER. However, they do not seem specific or different from other principal-agent problems between shareholders and managers. Thus, this does not merit specific regulatory solutions because the traditional remedies for the principal-agent problem prescribed in the corporate governance literature can be applied.

7 Concluding Remarks and Implications for China

We started by presenting CER as a form of so-called private environmental governance, showing that CER and CSR may appear under a variety of different identities. No matter how one defines CER and regardless of which examples one presents, the bottom line is that CER is always going beyond mere compliance with mandatory standards. Standards that merely internalise environmental externalities always have to be complied with via mandatory rules.

In this chapter, we did not take a position in the debate whether CER should be imposed upon corporations. In fact, given the voluntary nature of CER it is inherently logic in CER that it is and will not be mandatory.

[110] Angara et al. (2010).

[111] Kitzmueller and Shimshack (2012), p. 76.

[112] See Sect. 4.

Although traditional economics presented CSR as a form of diverging from the profit maximisation objective of the corporation, we have indicated that there may be many reasons why corporations engage in CER which may to an important extent align with their goal of profit maximisation. Empirical evidence also increasingly indicates that CER and profit maximisation should not necessarily be opposite goals. Even beyond strategic CER (for increasing profitability) shareholders may be interested in CER based on an intrinsic motivation to do good. After all, shareholders may not only want dividends as a return on their investment, but also the feeling to have contributed in a useful way to society.

We argued that there is as such not much need to worry about CER from a law and economics perspective (in the sense that it would require regulatory intervention). The purpose of our contribution was primarily to see whether the increased interest in CER in the business community could be reconciled with the traditional aversion against CER in the law and economics literature. We argued that this is the case because profitability and CER should not necessarily be considered as opposites. However, there may be problems in realising CER, for example related to principal-agent problems between managers and shareholders or resulting from information asymmetry and green-washing (in the case of eco-labelling). In that case, some form of regulation may be necessary to support CER, although to a large extent this support could be provided via self-regulation as well. To the extent that government oversees this self-regulatory process (e.g., of sustainability reporting, eco-labelling and certification), government regulation would merely play a supplementary role. It then fits into what is referred to as conditional self-regulation.

The mere fact that CER does not immediately necessitate a call for government regulation does not mean that there are no interesting points to be examined in further research. One point for example relates to the relationship between public regulation and CER. The question arises whether very detailed government regulation would lead to a crowding out of CER or whether, to the contrary, CER could supplement weak government regulation. Those interdependencies between government regulation and CER definitely merit further research. Moreover, the point mentioned in the previous section concerning the North-South relationship also merits further debate: is it really useful to create a legal obligation, forcing multinational corporations to apply CER in their businesses in developing countries in the South, or would that to the contrary amount to a paternalism which could also run counter to the interest of developing countries?

The role and function of CER is also fascinating as far as the case of China is concerned. One can notice that in China CER is high on the agenda of the business community. If one looks at either websites of large private commercial companies[113] or state-owned enterprises,[114] one will see explicit and detailed references to corporate social responsibility, whereby the companies explain in detail how well they have done as far as CSR is concerned. However, in the case of China one particular worry may arise where state-owned enterprises engage in CSR. Under the heading of their social obligations state-owned enterprises could (and do) engage for example in building and running a variety of public services such as local schools, public hospitals etc. Even stronger: the Chinese government may have the tendency to call on (both public and private) enterprises to ask them to engage in the provision of these kind of public services, calling on their social responsibility. That may, however, lead to a curious blurring of the functions of the Chinese state: the state may on the one hand be engaged as profit maximising business operator in state-owned enterprises but on the other hand, require the same state-owned enterprises to provide public services which the state is in fact supposed to provide. Hence, more particularly with regard to the specific case of state-owned enterprises in China, the question arises how one should interpret CSR if this would, in the end, only result in states withdrawing from their primary obligation to provide public services. Moreover, within the context of China the question of course arises to what extent CER could indeed supplement the traditionally weak government regulation and weak enforcement. These and other issues hence undoubtedly merit further research.

References

Akerlof GA (1970) The market for "lemons": quality uncertainty and the market mechanism. Q J Econ 84(3):488–500

Ambec S et al (2013) The Porter hypothesis at 20: can environmental regulation enhance innovation and competitiveness? Rev Environ Econ Policy 7(1):2–22

[113] Such as, for example, Ping An Insurance (Group) Company of China ("Ping An"): Ping An is the first insurance company in China to adopt a shareholding structure. By following its philosophy of "Expertise creates value", Ping An actively fulfils its commitment to corporate social responsibility, pursuing win-win cooperation and progressing in step with all stakeholders. The Group continues to step up its efforts in major disaster relief, the environment, education, the Red Cross, communities and other worthy causes. Ping An has received numerous awards and accolades in recognition of its charitable work, including "The Most Respected Companies of China Awards" for 12 consecutive years, "Best Chinese Corporate Citizen" for 8 consecutive years, and a top ranking in social responsibility reports by listed companies for 5 consecutive years. More information about Ping An in the field of CSR can be accessed at http://about.pingan.com/shehuizeren/jianjie.shtml.

[114] Such as for example the Bank of China (BOC): BOC is one of the largest commercial banks in China and has given due regard to corporate social responsibility as an important strategy and commitment to society and will resolutely implement the policies of the state, service the customers, strengthen corporate governance, carry forward excellent culture and support social undertakings to push forward the harmonious development of economy and society and make concerted efforts with the stakeholders to create a harmonious society and become a world-class provider of sustainable financial services. The information above and more information about BOC in the field of CSR can be accessed at: http://www.boc.cn/aboutboc/boccsr/.

Angara R, Babu PG, Eger T, Schäfer HB, Somashekhar TS (2010) Economic analysis of law in India: theory and application. Oxford University Press, Oxford
Arlen J, Kraakman R (1997) Controlling corporate misconduct: an analysis of corporate liability regimes. N Y Univ Law Rev 72:687–779
Bai Y, Faure M, Liu J (2014) The role of China's banking sector in providing green finance. Duke Environ Law Policy Forum 24:102–150
Barrett S (1994) Self-enforcing international environmental agreements. Oxf Econ Pap 46:878–894
Beyer S (2006) Environmental law and policy in the People's Republic of China. Chinese J Int Law 5(1):185–211
Carroll AB (1999) Corporate social responsibility evolution of a definitional construct. Bus Soc 38 (3):268–295
Carroll AB, Shabana KM (2010) The business case for corporate social responsibility: a review of concepts, research and practice. Int J Manag Rev 12(1):85–105
Chatterji AK, Levine DI, Toffel MW (2009) How well do social ratings actually measure corporate social responsibility? J Econ Manag Strategy 18(1):125–169
Cheffins BR (1997) Company law: theory, structure and operation. Clarendon, Oxford
Choukroune L (2013) Corporate liability for human rights violation. The Exxon Mobil case in Indonesia. In: Faure M, Wibisana A (eds) Regulating disasters, climate change and environmental harm. Lessons from the Indonesian experience. Edward Elgar, Cheltenham, pp 50–80
Coase RH (1960) The problem of social costs. J Law Econ 3:1–44
Crane A (ed) (2008) The Oxford handbook of corporate social responsibility. Oxford Handbooks Online, Oxford
Dewees D, Duff D, Trebilcock M (1996) Exploring the domain of accident law: taking the facts seriously. Oxford University Press, New York
Dommerholt E (2012) Validity and compatibility of the SAM and KLD screening instruments. Dovenschmidt Q 1:45–64
Eijsbouts J (2011) Corporate responsibility, beyond voluntarism. Regulatory options to reinforce the licence to operate. Maastricht University Press, Maastricht
Elkington J (1998) Cannibals with forks: the triple bottom line of sustainability. New Society, Gabriola Island
Engel DL (1979) An approach to corporate social responsibility. Stanford Law Rev 32(1):1–98
Esty DC, Porter ME (2005) National environmental performance: an empirical analysis of policy results and determinants. Environ Dev Econ 10(4):391–434
Faure M, Johnston JS (2009) Law and economics of the environmental federalism: Europe and the United States compared. Virginia Environ Law J 27:205
Faure M (2011) Does environmental law matter? In: Faure M, Smits J (eds) Does law matter? On law and economic growth. Intersentia, Antwerp, pp 385–416
Faure M (2012) Effectiveness of environmental law: what does the evidence tell us? William Mary Environ Law Policy Rev 36(2):293–336
Faure M, Weishaar SE (2012) The role of environmental taxation: economics and the law. In: Milne JE, Andersen MS (eds) Handbook of research of environmental taxation. Edward Elgar, Cheltenham, pp 399–421
Frey BS (1997) Not just for the money: an economic theory of personal motivation. Edward Elgar, Cheltenham
Frey BS (1999) Morality and rationality in environmental policy. J Consum Policy 22:395–408
Friedman M (1962) Capitalism and freedom. University of Chicago Press, Chicago
Friedman M (1970) The social responsibility of business is to increase its profits. The New York Times Magazine, New York, 13 September 1970
Heyes A, Rickman N (1999) Regulatory dealing – revisiting the Harrington paradox. J Public Econ 72:361–364
Jaffe AB et al (1995) Environmental regulation and the competitiveness of US manufacturing: what does the evidence tell us? J Econ Lit 33:132–163

Johnston JS (2007) Tradable pollution permits and the regulatory game. In: Kolstad C, Freeman J (eds) Moving to markets in environmental regulation: lessons from twenty years of experience. Oxford University Press, Oxford, pp 353–385

José S, Husted BW (2008) Principals and agents: further thoughts on the Friedmanite critique of corporate social responsibility. In Crane A (ed) The Oxford handbook of corporate social responsibility. Oxford Handbooks Online, Oxford

Kerr M, Richard J, Pitts C (2009) Corporate social responsibility: a legal analysis. LexisNexis, Canada

Kitzmueller M, Shimshack J (2012) Economic perspectives on corporate social responsibility. J Econ Lit 50(1):51–84

Lyon TP, Maxwell JW (2008) Corporate social responsibility and the environment: a theoretical perspective. Rev Environ Econ Policy 2(2):240–260

Lyon TP, Maxwell JW (2011) Greenwash: corporate environmental disclosure under threat of audit. J Econ Manag Strategy 20(1):3–41

Ma X, Ortolano L (2000) Environmental regulation in China: institutions, enforcement, and compliance. Rowman & Littlefield, Lanham

Margolis JD, Elfenbein HA, Walsh JP (2009) Does it pay to be good. . .and does it matter? A meta-analysis of the relationship between corporate social and financial performance (1 March 2009). Available at SSRN: http://ssrn.com/abstract=1866371

Martinez Gandara A (2013) The law and economics of eco-labels. Erasmus University Rotterdam, Rotterdam

Moon J, Vogel D (2008) Corporate social responsibility, government, and civil society. In: Crane A (ed) The Oxford handbook of corporate social responsibility. Oxford Handbooks Online, Oxford, pp 303–326

Oded S (2013) Corporate compliance: new approaches to regulatory enforcement. Edward Elgar, Cheltenham

OECD (2006) Environmental compliance and enforcement in China: an assessment of current practices and ways forward. OECD, Paris

Olaerts M, Schwarz CA (eds) (2012) Shareholder democracy. An analysis of shareholder involvement in corporate policies. Eleven International Publishing, The Hague

Orts EW, Deketelaere K (eds) (2001) Environmental contracts: comparative approaches to regulatory innovation in the United States and Europe, vol 1. Kluwer Law International, Alphen aan den Rijn

Philipsen NJ (2003) Regulation of and by pharmacists in the Netherlands and Belgium: an economic approach. Intersentia, Antwerpen

Porter ME (1991) Towards a dynamic theory of strategy. Strateg Manag J 12(S2):95–117

Porter ME, Van der Linde C (1995) Toward a new conception of the environment-competitiveness relationship. J Econ Perspect 9(4):97–118

Posner R (2003) Economic analysis of law, 6th edn. Aspen, New York

Ryan HE Jr, Wiggins RA III (2004) Who is in whose pocket? Director compensation, board independence, and barriers to effective monitoring. J Financ Econ 73(3):497–524

Scalet S, Kelly TF (2010) CSR rating agencies: what is their global impact? J Bus Ethics 94 (1):69–88

Shavell S (1980) Strict liability versus negligence. J Legal Stud 9:1–25

Shavell S (1984) Liability for harm versus regulation of safety. J Legal Stud 13:357–370

Van Dam C (2011) Tort law and human rights: brothers in arms on the role of tort law in the area of business and human rights. J Eur Tort Law 2(3):221–254

Van den Bergh MP (2013) Private environmental governance. Cornell Law Rev 99:129–199

Van Rooij B (2006) Implementation of Chinese environmental law: regular enforcement and political campaigns. Dev Change 37(1):57–74

Vogel D (2006) The market for virtue: the potential and limits of corporate social responsibility. Brookings Press, Washington

Wang C (2006) Chinese environmental law enforcement: current deficiencies and suggested reforms. Vermont J Environ Law Symp 8:159–194

[illegible]

Self-Regulation Versus Public Regulation: An Analysis of Environmental and Safety Standard Setting in the Oil and Gas Pipeline Sector

Mehdi Piri Damagh and Michael Faure

1 Introduction

Pipelines are widely used for transporting gas, oil or other substances. They can run onshore, underground and offshore and often cross territories of different countries. Unfortunately, accidents occur with these pipelines, which then cause a lot of public attention. An accident that caused quite a bit of turmoil in Belgium happened in Ghislenghein[1] on 30 July 2004.[2] From that accident, 24 people died and more than 134 were injured. Gas line accidents with serious consequences happen all over the world. Lately, in the city of Kaoshiung in Taiwan an accident occurred causing more than 30 deaths, many injured and substantial property damage.[3] In another incident, an oil pipeline, which exploded in east China's Shandong Province in 2013, caused more than 52 deaths and many more injured.[4] These accidents often raise the question what the precise causes are of those accidents. According to

[1] In Dutch pronounced as "Gellingen".

[2] For further discussion, see Bruggeman (2010), pp. 269–271.

[3] See South China Monitoring Post (2014) Owners never inspected the Taiwan gas pipeline, http://www.scmp.com/news/china/article/1566101/owner-pipeline-caused-deadly-blasts-kaohsiung-never-inspected-it. Accessed 6 October 2014.

[4] See Xinhau (2013) Death toll from China oil pipeline blast rises to 52, 11 missing, http://news.xinhuanet.com/english/china/2013-11/24/c_132913391.htm. Accessed 6 October 2014.

M. Piri Damagh (✉)
Maastricht University, Faculty of Law, METRO, Maastricht, The Netherlands
e-mail: m.piridamagh@maastrichtuniversity.nl

M. Faure
Maastricht University, Faculty of Law, METRO, Maastricht, The Netherlands

Erasmus University School of Law, Rotterdam, The Netherlands
e-mail: michael.faure@maastrichtuniversity.nl

N. Philipsen et al. (eds.), *Market Integration: The EU Experience and Implications for Regulatory Reform in China*, China-EU Law Series 2,
DOI 10.1007/978-3-662-48273-5_11

technical literature, many accidents occurred because of technical failures, poor maintenance or external impacts, and were in that sense preventable.[5] For example, there is literature claiming that according to post-Soviet Russian statistics the rate of pipeline accidents, e.g., in Russia,[6] is seven times higher than with European pipelines, mainly because of low monitoring and enforcement.[7] Also concerning the trans-Alaska pipeline (operated by BP) there were accusations of poor maintenance which would have led to several oil leaks in 2006.[8] It was held that BP would have economised on the maintenance of the pipeline.

These type of accidents inevitably raise the question how adequate incentives can be provided to operators to prevent the various types of damage that could result from either leakage (usually leading to environmental damage) or explosions (usually leading to personal injury and property damage). One answer is that economic operators will have incentives to invest in safety of pipelines because a malfunctioning of a pipeline (either a leakage or explosion) will anyway lead to a loss of product and hence to economic losses that operators wish to avoid. However, the history shows that quite an impressive number of pipeline accidents has occurred in the past,[9] showing that the mere economic incentive of wishing to avoid a loss of product apparently does not suffice. One traditional remedy often advanced to deal with damage towards third parties is a liability rule.[10] Liability rules could provide a deterrent effect and hence provide operators with the necessary incentives to invest in optimal preventive technology. However, it has equally been established in the literature that under particular circumstances liability rules may not be able to exercise their deterrent effect.[11] In some cases operators may lack appropriate information on optimal preventive technologies, limited wealth may reduce their incentives to take appropriate preventive measures, and victims may in some cases for a variety of reasons not bring a liability suit at all. Especially because pipelines often have a transboundary nature, the barriers to access to justice may be considerable. For that reason, standard setting via regulation may be a more appropriate instrument to guarantee the safety of pipelines, and more particularly cross-border pipelines.

Looking at the practice of standard-setting in this domain, a wide variety of different types of standards can be found from different sources. In some cases, governmental bodies set environmental and safety standards. In many cases

---

[5] See Montiel et al. (1996); see also Burgherr and Hirschberg (2008).

[6] For example, because of an oil pipeline accident in 1984 in a section between Almetyevsk and Novgorod in Russia nearly 127 tonnes of oil spilled into the Volga River. See on that Cherniaev et al. (1998), p. 246.

[7] Cherniaev et al. (1998), p. 222.

[8] Kandiyoti (2012), p. 36.

[9] See for more information on gas pipeline accidents: Hirschberg et al. (2004); Muhlbauer (2004); Burgherr and Hirschberg (2005); Hirschberg et al. (1998); Montiel et al. (1996); for oil pipeline accidents, see Eckle and Burgherr (2013); Davis et al. (2006).

[10] Shavell (1980).

[11] Shavell (1983).

standards have been incorporated in regulations. In cross-border pipelines, the parties mainly determine the applicable safety and environmental standards in relevant agreements and contracts. An important feature of those contracts is that they often are concluded between states or state-owned enterprises. They hence possess the sovereign power to determine which type of standards will apply. In addition, voluntary standards, prepared by firms or private standard setting bodies, have also been designed and used to mitigate the risks of oil and gas pipeline accidents. This fragmented regulatory space poses serious questions for the effective design and implementation of safety and environmental regulations. In fact, high quality regulations, if they cannot be fully implemented, are nothing but empty shells.

Hence, it is obvious that standard-setting and enforcement play significant roles to protect and improve the safety of the public and the environment. Standard setting and enforcement could equally affect market integration. For instance, the harmonisation of standards is one of the core issues which the EU has faced in developing market integration.[12] Indeed, regulatory reform is one of the central elements to overcome market failures in market integration.[13] Standard-setting and regulation, also in this domain, are crucial elements of market integration. Indeed, in the literature regulatory reforms have been described as one of the promising areas of the supply of energy in market integration progress. Furthermore, the issue of standard setting is of importance for countries in the process of market integration. Indeed, in the EU several steps have been made to harmonise safety and environmental regulations e.g., Directive 2014/52/EU of the European Parliament and of the Council of 16 April 2014 amending Directive 2011/92/EU on the assessment of the effects of certain public and private projects on the environment or Directive 2013/30/EU of the European Parliament and of the Council of 12 June 2013 on safety of offshore oil and gas operations and amending Directive 2004/35/EC. The question arises what type of specific regulation (more particularly public, private or a mix) can pursue market integration in an optimal way. Oil and gas markets are obviously of crucial importance to the economy and safety and environmental standards regulating oil and gas pipelines also play a crucial role in the market integration process. Therefore, as the central focus of this chapter, the environmental and safety standard setting in the oil and gas pipeline sector will be examined. As we will show, societal goals (like the protection of the public at large against personal injury and the protection of the environment) can be achieved through various types of both public and private standards. It is precisely this mix of public and private standards as well as the use of a variety of different standards to regulate the safety of oil and gas pipelines that will be the subject of this chapter. Standard setting for oil and gas pipelines is of great importance both for China and for the EU. The simple practical reason is that pipelines are often used both in the EU and in China for the transport of oil and gas. If we look at the standard setting in China and the EU we can see that oil and gas pipelines have been extensively

---

[12] Barnard (2013), pp. 656–660.

[13] Pelkmans (2012).

regulated in different forms.[14] For instance, in China there exist four levels of standards, including national standards, professional standards, local standards and enterprise standards.[15] These standards are mostly based on international standards such as ISO standards.[16] Meanwhile, in practice there are cases in which foreign investors could not reach an agreement with Chinese government or state-owned oil companies for the construction of a proposed oil pipeline, mainly because of different approaches of parties involved in relation to safety and environmental standards.[17] Complying with international standards in oil and gas pipeline projects may also be required in cross-border pipelines. One example constitutes the China–Myanmar gas pipeline which links Myanmar to China.[18] In the project, the Chinese developer of the project was criticised for not complying with international standards. Thus, by considering the current progress of market integration in China, analysing environmental and safety standard setting in the oil and gas pipeline sector seems necessary.

First, we will describe the various types of technical, environmental and safety regulations aimed at ensuring the safe operation of oil and gas pipelines. We will describe these different types of standards and provide examples of the extent to which they are effectively used in the regulation of the safety of oil and gas pipelines (Sect. 2). Next, we will provide a theory of standard-setting, distinguishing between public regulation, private regulation and co-regulation (Sect. 3). From that distinction, we will provide a critical analysis of technical, safety and environmental standards and propose an alternative "smart mix" of public and private regulation in this domain (Sect. 4). Section 5 concludes.

[14] See for more information on oil and gas pipeline standards in the EU, the European Commission Directorate-General Environment report 2011. See also Papadakis (2000).

[15] Schaffer et al. (2014), p. 329.

[16] Zhaojie (2008), pp. 172–173.

[17] For example in the west-East Pipeline Project which is a 4000 km gas pipeline originating in Xinxiang and ending in Shanghai, Shell was selected as a preferred partner for further negotiations. At the end, given the fact that the project was one of the major infrastructure projects, the Chinese party (PetroChina) was under pressure to conduct the project on time, hence PetroChina didn't negotiate safety and environmental issues which could decelerate the project. On the other side, within the period of negotiation, Shell examined the EIAs conducted by PetroChina. After examination it became clear for Shell that there are significant environmental and safety issues which should be dealt with, unless the participation in the project would be difficult. In the end, although Shell was never appointed legally as a financial partner in the project, Shells participation in the project to some extent improved the quality of the EIAs and other assessments. See for more information Stalley (2010), pp. 119–125.

[18] Burmese officials claimed that cracks have been found at several points on the pipeline and thus the construction of the pipeline does not comply with international standards. See About Oil (2014), China–Myanmar, breach of standards: new pipeline woes, http://www.abo.net/oilportal/topic/view.do?contentId=2200566. Accessed 10 November 2014.

2 Types of Standards

There exists a wide range of policy instruments that can be used to prevent or minimise environmental damage.[19] Because of the characteristics of oil and gas pipelines, however, they are mainly furnished with safety and environmental regulations.[20] This might be because it is generally assumed that most pipeline risks can be prevented by the direct involvement of government. From the outset it is important to establish what is meant by regulation. According to Dudley and Brito, regulations are specific standards or instructions concerning what individuals, businesses, and other organisations can or cannot do.[21] Many scholars point out the key role of public or governmental authority in exercising control over public or private activities.[22] However, scholars such as Julia Black take a wider approach to define regulation.[23] Black defines regulation as the intentional use of authority to affect the behaviour of a different party according to set standards, involving instruments of information gathering and behaviour modification.[24] The latter approach seems more general and covers self-regulation as well. In this chapter, the regulation of oil and gas pipelines will be examined according to the latter approach. Not all types of regulation are of interest in this context: technical, environmental and safety regulations will be the focal point of our research.

Regulations by subject can be divided into technical standards and safety and environmental regulations.[25] Technical standards largely refer to those standards that govern design, construction, operation and maintenance of natural gas and hazardous liquid transmission pipelines.[26] Of course, technical standards to a large extent overlap with safety standards, given that the inherent purpose of technical standards is to keep the pipeline safe.[27] Hence safety standards in this research mainly refer to regulations particularly aimed at ensuring the optimum level of safety of pipelines' facilities and their crews from non-technical concerns and preventing pipelines from causing loss of life and serious property damage to people living nearby. Pipelines are often subject to various forms of environmental

[19] Livermore and Revesz (2014).

[20] For a detailed study on the need for and justification of safety and environmental standards, see Faure (2012). For a specific study on pipelines, see Perry and Haynes (1993).

[21] Dudley and Brito (2012).

[22] See Selznick (1985), p. 363; den Hertog (2003).

[23] Black (2001).

[24] Black (2001).

[25] In principle, regulation can be divided into social regulation and economic regulation. Social regulation refers to environmental and safety regulation, consumer protection and labour law. Economic regulation, on the other hand, is mainly used for regulating markets. For more discussion, see Baron (1995), pp. 10–11 and 33; Ogus (2004); den Hertog (2003), pp. 7–8.

[26] Meyer et al. (2008).

[27] As indicated by Fliess et al. (2010), technical regulations cannot be broken down by safety and quality.

threats in the construction and operation periods. In principle, environmental risk prevention is, to a large extent, incorporated in technical and safety standards, because obviously they are aimed at avoiding pipeline failures. Nevertheless, there exists a certain amount of concern that requires considering environmental regulation separately. Taking the potential environmental risk of pipelines into account in the decision-making procedure, establishing minimum requirements to prevent environmental (ecological) damage throughout the operational period and ensuring that pipelines are maintained in compliance with their permits are some of the major problems reflected by this argument.

From a review of existing literature and a few cross-border pipeline agreements, we can deduce that safety, technical and environmental regulations have been incorporated into agreements under separate categories.[28] In addition, in some countries, separate laws have been enacted for each category.[29] Therefore, definitions, scope, monitoring and enforcement programs for each category may vary to a large degree. As a consequence, each category should be described individually.

We will now distinguish technical, safety and environmental standards in further detail, whereby we first describe the nature of the standard and next provide examples of those specific types of standards for the regulation of oil and gas pipelines. In that respect, we will pay specific attention to the question of whether the source of the particular standard is public (government) or private (industry).

2.1 Technical Codes and Standards

2.1.1 Description

Technical standards[30] can be defined as a set of technical definitions and engineering codes of conduct. These codes specify minimum operating design levels, pre-construction and post construction standards for pipelines and their components.[31] These standards define the pipeline's design, route selection, installation methods, equipment quality, welding, fabrication, installation, testing, operation and maintenance and safety requirements.[32] Technical standards can be divided

---

[28] For example, in the BTC oil pipeline and SCP gas pipeline. Wawryk (2003) divides international oil and gas safety and environmental standards into three categories: standards for equipment and products, standards for environmental practices and standards to improve environmental performance.

[29] For instance, in US pipelines, safety concerns are generally addressed by the Pipeline Safety Improvement Act of 2006. For environmental concerns, actors should comply with the National Environmental Policy Act and other regulations. See Jewell (2007).

[30] It is necessary to mention that the literature sometimes refers to technical codes and sometimes to technical standards; in this chapter both concepts are used interchangeably.

[31] Committee on the Safety of Marine Pipelines (1994), p. 46.

[32] Bai and Bai (2012), pp. 892–900.

into two general categories: process and product standards.[33] Process standards can be defined as technical codes which are used for the design, construction, inspection of pipeline's projects and other operational issues.[34] Product standards, on the other hand, are codes which define the materials used for the pipelines.

In addition, technical standards specify the requirements and give recommendations for the design, materials, construction and testing of pipelines which all have a positive effect on preventing pipeline accidents. The setting of technical standards is usually done by a group of experts representing interested parties and takes its lead from established industry or business practices. Pipeline technical standards are not static subjects, they are periodically updated. Thus, in pipeline engineering literature, it is not advised to utilise the term best international standard or standards for qualifying pipelines.[35] Nevertheless, pipeline technical standards may vary in their requirements. For example the wall thickness, location based on design factors, minimum yield strength of pipe steel and class location of pipelines[36] may differ in various technical standards. On the other hand, the cost of pipelines greatly depends on safety measures. For instance, Menon argues that normally 10–15 % of the total cost of a pipeline project comprises environmental and permitting costs.[37] The capital costs of a pipeline greatly depend on the geological conditions. Therefore, laying a pipeline subsea or even an onshore pipeline in a populated area or in sensitive environmental area will cost much more than a normal land-based pipeline.[38]

2.1.2 Examples and Sources

Technical standards *inter alia* address the way in which pipelines should be designed. It is interesting that between the different standard setters (usually private institutions) the standards can substantially differ. A discussion of the standards for liquids and for gas for different classes can illustrate those differences as Table 1 illustrates.

---

[33] See Wawryk (2003).

[34] Antaki (2003), p. 23.

[35] Kuprewicz (2007).

[36] As stated by Braestrup et al.: "Design of the pipeline wall thickness is based on the classification of the pipeline". The classification of pipeline into safety classes (location class) is mainly based on the location (human density) and transport medium. In fact, the pipeline must be designed with a sufficient wall thickness to withstand anticipated external pressures and loads in areas with more human activity. At the higher class, the more yield strength is required for the maximum design pressure because in the higher class, the greater number of buildings intended for human occupancy are located. See generally Braestrup et al. (2009), pp 78–79; and Hopkins (2005).

[37] Menon (2005), p. 334. See for a detailed discussion of capital and operation costs of pipelines Omonbude (2012), pp. 13–14.

[38] Seddon (2006), pp. 87–88.

Table 1 Typical maximum design factors for transmission pipelines (Kuprewicz 2007; design factors are determined based on the class location of the pipeline)

	Liquids (no classification)	Gas Class 1 location	Gas Class 3 location
US (ASME B31.8 (ASME standards for the American Society of Mechanical Engineers. B31.8 is the code of transmission and distribution pipeline systems, see Escoe 2006, pp 66–68.))	0.72	0.72	0.5
Canada (CSAZ662) (The Standards Council of Canada (SCC) coordinates the National Standards System. CSA develops the Z662 Oil and Gas Pipeline Systems standards for pipelines. See for more information Meyer et al. 2008.)	0.8	0.8	0.56
Australia (AS2885) (This standard was developed by a working group from both industry and government. AS2885 relates to design, construction, testing, operations and maintenance of gas and petroleum pipelines that operate at pressures in excess of 1050 kPa. See for more information Standard Australia (2014) http://www.standards.org.au/Pages/default.aspx. Accessed 08 October 2014. Standards Australia is the nation's peak non-government Standards organisation. See for more information. http://www.standards.org.au/Pages/default.aspx. Accessed 08 October 2014.)	0.72	0.72	0.72
UK (BS8010) (This Part of BS 8010 gives recommendations for the design, construction, installation, testing and commissioning of subsea pipelines constructed from steel and metallic reinforced polymers. See for more information BSI 2009)	0.72	0.72	0.3
ISO 13623	0.77	0.83	0.67

Class locations are basically determined by calculating the number of buildings in the area where a proposed pipeline is envisaged to be positioned. See for more information McAllister (2013), p. 161. Class locations are usually determined by the relevant safety regulation. In general, class location is determined based on the population density in the vicinity of the pipeline. See Menon (2005), pp. 208–209. For instance, according to DOT 49 CFR Part 192(US), a Class 1 location is allocated to areas that have 10 or fewer residential buildings. Class location 2 is for an area with more than 10 but less than 46 residential buildings. Class location 3 is for an area with more than 46 buildings or within 100 yards of a public assembly. Class location 4 is for buildings with four or more shops. See for more information Menon (2005), pp. 208–210. See also Antaki (2003), p. 84

This table already illustrates the wide variety that exists with respect to these technical standards for pipelines.[39] Let us now focus on the sources of those standards, i.e., the organisations that prepare, issue and publish those standards.

[39] For more discussion on the differences between technical standards of oil and gas pipelines see Meyer et al. (2008); Kuprewicz (2007); Muhlbauer (2004), p. 235. See also AdvancePipeliner (2010) Major Codes and Standards for Designing Pipelines. http://advancepipeliner.com/site/

Pipeline technical standards may be published by professional societies, trade associations, testing and certification organisations, standards developing organisations, governmental bodies and companies.[40] Therefore, private entities as well as public agencies may develop technical standards. Each of these entities may develop standards at national, regional or international levels. For instance, the International Organization for Standardization (ISO) is an international standard setting body for promulgation of standards for businesses, governments and societies. This organisation is composed of representatives from different national standard entities; nonetheless it is a private institution and develops voluntary standards. ISO 13623 code is the first international code prepared for liquid and gas pipeline transportation systems and is provided by the International Organization for Standardization.[41]

In China, the oil and gas sector is mainly regulated by national standards and professional standards. For example, GB 50423-2007 is the *Code for design of oil and gas transportation pipeline crossing engineering*. And GB 50424-2007 is the *Code for design of oil and gas transmission pipeline crossing engineering*. Both of these standards are national standards which are drafted by China Petroleum Pipeline Engineering.[42] In addition, there are several technical standards which are categorised as professional standards and drafted by professional institutions and administered by governmental bodies.[43] For instance, the *Code for quality acceptance of oil and gas construction engineering* is drafted by the China Petroleum Group Engineering Technology Research Institute and administrated by the Petroleum Engineering Construction Standardization Committee.[44]

Professional societies, trade associations and testing and certification organisations are mainly private entities which contribute to producing and integrating technical standards.[45] These types of institutions, although they have multiple clients worldwide, basically are country-based institutions. Examples include DNV (Det Norske Veritas) and the American Society of Mechanical Engineers

index.php/component/content/article/131-allcategories/16-major-codes-and-standards-for-designing-pipelines.html. Accessed 14 October 2014.

[40] Antaki (2003), pp. 10–11.

[41] Braestrup et al. (2009), p. 73.

[42] See Chinese Standards (2007) Code for design of oil and gas transmission pipeline crossing engineering. http://www.chinesestandard.net/PDF-English-Translation/GB50423-2007.html. Accessed 11 November 2014.

[43] For the complete list of the Chinese technical standards in the oil and gas sector see Chinese Standards (2014) List of Chinese Industry Standard. http://www.chinesestandard.net/List-PDF/SY.aspx. Accessed 11 November 2014.

[44] See Chinese Standards (2007) Code for quality acceptance of oil and gas construction engineering. http://www.chinesestandard.net/PDF-English-Translation/SY4200-2007.html. Accessed 11 November 2014.

[45] In China, professional standards are formulated by competent administrative authorities and should be confirmed by the standardisation committee (under the State Council). See Shen (2014), pp. 36–37.

(ASME). DNV is an independent Norwegian foundation with the purpose of safeguarding life, property, and the environment. This foundation has proposed a variety of industry safety standards in particular for offshore oil and gas pipelines and facilities. For example, the Blue Stream offshore gas pipeline, which connects Russia to Turkey through the Black Sea, is constructed based on the DNV technical codes.[46] ASME is a not-for-profit professional organisation that has a leading role in publishing and promoting technical standards.[47] The ASME standard, more specifically ASME B31, is one of the most widely used technical standards worldwide.[48] ASME standards have been used in many cross-border pipelines such as the BTC or SCP.[49]

It may be clear from the previous that most of those technical standards are set by private organisations specialised in standard setting such as ISO, DNV or ASME. However, these standard setting organisations and the standards they impose do not function in a legal vacuum. In practice each country has its own standard setting body. These standard bodies may write their own standards, but they mostly accredit standards written by standards setting institutions, whether published by domestic or international standard institutions. For example in Japan, the Japanese Industrial Standards Committee, which is authorised by the law of industrial standardisation 1949, has conducted affirmation and development of standards in Japan that have been suggested both from academia, companies and also international bodies such as ISO.[50]

Formal regulators hence rely on those (private) standards. Indeed, private standards have to an important extent been recognised by national legislation as legally and forcible standards and national legislation often refers to the standards.

---

[46] Grishin (2005).

[47] See for more information ASME official site: https://www.asme.org/about-asme. Accessed 23 November 2014.

[48] Antaki (2003), p. 15.

[49] See for example, Appendix 5, the code of practice of the Host Government Agreement Between and Among the Government of The Republic of Turkey and the State Oil Company of the Azerbaijan Republic BP Exploration (Caspian Sea) LTD. Statoil BTC Caspian AS Ramco Hazar Energy Limited TURKIYE Petrolleri A.O. Unocal BTC Pipeline, LTD. ITOCHU OIL Exploration (Azerbaijan) INC. Delta HESS (BTC) Limited. Accessible at the following address: http://www.gib.gov.tr/fileadmin/CifteVergilendirme/TC_MEP_anlasma.htm. Accessed 12 December 2013; Appendix 4, Host governmental agreement between and among the Government of Georgia and state oil company of the Azerbaijan Republic BP exploration (Azerbaijan) limited, Total finaelf E&P Caucasian Gas SA, Lukagip N.V., Statoil Azerbaijan a.s., Naft Iran Intertrade Co (Nico) limited, Turkish Petroleum Overseas Company Limited, Appendix 7, Gas sale agreement. See: http://subsites.bp.com/caspian/SHA/Eng/HGA/Host%20Government%20Agreement%20Georgia%20-(English).pdf. Accessed 16 July 2013.

[50] See for more information Japanese Industrial Standards Committee (2014) http://www.jisc.go.jp/eng/index.html. Accessed 14 July 2014. In Australia, specific standards are provided by the public standards setting organisation for pipelines. The standards series of AS 2885 are specifically generated in relation to onshore pipelines. See note 35.

In Nigeria for example the American Petroleum Institute (API) Codes and the American Society of Mechanical Engineers (ASME). Codes are considered by law as good oil field practice. In particular, in the absence of internal regulation concerning pipeline standards, foreign standards, whether private or public are regulated by the competent authorities as public standards. For example, Steiner mentions that in Nigeria, if the operator does not comply with good oil field practice, the Petroleum Act of 1969 grants the Minister of Petroleum Resources the statutory authority to revoke an oil operator's license to operate.[51] In the Mineral Oils Regulations of 1962, it is indicated that good oil field practice means compliance with the petroleum safety codes provided by the API or ASME. Both are private standards and also the technical standards of Shell Company,[52] which is one of the main operators of the oil industry in Nigeria.

In addition, there is a variety of standard setting organisations which has originally been established for producing or accrediting domestic standards; subsequently their standards are used by other countries as well. An example constitutes the standards produced by BSI.[53] BSI is the UK's National Standards Body (NSB), which has 64,000 clients worldwide.[54] The BS 8010 code contains three parts covering onshore and offshore oil and gas pipelines. The code has been developed over a period of more than 40 years. This code is provided by the UK's National Standards Body (NSB) and has been used at many pipelines worldwide.[55] As mentioned above, technical standards are mainly produced by professions, industries and associations. Hence, the involvement of public regulators is mostly limited to accrediting standards written by standard setting institutions whether by recognising the regulator or specific rules enacted by the private regulator.[56]

---

[51] Steiner (2010).

[52] Steiner (2010).

[53] The British Standards Institution (BSI) standards are developed by committees consisting of government departments, research organisations, industries and so on. The British Standards Institution is termed a "non-profit distributing company" because profits are re-invested back into the business. For more information about BSI standards see Company Profile, accessible at the following address: http://www.bsigroup.com/en-GB/about-bsi/governance/. Accessed 14 October 2014. Although BSI is a private entity, it is recognised as the UK National Standards Body (NSB) by the UK Government. This status is formally codified in the Memorandum of Understanding (MoU) between the United Kingdom Government and the British Standards Institution in respect of its activities as the United Kingdom's National Standards Body.

[54] See for more information the official website of the Chinese Standards at the following address: http://www.bsigroup.com/. Accessed 14 July 2014.

[55] For example, BS standards have been set by the parties of the CPS and BTC pipelines as one of the technical standards (Azerbaijan, Turkey and Georgia host governmental agreements through Baku–Tbilisi–Ceyhan pipeline), see note 43. It is worth mentioning that in accordance with the CEN rules, BS 8010-1:1989, BS 8010-2.8:1992 and BS 8010-3:1993 have been replaced by EN 14161 since 2003. See BRITISH STANDARD. Petroleum and natural gas industries—Pipeline transportation systems, 2003. http://www.cngspw.com/Doc/WebNote/201108/Y2011M08D04H11m01s49/bs20en2014161-200320u77F3u6CB9u548Cu5929u7136u6C14u5DE5u4E1A.pdf. Accessed 14 October 2014.

[56] See Cafaggi (2006), pp. 16–17.

Although the standards setting organisations mainly draft technical standards in the way we defined above, the literature mentions that in designing technical standards, environmental and safety concerns are also taken into consideration.[57] Finally, in this respect it should also be mentioned that not only national regulators, but also regional or international treaties often refer to private standards.[58] An example is provided by the Seventh Meeting of the Parties to the Basel Convention on the control of transboundary movement of hazardous waste. At this meeting, the Parties referred explicitly to ISO standards as appropriate international standards.[59]

2.2 *Safety Standards and Guidelines*

2.2.1 Description

With safety standards within the context of this contribution we refer to standards that are meant to protect pipeline facilities more specifically from external impacts. Safety in this context hence refers to the freedom from danger, risk or injury and to a management of risk to acceptable levels. For the purposes of this chapter it is important to distinguish the technical standards we have just discussed from the safety standards. Safety standards more particularly aim at preventing external impacts and third party interference. In fact studies show that those constitute the main causes of failure in pipeline accidents. In a review of hazardous pipeline incidents in the US during 1991, 60 % of fatalities and 35 % of injuries occurred because of damage caused by third party interference.[60] This type of incidents can be prevented or at least minimised by applying more precise, stringent and of course costly regulation.[61] Therefore, in this contribution, safety standards are defined as measures that are envisaged to keep pipelines, including their facilities and crews, safe from external impacts and non-technical failures.

Safety standards hence can refer both to *ex ante* as well as to *ex post* safety measures. *Ex ante* measures aim to prevent accidents; *ex post* measures aim to minimise the after-effect of an accident and are hence included in the definition of safety standards.[62] Indeed, safety standards encompass a broad range of rules, enacted to different degrees at national levels and industry levels. Most of these measures are established and improved to reduce the number and consequences of accidents. Safety regulation should be differentiated from technical standards mainly because technical standards are private regulations carried out

[57] See Dux (2011), pp. 116–117.

[58] See the examples provided by Oliva (2015), p. 288 and by Schaffer et al. (2014), p. 17.

[59] United Nations Environment Programme, Ozone Secretariat (2006), p. 92.

[60] Perry and Haynes (1993).

[61] Kandiyoti (2012), pp. 32–33.

[62] Boss et al. (2004).

autonomously by industries, associations etc. (all private actors), aiming to regulate their own activities. On the other hand, safety regulations are adopted not only to control the behaviour of industries but also to make provisions against risks arising out of the acts of third-parties. Safety standards are hence mostly issued by public regulators.

2.2.2 Examples and Sources

Examples of preventive measures include safety management systems, risk assessment, technical safety management measures, prevention of third parties interference and land use planning. Mitigating measures include informing public authorities soon enough after accidents and emergency plans.[63] Muhlbauer defines risk assessment as a process that uses available information to measure risks involved in pipeline construction and operation.[64] Perry & Haynes suggest a more complete definition: identifying pipeline risks, evaluating identified risks, and managing those risks by estimating priorities through prevention and detection of the characteristics of an accident and relating them to the consequence of the incidents in terms of public safety and property damage.[65] This assessment can be done either without using any measured performance-based risk threshold benchmarks such as the model which has been used in U.S. regulations and can also require additional detailed or numerical methods, such as specific risk benchmarks, or quantified risk acceptance criteria thresholds for pipelines such as in the Netherlands and Malaysia.[66]

Safety measures during the planning and construction phases of a pipeline encompass a variety of rules. Some are integrated into technical standards, such as wall thickness and pipeline location. In China, many safety standards are classified as professional standards (Industry Standard). For instance, the *Safety specifications for oil products transportation pipeline* is drafted by the Daqing Oilfield Engineering Design Technology Development Co., Ltd. and administrated by the Oil and Gas Fields and Pipeline Construction Design Professionals Standardization Committee.[67]

---

[63] See for more information the European Commission report prepared by Directorate-General Environment, Assessing the case for EU legislation on the safety of pipelines and the possible impacts of such an initiative, 2011 (hereafter the European Commission Report 2011).

[64] Muhlbauer (2004), p. 9.

[65] Perry and Haynes (1993).

[66] In the Netherlands via NEN 3650. See Kuprewicz (2007). In the Malaysian Quantified risk assessment model, data including, pipeline attributes relating to design, construction, operating pressure, damage/failure histories, in-line inspection, close internal potential survey, and others will be quantified. The risk then will be assessed because of: probability of Failure x Consequence of Failure. See for further discussion bin Mohd Ali Napiah (2009).

[67] See Chinese Standards (2004) Safety regulations for heaters used in petroleum industry. http://www.chinesestandard.net/PDF-English-Translation/SY0031-2004.html. Accessed 11 November 2014.

A number of safety rules relate to third party interference prevention such as determining the location of pipelines and the safety zone around these. In addition, in some cases, safety regulations should be respected and enforced by the third parties. For example, Federal pipeline safety regulations of the US (49 CFR 192.616 and 49 CFR 195.440) require pipeline operators to develop and implement public awareness programs that follow the guidance provided by the American Petroleum Institute (API) Recommended Practice (RP) 1162: Public Awareness Programs for Pipeline Operators.

Safety management systems or pipeline integrity management systems are methods ensuring long term sustainability of safety and enforcement performance.[68] A safety management system requires operators to identify, prioritise, assess, evaluate, repair and validate the integrity of pipelines and continuously evaluate and manage a database of information concerning their pipeline to ensure that the pipe integrity remains safe, in particular, in high consequence areas.[69] Pipeline integrity management programs are to be developed in response to the pipeline's threats.[70] These threats are derived from previous accident reports.

Many regulators moreover impose mitigating measures aiming at the reduction of damages after the accident occurred. One of the most commonly used measures in this category is preparing emergency response plans. The aim of these plans is to detail the necessary actions to minimise the consequences of accidents. These plans encompass a variety of measures, including but not limited to preparing pipeline maps, shut-down valves on certain major pipeline accidents, notifying competent authorities and clean-up of oil contamination.[71]

These safety standards, different from the technical standards we discussed before, are hence mainly issued by public regulators. Still, there are also a few private standards that focus on safety. The compliance with those standards is in some cases mandated by law as well.[72] Within the context of cross-border pipelines the applicable law, as agreed by the parties in the contract, will determine the applicable safety regulations. A striking feature is that in some cases the parties involved (States) explicitly exclude the applicability of their national safety law. This for example happened in the case of the BTC pipeline between the

---

[68] Singh (2013), pp. 133–135.

[69] Singh (2013), pp. 13–14.

[70] Boss et al. (2004).

[71] See for example Muhlbauer (2004), pp. 162–165. For instance in the UK, the duty holder shall prepare the emergency response plan and submit it to the Department of Energy and Climate Change (DECC). This plan should be confirmed by the DECC. The Offshore Installations (Prevention of Fire and Explosion, and Emergency Response) Regulations 1995 came into force on 20th June 1995. According to the UK Pipelines Safety Regulations 1996, before the pipeline is first used, the local authority shall prepare an adequate plan detailing how an emergency relating to a possible major accident in its area will be dealt with. See the Pipelines Safety Regulations 1996 come into force on 11th April 1996, PART III MAJOR ACCIDENT HAZARD PIPELINES, para 25.

[72] See on that, for example, Felix and Sebastian (2012).

Government of the Azerbaijan Republic and investors where the standards decreed by the investment agreements were declared applicable.[73] Moreover, as with the case of the technical standards, also as far as safety standards is concerned, international or regional organisations can, via treaties, oblige their members to comply with particular safety standards, even if they would have been issued by private organisations.[74]

2.3 *Environmental Standards and Regulations*

2.3.1 Description

Whereas the safety standards just mentioned aim at protecting the safety of the pipeline, as well as the individuals and property surrounding the pipeline (more particularly from external impacts), environmental standards generally aim at the protection of environmental resources such as water, air and soil. Pipelines, as mentioned before, have the potential to create substantial environmental risks. Hence, regulation has been widely used to address the possible negative impacts of the oil and gas pipeline projects. Generally, Kiss and Shelton define environmental standards as "perspective norms that govern products or processes or set limits on the amount of pollutants or emissions produced".[75] If one takes the definition as given, the regulatory space relating to oil and gas pipelines contains a number of mandatory and voluntary regulations that assist in protecting the environment. International and regional conventions as well as national laws contain legal requirements which are adopted for environmental performance. Nevertheless, because of the difficulties in reaching international agreements and the high degree of variation of effectiveness and enforcement of national law around the world there is a gap which can only filled by voluntary and non-legal environmental standards.[76] There is no international treaty dealing directly with environmental standards applicable to pipelines. There are, however, quite a few environmental standards, to be found in either national, regional or international regulations that may have some importance for pipelines that we will briefly touch

[73] See for example Article 10 of the Host governmental agreement between and among the Government of the Azerbaijan Republic and the state oil company of the Azerbaijan Republic BP exploration (Azerbaijan) limited, Total finaelf E&P Caucasian Gas SA, Lukagip N.V., Statoil Azerbaijan a.s., Naft Iran Intertrade Co (Nico) limited, Turkish Petroleum Overseas Company Limited, appendix 7, Gas sale agreement. http://subsites.bp.com/caspian/BTC/Eng/agmt1/agmt1.PDF. Accessed 19 November 2013.

[74] The WTO Agreement on Technical Barriers to Trade (TBT Agreement), gives privileged status to international standards produced by the International Organization for Standardization (ISO). WTO members are thus required to comply with ISO standards, which is a private standards setting. See for a more detailed discussion Alvarez (2005), pp. 220–222.

[75] Kiss and Shelton (2007), p. 121.

[76] For a more detailed discussion, see Wagner and Armstrong (2010).

upon. However, it should be kept in mind that those environmental standards are usually not drafted specifically for pipelines, but with a much broader aim.

2.3.2 Examples and Sources

A first group of environmental standards, often to be found in domestic environmental law, in regional or international treaties could be directly or indirectly applicable to pipeline activities.[77] For instance, at international level, the Ramsar Convention on Wetlands, as amended in 1982 and 1987, obliges each Contracting Party to consider its international responsibilities for the conservation, management and wise use of migratory stocks of waterfowl within its territory.[78] In that case, although the convention doesn't directly include any norm concerning the construction and operation of pipelines, involved parties are obliged to use such registered wetlands in a wise manner. Even concerning cases of urgent national interest, if states delete or restrict the boundaries of wetlands already included in the convention, they shall, as far as possible, compensate for any loss of wetland resources.[79] The same approach has been followed by Council Directive 92/43/EEC on the Conservation of Natural Habitats and of Wild Fauna and Flora[80] and the Convention on the Protection and Use of Transboundary Watercourses and International Lakes Helsinki of 1992.[81] Hence, it could be argued that the Ramsar Convention, Council Directive 92/43/EEC on the Conservation of natural habitats and of wild fauna and flora and the Convention on the Protection and Use of Transboundary Watercourses and International Lakes Helsinki have an indirect relevance to the construction and operation of pipelines. At national level, for instance, the prohibition against the destruction of critical habitats, the prohibition of the deposit of a substance that is harmful to migratory birds into waters or areas frequented by migratory birds or permit for disposal at sea which may be required

[77] An integrated assessment of all environmental standards potentially applicable to pipelines would obviously go beyond the scope of this chapter. We will therefore suffice with providing a few examples of environmental standards, especially focussing on the particular nature of those standards and the sources.

[78] Article 2 of the Convention on Wetlands of International Importance. Ramsar (Iran), 2 February 1971. UN Treaty Series No. 14583; 11 ILM 963 (1972); hereafter referred to as the Ramsar Convention on Wetlands. It pays particular attention to the Waterfowl Habitat.

[79] Article 4 of the Ramsar Convention on Wetlands.

[80] Article 6 of the Council Directive 92/43/EEC on the Conservation of natural habitats and of wild fauna and flora. Council Directive 92/43/EEC of 21 May 1992 on the conservation of natural habitats and of wild fauna and flora. Official Journal L 206, 22/07/1992 P. 0007-0050); hereafter the Council Directive 92/43/EEC.

[81] Article 3 of the Convention on the Protection and Use of Transboundary Watercourses and International Lakes 1936 UNTS 269; 31 ILM 1312 (1992); hereafter the Helsinki Convention.

for dredging, all require compliance with special environmental norms and permits.[82]

On the other hand, according to several domestic and international regulations, developers are required to conduct feasibility studies to evaluate the current and future impact of pipelines. In the area of environmental management and procedure systems, several practices have emerged and have been regulated by regulators. These practices can be listed as environmental impacts assessment,[83] environmental management system,[84] environmental performance evaluation, environmental monitoring and auditing and environmental reporting.[85] These practices are mainly developed by standard setting organisations such as ISO and therefore have a non-binding nature, unless they became mandatory by the public regulator or through contracts.[86]

One environmental instrument that does indeed play an important role, also in the standard setting concerning pipelines is the Environmental Impact Assessment (EIA). At the international and regional level, several instruments expressly oblige their member parties to conduct (transboundary) EIA. Examples include the Convention on the Environmental Impact Assessment in a Transboundary Context (Espoo, 1991)[87] and the EU Directive on Environmental Impact Assessment 2011/92.[88] For instance, The Nord Stream Gas Pipeline (NSGP) was subject to Article 3 of the Espoo Convention and hence an elaborated transboundary EIA was prepared by the developer.[89] On the other hand, several international funding organisations mandate conducting an EIA according to their guidelines for projects that will be financed by them. Example includes the West African Gas Pipeline

---

[82] For instance in Canada, the Species at Risk Act, the Migratory Birds Act and the Canadian Environmental Protection Act include several norms relating to the construction and operation of pipelines. In Iran, the Law of Conservation of Natural Resources and Forest Reserves (1992) prohibits cutting, destroying or injuring plants or growing trees. As a consequence, offenders may be formally charged unless they have been awarded certain permits.

[83] Environmental impact assessment can be categorised as management-based regulation, Coglianese and Lazer (2003).

[84] For example, the environment management system (ISO 14001) was used in the Interconnector UK-Belgium offshore gas pipeline. See for more information the official website of the operator, at http://www.interconnector.com. Accessed 21 May 2014.

[85] Wawryk (2003).

[86] For instance ISO 14001 for environmental management system and ISO 14031 for environmental performance evaluation.

[87] Large diameter oil and gas pipelines are included in the list of the hazardous activities in the Appendix I of the Espoo Convention. Convention on Environmental Impact Assessment in a Transboundary Context (1991), 5 February 1991, 30 I.L.M. 800; hereinafter referred to as the Espoo Convention.

[88] Gas and oil pipelines with a diameter of more than 800 mm and a length of more than 40 km are included in Annex I of the Directive. Directive 2014/52/EU of the European Parliament and of the Council of 16 April 2014 amending Directive 2011/92/EU on the assessment of the effects of certain public and private projects on the environment Text with EEA relevance OJ L 124, 25.4.2014, pp. 1–18.

[89] See for more discussion Koivurova and Polonen (2010).

which is supported by the World Bank. In that case, the World Bank required preparing an environmental impact assessment according to the World Bank standards.[90]

At national level, in many countries such as Iran,[91] the US,[92] the UK,[93] China[94] and Canada,[95] a national EIA is mandatory for garneting oil and gas pipeline projects. An example could be the case of the new Swiss section of the North Sea-Italy Pipeline (Transitgas pipeline) which was commissioned in 2003.[96] In that case the federal environmental protection law of Switzerland, as a transit state, has been applied to the pipeline. Therefore, before the construction of the pipeline, a risk assessment based on the safety regulation of the transit country, Switzerland, was conducted. Because of that risk assessment, for the unacceptable zone, the route was changed into a tunnel and for intermediate zones preventive measures, such as increasing the depth of cover of the pipeline, concrete slab covering and increasing pipeline thickness, were applied to minimise the risks of an accident and of pollution.[97]

When, at the national and international level there are treaties which mandate preparing EIAs for large diameter oil and gas pipelines, intergovernmental agreements and in particular host governmental agreements play the key roles in formulating the EIAs details, particularly for cross-border pipelines.[98] Having considered

[90] Mujih (2008).

[91] The Iranian regulation on Environmental Impact Assessment of the major construction, manufacturing and services projects as amended (2011).

[92] In the US, National environmental Policy Act as amended (2007) 1 42 U.S.C. § 4321 et seq.

[93] The Pipe-line Works (Environmental Impact Assessment) Regulations 2000.

[94] According to the Environmental Impact Assessment Law of the People's Republic of China, an EIA is required for any project that can have negative environmental impacts, regardless of which sector the project may fall under including oil and gas pipeline. See the Environmental Impact Assessment Law of the People's Republic of China. (Adopted at the 30th Meeting of the Standing Committee of the Ninth National People's Congress on 28 October 2002, promulgated by Order No. 77 of the President of the People's Republic of China on 28 October 2002, and effective on 1 September 2003). Accordingly, in several national and international pipeline projects, EIAs have been implemented by project developers, e.g. the West-East pipeline project (supra note 17) or the China–Myanmar gas pipeline (supra note 18).

[95] Final Report of the National Energy Board Action Plan on Safety and Environmental Protection (2011–2012). http://www.neb-one.gc.ca/clf-nsi/rsftyndthnvrnmnt/sfty/ctnplnrprtprgrss/prtprgrssfnl2013-eng.html. Accessed 16 October 2014.

[96] At present, the Transitgas Pipeline system consists of 292 km (two parallel lines), which crosses Switzerland from north to south. For more information see Transitgas AG (2014) The pipeline system. http://www.transitgas.org/EN/pipeline.aspx. Accessed 10 December 2014. Indeed, in 1974 the 164 km Transitgas Pipeline (the Swiss section of the North Sea-Italy pipeline) was officially put into service. In 1997, because of the increasing demand for natural gas in Italy, the Italian natural gas company SNAM SpA decided to expand the complete transport system. This new section, which was commissioned in 2003, includes 185 km of 36 in. and 48 in. pipelines.

[97] Plüss et al. (2000).

[98] Examples include the BTC, SCP and Chad-Cameron pipelines. For further discussion, see Piri Damagh and Faure (2014). See also Mujih (2008).

a few host governmental agreements between investors and host states, it can be argued that the scope, structure and permitting process will be to a large extent dependent on the contractual obligations of developers.[99] This issue creates several questions concerning the effectiveness of environmental regulations adopted through host governmental agreements.[100]

As indicated, environmental regulations relating to oil and gas pipelines may vary according to applicable law which can be national or international law. At least two distinctive approaches with a slight overlap can be examined. In the first approach, at either the international or national level, the relevant legally binding law may require oil and gas pipeline developers to comply with certain standards as a minimum environmental performance. These standards can be enacted by public regulators such as the UK Offshore Petroleum Production and Pipe-lines (Assessment of Environmental Effects) (Amendment) Regulations 2007 at domestic level or the Environmental Impact Assessment Law of the People's Republic of China. Examples at regional and international level include the Espoo convention 1991 and the EU Directive on Environmental Impact Assessments 2011.[101] On the other hand, initially non-binding standards such as ISO standards can be transformed to binding law by the authorisation of public regulators or by incorporation in international or regional treaties.[102] In the second approach, at both the international and national levels, developers may be required to exercise the best international practice, best available technology[103] or best practice. In that case the applicable law does not require compliance with certain standards. Instead, in case of litigation the judicial body will, by using international or national standards and guidelines, interpret whether the developer has used the best practice or not. Therefore in the latter approach, developers may comply with their own standards or even prepare environmental impact assessment without any specific legal obligation to perform such practices, but in litigation against such a developer, the relevant adjudication body will decide whether the developer in charge has already complied with best practice or not. At domestic level, examples include the Australian Petroleum Act 1967[104] or in Nigeria, the Petroleum Act of 1969, which grants the Minister of

[99] For instance, according to the BTC host governmental agreement, the host state can only approve the EIA and other assessments in accordance with the terms of the relevant agreement and not according to the domestic regulations of the host state. Interestingly, in the BTC pipeline, the Environment Ministry of Georgia criticised BP's EIA, accusing BP to give little weight to risks endangering the Bajori protected area which had been chosen as the route of the pipeline. See Waters (2003).

[100] See Piri Damagh and Faure (2014).

[101] See also the Protocol on Environmental Protection to the Antarctic Treaty 1998.

[102] Supra notes 46 and 54.

[103] According to Kiss and Shelton this comes from the customary international law obligation of due diligence. Kiss and Shelton (2007), p. 120.

[104] Kiss and Shelton (2007), p. 120.

Petroleum Resources the statutory authority to revoke an oil operator's license to operate if the operator does not comply with "good oil field practice".[105] At international level, several international instruments oblige parties to apply best international practice. An example includes the Helsinki Convention.[106]

Either of these approaches to regulating environmental concerns has its own advantages or disadvantages which of course is beyond the scope of this research.[107] A critical issue in this regard is the relationship between the governance structure of the regulation and enforcement mechanism in either of these approaches. In other words, based on the regulatory governance by which such environmental regulation will have been created and the enforcement mechanism which will be applied by the competent authorities, distinctive results may be gained.

In a cross-border pipeline, however, the environmental norms can be implemented in accordance with the applicable law, which could be domestic law, regional or international conventions or bilateral or multilateral agreements and finally host governmental agreements. As a matter of fact, cross-border pipelines may cause transboundary damage as well; hence the relevant rules for preventing transboundary environmental damage may also apply when considering environmental regulations applicable to cross-border pipelines.

3 A Theory of Standard Setting

The previous overview of the different types of standards used to regulate cross-border pipelines shows not only a large variety of standards with different goals (technical, safety and environmental standards), but also standards coming from a wide variety of sources: private, public and mixed. Moreover, an additional complication is that in some cases the applicable standards are simply determined in contractual arrangements between the parties (often being the States). The question, crucial to our analysis in this chapter, is obviously whether the current structure of standard setting with respect to pipelines guarantees an optimal internalisation of externalities and the implementation of optimal preventive technologies. To address that question we will first look at the arguments in favour of public or private regulation and the arguments in favour of co-regulation, which will be applied in Sect. 4 to the choice between technical, safety and environmental standards.

[105] Steiner (2010).

[106] Article 2 of the Helsinki Convention also recognises seabed pipelines as a source of potential pollution in the marine environment.

[107] See for more discussion on that Wawryk (2003).

3.1 Public Regulation

It is well known that in economic theory two seemingly competing approaches have been presented with respect to regulation. In a first approach it is assumed that the government will act in the public interest and criteria are hence advanced to determine when such a public intervention would be in that public interest. Others have, however, stressed that regulation is not (always) made in the public interest but serves the interest of particular pressure groups. Politicians would award benefits to pressure groups (often referred to as so-called rents) in exchange for support in re-election.[108] In addition, regulation is sometimes used by particular groups to create barriers to market entry. Because incumbents could easily follow particular rules, following those rules (e.g., licensing requirements) may be difficult for newcomers, which would thus effectively limit entry into the markets.[109] For now we will mainly look at the public regulation model, coming back to the private interest explanation when discussing private and co-regulation.

The reasons for environmental and safety regulations, and the need for government intervention generally, have been well-acknowledged in the literature.[110] In the so-called command and control regulations (CCRs) uniform technology-based or performance-based standards are imposed by public regulators. As Steinzor notes command and control regulations impose legally enforceable limits, conditions and requirements on operations which may generate environmental pollution.[111] In CCRs, the complete regulatory process is performed by public regulators. Literature has for a long time, and in depth, studied the effectiveness of CCRs in protecting environmental interests.[112] This chapter does not aim to discuss CCRs in further detail, but it is necessary to mention that one of the main arguments of interest for environmental regulations in the form of environmental law is the need for government intervention when there is a market failure and the costs of pollution could be externalised to the community and not the actor involved.[113] This is clearly based on the public interest theory of regulation, which we just introduced.[114]

Based on the public interest theory of regulation, public regulation limits the freedom of the economic activity in the public interest.[115] Hence, the public

---

[108] This rent-seeking hypothesis has been strongly defended in the well-known work of Nobel Prize winner James Buchanan et al. (1980).

[109] It is a point a view that has been strongly defended by (again) Nobel Prize winner George Stigler (1971). For an excellent summary of both theories of regulation see the various publications of Philipsen. Philipsen and Faure (2002); Philipsen (2007, 2010).

[110] For a summary see *inter alia* Macrory (2008), pp. 157–160.

[111] Steinzor (1998).

[112] See, for example, Stewart (1991); Hackett (2011), pp. 222–226; Macrory (2008), pp. 157–160.

[113] See, for example, Macrory (2008), p. 157.

[114] See Posner (1974).

[115] See Posner (1974).

regulators should ensure that their regulatory process is performed in accordance with the public interest and with due regard to the rights and interests of the affected community.[116] This so called "democratic oversight" can be found in a wide range of arrangements and during the planning, construction and operation of the activities in question. In particular, in the planning and permitting process, environmental and safety regulations often require the participation of the affected community in the process of environmental impact assessment. The participation of affected parties not only incorporates concerns of the community through the permitting process, but also upholds the legitimacy of such assessments.

As we have indicated above[117] public regulation is widely used to prevent the potential damage associated with oil and gas lines through safety and environmental standards. Such regulations are mainly aimed at the protection of safety and environmental interests or the development of natural resources. In general, in many countries, the environmental law system does not operate alone. In other words, although there may be an important environmental law relating to the safety of the oil and gas pipelines, other laws complement the obligations of the specifically regulated industry.[118] For instance, in the US, the Gas Pipeline Safety Act is related specifically to the safety of gas pipelines, but at the same time construction of the gas pipelines is subject to the national environmental policy act.[119] Therefore, a number of safety and environmental regulations could be applicable to oil and gas pipelines.

Public regulations are usually enforceable under the sovereignty of the related state. With cross-border pipelines however, parties may agree to accept the national law of a third country as the applicable law for the host governmental agreements.[120] Therefore the enforcement of national law may be extended beyond the territory of the origin state via contractual means. The rationality behind this decision is an open question which should be solved by considering any other circumstances which are accepted as a justification.

However, notwithstanding the point that safety and environmental interests surely merit public regulation and the fact that in the area of pipelines one can notice extensive use of safety and environmental standards through public regulation, still a lot of inefficiencies may occur. One question that arises is whether the public regulator always possesses detailed information to be able to set efficient standards in this highly complicated and technical area. Capacity of public regulators may in some cases be lacking to set adequate standards. Another problem is

---

[116] Oliver (2010), pp. 243–245.

[117] See more particularly Sects. 2.2 and 2.3 above.

[118] See Steinway et al. (2011), pp. 5–6.

[119] Fang (2012).

[120] See for example the BTC pipeline case, in which according to Articles 17 and 23 of the Host Governmental Agreement between and among the Government of the Azerbaijan Republic and the investors, the agreement shall be governed in accordance with the substantive law of England. Supra note 78.

that, as indicated, the effectiveness of public standards is always dependent upon enforcement. Enforcement requires investments in monitoring and again requires capacity building because monitoring the safety of pipelines requires high knowledge and expertise. Again, that may often be lacking with public authorities. Moreover, as indicated, there is always a danger that standards are not set in the public interest, but that interest groups play a role, affecting the efficiency of the standards. There may in some, be regulatory deficits in public regulation which could affect the effectiveness of those standards set by public regulators.[121]

Precisely because of those regulatory failures in the public standard setting system we have noticed when describing the various standards used for pipeline activities that frequently private institutions set those standards. Let us now address how this private standard setting fits into a theoretical framework.

3.2 *Private Regulation*

The law and economics literature has for a long time recognised that even when private law may fail to internalise externalities, there still is not necessarily a role for public regulation to the extent that self-regulation by private actors could provide an adequate remedy. A classic article in that domain comes from Anthony Ogus who provided three justifications (from a public interest perspective) for using self-regulation: (1) lower information costs for the standard setting itself through industry; (2) lower monitoring and enforcement costs and (3) lower administrative costs, also in amending the rules because of larger flexibility.[122]

In a later publication Ogus also referred to the possibility that public authorities delegate regulatory powers to private agents because they "command a great degree of expertise and technical knowledge of practices and innovatory possibilities".[123] Also Gunningham and Rees have stressed the strengths and weaknesses of self-regulation.[124] Like Ogus they equally mention speed, flexibility and lower costs as advantages, but they also see the danger that self-regulation would advance rather the interests of the particular group concerned than the public interest at large. Later literature, especially with respect to professional regulation, has stressed that with

[121] For instance, Eaton argues that in Nigeria, in particular in the period until 1988, no comprehensive federal environmental enforcement agency existed. The Nigerian National Petroleum Corporation, the State-owned petroleum company, was also responsible for environmental protection in the petroleum industry. Since 1988 Nigeria adopted a comprehensive environmental protection system. But still because of inadequacy of sanctions, ineffective monitoring, the lack of enforcement and so on, environmental law (public law) failed to protect the environment and oil pollution in the Niger Delta continued. See Eaton (1997). For further discussion on regulatory failure of public standards, see James (2000).

[122] Ogus (1995).

[123] Ogus (2000), p. 591.

[124] Gunningham and Rees (1997).

self-regulation by professional groups (like architects and lawyers) there are substantial dangers that the self-regulatory framework will restrict competition and only promote the interests of the group rather than the public interest.[125]

Self-regulation is hence seen as rules made by professionals to basically govern their own activities. The rules we refer to at this stage with respect to pipeline activities are not always self-regulation, but can rather be considered as private regulation and in that case it concerns rules drafted by a private actor, but not only through regulate its own behaviour, but also of other actors.[126] Recent literature also has paid broad attention to the news of this so-called private regulation. The advantages are similar to self-regulation (better information, more flexibility and lower administrative cost). But several disadvantages of private regulation are also matched, more particularly concerning the legitimacy and accountability of the standards drafted by the private regulators[127] and questions concerning the independence of those private regulators.[128] Interestingly, also with respect to private regulation the literature holds that it remains important that public regulators, when they make use of private regulators, fix the conditions under which private regulation can function and monitor the functioning of the private regulators.[129] This hence points at the desirability of having some form of co-regulation.

This literature is quite relevant also in the framework of regulation of pipeline activities. Private regulators, whether at the national or transnational level can be found as well. Professional associations such as the ASME and standards setting organisations such as ISO are the main developers of oil and gas pipeline technical standards worldwide.[130] Some of these private regulations can be characterised as a voluntary code of conduct (self-regulation) which mainly represents the interests of the society members. An example is the ASME, which is a non-profit organisation producing voluntary technical standards. Although compliance with ASME standards can be mandated by legislation or contractual arrangements, these standards are voluntary in nature.[131] Therefore a voluntary code of conduct (self-regulation) basically serves private interests, while it could be recognised by legislation, contracts and the courts to define the minimum regulatory objectives. A distinction, however, should be made where such private standards are only produced by

[125] See the contributions in Faure et al. (1993), Faure and Van den Bergh (1991), and Philipsen (2010).

[126] See for example Scott et al. (2011).

[127] See Curtin and Senden (2011).

[128] Scott et al. (2011), p. 13.

[129] Scott et al. (2011), p. 19.

[130] See for more information The International Association of Oil & Gas Producers (2012) Catalogue of international standards used in the petroleum and natural gas industries. http://www.ogp.org.uk/pubs/362.pdf. Accessed 15 October 2014; Kuprewicz (2007); Wawryk (2003).

[131] In the US, for instance, 49 CFR Parts 192, 193, and 195 expressly refer to more than 60 technical standards, including and not limited to API, ASME, ASTM, American Gas Association (AGA). The BTC and Chad-Cameron pipelines are examples where voluntary standards were mandated through contractual means.

participation of a regulatee and when they are created by the involvement of affected communities. Of course, participation of a regulatee in the regulatory process could ensure the effectiveness of regulations[132]; nevertheless, what should be taken into consideration is the participation of affected communities in the regulatory process. As private regulators may mainly seek to maximise their own benefits, without the participation of third parties which will be affected by the regulation, they may externalise the costs of their regulation towards third parties.[133]

3.3 Co-Regulation

Co-regulation is defined by the European Parliament Council Commission Inter institutional Agreement on Better Law-Making (2003) as "*the mechanism whereby a Community legislative act entrusts the attainment of the objectives defined by the legislative authority to parties which are recognized in the field*" (such as economic operators, the social partners, non-governmental organisations, or associations). Therefore, co-regulation, unlike pure self-regulation, involves participation of public authorities. Co-regulation hence constitutes the compromise between two extremes. At one end of the spectrum, all of the regulatory functions are carried out by the public regulator and at the other end of the spectrum; the entire regulatory system is performed by private regulators. The so called co-regulation or co-regulatory approach falls somewhere in between. In fact, co-regulation can be defined as a legal model in which regulatory functions are not exercised by the sole regulator, rather by a number of players. Both public and private regulators are involved in the regulatory process.[134] It can be argued that the emergence of co-regulation is to remedy deficiencies experienced by using command and control and purely private regulations.[135]

Co-regulation can be based on various regulatory structures. Co-regulation can be established through participation by civil society organisations, intergovernmental organisations, trade unions, and governmental agencies and so on. Indeed co-regulation can be observed as public-private or civic-private regulatory models.[136] Public-private co-regulation is a product of cooperation between public and private regulators in a way that the objectives are defined by the public regulators, and the private actors in the field will attain those objectives by their own initiatives and finally the public regulator will monitor the outcome.[137] The

132 See Cafaggi (2006), p. 3.

133 Cafaggi (2006), p. 3.

134 Frydman et al. (2012), p. 133.

135 See Gunningham (2009).

136 Albareda (2008).

137 Senden (2005).

civic-private regulatory model, on the other hand, is the outcome of cooperation between private actors, NGOs and other stakeholders such as the affected community. An example is UN Global Compact, which encourages multinational corporations to adopt sustainable policies.[138] Unlike the first model of co-regulation, the second model does not involve the participation of public regulators. In essence, the second model is a private model of regulation which is created by the participation of civil society organisations potentially affected by the regulation, together with representatives from industry. A distinction should be made between the situation where private regulations are ex-post recognised by statute, court decisions or even contracts as due diligence and where there is ex ante coordination between private and public regulators in which private regulators develop the regulations and the public regulator monitors the compliance with the regulations. Indeed, the first is private regulations and the latter is co-regulation. Such *ex-post* regulation can be recognised in two different manners: in some cases, a private regulatory body could be recognised by legislation such as the UK standards body (BSI) which indeed is a private regulator but has been recognised officially as the UK standard setting organisation.[139] On the other hand, there are a number of private regulations that have been developed by coordination of public and private regulation such as the regulatory self-management.[140]

In the area of cross-border pipelines, management-based regulation can be cited as a model of co-regulation. Examples include the pipeline integrity management system, risk assessment and environmental impact assessment.[141] In this type of regulation, the regulatory goals are mostly defined by public regulators, while private actors develop their internal practice to attain such regulatory objectives. Of course, a distinctive approach can be adopted by public regulators to set regulatory objectives. For instance, in the Iranian regulations on the EIA, the type of activity needs to be assessed based on the location and size of the projects that are listed before a permission is granted. In addition, the scope and the framework of the EIA report are clearly determined by law.[142] Developers are hence required to carry out the EIA assessment and produce an environmental statement in accordance with the framework provided by the public regulator. By reasoning that such management-based regulations often require participation of the affected community in the EIA process, this type of regulation could be also characterised as civic-private co-regulation.

---

[138] Utting (2005). See for more information: The UN Global Compact's Principles (2000). http://www.unglobalcompact.org/abouttheGc/TheTenprinciples/index.html. Accessed 01 July 2014.

[139] See Büthe and Mattli (2011), p. 153.

[140] See Priest (1997).

[141] Gunningham (2009).

[142] The Iranian Regulation on Environmental Impact Assessment of the major construction, manufacturing and services projects (2011).

Co-regulation in either public-private or civic-private mechanisms could be institutionalised at national or international levels. Indeed, public-private co-regulation is the outcome of cooperation between public and private regulators. With cross-border pipelines, if the host state requires the developer (an MNC) to carry out an EIA or other management-based regulations in accordance with the national legislation of the host state, this can be characterised as public-private co-regulation.[143] On the other hand, if a developer voluntarily and in response to NGOs or concerns arising out of the activity conducts an EIA with the participation of civil society groups, it may constitute civic-private co-regulation.[144] This could be required at the request of investment bodies such as the World Bank or the IMF. It can be argued that even though the public regulator of the host state is excluded from participation in such management-based regulations, international NGOs or investment bodies may compel MNCs to involve affected communities in the EIA or other relevant assessments.

3.4 Summary

In Sect. 2 we described that pipeline activities need and do use a variety of technical, safety and environmental standards. We indicated that they sometimes are determined by public regulations and in other cases by private organisations (private standards). But even in the latter case often the government relies (*ex ante* or *ex post*) on the private standards, thus using a model of co-regulation.

In this section we briefly summarised the theoretical foundations for public, private and co-regulation and apply this generally to where these forms of regulation could be found in the area of pipeline activities. In the next section we will relate the two issues. This means that we will basically ask the question if there are reasons to distinguish between public, private and co-regulation as far as technical, safety and environmental standards are concerned. In other words: are the arguments in favor of public, private or co-regulation different when it concerned for example technical rather than safety or environmental standards? Based on criteria that we will further discuss we will argue that this is indeed the case.

---

[143] An example of this is the new Swiss section of the North Sea-Italy Pipeline (Transitgas pipeline) which was commissioned in 2003. Plüss et al. (2000).

[144] For instance, the Chad-Cameroon Pipeline Project. See on that Mujih (2008). There are several cases, in which MNCs as a consequence of pressure from influential NGOs responded to environmental concerns by conducting EIA. See Garvey and Newell (2005).

4 A Critique and Alternative

4.1 Criteria Affecting the Optimal Regulatory Model

We mentioned that regulatory reform is one of the core issues in market integration. In this section an attempt will be made to analyse different regulatory models to find out which of these regulatory instruments can better ensure the protection of the safety of the public and the environment. As indicated there are a wide range of regulatory instruments applicable to oil and gas pipelines. A question arises as to which type of these regulatory instruments can better fit with safety and environmental regulations of cross-border pipelines. To assess alternative instruments, certain criteria can be introduced by reviewing the literature.

Cafaggi and Renda identify four criteria to evaluate the public and private regulatory models: effectiveness, quality, legitimacy and enforcement.[145] As noted by Revesz and Stavins, the first criterion for choosing a policy instrument is achieving the stated goal.[146] This criterion can play a role in oil and gas pipelines as well. Therefore, the first criterion is what sort of regulatory model can prevent transboundary and transnational damage (effectiveness). The second criterion concerns expertise and flexibility: who has the better knowledge of creating safety and environmental regulations with high quality at lower cost?[147] The second criterion hence deals with the quality of regulations. The third criterion is the enforcement and monitoring of regulations. Enforcement of regulations has a great impact on the ultimate result.

Cohen argues that in a case of pollution control, if a new, stricter regulation is imposed by regulator, but less attention has been paid to monitoring and enforcement, the result will be more pollution.[148] The fourth criterion is legitimacy. According to Bernstein, "legitimacy can be defined as the acceptance and justification of a shared rule by a community".[149] This definition encompasses both the legitimacy of the regulator and the acceptance of the regulation by the community.

We will now use those criteria to examine the choice between private, public and co-regulation more particularly with respect to the question which of those regulatory models would be more appropriate for regulating technical, safety or environmental standards in the domain of oil and gas pipelines.

---

[145] Cafaggi and Renda (2011).

[146] Revesz and Stavins (2007), p. 535.

[147] See generally Gunningham (2009).

[148] Cohen (1999).

[149] Bernstein (2004), p. 142.

4.2 Effectiveness

Effectiveness, as commentators suggest, is reaching the desired goals of regulations. The effectiveness of environmental regulations can be examined by illustrating the degree to which regulations can solve the environmental problems.[150] In the same line of reasoning, with oil and gas pipelines, the effectiveness of the regulations should be appraised by considering their impact on reducing environmental damage.

To demonstrate which of the regulatory structures is more effective at preventing pipeline incidents, a regulatory relationship is built to compare the effectiveness of regulatory models on different types of technical standards and environmental and safety regulations. Technical standards are codes which specify minimum operating design levels, pre-construction and post-construction. These standards have a great impact on the safe operation of pipelines, but they usually do not regulate the behaviour of third parties. For instance, the safety zone around pipelines, where unauthorised persons or vessels are prohibited from entering into the mentioned zone, is always established by the public regulations.[151] This can also be a case for the one call notification system.[152] Therefore, by now it should be clear that although technical standards which codify the construction and operation of pipelines can be established by private regulators, the bilateral dimension of pipeline incidents requires the presence of public regulation with the authority to regulate third parties. In fact the protection against third-party interference is regulated by public regulators as a part of national legislation in most of the EU member states.[153]

An additional element is that there still is considerable uncertainty about the adverse impacts of the construction and operation of oil and gas pipelines. Consequently, this may lead to ambiguity in relation to the threshold of damage caused by oil and gas pipelines. In other words, although there is a serious threat of environmental damage, lack of full scientific certainty precludes the recognition of certain forms of damage caused by oil and gas pipeline in legal terms. As Feintuck argues, in regulatory contexts there is a trade-off between non-pecuniary interests and economic interests and technological imperatives with regard to the precautionary principle.[154] Indeed, two narratives, namely public choice and public interest, are

---

[150] Victor et al. (1998), p. 1.

[151] In the UK, for instance under the petroleum act 1987, see Kraska and Pedrozo (2013), p. 84. In Iran, the law on the prohibition of building around gas pipelines, 1971.

[152] See for instance Article 2(d) of the pipeline safety act 2006: "(1) A person who engages in demolition, excavation, tunnelling, or construction—may not engage in a demolition, excavation, tunnelling, or construction activity in a State that has adopted a one call notification system without first using that system to establish the location of underground facilities in the demolition, excavation, tunnelling, or construction area".

[153] See the European Commission Report (2011), pp. 48–50.

[154] Feintuck (2005).

competing in the precautionary principle domain.[155] First, the business-orientated narrative emphasises the operation of a market-based instrument and largely conflicts with the precautionary principle. Instead it is focused on insurance and compensation in the case of damage.[156] The latter, on the other hand, focuses more on environmental damage caused by the industry and more specifically by considering its long term impact on society. This calls for a form of decision making including collective social interests rather than private group interests.[157]

In general, according to Dovers, public regulators are often more responsible for conducting a deeper policy than the private sector.[158] If one takes this orientation as given, it can be argued that based on the economic theory which holds that operators will maximise their own utility and their own profits, private regulators will decline to prevent risks that are not known. Contrary to private regulators, based on the public interest narrative, the quintessential role of a public regulator is to protect citizens and the environment and may have a greater incentive to incorporate uncertain risks in their decision making.

4.3 Quality of the Regulation

The construction and operation of oil and gas pipelines could be subject to a wide range of standards. These standards, as mentioned, are being updated by the development of technical knowledge and practical experience. Pipeline regulations and standards are updated, among other things, based on experience and expertise of the pipeline industry. These standards will be updated periodically.[159] The question that arises is: who has better information and can provide more flexible regulatory space to incorporate the most recent technologies into the regulation? While the quality of environmental and safety regulation can be examined from different approaches, the two concerns raised above, i.e. information and flexibility, will be discussed in this section.

Public regulations, especially those of the so-called command and control type, are generally criticised as being inflexible. In particular, in relation to sectors which are very dynamic and need to respond quickly, public regulators sometimes become rigid when trying to update them.[160] Public regulators may face some other constraints such as budget, personal control and administrative procedures which prolong the regulatory process.[161] Therefore in theory, literature states that private regulation typically is more flexible than public regulation.

[155] Feintuck (2004), pp. 8–9.

[156] Morris (2000), p. 9.

[157] Feintuck (2005).

[158] Dovers (2006), p. 96.

[159] Kuprewicz (2007).

[160] See Cafaggi and Renda (2011) and Green and Hrab (2003).

[161] Priest (1997).

In respect of information and technical knowledge, literature argues in favour of private regulators. As Green argues, it is costly and difficult for governments to obtain and analyse all information required for the regulatory actions.[162] On the other hand, private regulators, more specifically trade-associations and industry self-regulators, tend to have more information and expertise on technical issues.[163] In addition, with private regulation, the regulator and the regulatee often coincide. This increases information and knowledge-sharing. Nevertheless, private regulatory decision making may pose a functional challenge, particularly when network regulators without a coordinator body, regulate activity which includes multiple participants and impact factors.[164]

In the context of oil and gas pipeline regulations, technical standards are mainly generated by private standard-setting, industry self-regulation and codes of conduct. As state practice shows, because of the highly technical nature of oil and gas pipelines, states often endorse the technical standards which are generated by private standard setting bodies or the industry's own self-regulation (performance and technology-based regulation).[165] Safety and environmental regulations however, should be viewed from a different perspective. First of all, one cannot easily argue in favour of private regulations in terms of information and then flexibility. Economic theory holds that the companies will invest their own money in environmental protection if they need a new technology or if market competitiveness requires it.[166] The fear of regulatory action by governments can also be added. Therefore, when environmental impacts of an activity could be externalised to the local community and there is no economic incentive for the developers, they may have no incentive to invest in gathering information needed to regulate environmental impacts of their activities effectively.[167] However, based on the public interest theory, the protection of citizens and the environment is primarily one of the duties of the governments.[168]

Summarising, it can be argued that although technical standards could be created by private regulators and be recognised ex-post by public regulators or adjudication

[162] Green and Hrab (2003).

[163] Ogus (1994); Cafaggi (2006), pp. 5 and 9.

[164] Black (2008).

[165] For instance, in the European Commission Directorate-General Environment report, 57 % of responding states requires that certain technical standards should be complied with and only 29 % refers to technical standards as being mere guidance. Of course these technical standards that national legislation refers to are mainly private standards such as ISO, DIN and BSI. See the European Commission Report (2011), pp. 50 and 69.

[166] Berg and Ferrier (1998), p. 90.

[167] Rugman and Verbeke (2000).

[168] In the same way, external emergency plans, protection against third party interference and safety management systems are widely regulated through public regulations in the EU member states, see European Commission Report (2011), pp. 47 and 52.

bodies, environmental and safety regulations should be created through cooperation of public and private regulators.

4.4 Compliance and Monitoring

Public direct regulations have been criticised for two main reasons. First, they impose excessive compliance costs on industries.[169] Second, they are ultimately ineffective at encouraging regulatees to comply with regulatory objectives. This is mainly because they impose uniform sets of rules for all regulatees, sometimes including rules that are meaningless for the regulatee, and failures of the regulator to consider the expectation of the regulated industries.[170]

Some commentators argue that because the regulatee is involved in the decision-making process in private regulations (more specifically self-regulation), this participation will result in a higher level of compliance.[171] This argument can be complemented by pointing to the fact that where the regulatee understands the rationality of regulation (because the regulatee has been part of the regulatory process), a higher level of compliance is expected.[172] Nevertheless, the compliance with rules may not be monitored properly, when the industry's interests conflicts with society's interests.[173] Indeed, monitoring is costly; the monitor will invest in monitoring merely to the point that the marginal cost of monitoring equals its benefits.[174]

In the context of the oil and gas pipelines technical standards are often based on self-regulation made by industry. It could be argued that because a proper performance of technical standards will increase the productivity of the project, the compliance with standards is in the operator's interest. Therefore, even if the self-audits serve as a monitoring agency, the regulatory objective could be achieved.

In relation to safety and environmental regulations, as Kandiyoti notes, safety of pipelines can only be achieved by paying an expensive price which not all operators may be inclined to pay.[175] This will lead to an early conclusion that the level of compliance with safety and environmental regulations highly depends on the

[169] Hackett (2011), p. 225. For example in the case of EPA-Amoco York Town Project an Amoco refinery assessed that they could be able to attain the regulatory objectives (emissions reduction) at a quarter of the cost, if it were able to use its own instruments instead of the regulatory requirements. See Amoco/EPA Yorktown Project, Lessons Learned and Future Steps (undated). http://www.fischer-tropsch.org/DOE/_conf_proc/MISC/CONF-94013319/CONF-94013319,%20Tabs%2012%20-%2018%20%28pgs.%201-35%29.pdf. Accessed 10 July 2014.

[170] See for more discussion on that Parker (2002), pp. 8–10.

[171] For further discussion, see Priest (1997) and Cafaggi (2006).

[172] Miller (1985).

[173] Coglianese et al. (2004).

[174] Croley (1998).

[175] Kandiyoti (2012), pp. 32–33.

monitoring and enforcement regulations. As examples show, where the compliance with regulation was poorly monitored, and there is no fear of liability for environmental regulation violations, operators may decline to fully comply with safety and environmental regulations.[176] Therefore, the compliance with environmental and safety regulations should be monitored by public agencies as well as the affected community. The necessity of the participation of the affected community in the monitoring process complements the public auditors practically in the case of transnational performance of environmental and safety regulations.

4.5 Legitimacy and Accountability

Legitimacy as Weber et al. define is "the prestige of being considered binding".[177] Therefore, legitimacy is highly related to acceptance of stakeholders who are supposed to accept the regime. This is why Suchman argues that legitimacy motivates behavioural changes of those are supposed to accept the regulations.[178] Accountability, in simple words, means being responsible. It should be pointed out that although legitimacy and accountability are closely interrelated, they are different concepts. In fact, accountability of the regulatory organisations validates the perception of legitimacy.[179] By considering the combination of these two concepts, three questions emerge: who should be involved in the decision-making process, to whom the regulatory bodies should be accountable and by which means.

On the one hand, public regulations are the outcome of a rule making process in which representatives of the public will legislate rules based on majority voting.[180] On the other hand, public regulators are widely responsible for making rules before parliament, courts, NGOs and so on.[181] Although the legitimacy of the public regulatory mechanism could be criticised from various approaches,[182] it at least provides a minimum level of accountability. Private regulators, however, may be involved in the regulatory decision making as self-regulators or perform the regulatory functions which traditionally were performed by public regulators. While the private regulators are merely regulating internal organisational performance, including codes of conduct and the rule-making of trade associations, the regulatory process should be considered legitimate by those who are supposed to accept the rules and comply with them. On the other hand, if the private actors are exercising public powers which were basically performed by pubic regulators, the

[176] See for instance Eaton (1997); Cherniaev et al. (1998), p. 222.

[177] Weber (1978), p. 31.

[178] Suchman (1995).

[179] Black (2008).

[180] See, more generally, Lijphart (1984).

[181] Scott (2007).

[182] Scott (2000).

regulation should be considered legitimate by the public and the regulators should be accountable for their rule-making.

Technical standards of oil and gas pipelines are mainly codes of conduct which are created by standards-setting bodies as well as by trade associations. The legitimacy of this type of regulation lies in the relationship between different actors which, based on contact or constitutionally, authorises the regulators to impose standards. With respect to safety and environmental regulations, private regulators in fact exercise public powers; therefore the regulatory function should involve participation of affected communities to be considered legitimate.[183] Of course, the regulators could link themselves to other legitimate bodies to be considered by those affected by their decisions as legitimate.[184]

In sum, because public regulations are presumed to be established or authorised by the representatives of those regulated, they can be regarded as legitimate regulation. Moreover, public regulations are subject to judicial review, parliamentary scrutiny and executive auditors.[185] Private regulation has a different story. Self-regulation (technical standards in the case of oil and gas pipelines), where the regulatee and regulator coincides should be accepted merely by actors within the regulatory regime. However, the environmental and safety regulations could be considered legitimate when the actors inside and outside of the regulatory regime accept them. Although improving legitimacy increases the transaction and compliance costs, this cost will be paid for the public interest and to protect social and environmental interests.

4.6 Summary

The section argues that the effectiveness of oil and gas pipeline regulations in reaching their objectives is highly context-specific. In other words, depending on the subject of the regulation, distinctive forms of regulatory regimes could be suggested. Private regulations reduce the excessive cost of command and control regulations and provide more flexible forms of regulation. In private regulation, public administrative functions are delegated to private regulators. Therefore, an effective monitoring system is required to keep private firms accountable.[186] One of the advantages of the private regulatory model is the flexibility that a regulator may have in setting regulations. This decentralised nature of private regulation, however, may lead to functional challenges in the case of oil and gas pipelines. It can be concluded that the most effective way of creating technical standards is through private regulators. Safety and environmental regulations, on the other hand, should

[183] See on that Black (2008).

[184] Suchman (1995).

[185] See Cafaggi (2006) and Stewart (2004).

[186] Rhodes (1996).

be generated by cooperation of public regulators as well as participation of affected communities. This will increase the legitimacy and accountability of regulators, though at higher costs. Therefore, we can conclude that with a view on market integration, not one uniform type of regulation should be prescribed for the entire oil and gas sector; rather depending on the nature of the regulation, different regulatory regimes should be adopted to secure safety and environmental interests.

5 Concluding Remarks

This paper dealt with the regulation of oil and gas pipelines and cross-border pipelines in particular. As we showed in the introduction, this topic is not only of academic interest. Both in the EU and in China pipelines are used for the transport of oil and gas and both have unfortunately already been confronted with serious accidents resulting from such transport. Therefore, additional safety and environmental regulations may be necessary to increase the level of safety and to enhance enforcement of rules designed to prevent incidents. Those are precisely the standards that were crucial to this chapter that aim inter alia at the prevention of those accidents. We showed that a variety of different standards are used, more particularly technical standards, safety standards and environmental standards, and that those are emanating from different sources. It is striking that private standard-setting organisations play an important role in the standard-setting process in this domain. Moreover, they are often the contracting parties who determine in their contracts which types of (private) standards will apply to regulate the cross-border pipeline.

We provided an attempt to distinguish between technical, safety and environmental standards and, by using the economic literature on regulation, we argue that for some types of standards it may be necessary to have public regulation, or at least co-regulation, whereas in others private standard-setting may suffice. Based on criteria of effectiveness, quality, compliance and legitimacy we argued that technical standards can indeed to a large extent be subject to private standard-setting by private regulators. This allows benefiting from the well-known advantages of private standard-setting, i.e. better information, flexibility and lower costs. However, the same arguments no longer apply with respect to safety and environmental standards. For those, so we argued, the arguments in favour of public regulation, or at least co-regulation (whereby governments would monitor the use of private standards) would be indicated.

We equally noticed that even though pipelines can lead to accidents with substantial losses—personal injury, property damage and environmental damage—standard-setting in this area is, especially when it concerns technical and safety standards, often determined via private contracting. That obviously raises important questions of accountability and legitimacy, but also of monitoring capabilities. The latter is especially the case when contracting parties declare safety regulation applicable of another country than where the pipeline is actually laid. This does happen in practice.

Our contribution mainly focused on the regulation of pipelines in a national context. Different and potentially even more complex questions may arise in the case of cross-border pipelines. Cross-border pipelines generally seem to be a domain that is largely underexplored by lawyers. Nevertheless the data indicate that pipelines can pose substantial risks and losses. We do not argue that the nature of the standards applicable to pipelines today are a contributing factor to the (many) incidents that arise with cross-border pipelines. However, we have indicated that there are substantial weaknesses in the design of the legal framework applicable to cross-border pipelines. Precisely because it concerns an ultra-hazardous activity, it is important to analyse carefully the optimal mix of private, public and co-regulation that can guarantee the safe operation of pipelines.

The assessment of the safety and environmental standard-setting and the comparison with different regulatory models propose that different regulatory models should be used to guarantee personal and environmental safety. This need for having different standards should equally be considered in the regulatory reforms aiming at market integration. Indeed, not all types of safety and environmental standards should necessarily be harmonised; creating a harmonised safety level is only indicated when a lack of harmonised standards can affect the functioning of the internal market.

References

Albareda L (2008) Corporate responsibility, governance and accountability: from self-regulation to co-regulation. Corporate Governance 8(4):430–439

Alvarez JE (2005) International organizations as law-makers. Oxford University Press, Oxford

Antaki GA (2003) Piping and pipeline engineering: design, construction, maintenance, integrity, and repair. CRC, New York

Bai Y, Bai Q (2012) Subsea engineering handbook. Gulf Professional, Waltham

Barnard C (2013) The substantive law of the EU: the four freedoms. Oxford University Press, Oxford

Baron D (1995) The economic and politics of regulation. In: Banks JS, Hanushek EA (eds) Modern political economy: old topics, new directions. Cambridge University Press, Cambridge

Berg DR, Ferrier G (1998) The U. S. environmental industry: meeting the challenge: U. S. industry faces the 21st century. DIANE Publishing, Darby

Bernstein S (2004) Legitimacy in global environmental governance. J Int Law Int Relat 1:139–167

Bin Mohd Ali Napiah MN (2009) Development and customisation of integrated pipeline integrity management system. In: 4th pipeline technology conference 2009, Hannover Messe, Hannover

Black J (2001) Decentring regulation: understanding the role of regulation and self-regulation in a "post-regulatory" world. Curr Legal Probl 54(1):103–146

Black J (2008) Constructing and contesting legitimacy and accountability in polycentric regulatory regimes. Regul Governance 2(2):137–164

Boss T, Drake A, Leewis K, Selig B, Zurcher J (2004) The benefits of consensus standards: a pipeline case study. In: International Pipeline Conference, Volumes 1, 2, and 3, 4–8 October 2004, Calgary, AL

Braestrup M, Andersen JB, Andersen LW, Bryndum MB, Nielsen NJR (2009) Design and installation of marine pipelines. Wiley-Blackwell, Oxford
Bruggeman V (2010) Compensating catastrophe victims: a comparative law and economics approach. Kluwer Law International, Deventer
BSI (British Standards Institution) (2009) Codes for practice of pipelines. BSI Publication
Buchanan JM, Tollison RD, Tullock G (1980) Toward a theory of the rent-seeking society. Texas A&M University Press, Texas, College Station
Burgherr P, Hirschberg S (2005) Comparative assessment of natural gas accident risks. Paul Scherrer Institut, Villigen PSI, Switzerland
Burgherr P, Hirschberg S (2008) Severe accident risks in fossil energy chains: a comparative analysis. Energy 33(4):538–553
Büthe T, Mattli W (2011) The new global rulers: the privatization of regulation in the world economy. Princeton University Press, Princeton
Cafaggi F (2006) Rethinking private regulation in the European regulatory space (No. 13). European University Institute (EUI), Department of Law
Cafaggi F, Renda A (2011) Public and private regulation: mapping the labyrinth. Regulatory Policy (Working Documents), Centre for European Policy Studies, Brussels
Cherniaev VD, Vdovin GA, Yassin EM, Stavrovsky ER (1998) Oil transportation. In: Krylov N, Boksernan A, Stavrovsky E (eds) Oil industry of the former Soviet Union: reserves, extraction and transportation. Gordon & Breach Science, Amsterdam, pp 185–274
Coglianese C, Lazer D (2003) Management-based regulation: prescribing private management to achieve public goals. Law Soc Rev 37:691–730
Coglianese C, Keating EK, Michael ML, Healey TJ (2004) Role of government in corporate governance. N Y Univ J Law Bus 1:219–239
Cohen MA (1999) Monitoring and enforcement of environmental policy. In: Tietenberg T, Folmer H (eds) International yearbook of environmental and resource economics. Edward Elgar, Cheltenham, pp 44–106
Committee on the Safety of Marine Pipelines (1994) Improving the safety of marine pipelines. National Academies Press, Washington
Croley SP (1998) Theories of regulation: incorporating the administrative process. Columbia Law Rev 98(1):1–168
Curtin D, Senden L (2011) Public accountability of transnational private regulation: chimera or reality? J Law Soc 38(1):163–188
Davis PM, Dubois J, Olcese A, Uhlig F, Larivé JF, Martin DE (2006) Performance of European cross-country oil pipelines. Statistical summary of reported spillages 54, Concawe, Brussels
den Hertog JA (2003) Public and private interests in regulation: essays in the law and economics of regulation. Dissertation, Utrecht University Repository
Dovers S (2006) Precautionary policy assessment. In: Fisher EC, Jones SJ, Schomberg RV (eds) Implementing the precautionary principle: perspectives and prospects. Edward Elgar, Cheltenham, pp 88–109
Dudley SE, Brito J (2012) Regulation: a primer. The Mercatus Center at George Mason University, Washington
Dux T (2011) Specially protected marine areas in the exclusive economic zone (EEZ): the regime for the protection of specific areas of the EEZ for environmental reasons under international law, vol 18. LIT Verlag, Münster
Eaton JP (1997) Nigerian tragedy, environmental regulation of transnational corporations, and the human right to a healthy environment. Boston Univ Int Law J 15(1):261–309
Eckle P, Burgherr P (2013) Bayesian data analysis of severe fatal accident risk in the oil chain. Risk Anal 33(1):146–160
Escoe K (2006) Piping and pipelines assessment guide, vol 1. Gulf Professional Waltham
European Commission Directorate-General Environment (2011) Assessing the case for EU legislation on the safety of pipelines and the possible impacts of such an initiative. Final Report ENV.G.1/FRA/2006/0073, COWI A/S, Lyngby

Fang L (2012) Environmental review problems of cross-border projects under NEPA: lessons from the Tar Sands Pipelines. Stanford Environ Law J 31:285–313
Faure MG (2012) Environmental regulation. In: Van Den Bergh RJ (ed) Regulation and economics. Edward Elgar, Cheltenham, pp 229–302
Faure MG, Van den Bergh R (1991) Self-regulation of the professions in Belgium. Int Rev Law Econ 11:167–182
Faure, MG, Finsinger J, Siegers J, Van den Bergh R (eds) (1993) Regulation of professions: a law and economics approach to the regulation of attorneys and physicians in the U.S., Belgium, the Netherlands, Germany and the U.K. Maklu, Antwerp
Feintuck M (2004) The public interest in regulation. Oxford University Press, Oxford
Feintuck M (2005) Precautionary maybe, but what's the principle? The precautionary principle, the regulation of risk, and the public domain. J Law Soc 32(3):371–398
Fliess B, Gonzales F, Kim J, Schonfeld R (2010) The use of international standards in technical regulation (No. 102). OECD
Felix BC, Sebastian RB (2012) Pipeline Integrity Management System. 18th world conference on non-destructive testing, 16–20 April 2012, Durban
Frydman B, Hennebel L, Lewekowicz G (2012) Co-regulation and the rule of law. In: Brousseau E, Marzouki M, Méadel C (eds) Governance, regulation and powers on the Internet. Cambridge University Press, Cambridge, pp 133–150
Garvey N, Newell P (2005) Corporate accountability to the poor? Assessing the effectiveness of community-based strategies. Dev Pract 15(3-4):389–404
Grishin N (2005) Environmental Impact Assessment of a transboundary pipeline in the Black Sea region (legal and environmental aspects). In: Workshop on the Prevention of Water Pollution due to the Pipeline Accidents (UNECE), Ecoterra Environmental Assessment Agency, Russian Federation
Green A, Hrab R (2003) Self-regulation and the protection of the public interest. Panel for the Role of Government, Canada. http://www.law-lib.toronto.edu/investing/reports/rp26.pdf. Accessed 16 Oct 2014
Gunningham N (2009) Environment law, regulation and governance: shifting architectures. J Environ Law 21(2):179–212
Gunningham N, Rees J (1997) Industry self-regulation: an institutional perspective. Law Policy 19(4):363–414
Hackett SC (2011) Environmental and natural resources economics: theory, policy, and the sustainable society. ME Sharpe, New York
Hirschberg S, Spiekerman G, Dones R (1998) Severe accidents in the energy sector. Paul Scherrer Institut, Switzerland
Hirschberg S, Burgherr P, Spiekerman G, Dones R (2004) Severe accidents in the energy sector: comparative perspective. J Hazard Mater 111(1–3):57–65
Hopkins PHIL (2005) High design factor pipelines: integrity issues. J Pipeline Integrity 4(2): $32#69–97
James O (2000) Regulation inside government: public interest justifications and regulatory failures. Public Adm 78(2):327–343
Jewell MT (2007) Evolving pipeline regulations: historical perspectives and a new model for pipeline safety in the Arctic National Wildlife Refuge. Transportation Law J 34:167–184
Kandiyoti R (2012) Pipelines: flowing oil and crude politics. IB Tauris, London
Kiss A, Shelton D (2007) Guide to international environmental law. Martinus Nijhoff, Leiden
Koivurova T, Polonen I (2010) Transboundary environmental impact assessment in the case of the Baltic Sea gas pipeline. Int J Mar Coastal Law 25(2):151–181
Kraska J, Pedrozo R (2013) International maritime security law. Martinus Nijhoff, Leiden
Kuprewicz RB (2007) General observations on the myth of a Best International Pipeline Standard. AccuFacts Research Corporation, Washington
Lijphart A (1984) Democracies: patterns of majoritarian and consensus government in twenty-one countries. Yale University Press, New Haven
Livermore MA, Revesz RL (2014) Environmental law and economics. In: Polinsky AM, Shavell S (eds) Oxford handbook of law and economics, vol 1. Elsevier, Amsterdam, pp 499–582

Macrory R (2008) Regulation, enforcement and governance of environmental law. Cameron May, London
McAllister EW (2013) Pipeline rules of thumb handbook: a manual of quick, accurate solutions to everyday pipeline engineering problems. Gulf Professional, Waltham
Menon SE (2005) Gas pipeline hydraulics. CRC, USA
Meyer KJ, Smith RW, Murray A (2008) Comparison of US and Canadian transmission pipeline consensus standards. In: 7th international pipeline conference. American Society of Mechanical Engineers, pp 621–627
Miller D (1985) Psychological factors influencing compliance: study for the Federal Statutes Compliance. Department of Justice, Mimeo
Montiel H, Vílchez JA, Arnaldos J, Casal J (1996) Historical analysis of accidents in the transportation of natural gas. J Hazard Mater 51(1–3):77–92
Morris J (2000) Defining the precautionary principle. In: Morris J (ed) Rethinking risk and the precautionary principle. Butterworth-Heinemann, Oxford, pp 1–22
Muhlbauer WK (2004) Pipeline risk management manual: ideas, techniques, and resources. Gulf Professional, Waltham
Mujih E (2008) Regulation of multinational companies operating in developing countries: a case study of the Chad-Cameroon Pipeline Project. Afr J Int Comp Law 16:83–99
Ogus AI (1994) Standards setting for environmental protection principles and process. In: Faure MG, Vervaele JAE, Weale A (eds) Environmental standards in the European Union in an interdisciplinary framework. Maklu, Antwerpen, pp 25–36
Ogus AI (1995) Rethinking self-regulation. Oxf J Legal Stud 15(1):97–108
Ogus A (2000) Self-regulation. In: Bouckaert B, De Geest G (eds) Encyclopedia of law and economics. Edward Elgar, Cheltenham, pp 587–602
Ogus A (2004) Regulation, legal form and economic theory. Hart, Oxford
Oliva MJ (2015) Standards and the implementation of the Nagoya protocol: defining and putting in practice due diligence in the EU regulation on ABS. In: Coolsaet B, Batur F, Broggiato A, Pitseys J, Dedeurwaerdere T (eds) Implementing the Nagoya protocol: comparing access and benefit-sharing in Europe. Brill, Leiden, pp 280–307
Oliver D (2010) Regulation, democracy, and democratic oversight in the UK. In: Oliver D, Prosser T, Rawlings R (eds) The regulatory state: constitutional implications. Oxford University Press, Oxford
Omonbude EJ (2012) Cross-border oil and gas pipelines and the role of the transit country: economics, challenges and solutions. Palgrave Macmillan, London
Papadakis GA (2000) Assessment of requirements on safety management systems in EU regulations for the control of major hazard pipelines. J Hazard Mater 78(1):63–89
Parker C (2002) The open corporation: effective self-regulation and democracy. Cambridge University Press, Cambridge
Pelkmans J (2012) The economics of single market regulation. Bruges European Economic Policy Briefings, 25, https://www.coleurope.eu/nl/node/8345. Accessed 11 Dec 2014
Perry WD, Haynes KE (1993) Prioritizing regulatory policy in pipeline safety. J Contingencies Crisis Manag 1(2):90–100
Philipsen NJ (2007) The law and economics of professional regulation: what does the theory teach China? In: Eger T, Faure MG, Zhang N (eds) Economic analysis of law in China. Edward Elgar, Cheltenham, pp 194–251
Philipsen NJ (2010) Regulation and competition in the legal profession: developments in the EU and China. J Competition Law Econ 6(2):203–231
Philipsen NJ, Faure MG (2002) The regulation of pharmacists in Belgium and the Netherlands: in the public or private interest? J Consum Policy 25(2):155–201
Piri Damagh M, Faure MG (2014) The effectiveness of cross-border pipeline safety and environmental regulations (under international law). N C J Int Law Commercial Regul 40(1):55–134
Plüss C, Niederbäumer G, Sägesser R (2000) Risk assessment of the Transitgas pipeline. Pipes Pipelines Int 45(6):33–40

Posner RA (1974) Theories of economic regulation. Bell J Econ Manag Sci 5:335–358
Priest M (1997) The privatization of regulation: five models of self-regulation. Ottawa Law Rev 29:233–302
Revesz RL, Stavins RN (2007) Environmental law. In: Polinsky AM, Shavell S (eds) Handbook of law and economics. Elsevier, Amsterdam
Rhodes RAW (1996) The new governance: governing without government. Polit Stud 44(4): $32#652–667
Rugman A, Verbeke A (2000) Environmental regulations and the global strategies of multinational enterprises. In: Prakash A, Hart JA (eds) Coping with globalization. Routledge, London, pp 77–93
Schaffer R, Agusti F, Dhooge L (2014) International business law and its environment. Cengage Learning, Stamford
Scott C (2000) Accountability in the regulatory state. J Law Soc 27(1):38–60
Scott C (2007) Regulating private legislation. In: Cavaggi F, Muir-Watt H (eds) The regulatory function of European private law. Edward Elgar, Cheltenham, pp 254–268
Scott C, Cafaggi F, Senden L (2011) The conceptual and constitutional challenge of transnational private regulation. J Law Soc 38(1):1–19
Secretariat of the Vienna Convention for the Protection of the Ozone Layer & the Montreal Protocol on substances that Deplete the Ozone Layer (2006) Handbook for the Montreal protocol on substances that deplete the Ozone Layer, United Nations Environmental Programme. UNON, Kenya
Seddon D (2006) Gas usage & value: the technology and economics of natural gas use in the process industries. PennWell Books, Tulsa
Selznick P (1985) Focusing organizational research on regulation. In: Noll R (ed) Regulatory policy and the social sciences. University of California Press, California, pp 363–369
Senden L (2005) Soft law, self-regulation and co-regulation in European law: where do they meet. Electr J Comp Law 9(1):1–27
Shavell S (1980) Strict liability versus negligence. J Legal Stud 9:1–25
Shavell S (1983) Liability for harm versus regulation of safety. J Legal Stud 13:357–374
Shen W (2014) People's Republic of China. In: Campbell D (ed) International consumer protection, 2nd edn. Juris, Huntington
Singh R (2013) Pipeline integrity handbook: risk management and evaluation. Gulf Professional, Waltham
Stalley P (2010) Foreign firms, investment, and environmental regulation in the People's Republic of China. Stanford University Press, Stanford
Steiner R (2010) Double standard: shell practices in Nigeria compared with international standards to prevent and control pipeline oil spills and the Deepwater Horizon oil spill. Milieudefensie (Friends of the Earth Netherlands), Amsterdam
Steinway DM, Ewing KA, Case DR, Nardi KJ, Brownell WF (2011) Environmental law handbook. Government Institutes, Plymouth
Steinzor RI (1998) Reinventing environmental regulation: the dangerous journey from command to self-control. Harv Environ Law Rev 22:103–202
Stewart RB (1991) Models for environmental regulation: central planning versus market-based approaches. Boston Coll Environ Aff Law 19:547–563
Stewart RB (2004) Global regulatory challenge to US administrative law. N Y Univ J Int Law Polit 37:695–762
Stigler GJ (1971) The theory of economic regulation. Bell J Econ Manag Sci 2(1):3–21
Suchman MC (1995) Managing legitimacy: strategic and institutional approaches. Acad Manag Rev 20(3):571–610
Utting P (2005) Corporate responsibility and the movement of business. Dev Pract 15(3-4): $32#375–388

Victor DG, Raustiala K, Skolnikoff EB (1998) Introduction and overview. In: Victor DG, Raustiala K, Skolnikoff EB (eds) The implementation and effectiveness of international environmental commitments: theory and practice. MIT Press, Massachusetts, pp 1–47

Wagner J, Armstrong K (2010) Managing environmental and social risks in international oil and gas projects: perspectives on compliance. J World Energy Law Bus 3(2):140–165

Waters CP (2003) Who should regulate the Baku-Tbilisi-Ceyhan pipeline. Georgetown Int Environ Law Rev 16:403–421

Wawryk AS (2003) International environmental standards in the oil industry: improving the operations of transnational oil companies in emerging economies. Oil Gas Energy Law Intell 1(1):1–27

Weber M (1978) In: Roth G, Wittich C (eds) Economy and society: an outline of interpretive sociology, vol 2. University of California Press, California

Zhaojie JL (2008) Commentary on China and the international legal system: challenges of participation. In: Clarke DC (ed) China's legal system: new developments, new challenges. Cambridge University Press, Cambridge

Part IV
Conclusions

Comparative and Concluding Remarks

Stefan E. Weishaar and Niels Philipsen

1 Background

In the introductory chapter we explained that this book is the result of a conference that was held in May 2014 in Beijing, organised jointly by the Research Center for Law and Economics of the China University of Political Science and Law, the Maastricht European Institute for Transnational Legal Research (METRO), and the Department of Law and Economics at the University of Groningen. That conference constituted a follow-up to two earlier conferences held in Beijing in 2012 and 2013, on economics and regulation in China, and the role of law and regulation in sustaining financial markets, respectively. For the 2014 conference, which was partly funded by the China-EU School of Law (CESL), the topic of market integration was chosen, again with a special focus on the role of regulation.

This book contains several contributions that examine how market integration and regulatory reform could help to unleash the economic forces of China to foster more sustainable economic growth and prosperity.[1] Because the European Union has a rich body of experiences in market integration, many contributors have selected Europe as a reference point. In some cases the European learnings suggest what Chinese legislators may wish to consider for China, while in others the European experience can be insightful for Chinese legislators in pointing to pitfalls and problems that one may wish to avoid.

[1] See for an elaboration on this Sect. 1 of the introduction to this book.

S.E. Weishaar (✉)
Faculty of Law, University of Groningen, Groningen, The Netherlands
e-mail: S.E.Weishaar@rug.nl

N. Philipsen
Faculty of Law, Maastricht University, Maastricht, The Netherlands
e-mail: niels.philipsen@maastrichtuniversity.nl

N. Philipsen et al. (eds.), *Market Integration: The EU Experience and Implications for Regulatory Reform in China*, China-EU Law Series 2,
DOI 10.1007/978-3-662-48273-5_12

The predominant methodology relied upon by the authors to examine law and regulation and their effect on market integration is Law and Economics. In addition, disciplines such as comparative law, financial economics, political science and sociology were used, bearing tribute to the fact that law and (economic) regulation are embedded in institutional environments that are influenced by a multitude of factors. Some authors went beyond positive analysis by providing carefully defined policy suggestions.

In this concluding chapter we seek to distil some central lessons from the analysis made in the previous chapters regarding market integration. These lessons will be grouped around four overarching issues.

- Different ways to address market integration
- Interplay of policy objectives/goals
- Actors: public, private, self-enforcement
- Critical reflections on market integration

2 Different Ways to Achieve Market Integration

Economic theory suggests that the integration of similar regional markets can lead to a reinvigoration of economic growth and societal prosperity, something that may in particular be relevant in times of economic crisis. There are a multitude of different areas of law and legal instruments that can support market integration. Market integration can for example be enhanced by establishing a 'level playing field' for factors of production and by enabling the free flow of goods and services. In the European Union market integration more particularly takes the form of facilitating the free movements of goods, capital, services and people. In this book Wenjing Li and Tianshu Zhou bear tribute to this by analysing capital markets, while Niels Philipsen and Qi Zhou analyse business restrictions in the legal professions. Guang Shen and Niels Philipsen address licensing barriers that can constitute an obstacle to the freedom of establishment, providing some support for the hypothesis that regulation is sometimes used as a barrier to entry, serving the interests of local companies. Moreover, Shen and Philipsen show that local public officials do not only consider social interests, but also private interests, including their own.

Another way to facilitate market integration is by opening up government markets to trade, such as public procurement markets. In this book Stefan Weishaar examines public procurement in the EU and China from a market integration perspective. He argues that European public procurement laws have been striving to achieve a better degree of market integration. So far, however, the market has been strongly resisting cross-border competition. The European experience also contains relevant insights for China. Not every advancement in fostering competition within a province (or Member State) actually leads to more cross-border market integration. This trade-off between more inter-regional and intra-regional trade will also have to be struck in the Chinese context. The EU seems to have chosen to emphasise intra-Member State competition over market integration in some areas—how the Chinese legislator will decide only the future will show.

A third way to enhance market integration is to prevent undue interference of the state in the market process. As examples of such practices, Mel Marquis examines state measures granting exclusive or special rights to particular market operators. In China, undue interference can stem, for example, from 'administrative monopolies' and from State Owned Enterprises. According to Marquis, some first steps to deal with public restraints on competition have already been taken in China. He points for example to the 'Work program to eliminate regional blockades and break industry monopolies', which is directed towards inter-regional trade issues and certain types of administrative monopolies. Marquis concludes his chapter by presenting a number of carefully drafted policy suggestions to further address the problem of administrative monopolies. These suggestions include: first, the introduction of mandatory legal rules and remedies to enhance the effectiveness of existing rules; and more broadly, the drafting of a multidimensional 'national competition strategy' that would reduce undue state support schemes and allow competition and the rule of law to take root in China. Jingyuan Ma also points out that administrative monopolies remain one of the major obstacles for China to establish an integrated and competitive domestic market. Binwei Gui and Guangdong Xu make a similar point: they argue that, without the financial rents created by China's distorted financial policies favouring SOEs over private enterprises, it is difficult or impossible for its SOEs to survive, not to mention develop or profit. SOEs' profits therefore do not come from the reorganisation and corporatisation or market openness. Furthermore, in the context of China's capital markets, Wenjing Li and Tianshu Zhou establish that the China Securities Regulatory Commission appears to grant regulatory subsidies in the form of devoting more resources into ex-ante cooperation and employing more discretion to central government controlled companies rather than local government-owned enterprises, thus undermining the level playing field and market integration.

3 Interplay of Policy Objectives/Goals

Policy makers in all parts of the world struggle to meet multiple policy objectives with the instruments they have at their disposal, from regulation and liability rules to market-based instruments such as taxes and emissions trading. Oftentimes individual instruments are charged with multiple goals at the same time, entailing that the attainment of the goals is being compromised.

Market integration has been one of the formidable goals of the European Union and has strongly influenced various policy areas. In this book, Jingyuan Ma examines the 'goal setting' of EU competition policy and compares it to its Chinese counterpart, the Anti-Monopoly Law. She argues that also in China the linkage between market integration and other goals of competition law should be considered within the framework of the corresponding legal provisions if market integration is taken as a goal. In this regard, in particular different conduct of administrative monopolies should be distinguished and more clearly defined. Mel Marquis appears to make a similar point in arguing that administrative monopolies affecting wide and diverse parts of the economy can best be addressed by having their eradication firmly inscribed as a higher ranking legal rule: unless there is clear determination, such mal-practices will prevail in their battle against narrowly conceptualised private interests.

In the context of public procurement rules Stefan Weishaar points out that the EU legislator follows a multi-objective approach where he tries to find a balance between more market integration and more competition at the same time.

Various contributors point to the fact that achieving the goal of market integration, or any other policy goal analysed in this volume (such as competition and environmental goals) is made even more difficult when considering factors like lobbying by interest groups, corruption, and the behaviour of politicians more generally. Guang Shen and Niels Philipsen provide an overview of the public choice literature on local protectionism and corruption and apply this to the specific case of business establishment in China. Niels Philipsen and Qi Zhou show that some of the arguments against allowing more competition in the legal professions (in the form of allowing alternative business forms) may be coloured by private interest rather than public interest considerations. Mengxing Lu and Michael Faure point to the problem of 'green washing' in eco-labelling, which may obscure the attainment of environmental goals.

4 Actors: Public, Private, Self-Enforcement

When addressing market integration there are a multitude of different actors that can be instrumental in supporting market integration processes. Above we already saw that the legislator and public institutions relating to competition and public procurement laws are important actors in shaping market integration. Yet whenever policy changes affect stake holders it is important to consider efficient means of law enforcement and the setting of efficient incentive structures to ensure that important stake holders work to 'entrench' the desired policy: market integration is no exception.

In this book several authors were reflecting upon the diversity of actors. In the context of competition law for example, Jingyuan Ma pointed out that China could learn from the EU by providing for both public as well as private enforcement instrument to secure a more effective enforcement of competition law provisions. In the EU effective competition law rules are viewed to be the 'natural complement' to the four freedoms because it prevents market actors to re-establish the boundaries that Member States sought to dismantle by creating the four freedoms. Effective enforcement of this body of law is thus tightly linked to and associated with market integration.

For the Chinese capital markets, Wenjing Li and Tianshu Zhou examine public enforcement in conjunction with ownership structures. The authors find that the public regulator in China enforces regulation without bias against either central-government owned companies or local government owned listed companies. Yet they find evidence that the China Regulatory Commission appears to grant regulatory subsidies to central government controlled companies. Because private enforcement is often based on public enforcement it is possible that the regulatory subsidies accruing to central-government owned companies are contributing to the relative scarcity of private enforcement cases of central-government owned companies. In any event the available data suggests that local government owned companies pay more compensation to private parties than central-government owned enterprises.

Besides public enforcement and private enforcement of regulation there are other stakeholders that can contribute to market integration outside the confines of an administrative or court procedure.

Mengxing Lu and Michael Faure examine the effects of corporate strategies: in the context of corporate environmental responsibility they point out that an increasing number of environmental labels could make it difficult for environmentally-minded companies to compete in an integrated market. The underlying argument is that the market could break down if consumers were unable to distinguish between high and low levels of environmental corporate responsibility (greenwashing). In such a situation the authors suggest that additional research into how government regulation could support such corporate activities would merit further research.

In the Oil and Gas Pipeline sector Mehdi Piri Damagh and Michael Faure contrast self-regulation to public regulation. With regard to environmental protection the authors argued for public regulation or at least co-regulation in the sense that governments would monitor private standards. With regard to technical and safety standards the authors found that private standard setting is widespread, particularly in the context of cross-border pipelines. Legislators should be mindful of such divergent regulatory regimes and standards if they embark upon the quest for market integration.

5 Critical Reflections on Market Integration

The contributors to this volume also pointed towards a series of critical issues concerning market integration. Jiye Hu and Shouji Sun point out that market integration does not extend to social welfare systems. In their chapter the authors show that ill-designed public pension schemes can undermine the fiscal sustainability of States and thereby the stability of the monetary framework and lead to disintegration. National debt burdens in Europe are a systemic risk for market integration, which is an issue that is very topical in the European debate about the Monetary Union. There is an emerging debate about officially complementing the Monetary Union with a 'fiscal union'.

Other authors remind us that market integration should not be an absolute goal in itself that blends out all rational thinking. Mehdi Piri Damagh and Michael Faure, as well as Stefan Weishaar, point out that harmonisation can be beneficial but can also have undesired consequences. Niels Philipsen and Qi Zhou make an explicit reference to the economic theory of federalism. According to this theory, moving decision-making to a higher level (e.g., European, federal) rather than regulating at national (or regional/provincial) level is recommended only if there are significant transboundary externalities, if transaction costs of having many different national (or regional/provincial) laws are higher than the costs of harmonising these different laws; or when there is a 'race to the bottom' between EU Member States setting lenient (safety, quality, environmental, etc.) standards to attract industry. In the alternative, a decentralised approach should be taken, because preferences of people are best represented at local or national level, provided that the four freedoms discussed in Sect. 2 are met. Philipsen and Zhou conclude that, at least for the specific case of business regulation in the legal services market, regulatory action at the European level seems warranted only when there is empirical evidence showing the negative effects of regulating at national or local level.

6 The Road Ahead

The chapters contained in this book have shown that there are several lessons that China can learn from the European experience, as well as from Law and Economics theory, if it wants to achieve further market integration and sustainable growth. One obvious example of such lessons is that policy goals need to be clearly defined and (if possible) non-conflicting. The contributions to this volume confirm that regulation, more particularly in the form of substantive law, can play an important role in achieving a level playing field, and that, ceteris paribus, a level playing field is the best environment in which to secure vibrant investment. Another lesson, following inter alia from the chapter by Mel Marquis, is that more faith and conviction in positive law, and an even-handed application of positive law (through a robust system of law and courts) will be necessary conditions for achieving such a level playing field.

The chapters also show that there are still various challenges facing China today. For example, as argued by many economists, governments often intervene too much in markets, e.g., in capital markets and in the banking sector (Xu and Gui in this book refer to this as 'financial repression'). Such over-regulation generally leads to distortions in other markets, also preventing market integration. There are many examples of these distortive effects, such as the rise of the shadow banking system in China, migration of workers, and black markets. The challenge is hence to find the right balance between market forces and government intervention.

It is not only challenging to examine the role of the (central) government; there are also other emanations of governmental bodies, such as SOEs and enforcement agencies, which are important economic actors that can impact market integration, as has been shown by various contributions to this book. This raises several questions. For example, do we need to apply the Anti-Monopoly Law also to large banks? Should it be applied more strongly against SOEs? And with respect to the level of government, a question (as hinted at in this book by Shen and Philipsen) is whether more competition between local governments would be a good form of competition, or rather a destructive kind of competition (i.e. a race to the bottom). And last but not least: is a reform towards a regulatory state even possible without structural reforms in the political system?

In sum, there are still challenges ahead. However, it is our hope and expectation, also based on the contributions to this book, that comparative legal analysis (EU–China) and Law and Economics can help finding the regulatory and other instruments that are best suited in facing some of these challenges.

[illegible]

MIX
Papier aus verantwortungsvollen Quellen
Paper from responsible sources
FSC® C105338

If you have any concerns about our products,
you can contact us on
ProductSafety@springernature.com

In case Publisher is established outside the EU,
the EU authorized representative is:
Springer Nature Customer Service Center GmbH
Europaplatz 3, 69115 Heidelberg, Germany

Printed by Libri Plureos GmbH
in Hamburg, Germany